C.B. Cebulski and Noriko Furuhata
Translation

Dan Nakrosis and Dano Ink Studios
Retouch and Lettering

Veronica Casson
Designer

Frank Pannone
Project Manager

Mike Lackey
Print Production Manager

Stephanie Shalofsky
Vice President, Production

John O'Donnell
Publisher

World Peace Through Shared Popular Culture™
www.centralparkmedia.com
www.cpmmanga.com

Nadesico Book One. Published by CPM Manga, a division of Central Park Media Corporation. Office of Publication – 250 West 57th Street, Suite 317, New York, NY 10107. Original Japanese Version "Meteor Schlachtschiff Nadesico Volume 1" © KIA ASAMIYA 1997. Originally published in Japan in 1997 by KADOKAWA SHOTEN PUBLISHING Co., Ltd., Tokyo. English version ©1999, 2000 Central Park Media Corporation. CPM Manga and logo are registered trademarks of Central Park Media Corporation. All rights reserved. Price per copy $9.99, price in Canada may vary. ISBN: 1-56219-901-3. Catalog number: CMX 62401MM. UPC: 7-19987-00624-9-99013. Printed in Canada.

CPM®
MANGA
New York, New York

NADESICO

BOOK ONE

KIA ASAMIYA
writer and artist

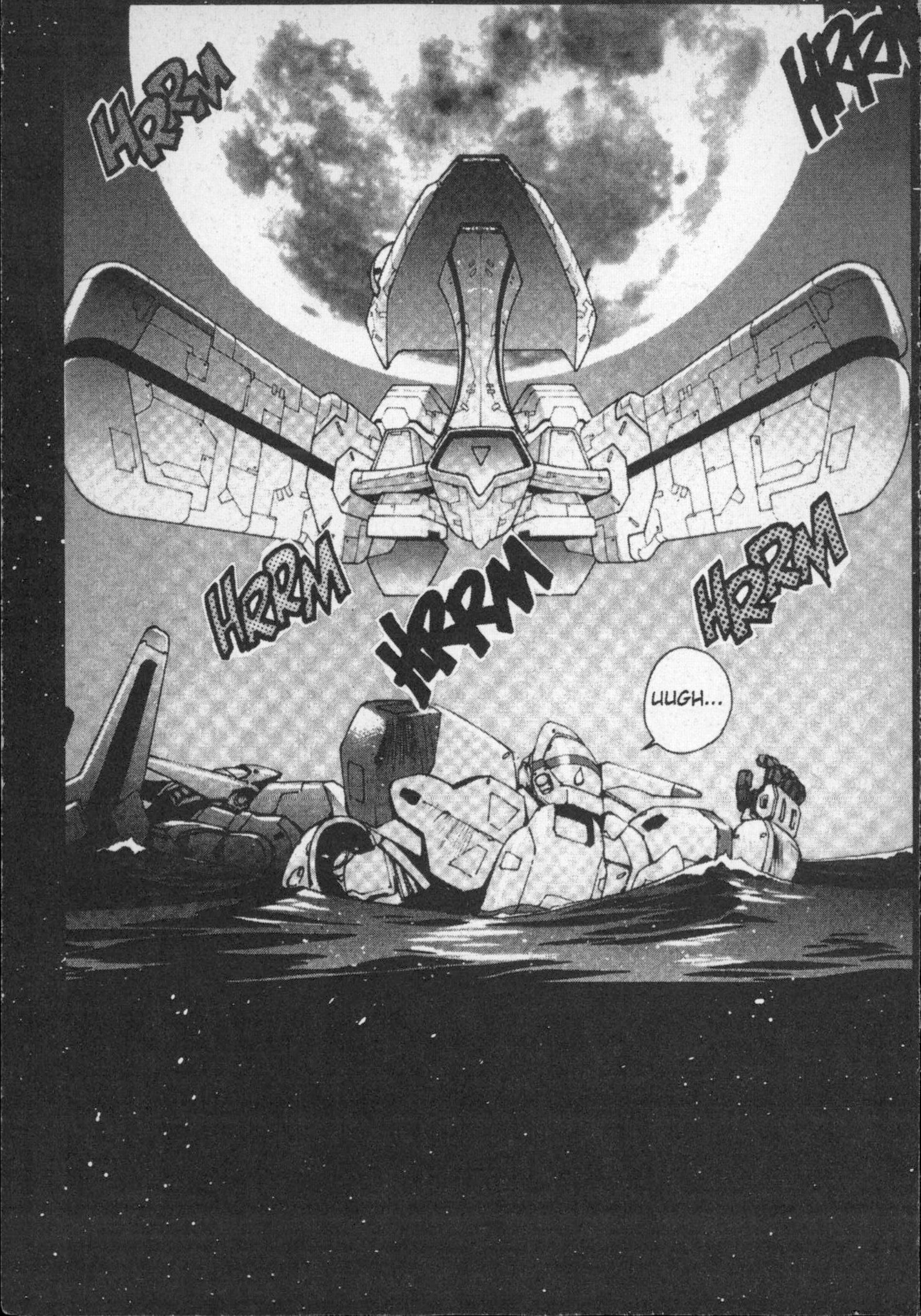
HRRM
HRRM
HRRM
HRRM
UUGH...

CONTENTS

Character Profiles 6
Chapter 1 – Let's Go 8
Chapter 2 - Meet Again 51
Chapter 3 - In the Space 77
Chapter 4 - Nadesico vs. Susano 99
Chapter 5 - Death in Outer Space 124
Chapter 6 - Under the Flag of Nadesico 147
About Kia Asamiya 176

CHARACTER PROFILES

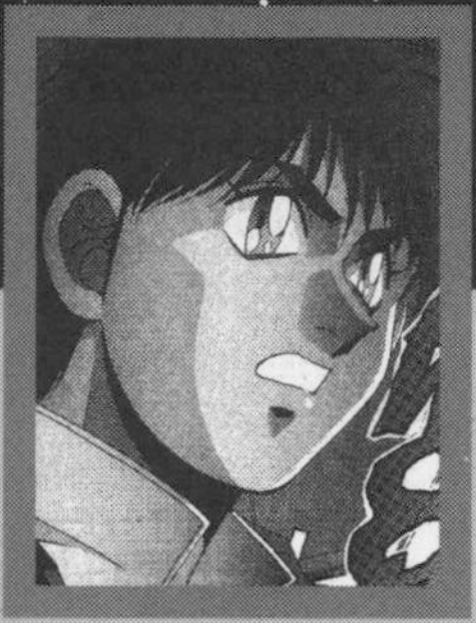

AKITO - This Martian immigrant is down on his luck on Earth. He's an out of work dreamer with few options left. Won't anyone give an unemployed Martian truck driver a break?

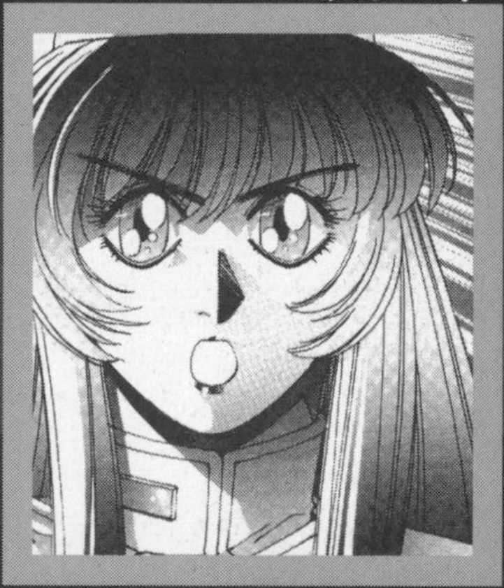

YURIKA - One of the most brilliant graduates of the military academy, she was never defeated in simulation battles. She's finally ready to assume the reins of leadership. Will war destroy her happy-go-lucky nature?

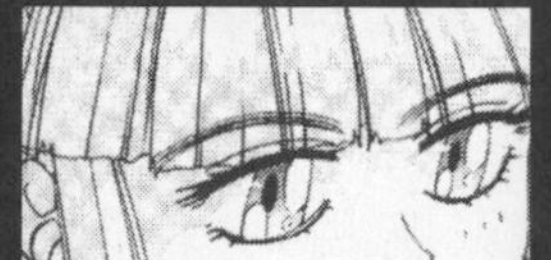

RURI - This cold and calculating youth is a genius, barely into her teens and already an officer on a space battleship. Will anything crack her machine-like exterior?

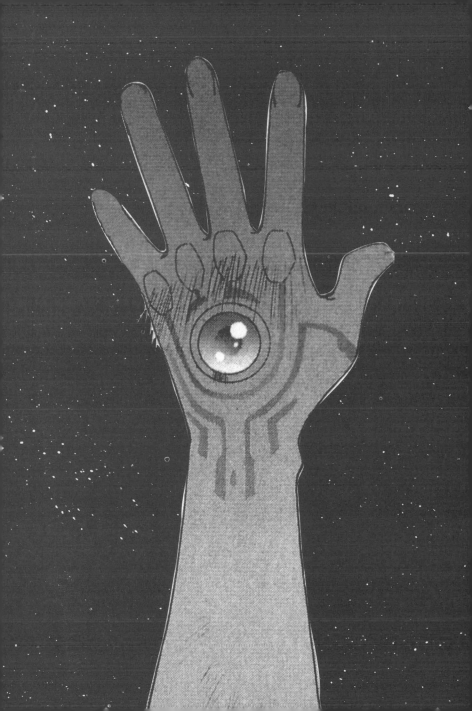

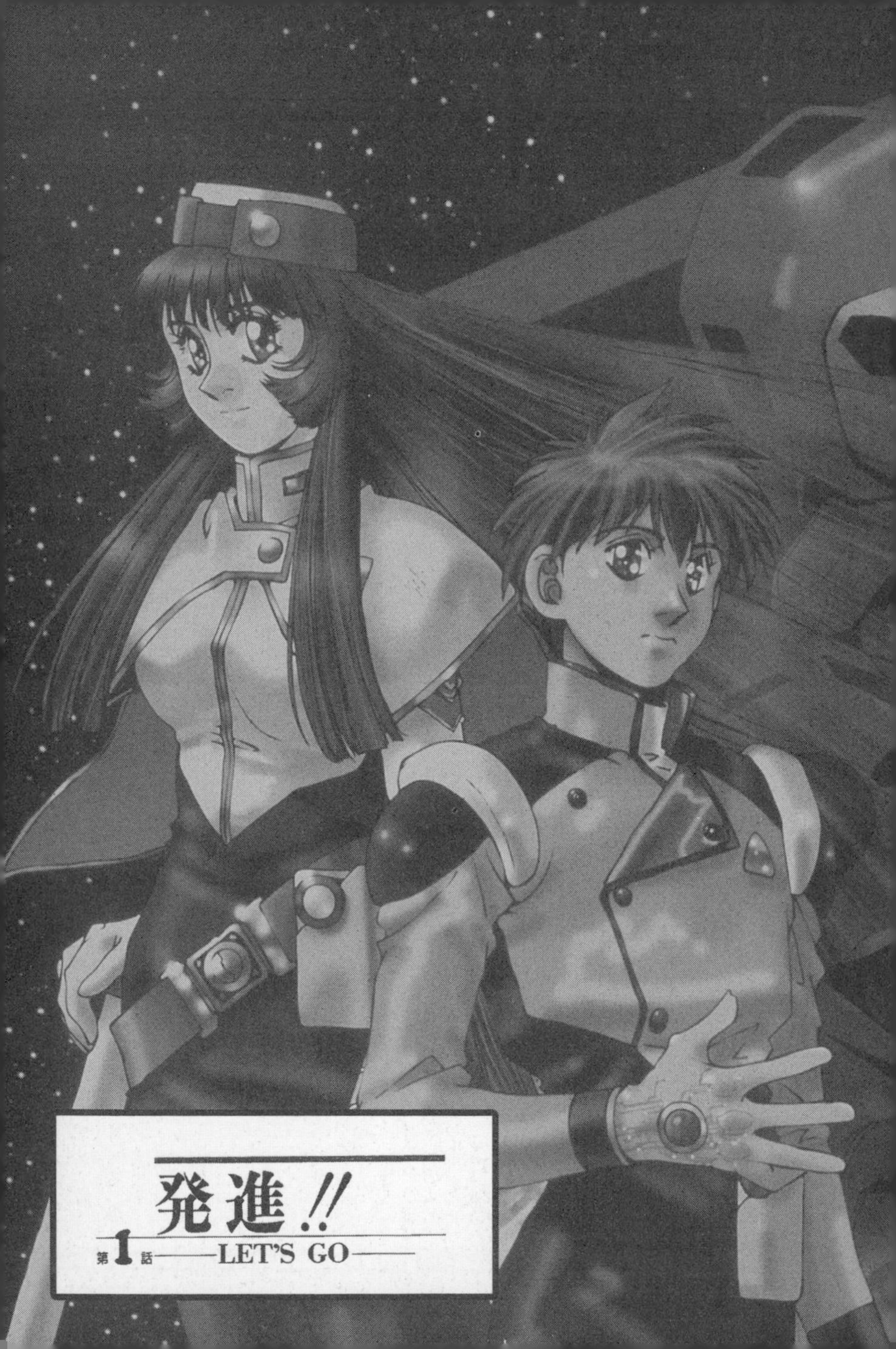
発進!!
第1話——LET'S GO——

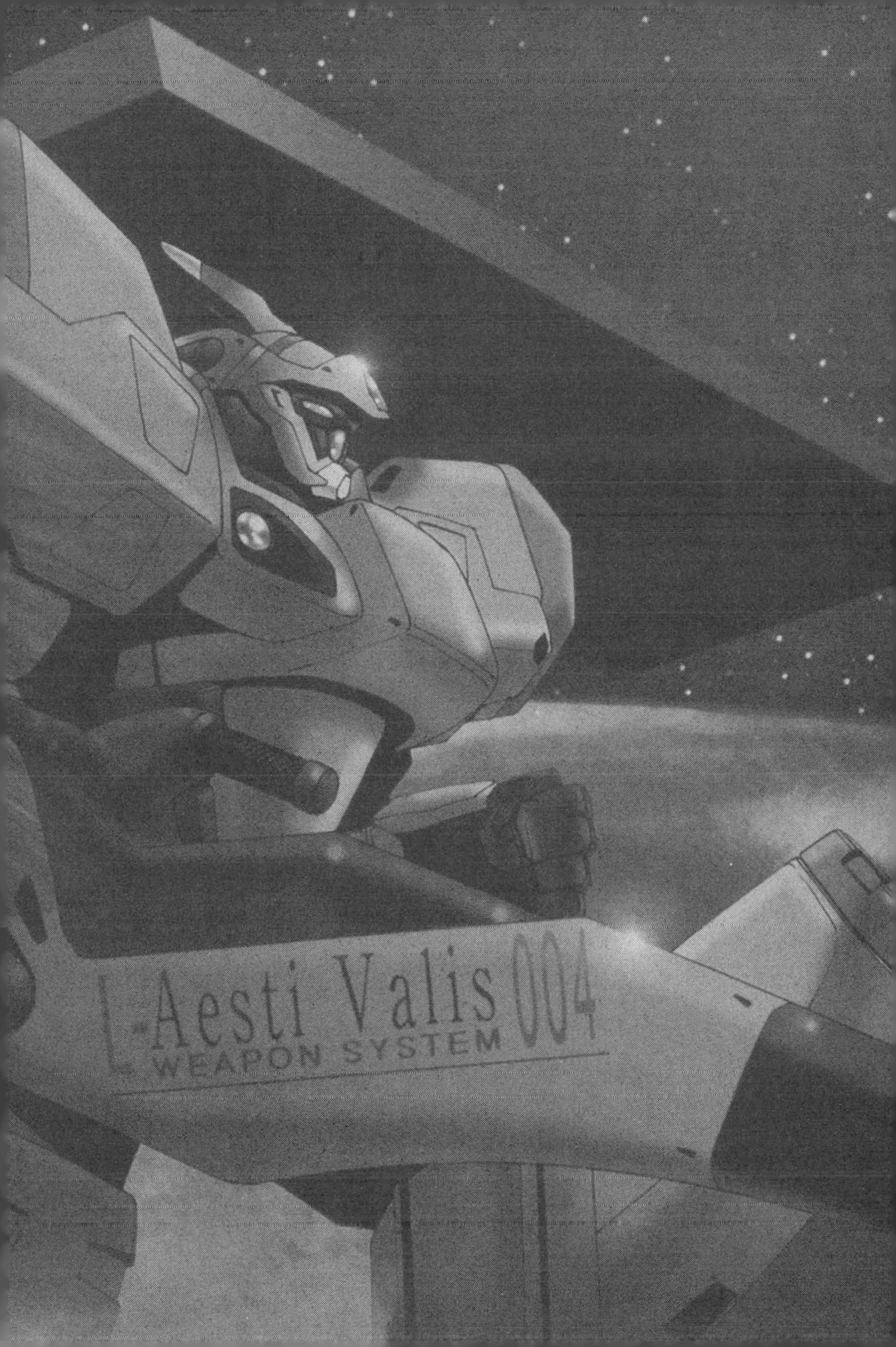
Aesti Valis 004
WEAPON SYSTEM

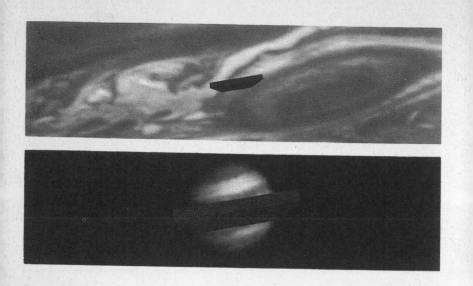

THERE... AN OBJECT FROM JUPITER...

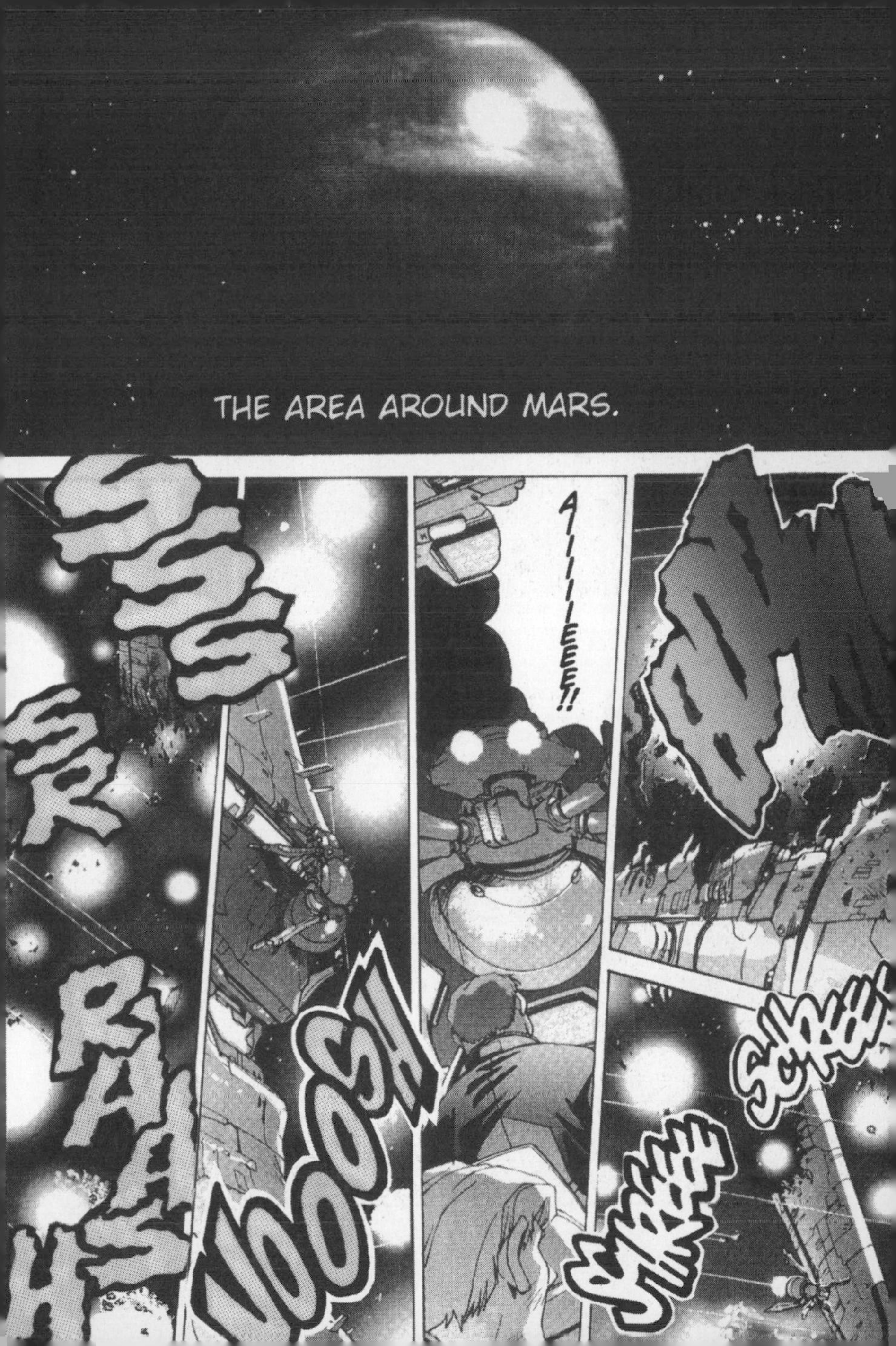
THE AREA AROUND MARS.
WHOOOSH
AIIIIIEEEE!!

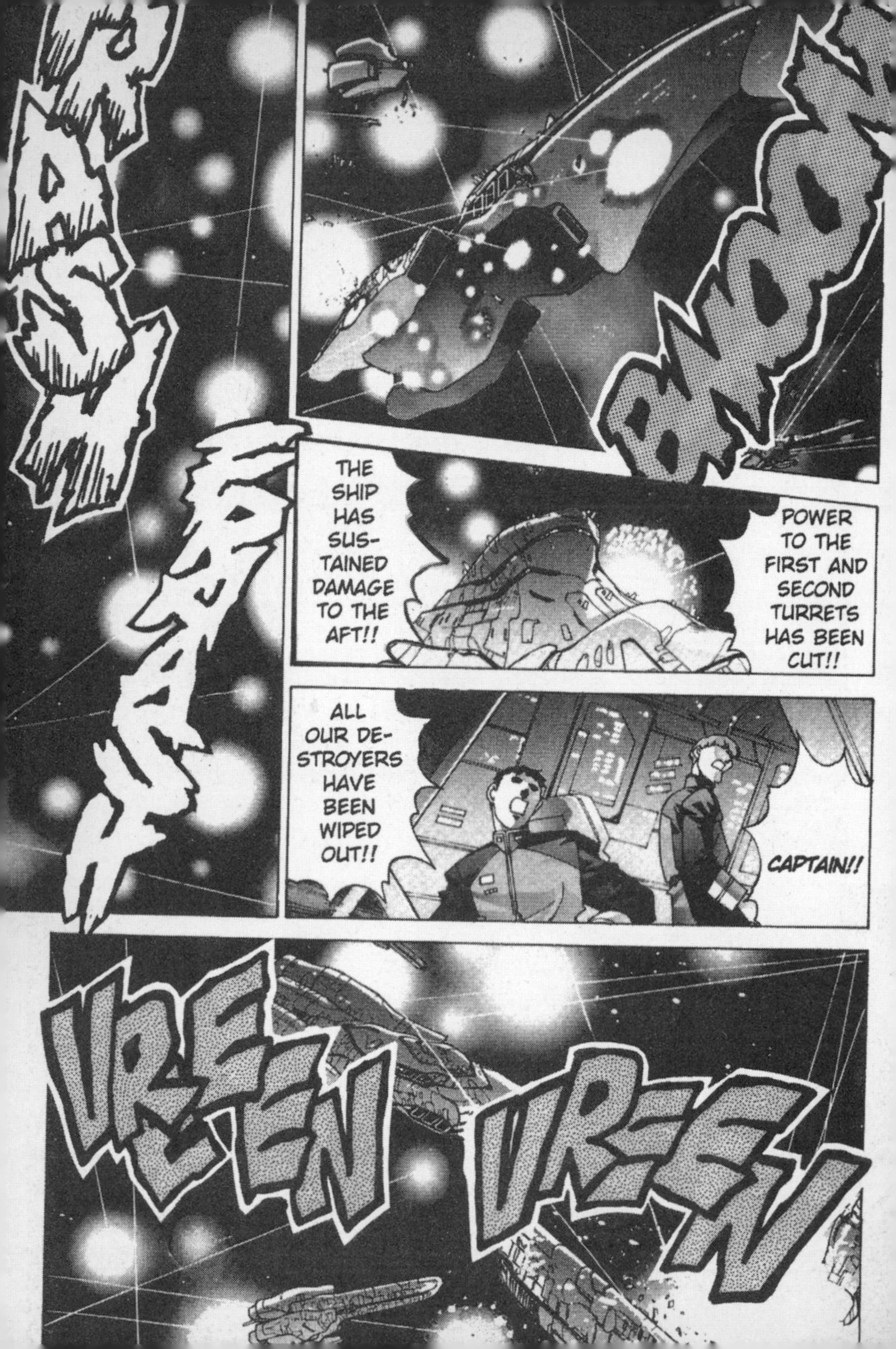
THE SHIP HAS SUSTAINED DAMAGE TO THE AFT!!
POWER TO THE FIRST AND SECOND TURRETS HAS BEEN CUT!!
ALL OUR DESTROYERS HAVE BEEN WIPED OUT!!
CAPTAIN!!

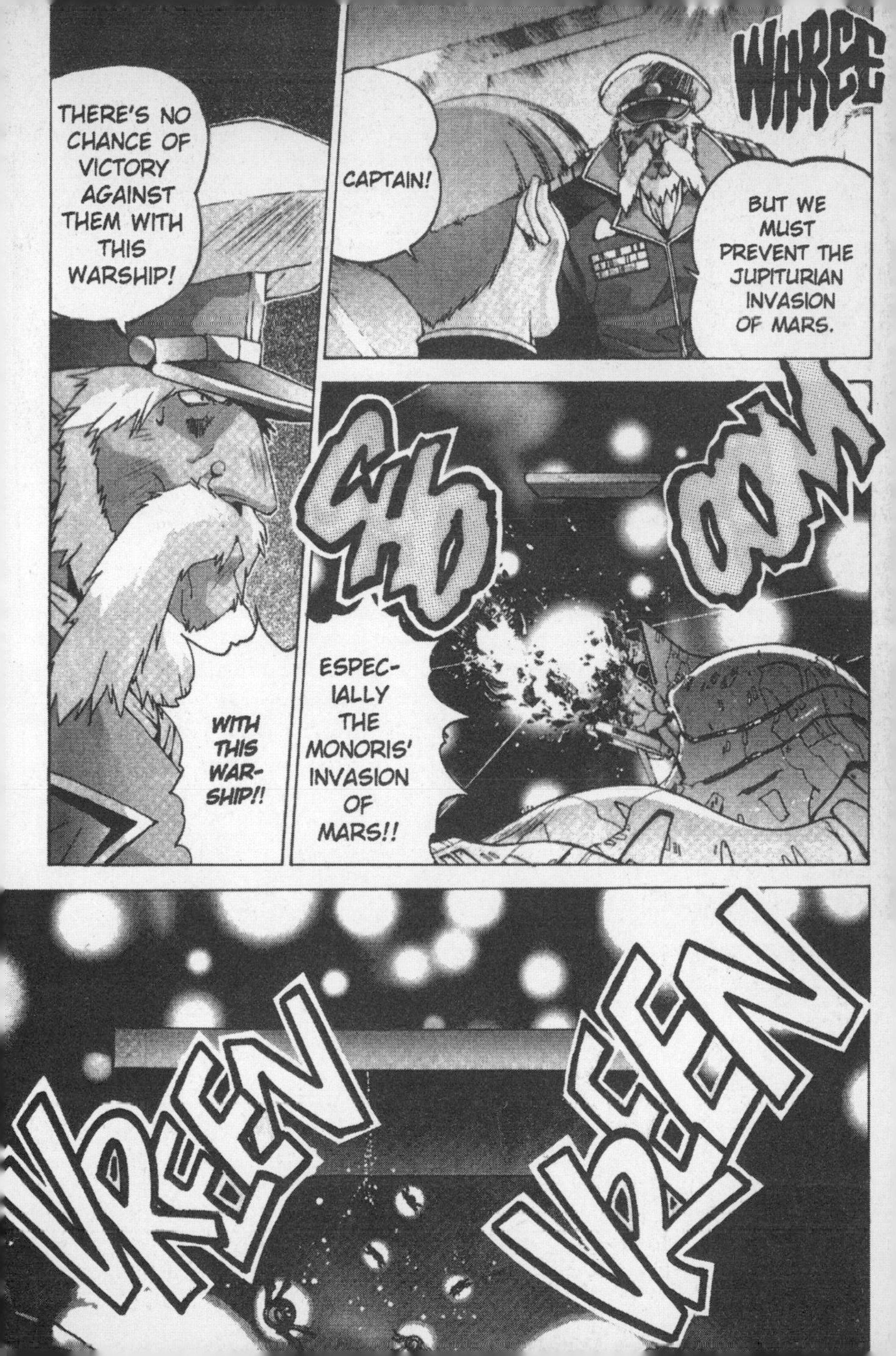
THERE'S NO CHANCE OF VICTORY AGAINST THEM WITH THIS WARSHIP!
WITH THIS WAR-SHIP!!
WHREE
CAPTAIN!
BUT WE MUST PREVENT THE JUPITURIAN INVASION OF MARS.
SHOOOM
ESPEC-IALLY THE MONORIS' INVASION OF MARS!!
VREEN
VREEN

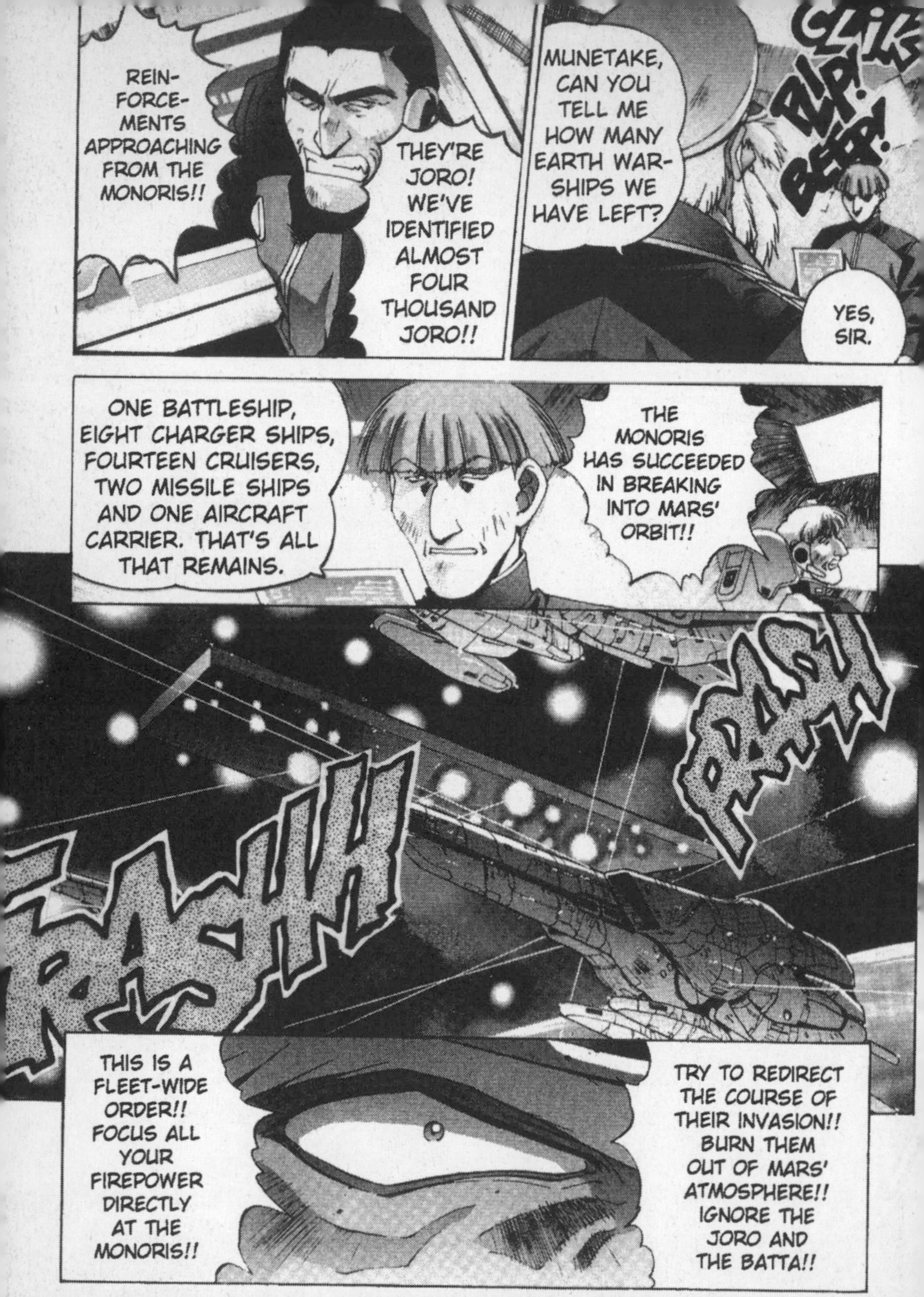
REIN-FORCE-MENTS APPROACHING FROM THE MONORIS!!
THEY'RE JORO! WE'VE IDENTIFIED ALMOST FOUR THOUSAND JORO!!
MUNETAKE, CAN YOU TELL ME HOW MANY EARTH WAR-SHIPS WE HAVE LEFT?
CLIK
BLIP!
BEEP!
YES, SIR.
ONE BATTLESHIP, EIGHT CHARGER SHIPS, FOURTEEN CRUISERS, TWO MISSILE SHIPS AND ONE AIRCRAFT CARRIER. THAT'S ALL THAT REMAINS.
THE MONORIS HAS SUCCEEDED IN BREAKING INTO MARS' ORBIT!!
RASH
BASHH
THIS IS A FLEET-WIDE ORDER!! FOCUS ALL YOUR FIREPOWER DIRECTLY AT THE MONORIS!!
TRY TO REDIRECT THE COURSE OF THEIR INVASION!! BURN THEM OUT OF MARS' ATMOSPHERE!! IGNORE THE JORO AND THE BATTA!!

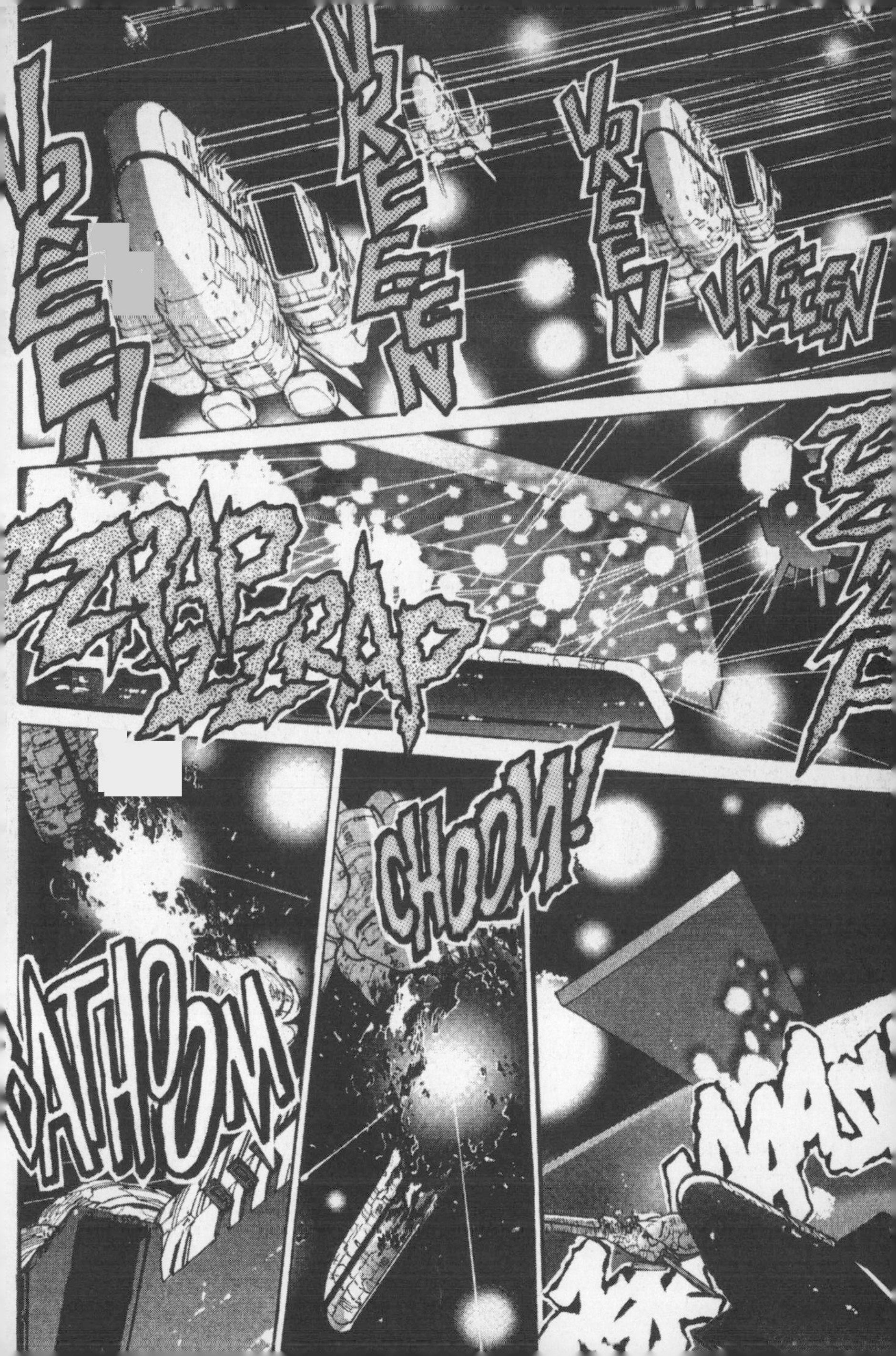
VREEN
VREEN
VREEN
VREEEN
ZZAP ZRAP
CHOOM!

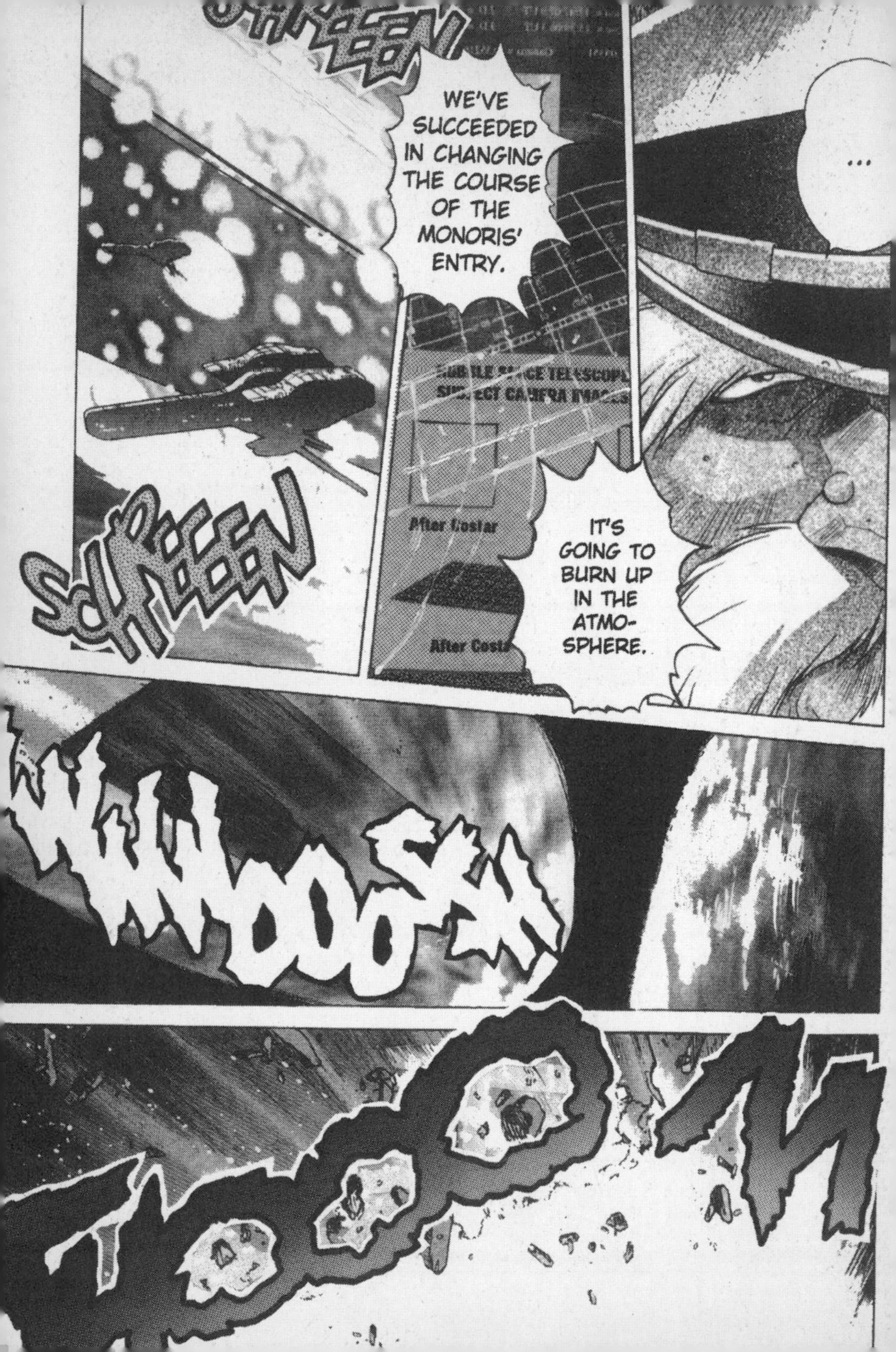

SCHREEEN
WE'VE SUCCEEDED IN CHANGING THE COURSE OF THE MONORIS' ENTRY.
After Costar
IT'S GOING TO BURN UP IN THE ATMOSPHERE.
...
WHOOSH
TOOOM

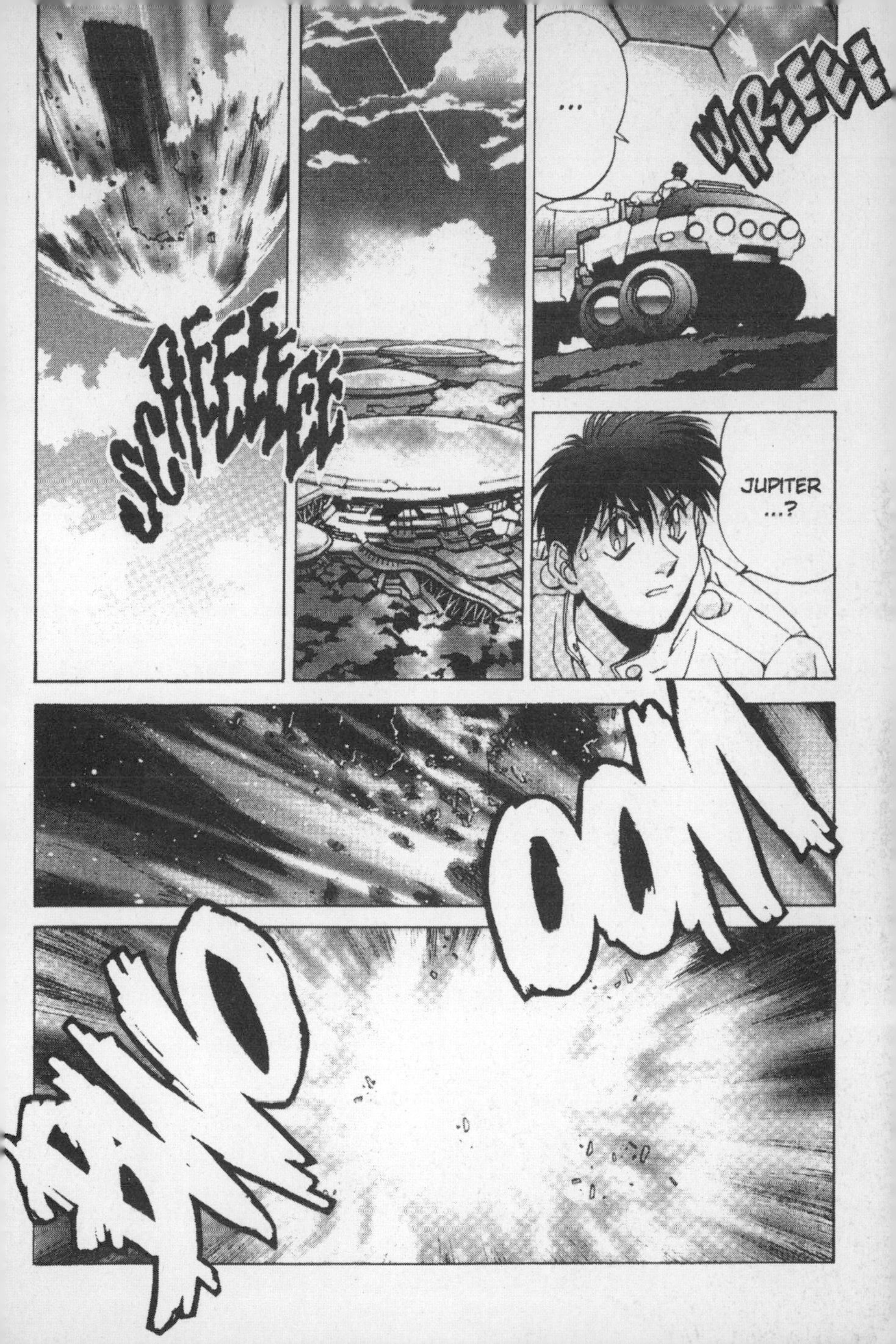

...
JUPITER ...?

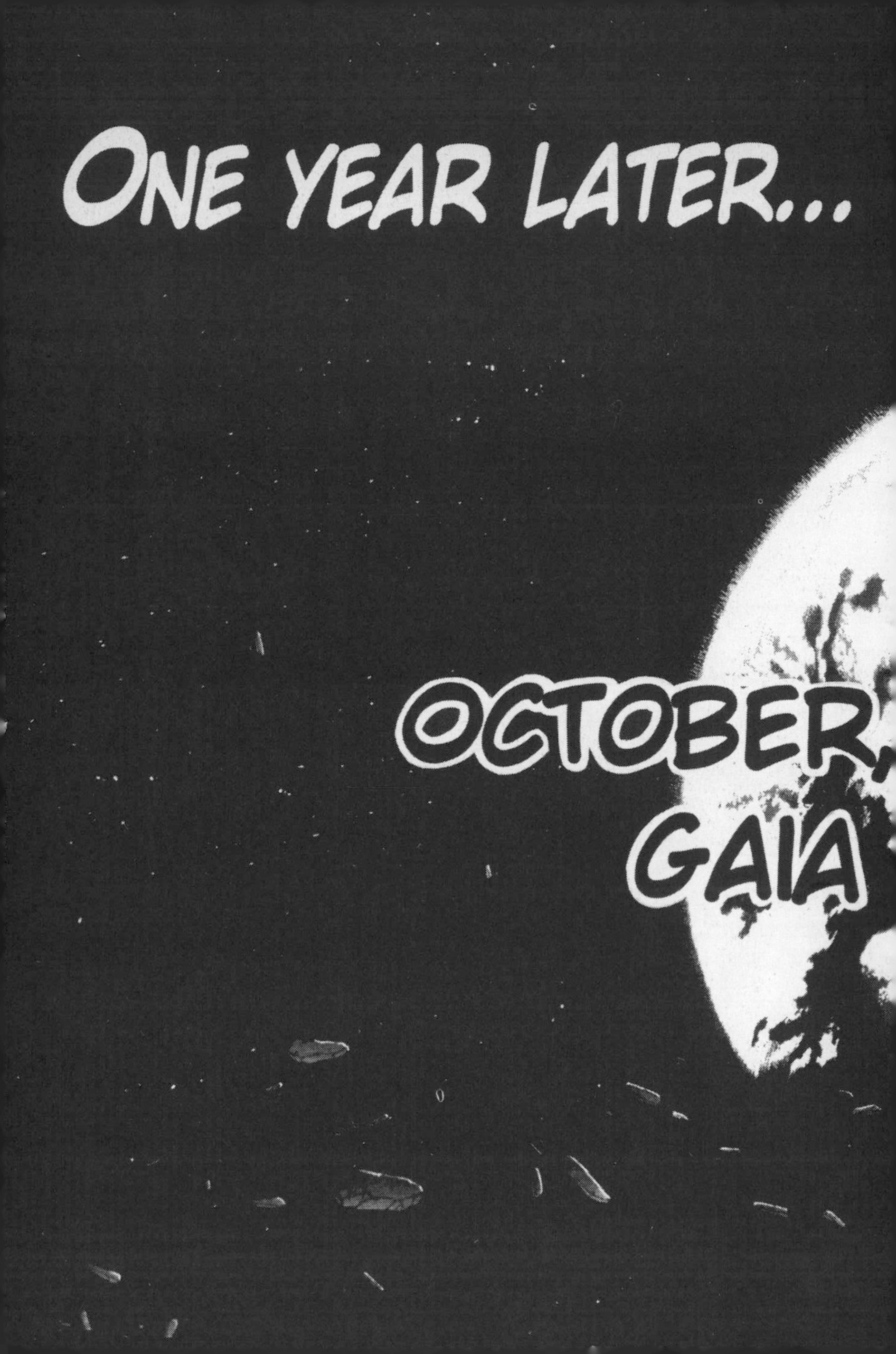
ONE YEAR LATER...
OCTOBER, GAIA

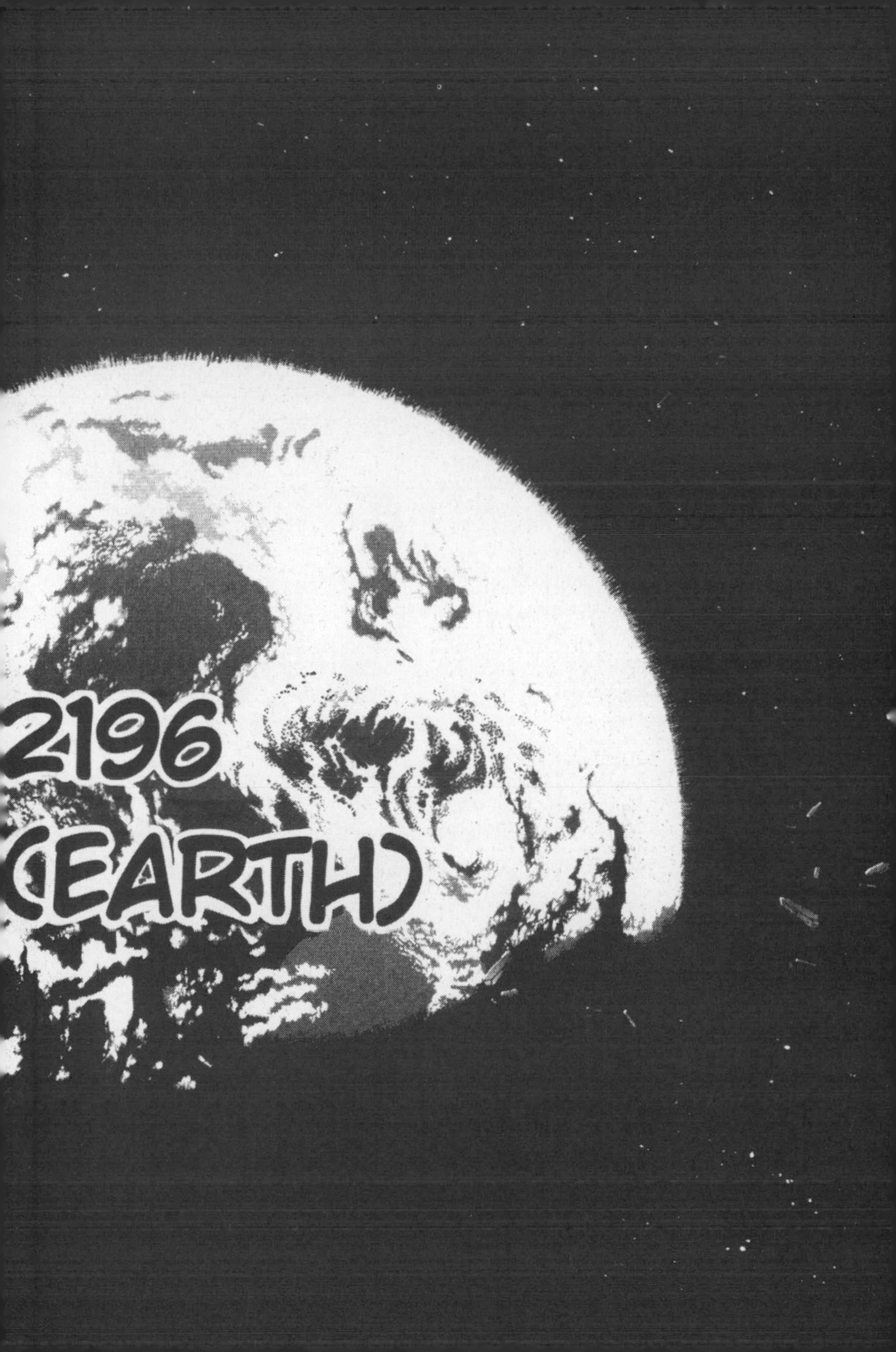
2196
(EARTH)

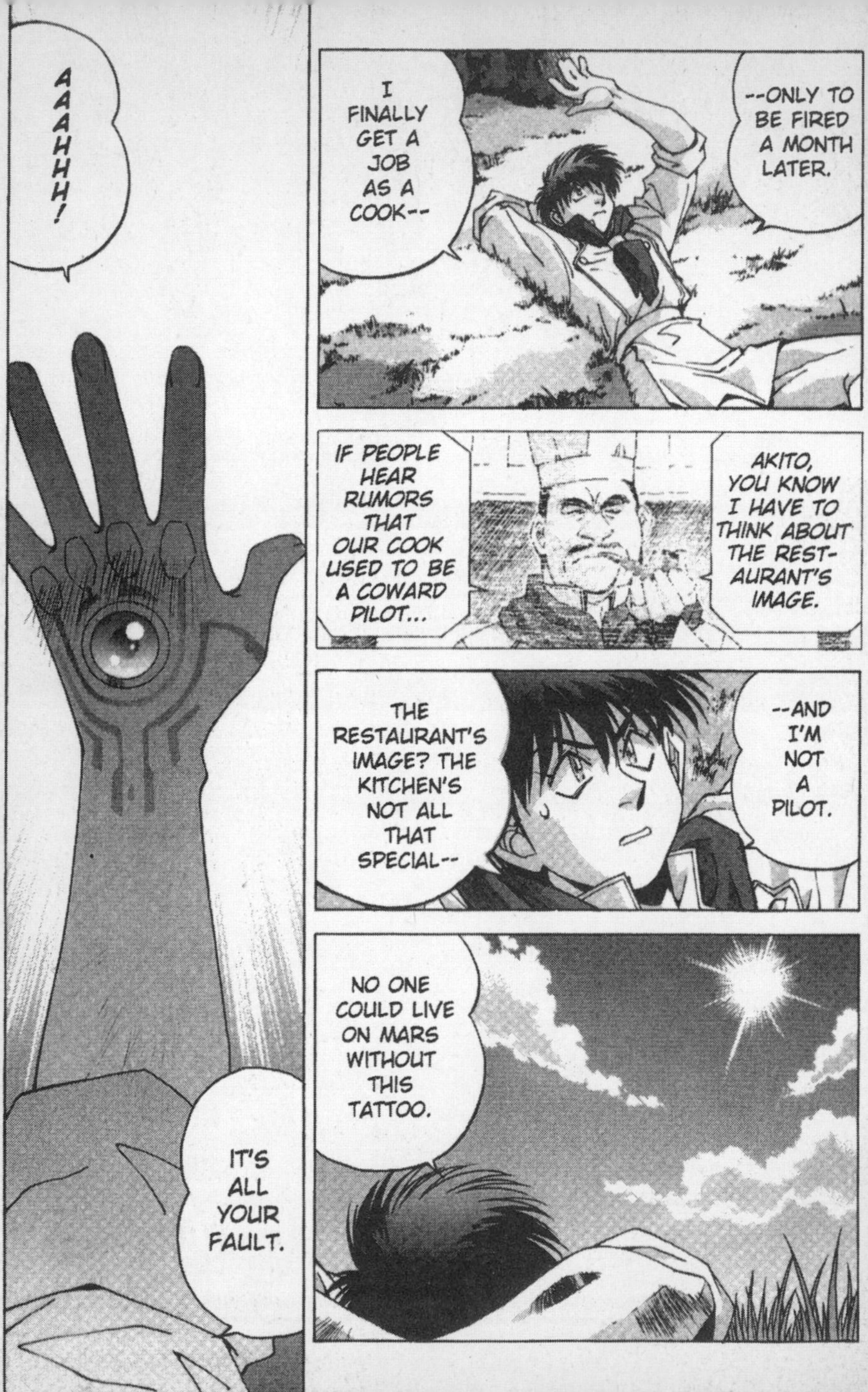
AAAHHH!
IT'S ALL YOUR FAULT.
I FINALLY GET A JOB AS A COOK--
--ONLY TO BE FIRED A MONTH LATER.
IF PEOPLE HEAR RUMORS THAT OUR COOK USED TO BE A COWARD PILOT...
AKITO, YOU KNOW I HAVE TO THINK ABOUT THE REST-AURANT'S IMAGE.
THE RESTAURANT'S IMAGE? THE KITCHEN'S NOT ALL THAT SPECIAL--
--AND I'M NOT A PILOT.
NO ONE COULD LIVE ON MARS WITHOUT THIS TATTOO.

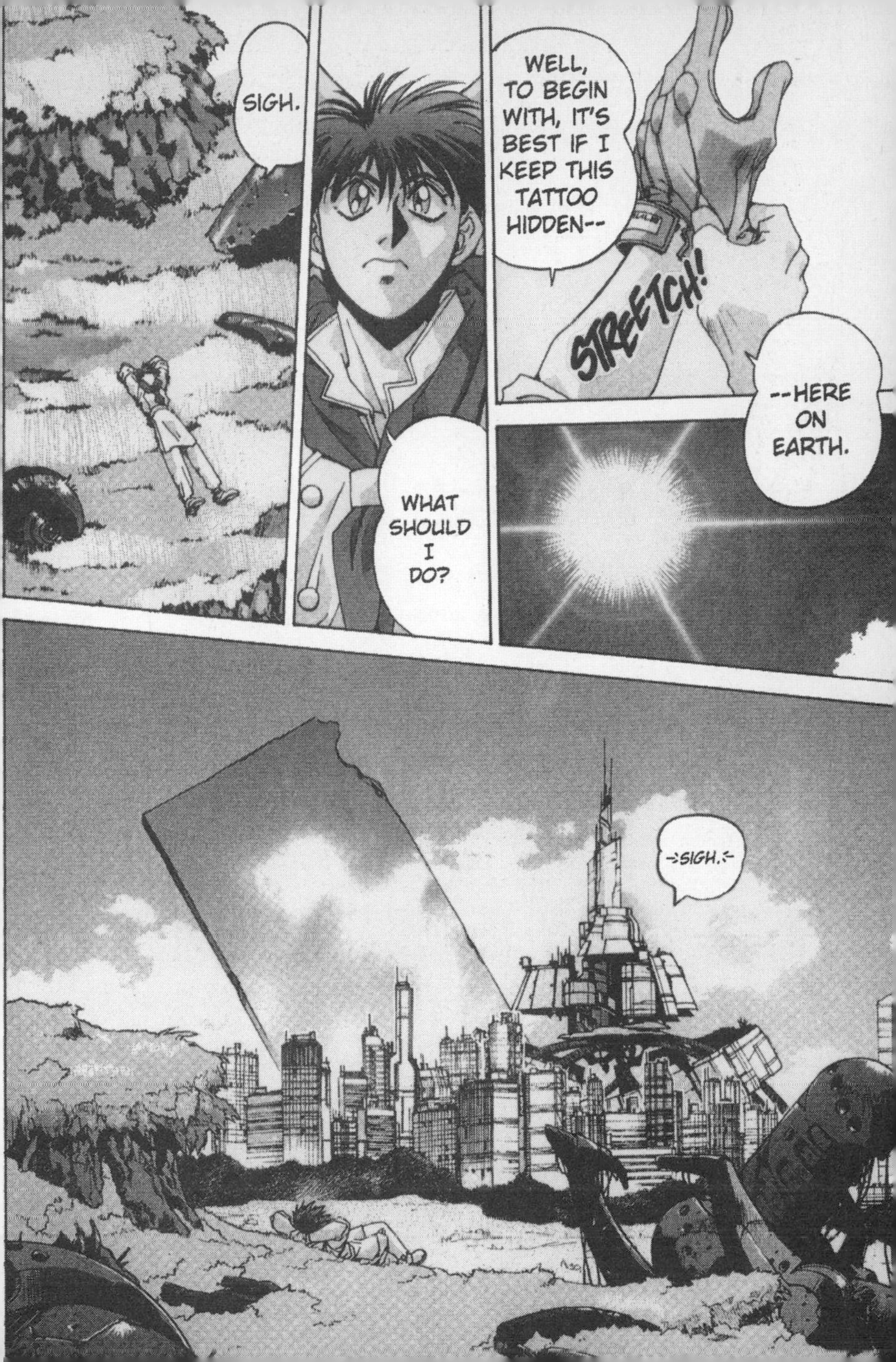
SIGH.
WHAT SHOULD I DO?
WELL, TO BEGIN WITH, IT'S BEST IF I KEEP THIS TATTOO HIDDEN--
STREETCH!
--HERE ON EARTH.
SIGH.

NERGAL CONGLOMERATE.

HAVE YOU HEARD OF THE SCAPARELLY PROJECT?

YES.

WE HAVE DECIDED TO PRIORITIZE THIS PROJECT AND STEP UP TO FULL SCALE CONSTRUCTION.

GORT, CERTAIN PEOPLE HAVE RECOMMENDED YOU FOR THIS POSITION BASED ON YOUR PAST WARTIME EXPERIENCES.

ME...?

IS THIS A MILITARY PROJECT?

PROSPECTOR WILL GIVE YOU ALL THE DETAILS.

THIS IS A DIRECT ORDER. YOU JUST DO AS HE SAYS.

PROSPECTOR...?

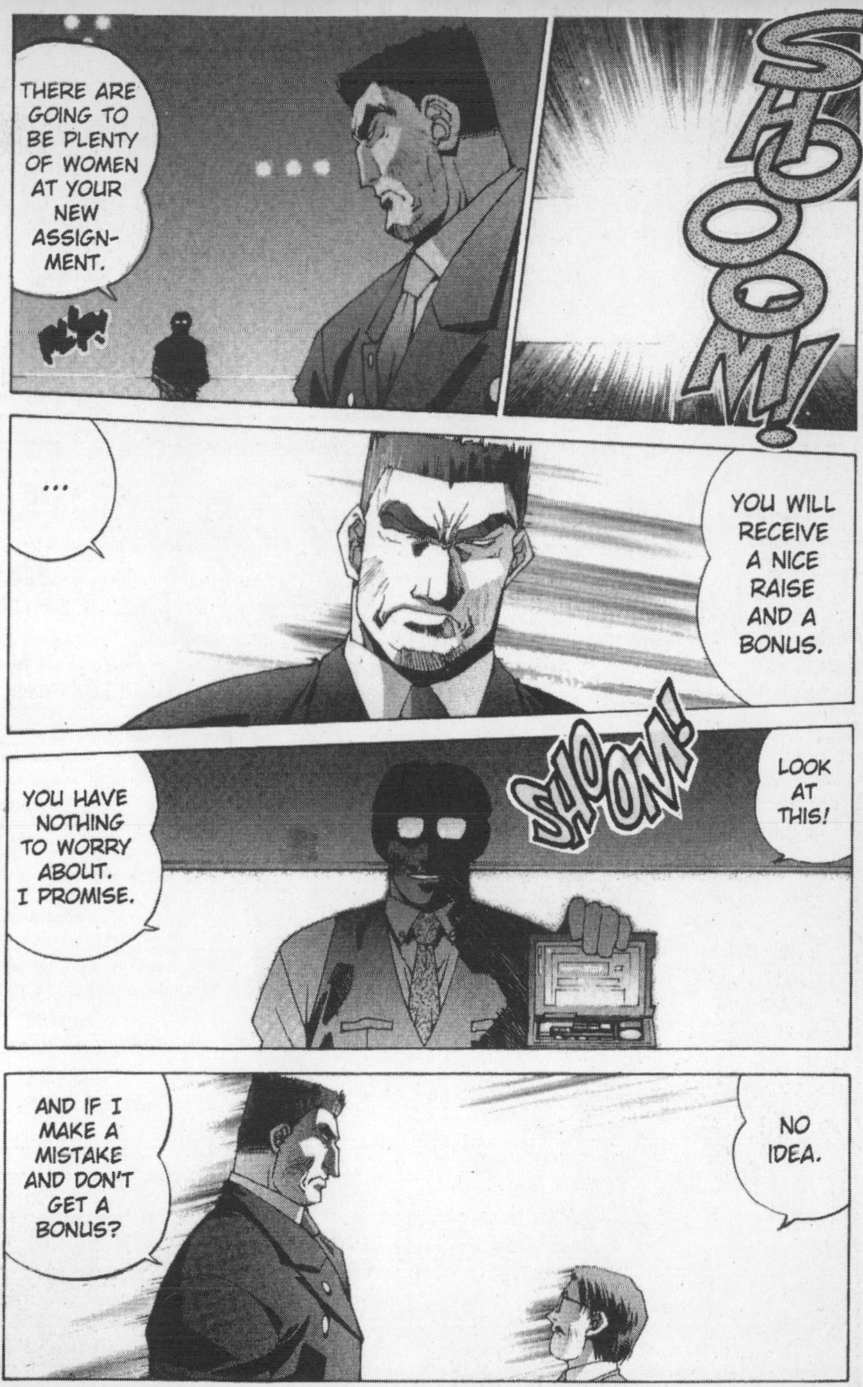
THERE ARE GOING TO BE PLENTY OF WOMEN AT YOUR NEW ASSIGN-MENT.
SHOOOOM!
...
YOU WILL RECEIVE A NICE RAISE AND A BONUS.
YOU HAVE NOTHING TO WORRY ABOUT. I PROMISE.
SHOOM!
LOOK AT THIS!
AND IF I MAKE A MISTAKE AND DON'T GET A BONUS?
NO IDEA.

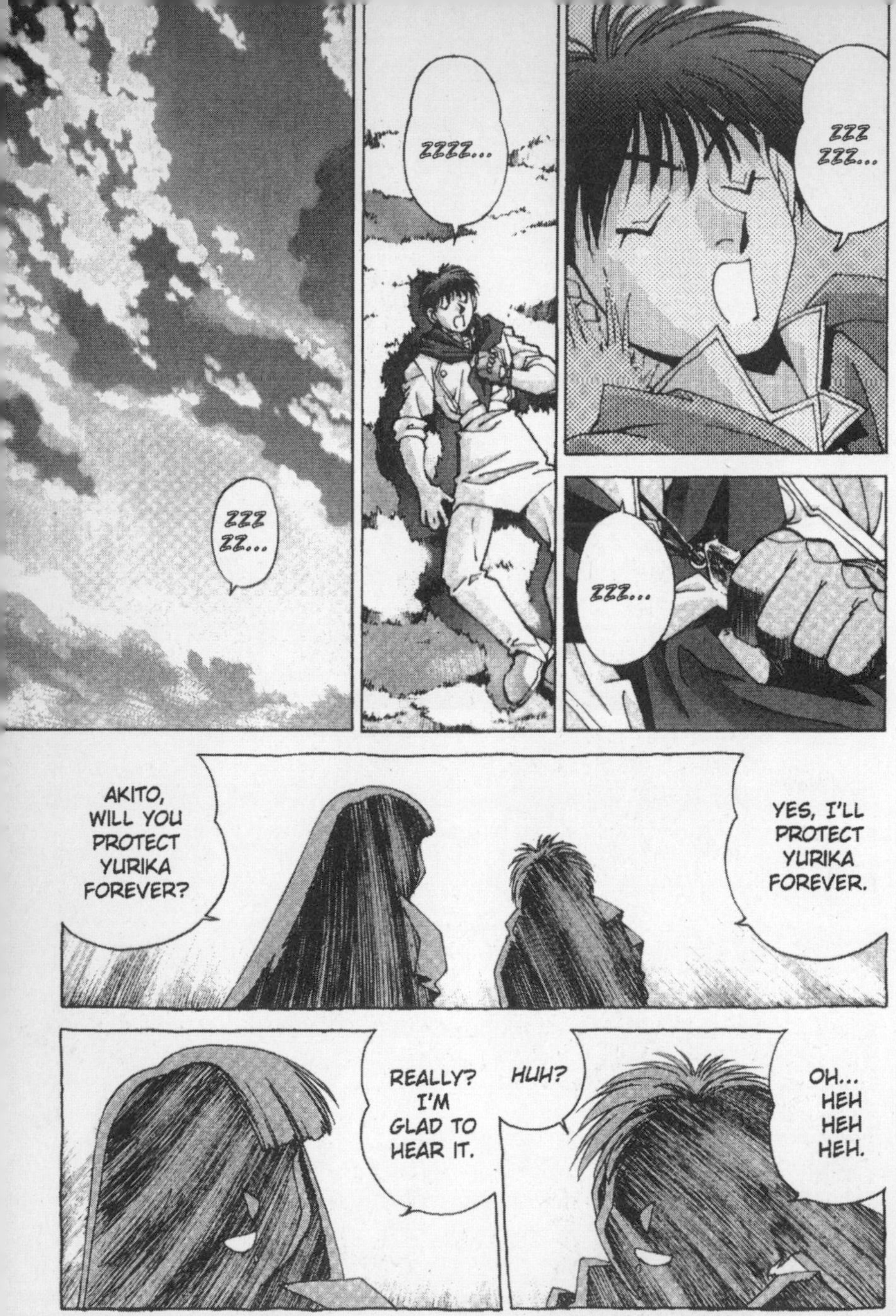
ZZZ
ZZ...
ZZZZ...
ZZZ
ZZZ...
ZZZ...
AKITO, WILL YOU PROTECT YURIKA FOREVER?
YES, I'LL PROTECT YURIKA FOREVER.
REALLY? I'M GLAD TO HEAR IT.
HUH?
OH... HEH HEH HEH.

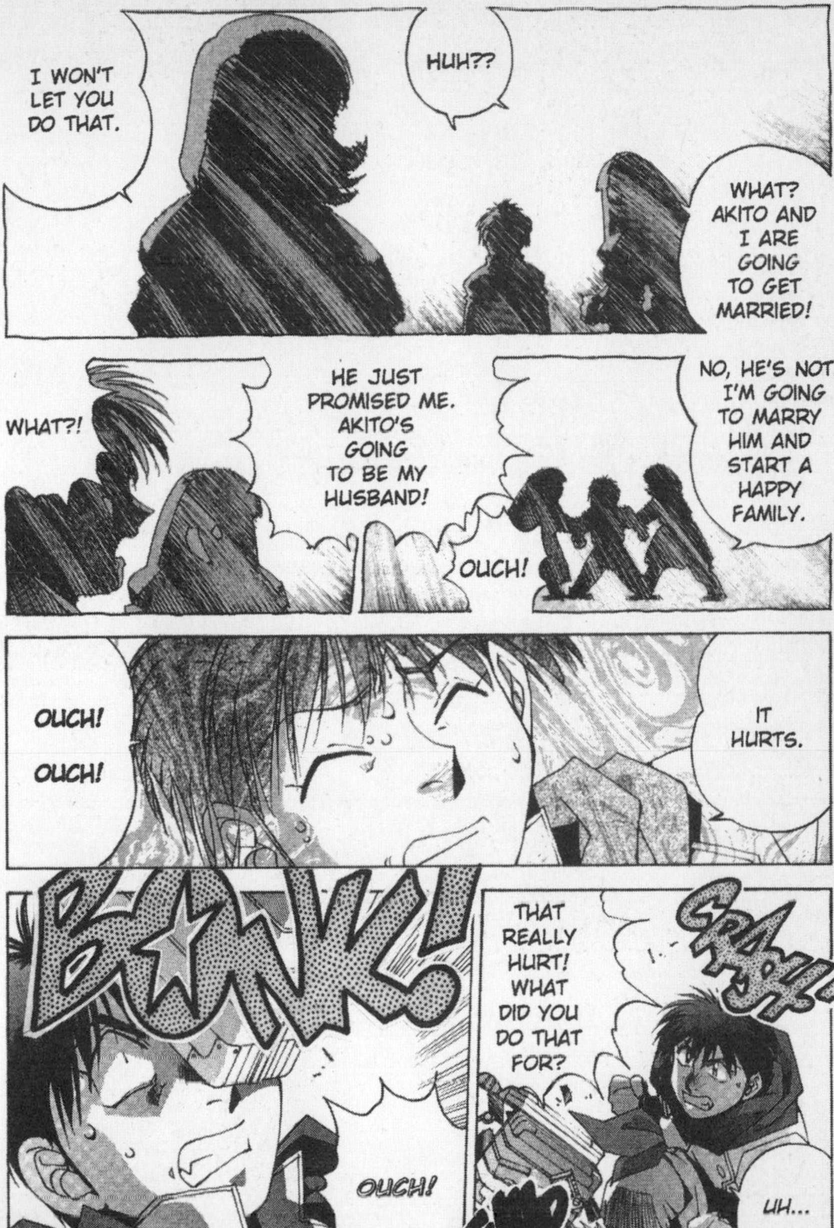
I WON'T LET YOU DO THAT.
HUH??
WHAT? AKITO AND I ARE GOING TO GET MARRIED!
WHAT?!
HE JUST PROMISED ME. AKITO'S GOING TO BE MY HUSBAND!
OUCH!
NO, HE'S NOT. I'M GOING TO MARRY HIM AND START A HAPPY FAMILY.
OUCH!
OUCH!
IT HURTS.
BONK!
OUCH!
THAT REALLY HURT! WHAT DID YOU DO THAT FOR?
CRASH!!
THUD
UH...

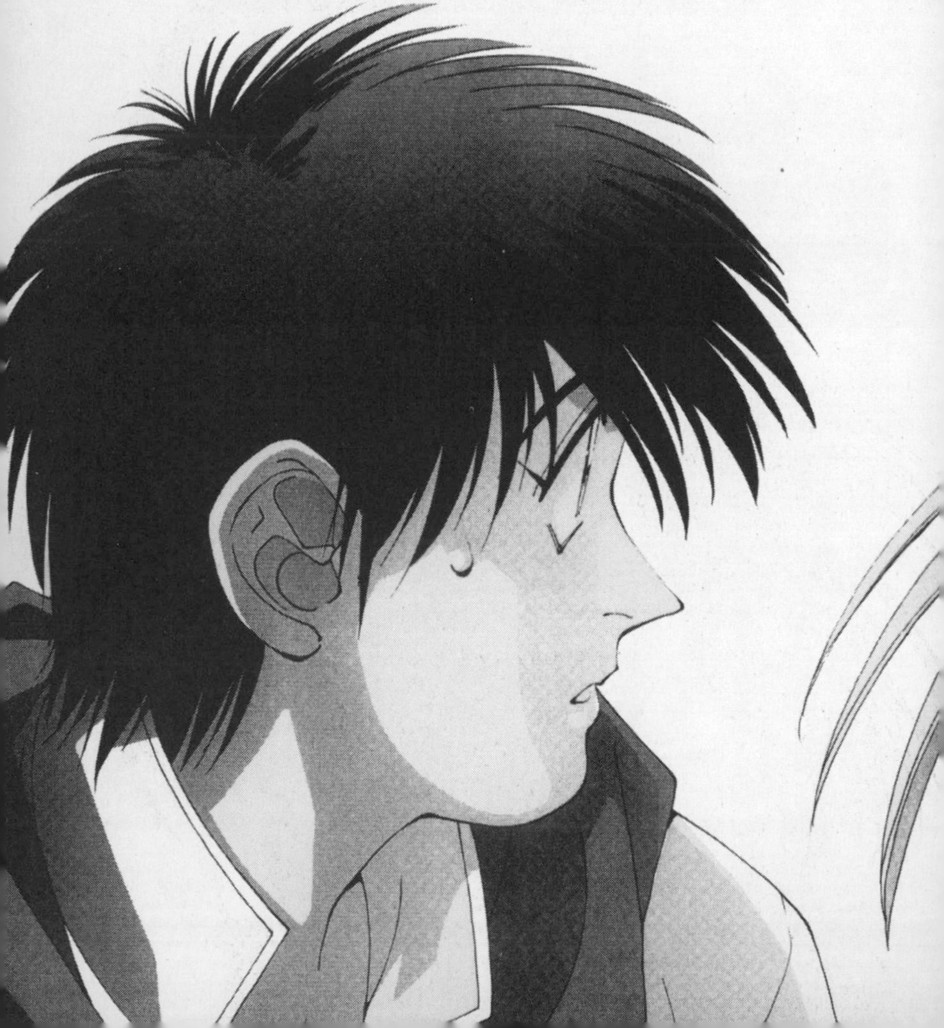

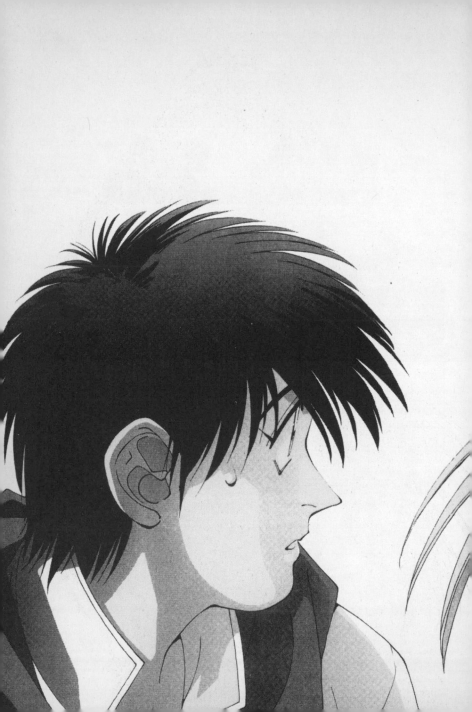

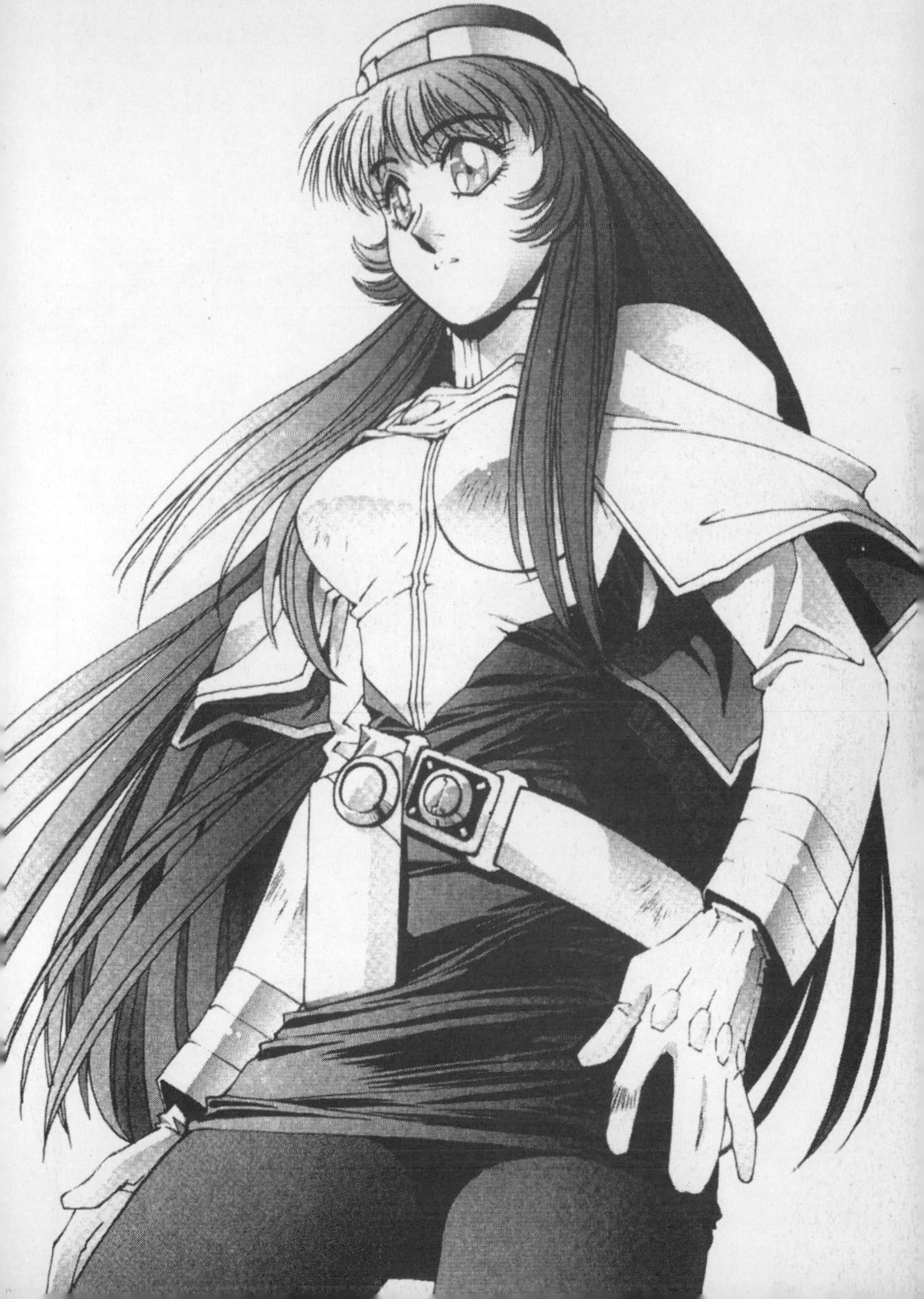

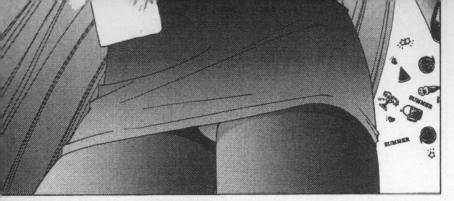

OOPS!

DRIBBLE!

THUD

KYAAAA!! YOU PERVERT!! HELP! PEEPING TOM!!

WAIT...

YOU SAW MY PANTIES AND NOW YOUR NOSE IS BLEEDING!!

NO, THAT'S NOT TRUE. SOMETHING HIT ME IN THE NOSE AND...

NOOOOO!! DON'T TOUCH ME! I'M GOING TO GET PREGNANT!!

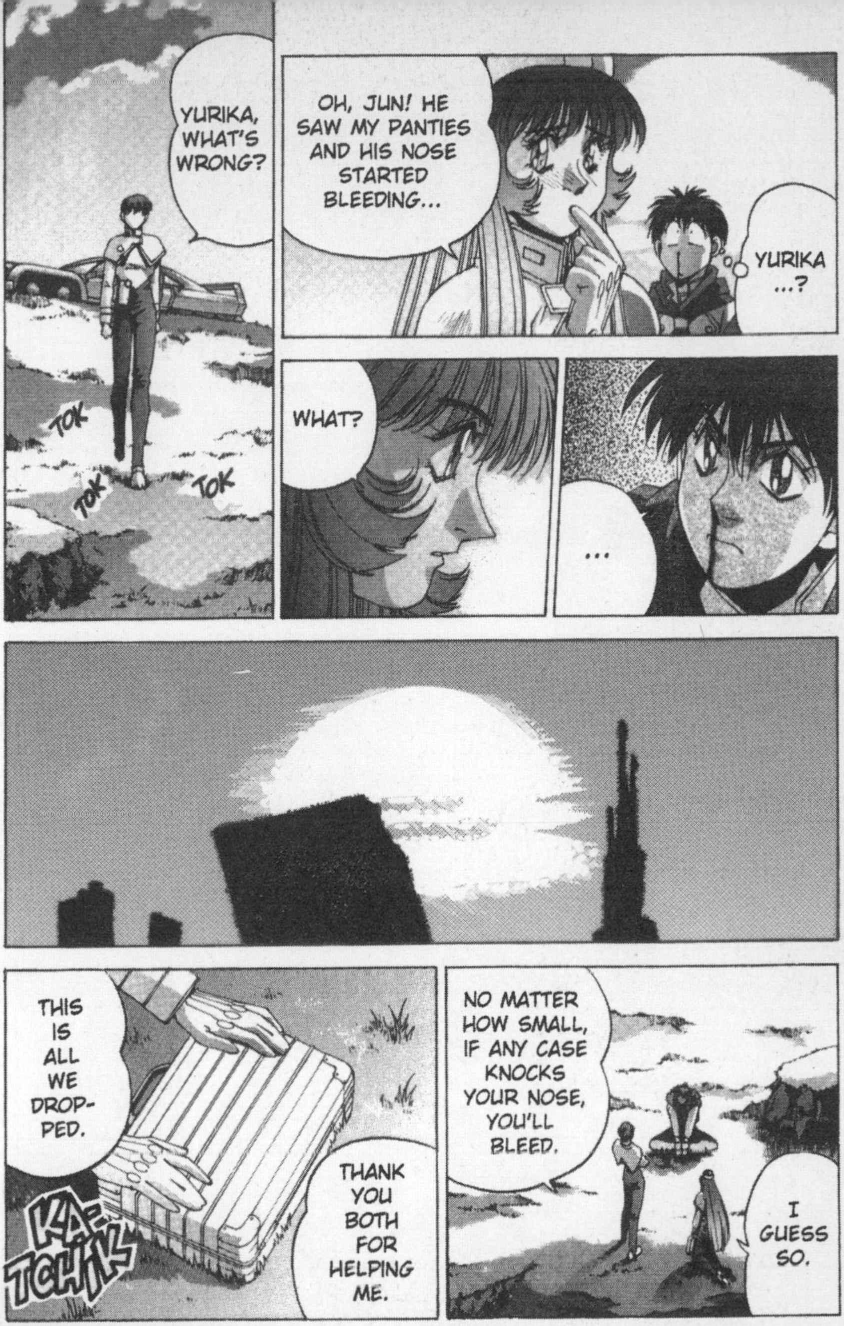
YURIKA, WHAT'S WRONG?
TOK
TOK
TOK
OH, JUN! HE SAW MY PANTIES AND HIS NOSE STARTED BLEEDING...
YURIKA ...?
WHAT?
...
THIS IS ALL WE DROP-PED.
KA-TCHIK
THANK YOU BOTH FOR HELPING ME.
NO MATTER HOW SMALL, IF ANY CASE KNOCKS YOUR NOSE, YOU'LL BLEED.
I GUESS SO.

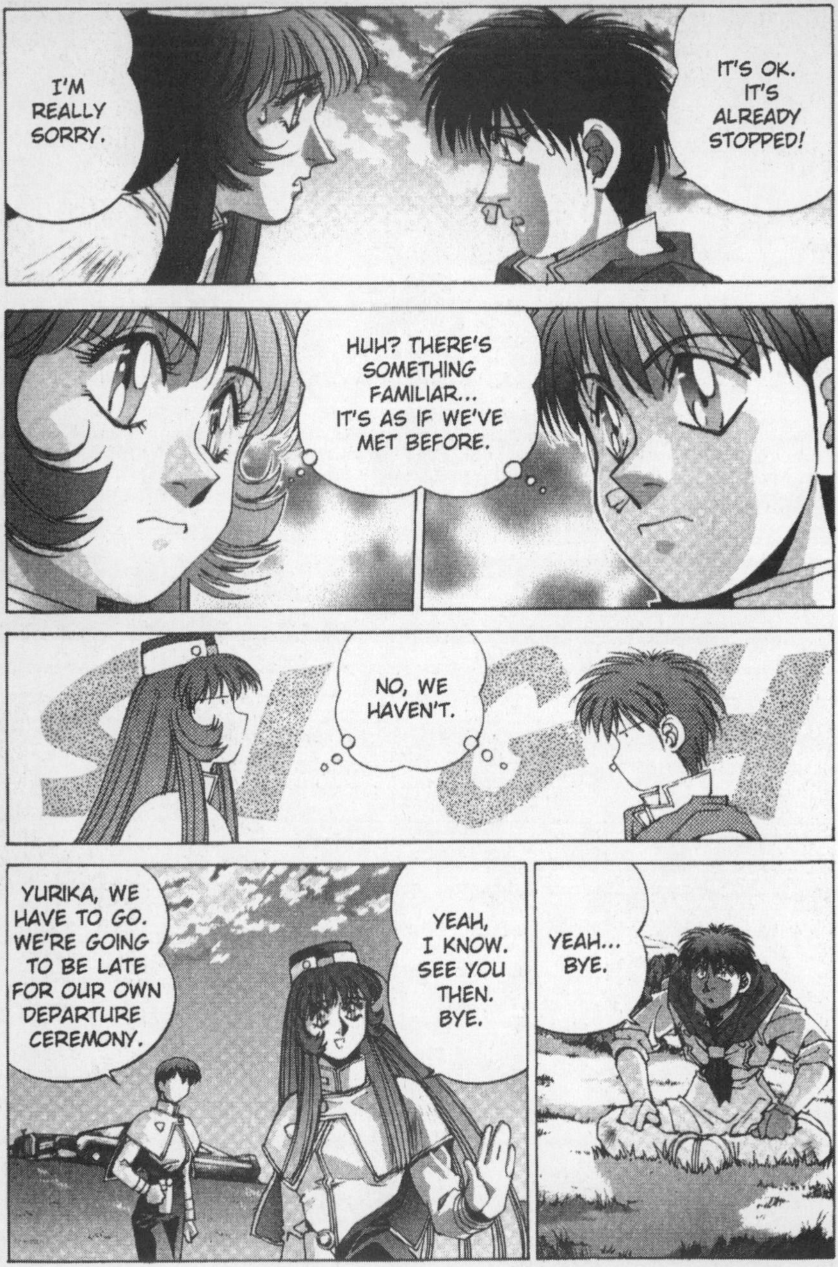
I'M REALLY SORRY.
IT'S OK. IT'S ALREADY STOPPED!
HUH? THERE'S SOMETHING FAMILIAR... IT'S AS IF WE'VE MET BEFORE.
SIGH
NO, WE HAVEN'T.
YURIKA, WE HAVE TO GO. WE'RE GOING TO BE LATE FOR OUR OWN DEPARTURE CEREMONY.
YEAH, I KNOW. SEE YOU THEN. BYE.
YEAH... BYE.

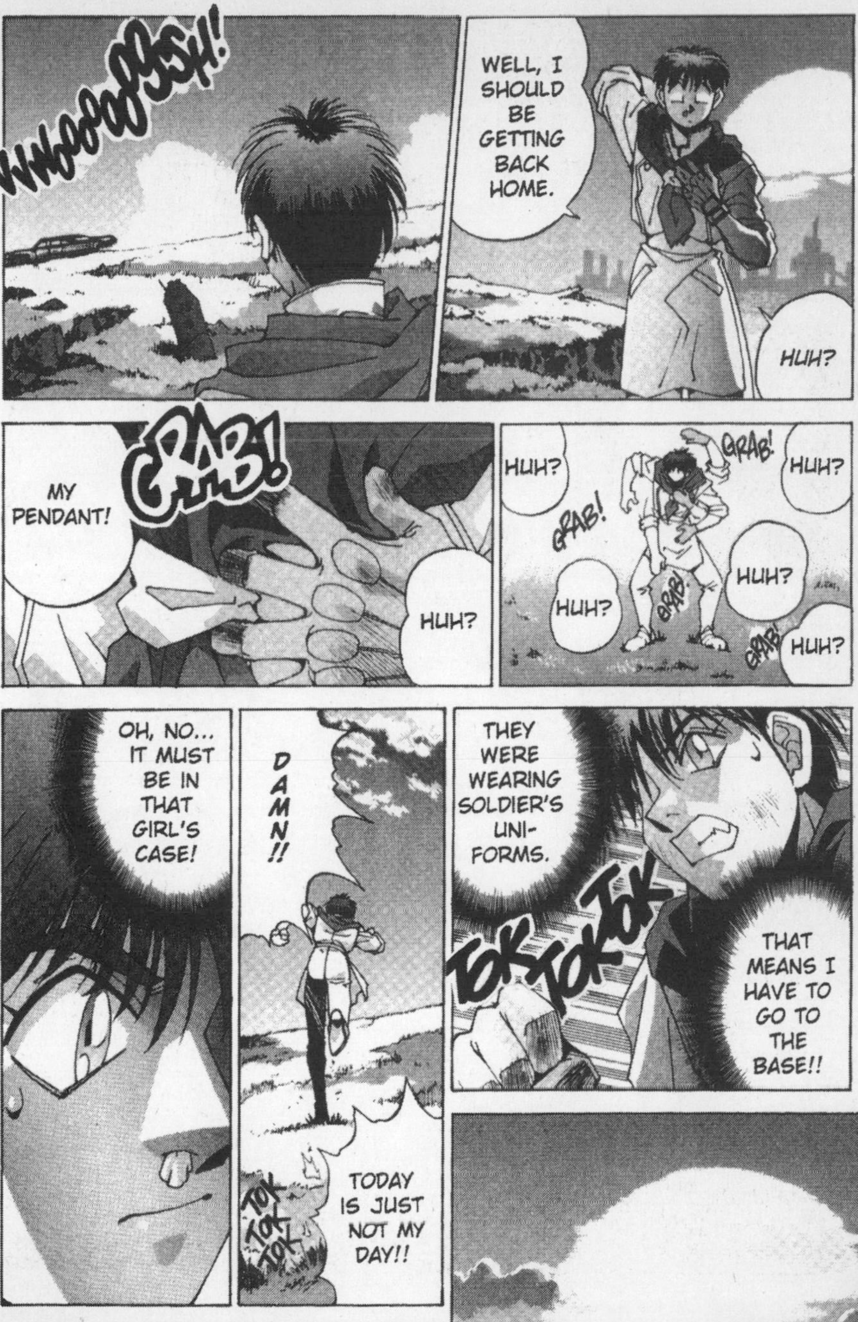
WELL, I SHOULD BE GETTING BACK HOME.
HUH?
MY PENDANT!
GRAB!
HUH?
HUH?
GRAB!
HUH?
GRAB!
HUH?
HUH?
GRAB!
GRAB!
HUH?
OH, NO... IT MUST BE IN THAT GIRL'S CASE!
DAMN!!
TODAY IS JUST NOT MY DAY!!
TOK TOK TOK
THEY WERE WEARING SOLDIER'S UNI-FORMS.
TOK TOK TOK
THAT MEANS I HAVE TO GO TO THE BASE!!

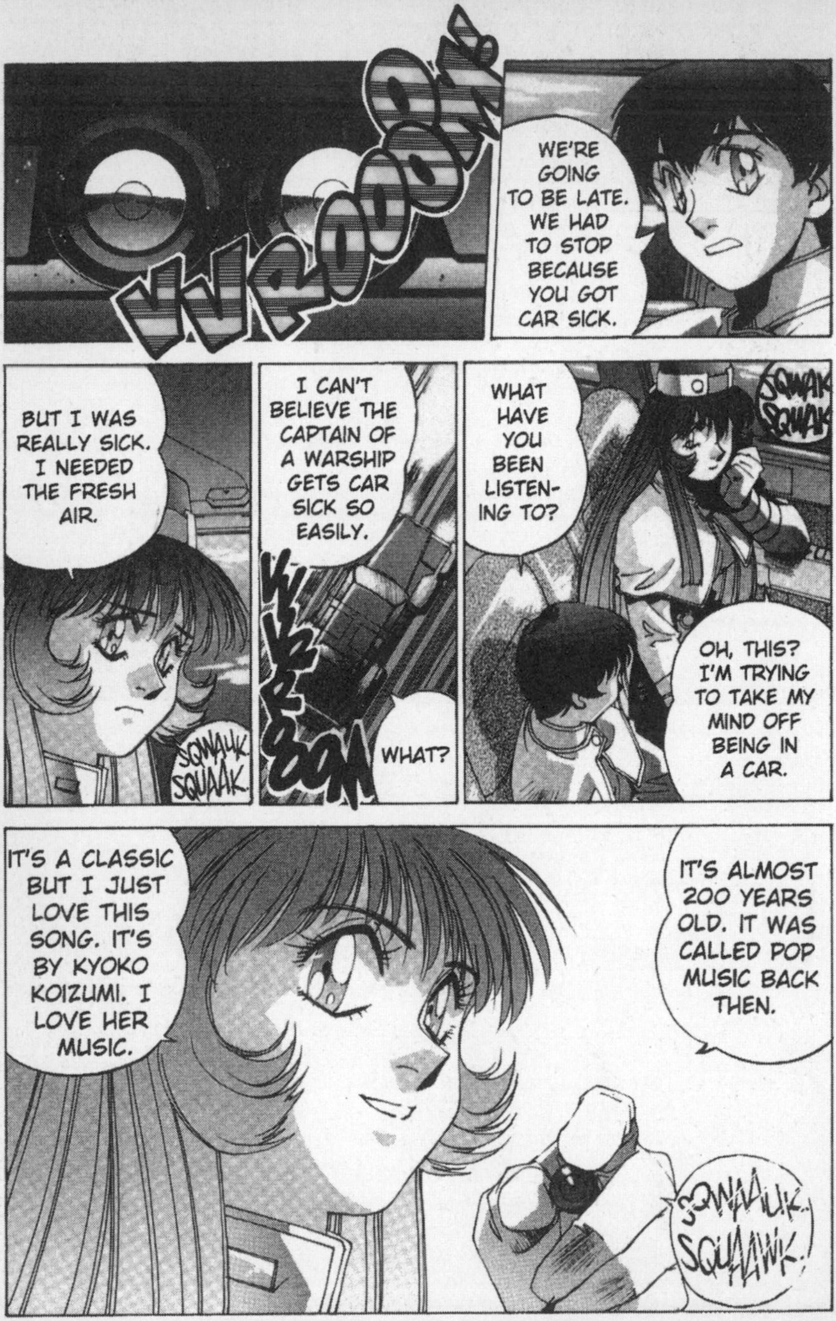
VVROOOOM
WE'RE GOING TO BE LATE. WE HAD TO STOP BECAUSE YOU GOT CAR SICK.
BUT I WAS REALLY SICK. I NEEDED THE FRESH AIR.
SQWAUK. SQUAAK.
I CAN'T BELIEVE THE CAPTAIN OF A WARSHIP GETS CAR SICK SO EASILY.
WHAT?
WHAT HAVE YOU BEEN LISTENING TO?
SQWAK SQWAK
OH, THIS? I'M TRYING TO TAKE MY MIND OFF BEING IN A CAR.
IT'S A CLASSIC BUT I JUST LOVE THIS SONG. IT'S BY KYOKO KOIZUMI. I LOVE HER MUSIC.
IT'S ALMOST 200 YEARS OLD. IT WAS CALLED POP MUSIC BACK THEN.
SQWAUK.. SQUAWK.

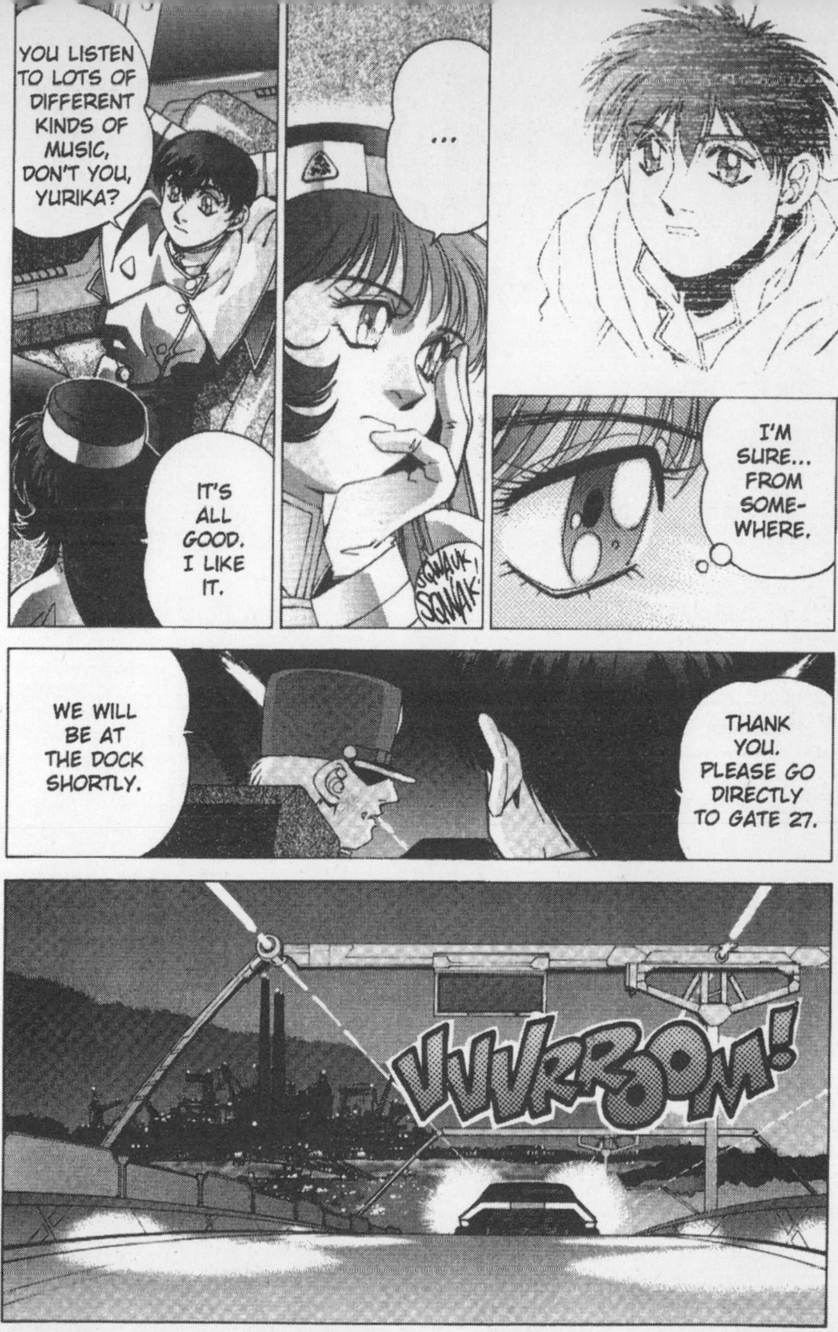
YOU LISTEN TO LOTS OF DIFFERENT KINDS OF MUSIC, DON'T YOU, YURIKA?
IT'S ALL GOOD. I LIKE IT.
...
SQWAWK SQWAWK!
I'M SURE... FROM SOME-WHERE.
WE WILL BE AT THE DOCK SHORTLY.
THANK YOU. PLEASE GO DIRECTLY TO GATE 27.
VVVRROOM!

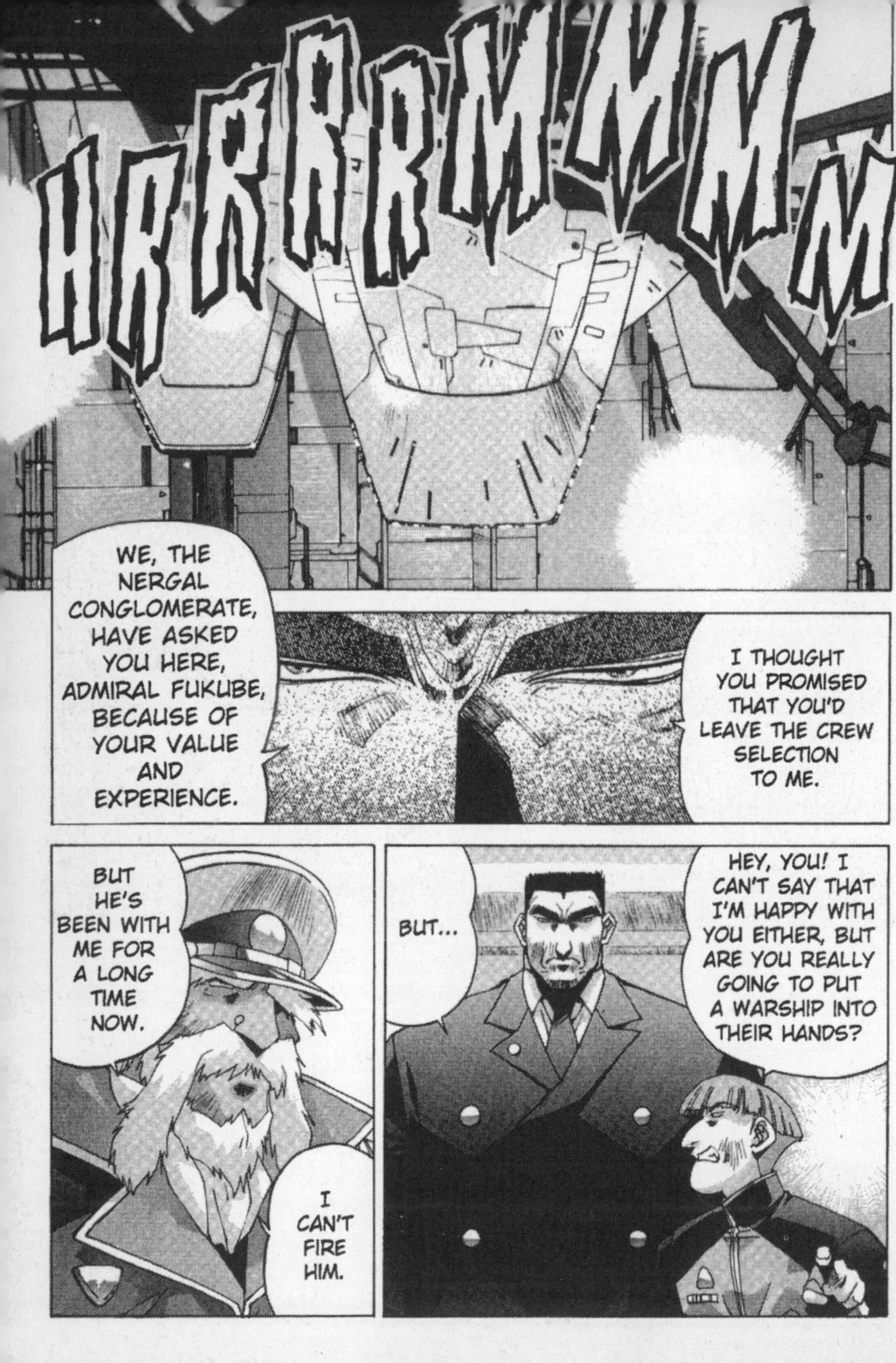
HRRRMMMMM
WE, THE NERGAL CONGLOMERATE, HAVE ASKED YOU HERE, ADMIRAL FUKUBE, BECAUSE OF YOUR VALUE AND EXPERIENCE.
I THOUGHT YOU PROMISED THAT YOU'D LEAVE THE CREW SELECTION TO ME.
BUT HE'S BEEN WITH ME FOR A LONG TIME NOW.
I CAN'T FIRE HIM.
BUT...
HEY, YOU! I CAN'T SAY THAT I'M HAPPY WITH YOU EITHER, BUT ARE YOU REALLY GOING TO PUT A WARSHIP INTO THEIR HANDS?

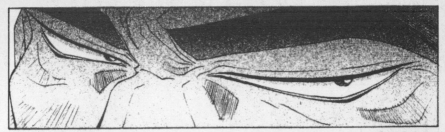

♪ LEAVIN' ON A JET PLANE ♪ DON'T KNOW ... I'LL BE BACK A...

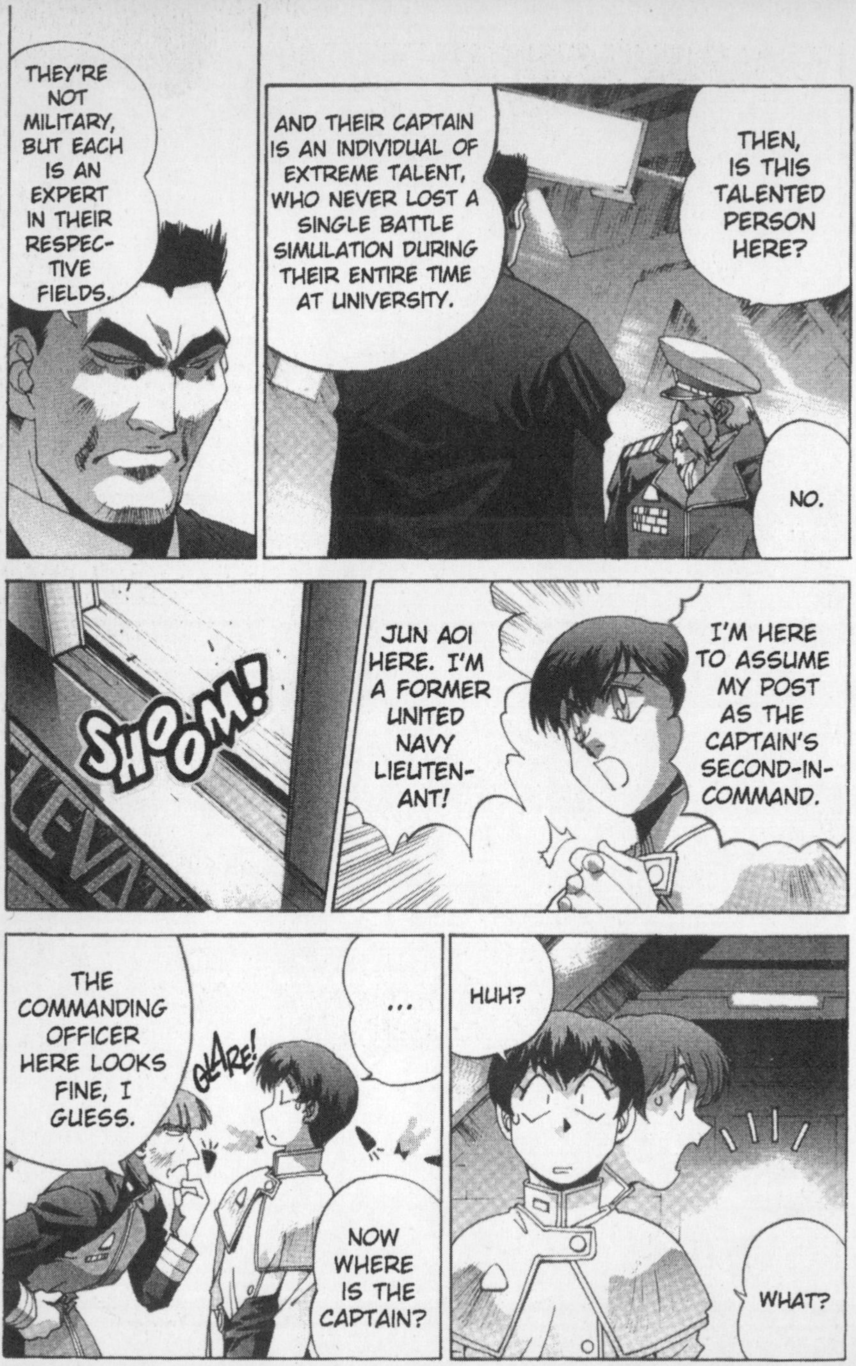
THEY'RE NOT MILITARY, BUT EACH IS AN EXPERT IN THEIR RESPEC-TIVE FIELDS.
AND THEIR CAPTAIN IS AN INDIVIDUAL OF EXTREME TALENT, WHO NEVER LOST A SINGLE BATTLE SIMULATION DURING THEIR ENTIRE TIME AT UNIVERSITY.
THEN, IS THIS TALENTED PERSON HERE?
NO.
SHOOM!
JUN AOI HERE. I'M A FORMER UNITED NAVY LIEUTEN-ANT!
I'M HERE TO ASSUME MY POST AS THE CAPTAIN'S SECOND-IN-COMMAND.
THE COMMANDING OFFICER HERE LOOKS FINE, I GUESS.
GLARE!
...
NOW WHERE IS THE CAPTAIN?
HUH?
WHAT?

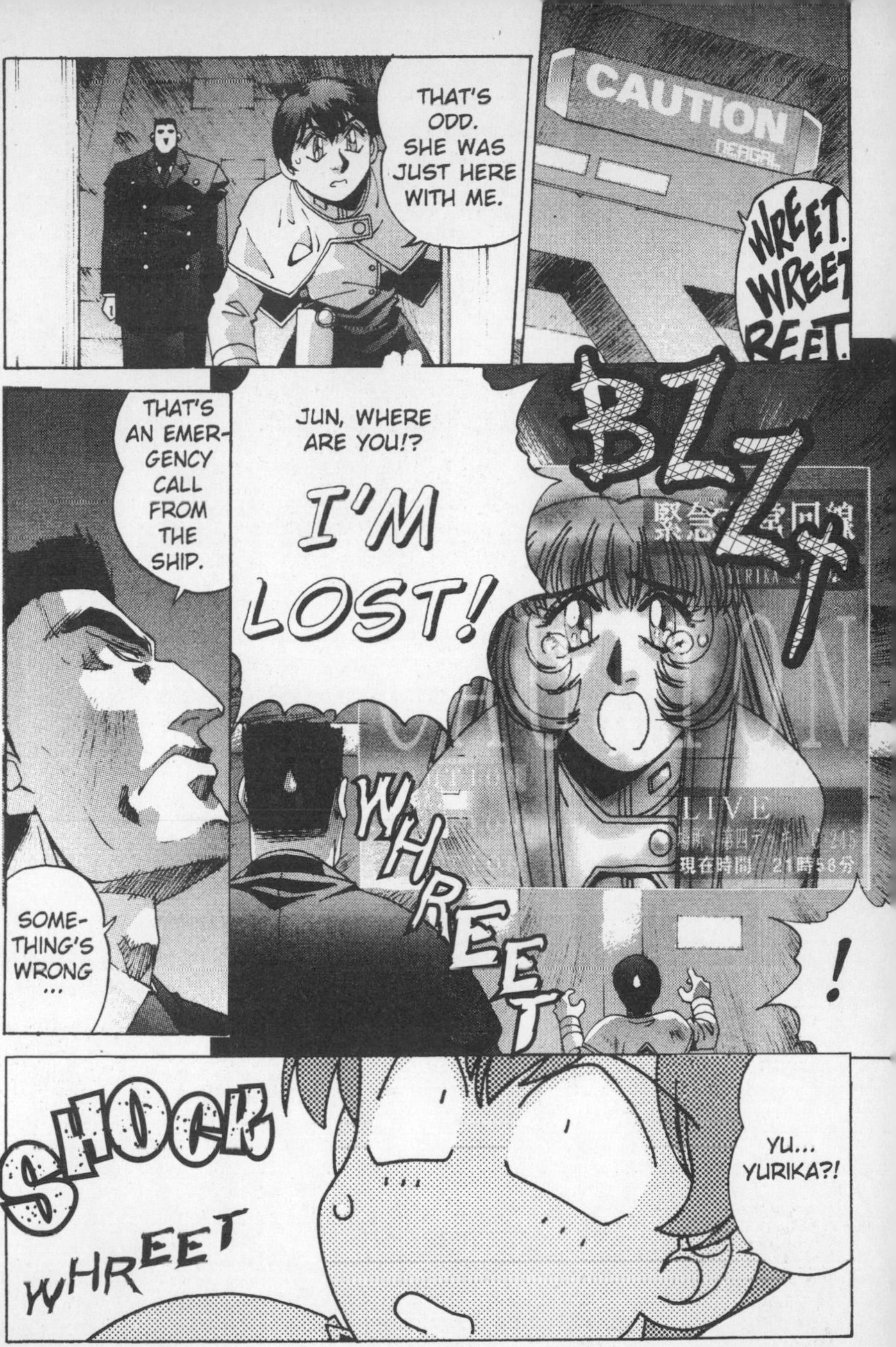
THAT'S ODD. SHE WAS JUST HERE WITH ME.
CAUTION
WREET. WREET. REET.
THAT'S AN EMERGENCY CALL FROM THE SHIP.
SOMETHING'S WRONG ...
BLZ
JUN, WHERE ARE YOU!?
I'M LOST!
LIVE
現在時間 21時58分
WHREET
!
SHOCK
WHREET
YU... YURIKA?!

I'M HERE BUT I HAVE NO IDEA WHERE SHE IS.

BUT...

...THAT PENDANT BELONGED TO MY DEAD FATHER.

I HAVE TO...

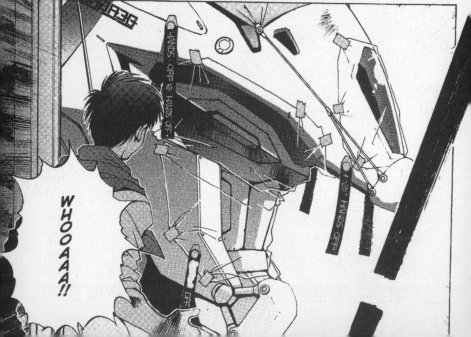

WHOOAAA!!

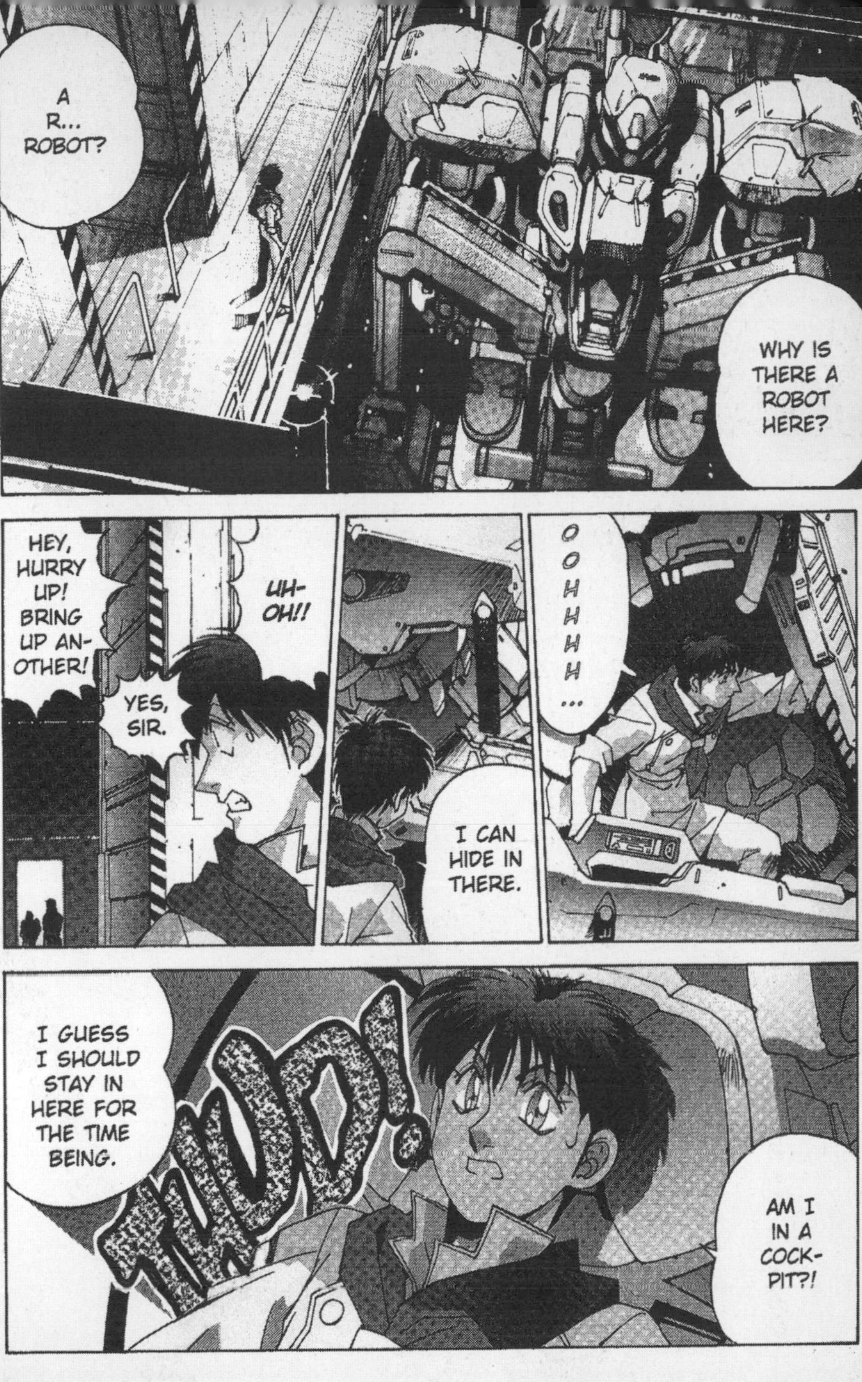
A R... ROBOT?
WHY IS THERE A ROBOT HERE?
HEY, HURRY UP! BRING UP AN-OTHER!
YES, SIR.
UH-OH!!
I CAN HIDE IN THERE.
OOHHHH...
I GUESS I SHOULD STAY IN HERE FOR THE TIME BEING.
THUD!
AM I IN A COCK-PIT?!

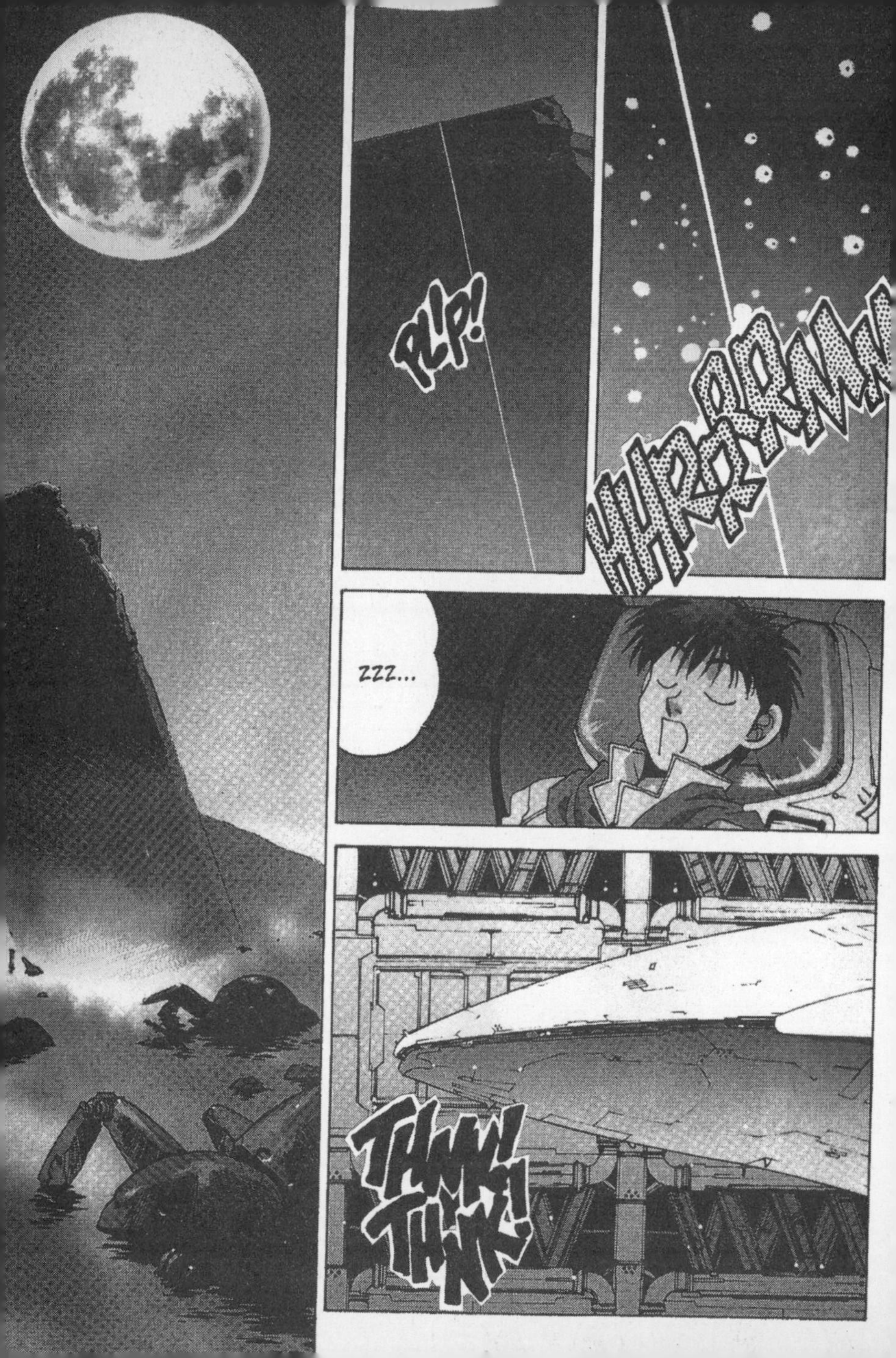
PLIP!
WHRRRRMM
ZZZ...
THUNK!
THUNK!

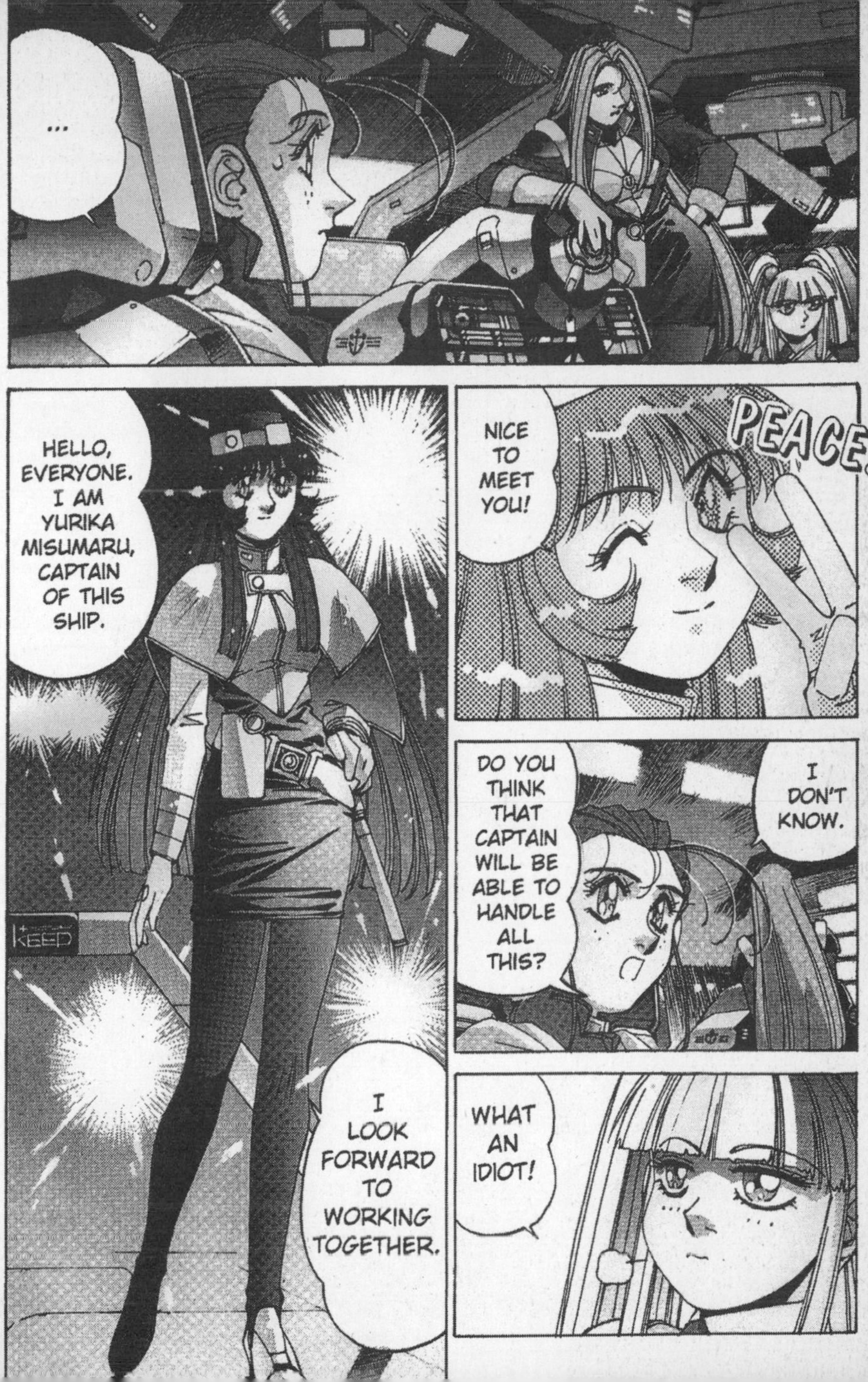
...
HELLO, EVERYONE. I AM YURIKA MISUMARU, CAPTAIN OF THIS SHIP.
I LOOK FORWARD TO WORKING TOGETHER.
NICE TO MEET YOU!
PEACE!
DO YOU THINK THAT CAPTAIN WILL BE ABLE TO HANDLE ALL THIS?
I DON'T KNOW.
WHAT AN IDIOT!

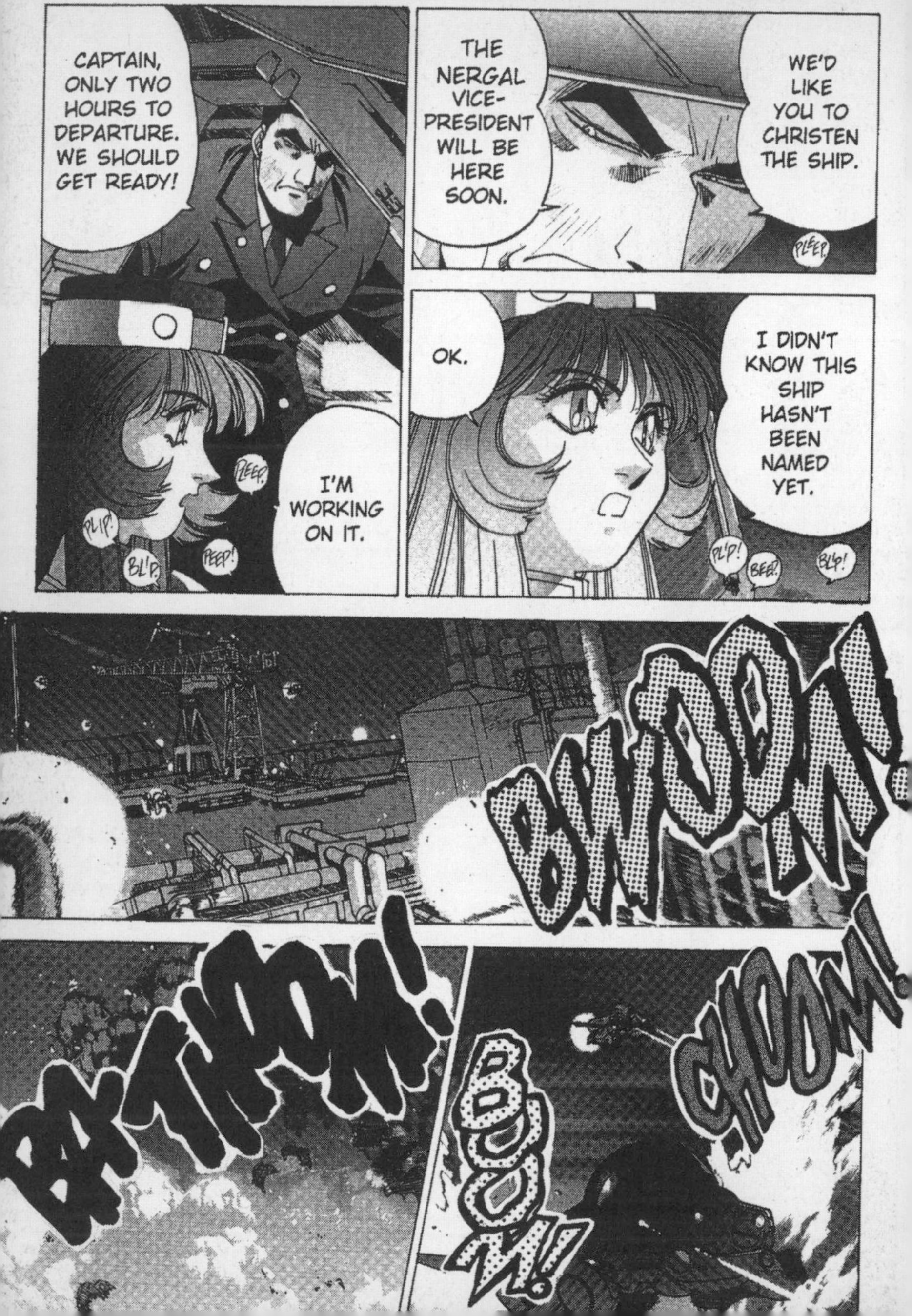
CAPTAIN, ONLY TWO HOURS TO DEPARTURE. WE SHOULD GET READY!
PLEEP!
PLIP!
BLIP!
PEEP!
I'M WORKING ON IT.
THE NERGAL VICE-PRESIDENT WILL BE HERE SOON.
WE'D LIKE YOU TO CHRISTEN THE SHIP.
PLEEP!
OK.
I DIDN'T KNOW THIS SHIP HASN'T BEEN NAMED YET.
PLIP!
BEEP!
BLIP!
BWOOM!
BA-THOOM!
BOOOM!
CHOOM!

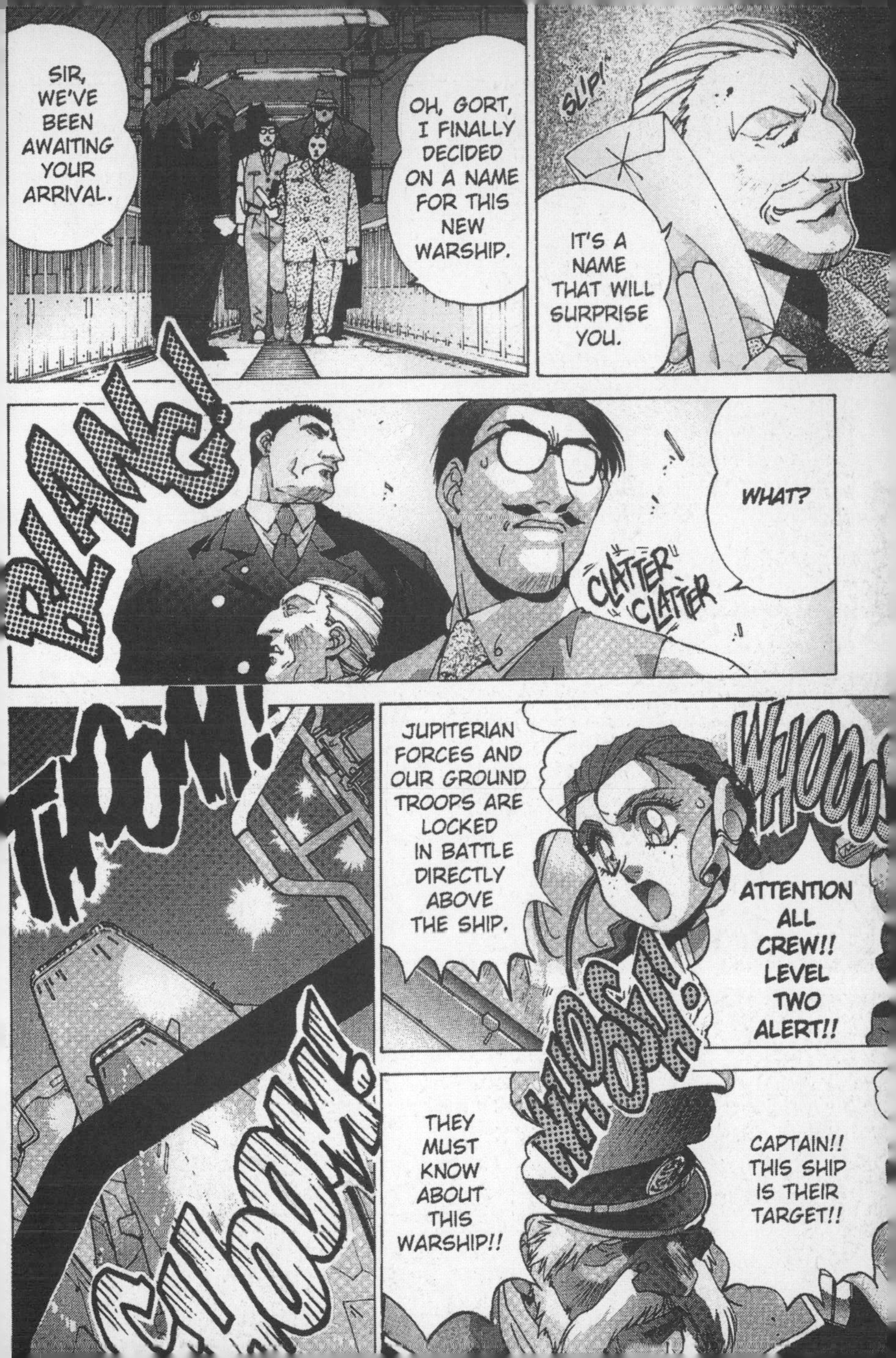
SIR, WE'VE BEEN AWAITING YOUR ARRIVAL.
OH, GORT, I FINALLY DECIDED ON A NAME FOR THIS NEW WARSHIP.
SLIP!
IT'S A NAME THAT WILL SURPRISE YOU.
BLAM!
CLATTER CLATTER
WHAT?
THOOM!
BOOM!
JUPITERIAN FORCES AND OUR GROUND TROOPS ARE LOCKED IN BATTLE DIRECTLY ABOVE THE SHIP.
WHOOOS
ATTENTION ALL CREW!! LEVEL TWO ALERT!!
WHOOSH!
THEY MUST KNOW ABOUT THIS WARSHIP!!
CAPTAIN!! THIS SHIP IS THEIR TARGET!!

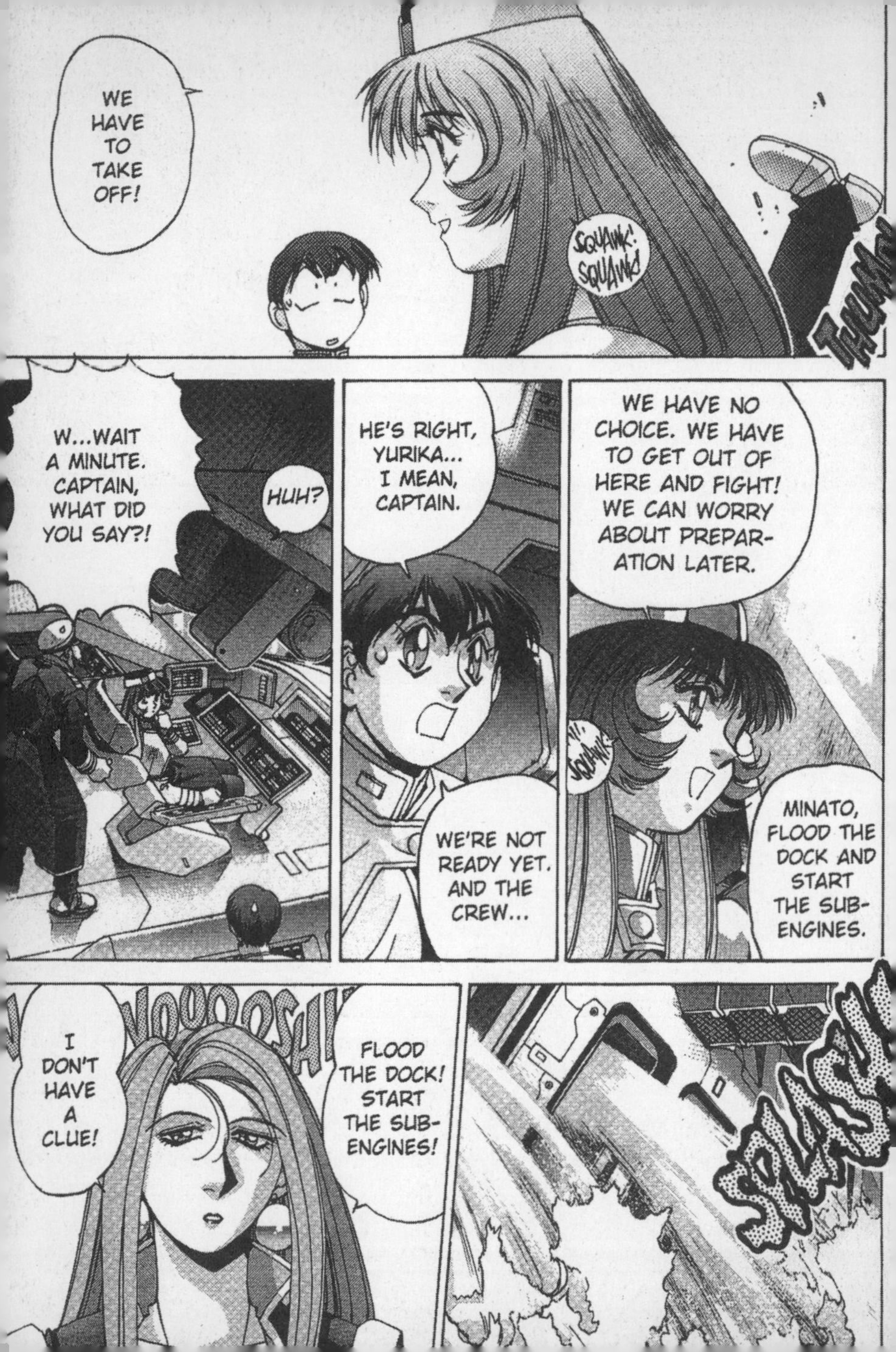
WE HAVE TO TAKE OFF!
SQUAWK! SQUAWK!
THUNK
W...WAIT A MINUTE. CAPTAIN, WHAT DID YOU SAY?!
HUH?
HE'S RIGHT, YURIKA... I MEAN, CAPTAIN.
WE'RE NOT READY YET. AND THE CREW...
WE HAVE NO CHOICE. WE HAVE TO GET OUT OF HERE AND FIGHT! WE CAN WORRY ABOUT PREPARATION LATER.
SQUAWK!
MINATO, FLOOD THE DOCK AND START THE SUB-ENGINES.
I DON'T HAVE A CLUE!
WOOOOOSH
FLOOD THE DOCK! START THE SUB-ENGINES!
SPLASH

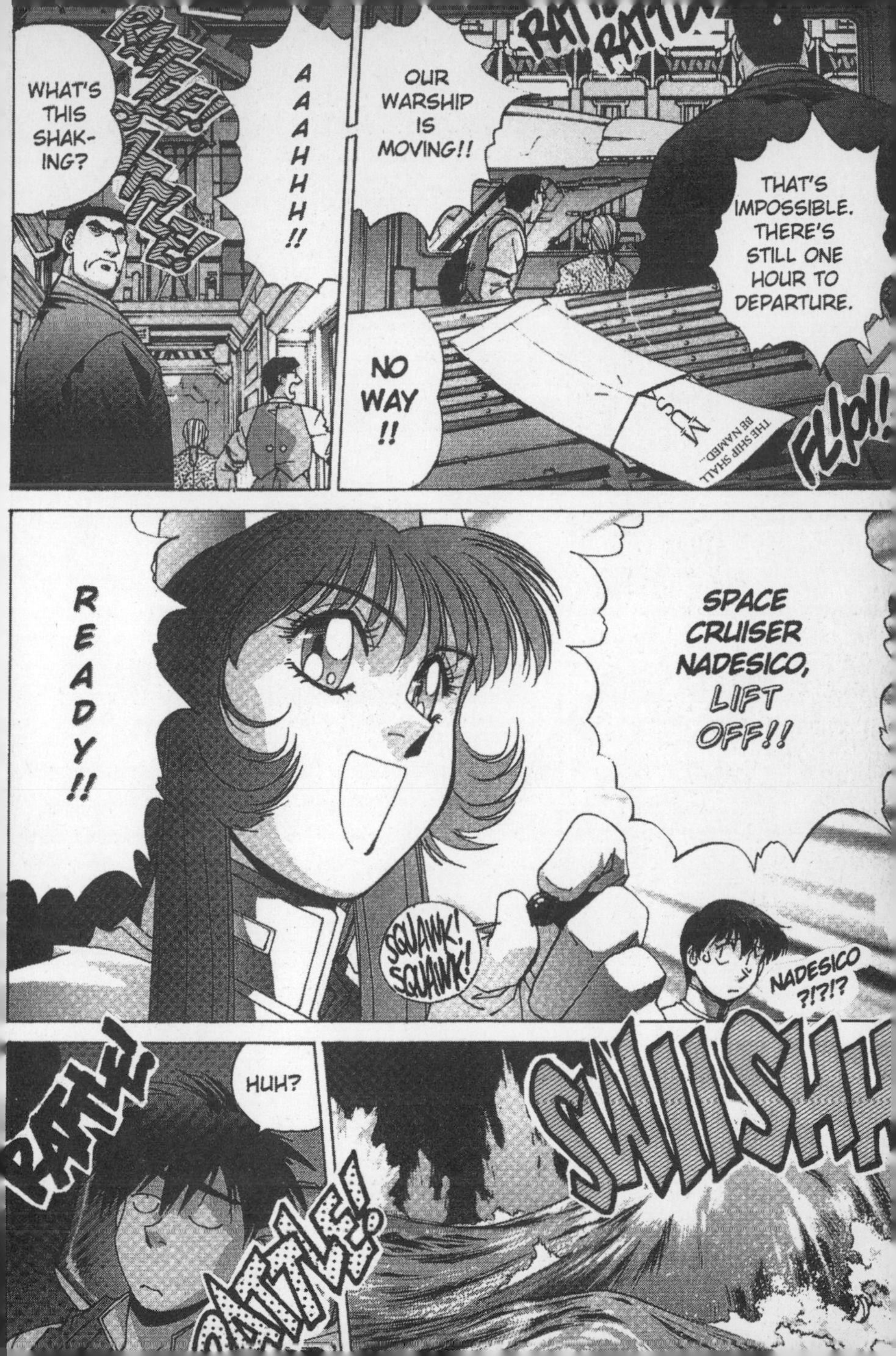
WHAT'S THIS SHAK-ING?
RATTLE! RATTLE!
AAAAHHHH!!
OUR WARSHIP IS MOVING!!
RAT... RATTLE
THAT'S IMPOSSIBLE. THERE'S STILL ONE HOUR TO DEPARTURE.
NO WAY!!
THE SHIP SHALL BE NAMED...
FLIP!!
READY!!
SPACE CRUISER NADESICO, LIFT OFF!!
SQUAWK! SQUAWK!
NADESICO?!?!?
RATTLE!
HUH?
RATTLE!
SWISH

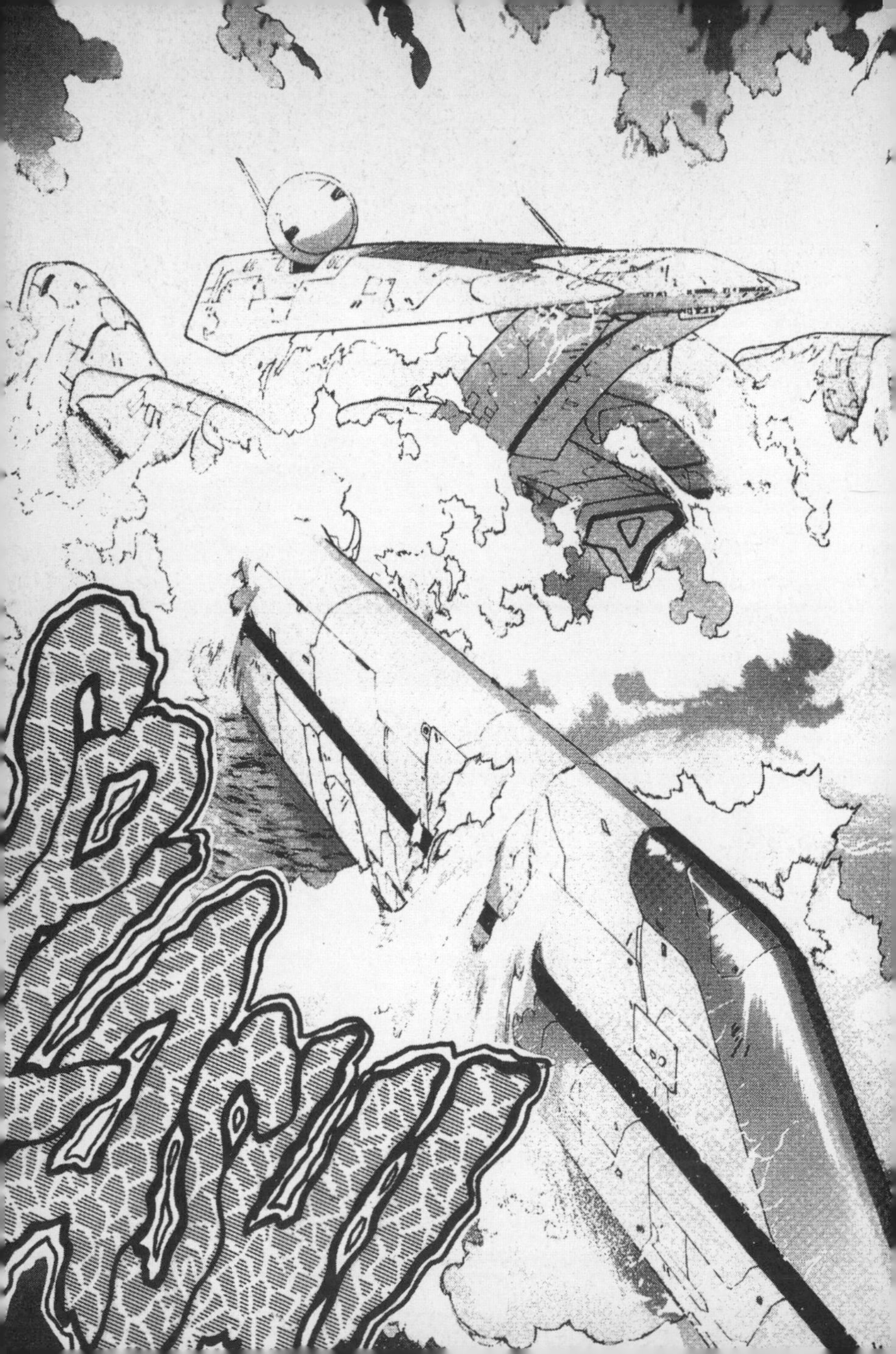

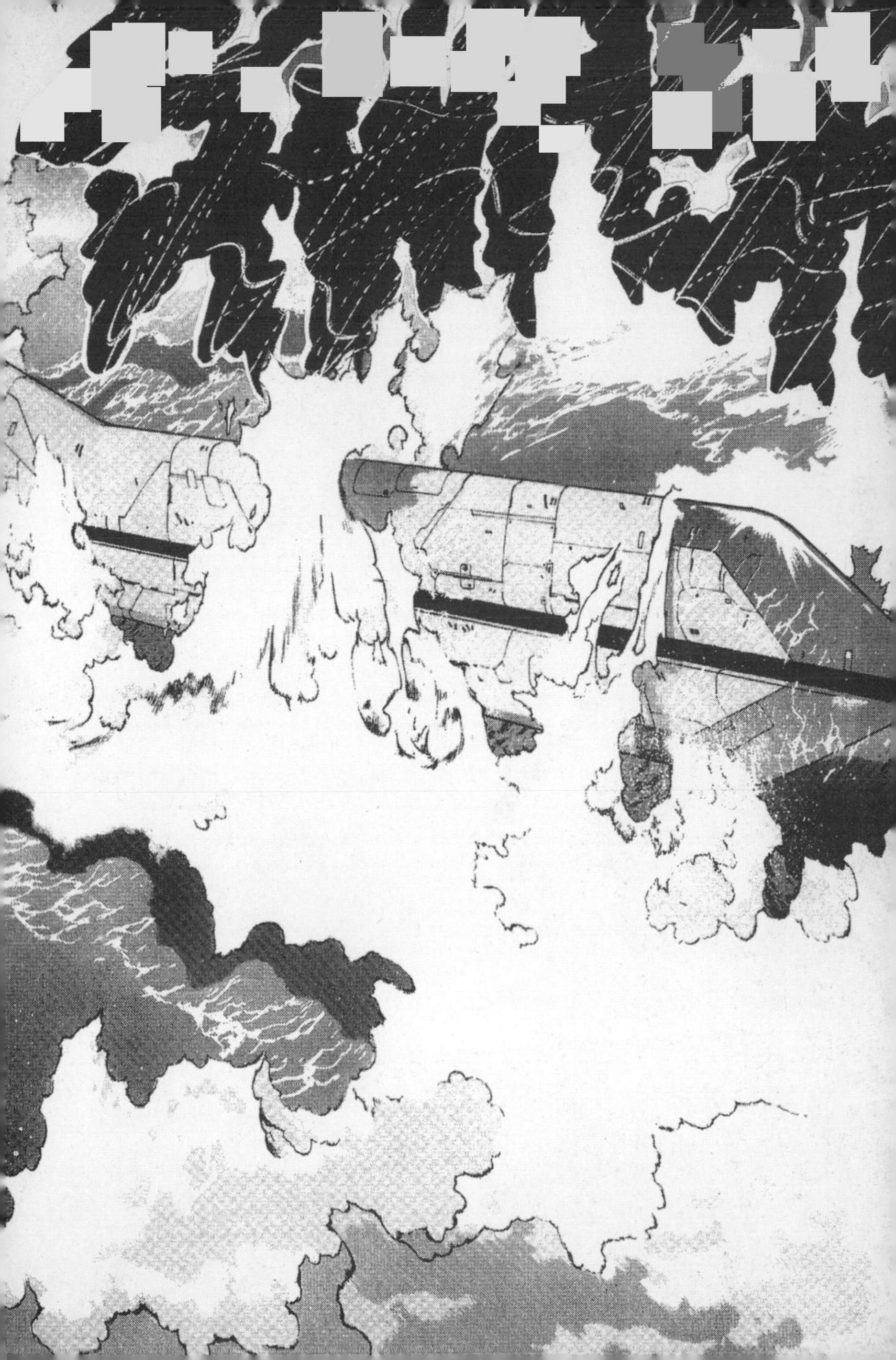

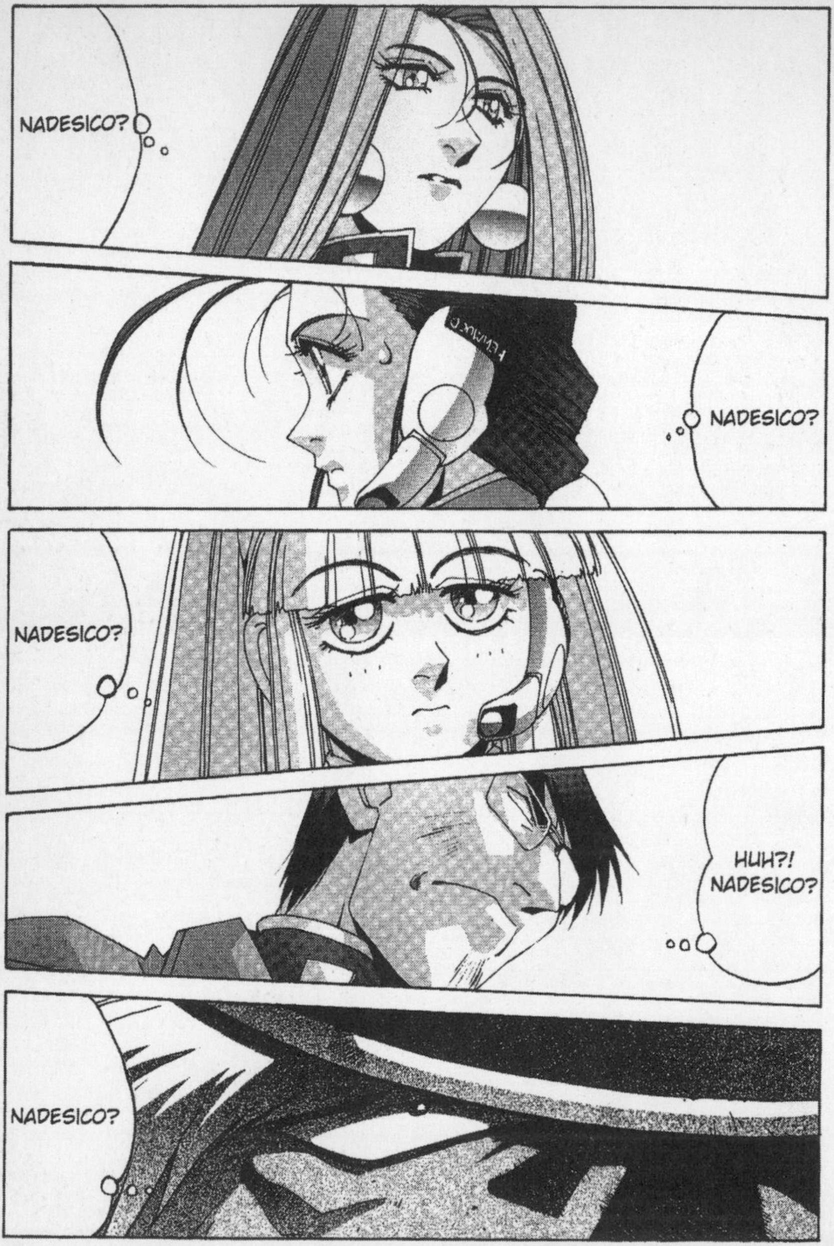
NADESICO?
NADESICO?
NADESICO?
HUH?! NADESICO?
NADESICO?

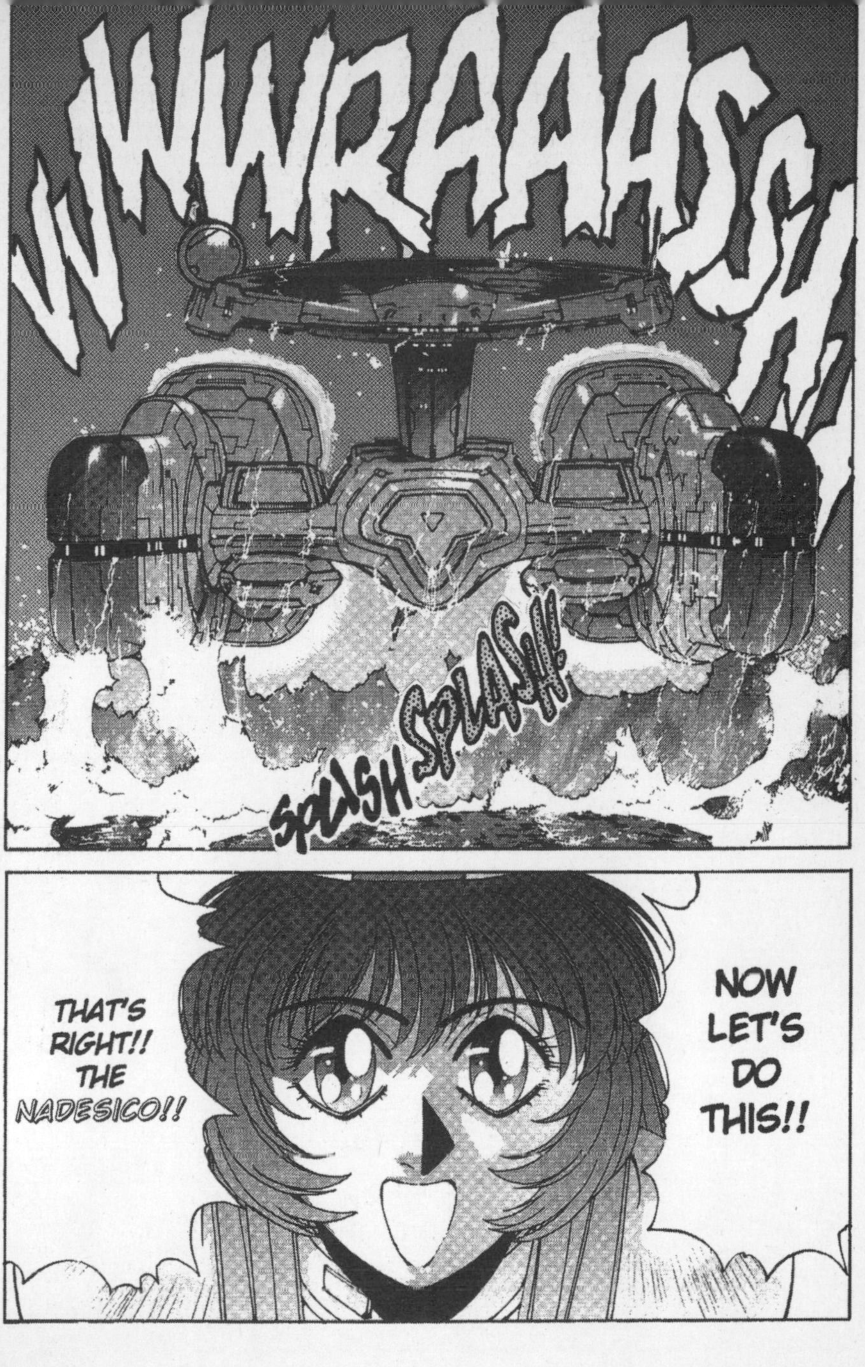
WWRAASH
SPLISH SPLASH!
THAT'S RIGHT!! THE NADESICO!!
NOW LET'S DO THIS!!

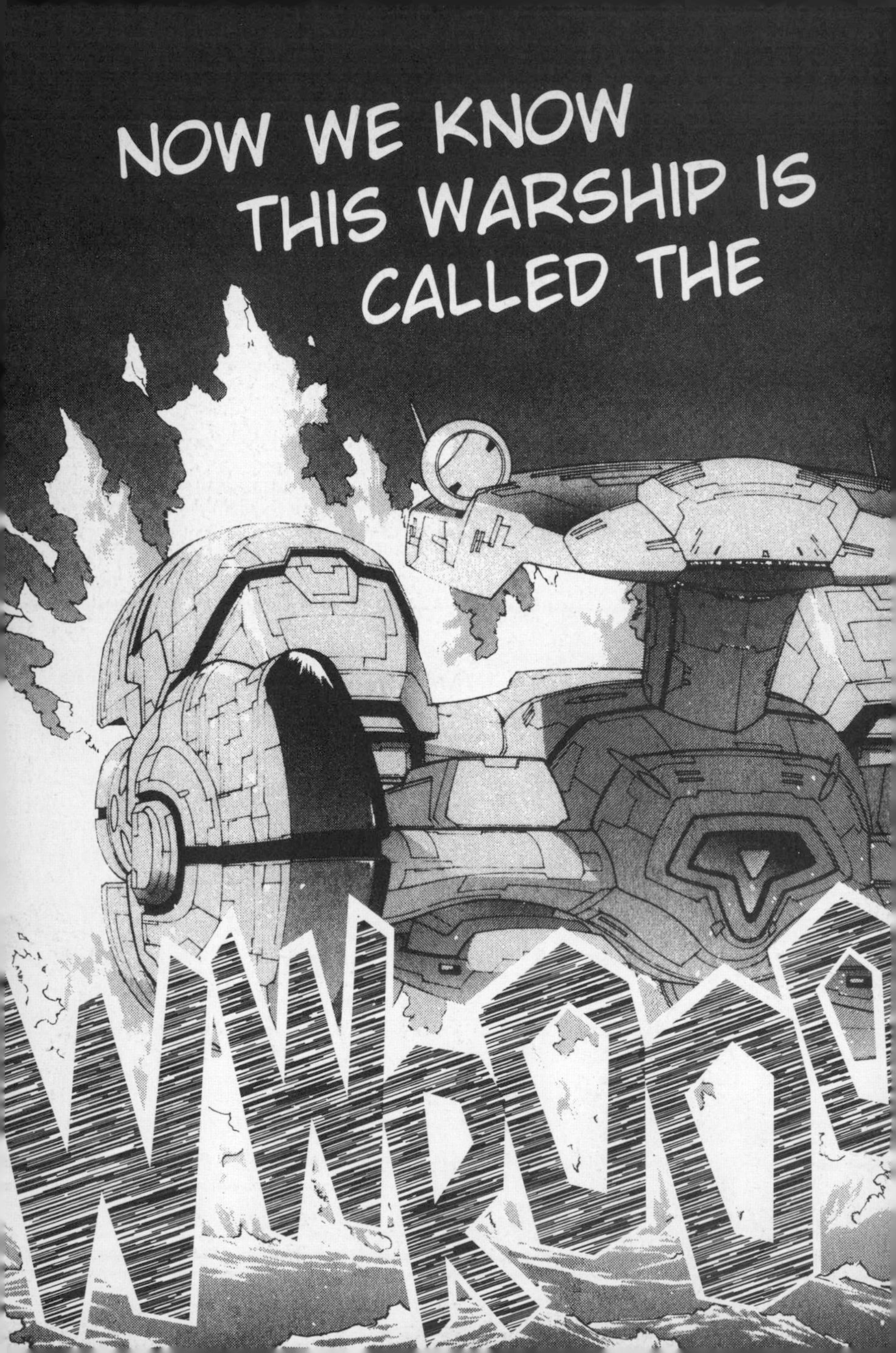
NOW WE KNOW
THIS WARSHIP IS
CALLED THE

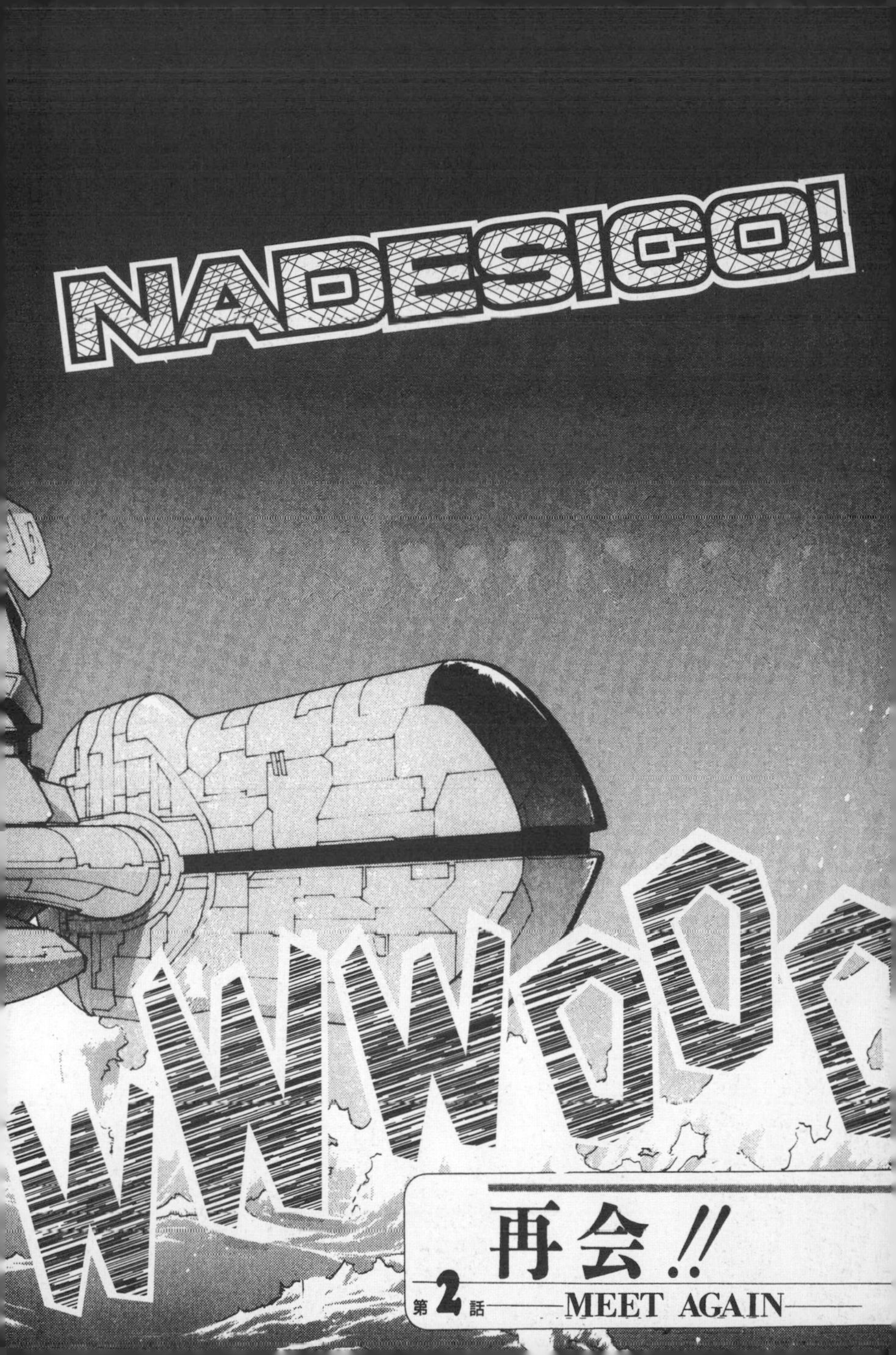
NADESICO!
WWWOOO
再会!!
第2話 MEET AGAIN

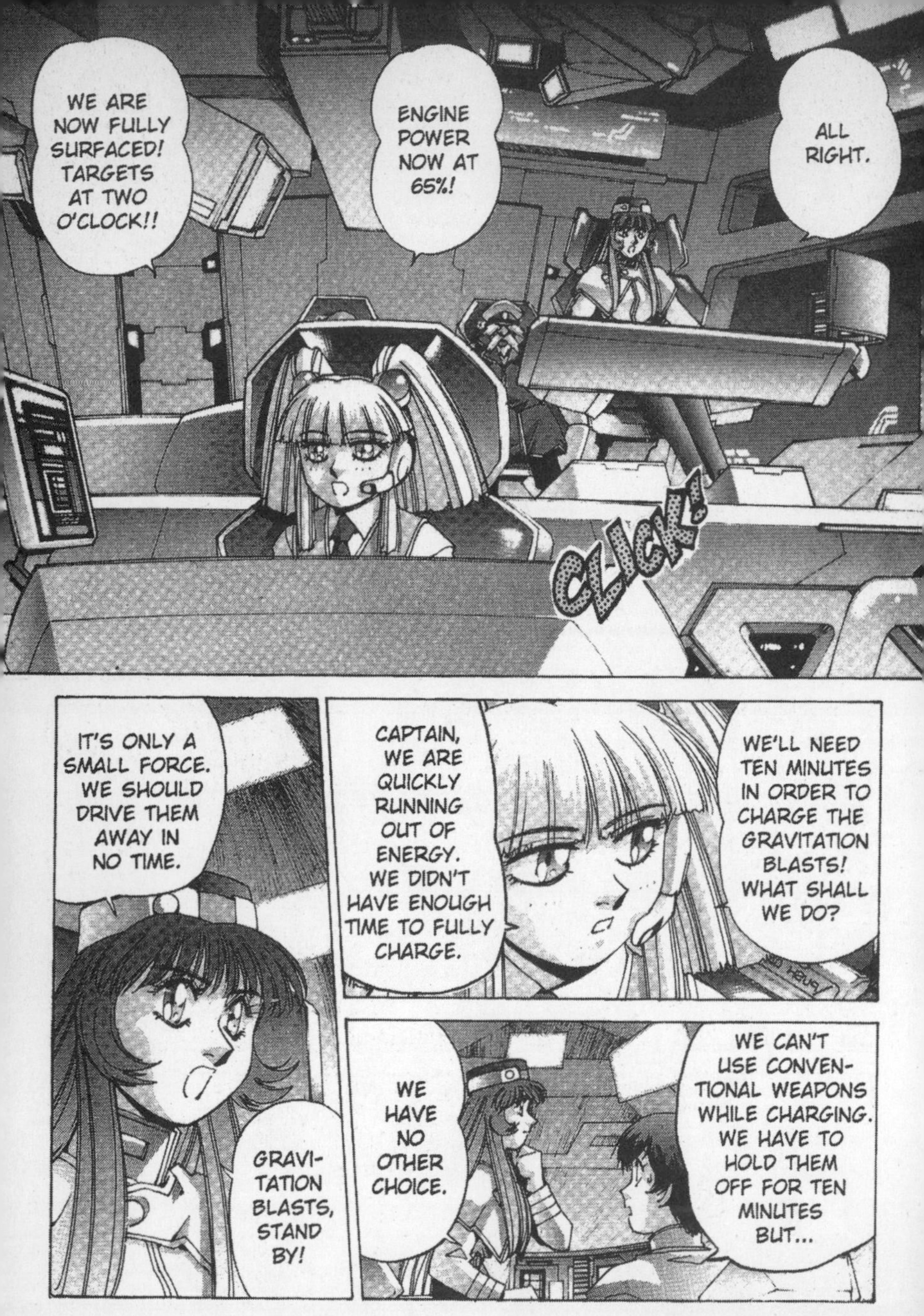
WE ARE NOW FULLY SURFACED! TARGETS AT TWO O'CLOCK!!
ENGINE POWER NOW AT 65%!
ALL RIGHT.
CLICK!
IT'S ONLY A SMALL FORCE. WE SHOULD DRIVE THEM AWAY IN NO TIME.
GRAVITATION BLASTS, STAND BY!
CAPTAIN, WE ARE QUICKLY RUNNING OUT OF ENERGY. WE DIDN'T HAVE ENOUGH TIME TO FULLY CHARGE.
WE'LL NEED TEN MINUTES IN ORDER TO CHARGE THE GRAVITATION BLASTS! WHAT SHALL WE DO?
WE HAVE NO OTHER CHOICE.
WE CAN'T USE CONVENTIONAL WEAPONS WHILE CHARGING. WE HAVE TO HOLD THEM OFF FOR TEN MINUTES BUT...

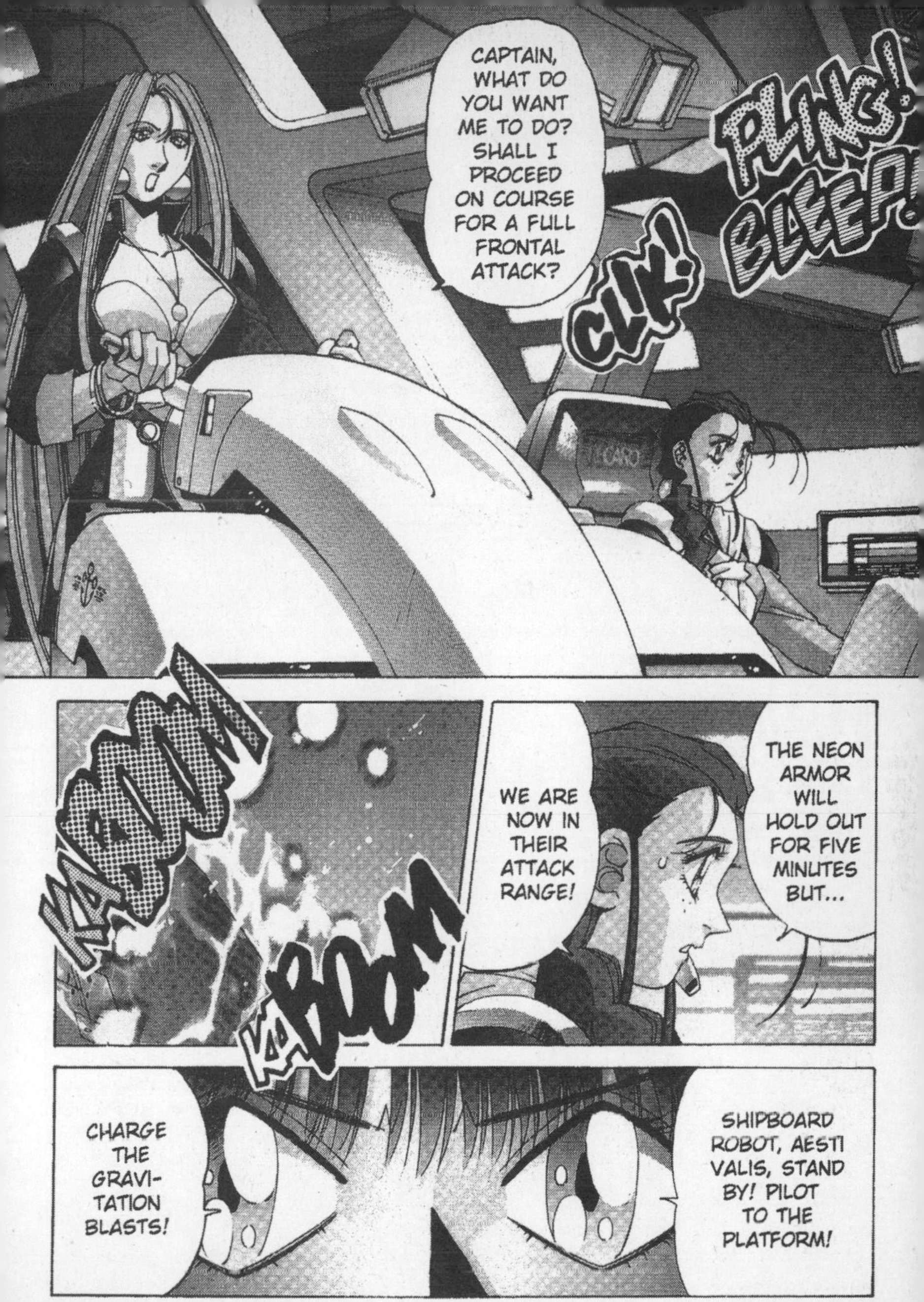
CAPTAIN, WHAT DO YOU WANT ME TO DO? SHALL I PROCEED ON COURSE FOR A FULL FRONTAL ATTACK?
CLIK!
PLING! BLEEP!
KABOOM
KABOOM
WE ARE NOW IN THEIR ATTACK RANGE!
THE NEON ARMOR WILL HOLD OUT FOR FIVE MINUTES BUT...
CHARGE THE GRAVI-TATION BLASTS!
SHIPBOARD ROBOT, AESTI VALIS, STAND BY! PILOT TO THE PLATFORM!

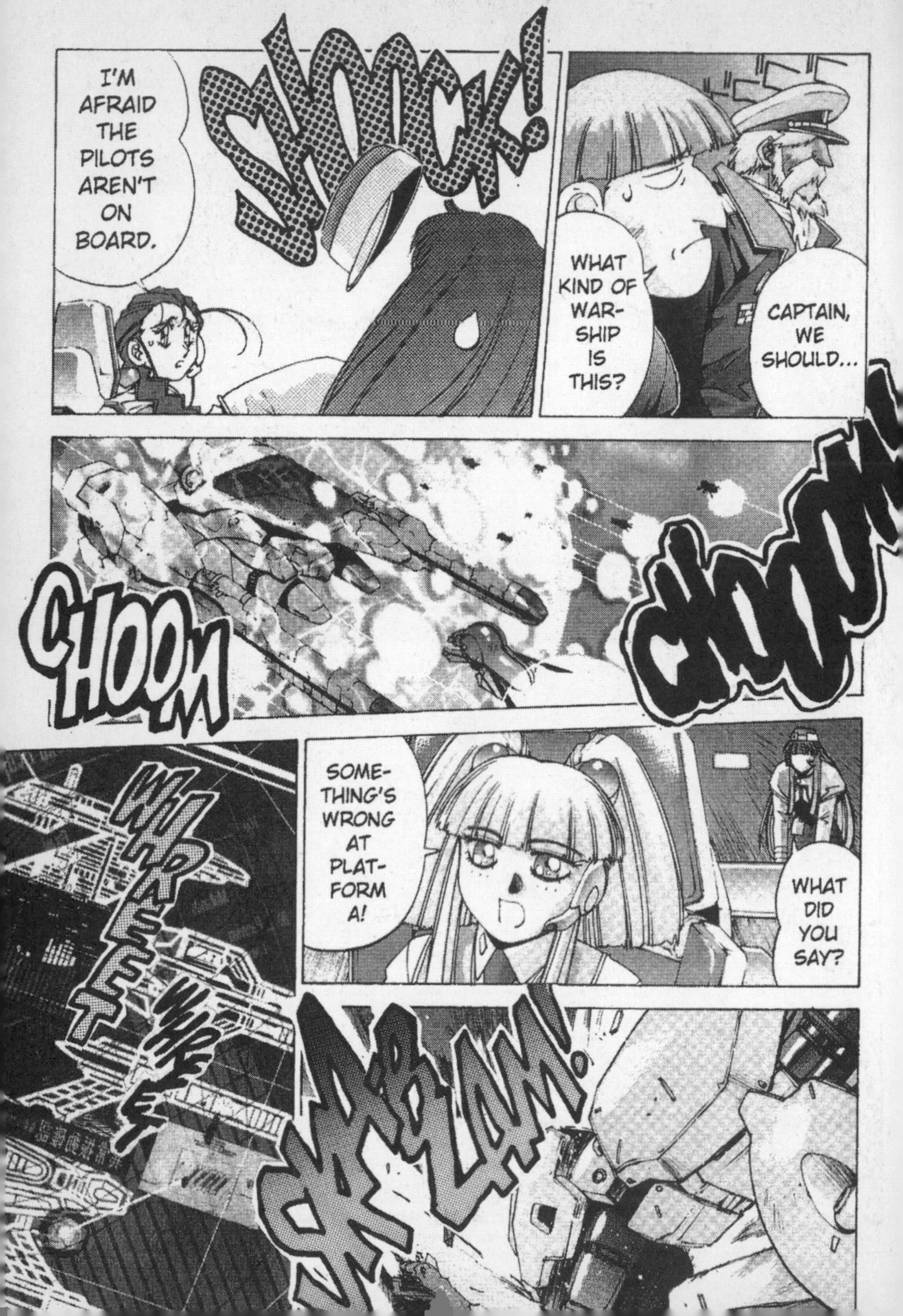
I'M AFRAID THE PILOTS AREN'T ON BOARD.
SHOOCK!
WHAT KIND OF WAR-SHIP IS THIS?
CAPTAIN, WE SHOULD...
CHOOM
CHOOM
SOME-THING'S WRONG AT PLAT-FORM A!
WHAT DID YOU SAY?
KA-BLAM!

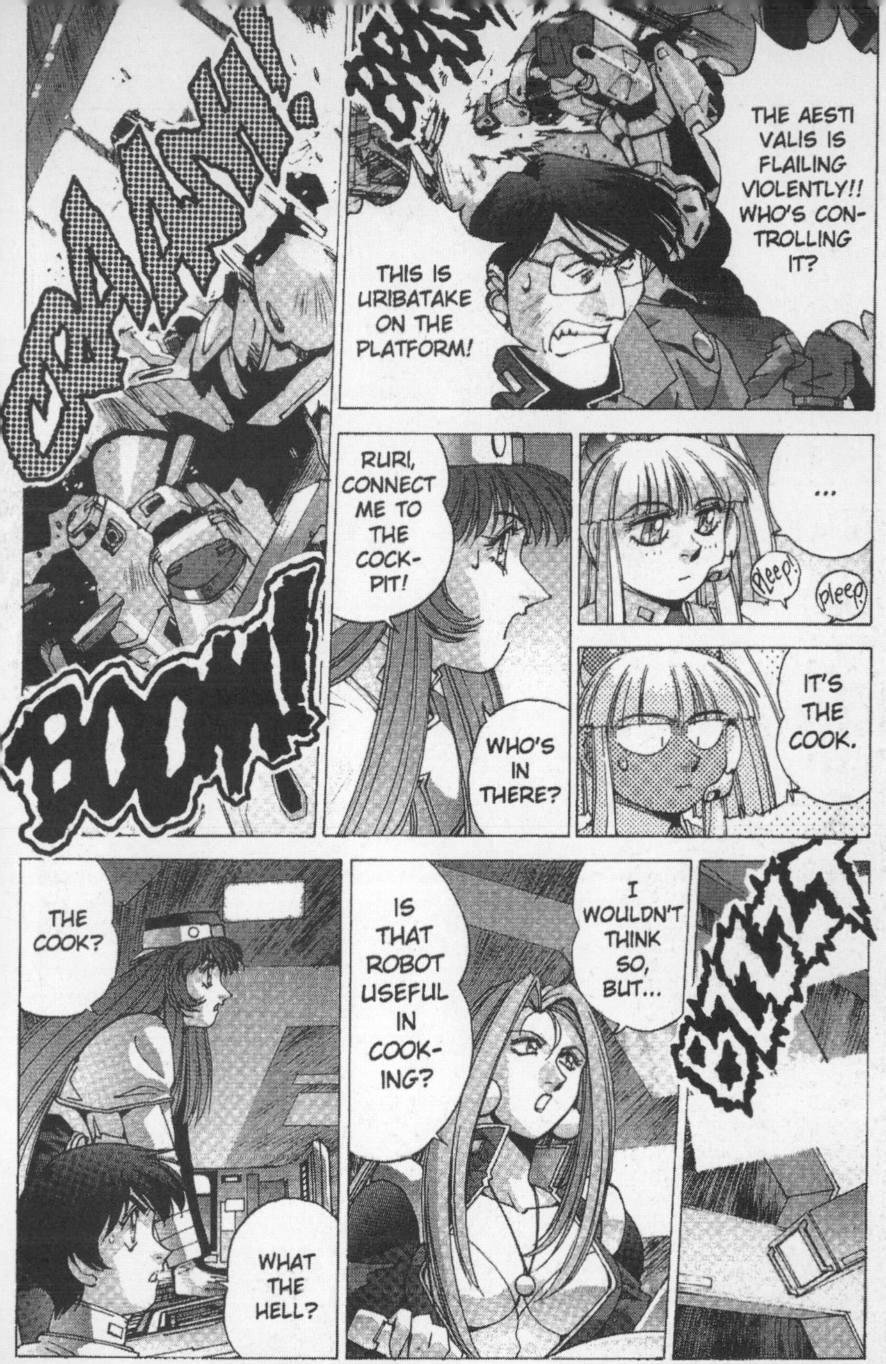
BOOM!
THIS IS URIBATAKE ON THE PLATFORM!
THE AESTI VALIS IS FLAILING VIOLENTLY!! WHO'S CON-TROLLING IT?
RURI, CONNECT ME TO THE COCK-PIT!
WHO'S IN THERE?
...
pleep!
pleep!
IT'S THE COOK.
THE COOK?
WHAT THE HELL?
IS THAT ROBOT USEFUL IN COOK-ING?
I WOULDN'T THINK SO, BUT...

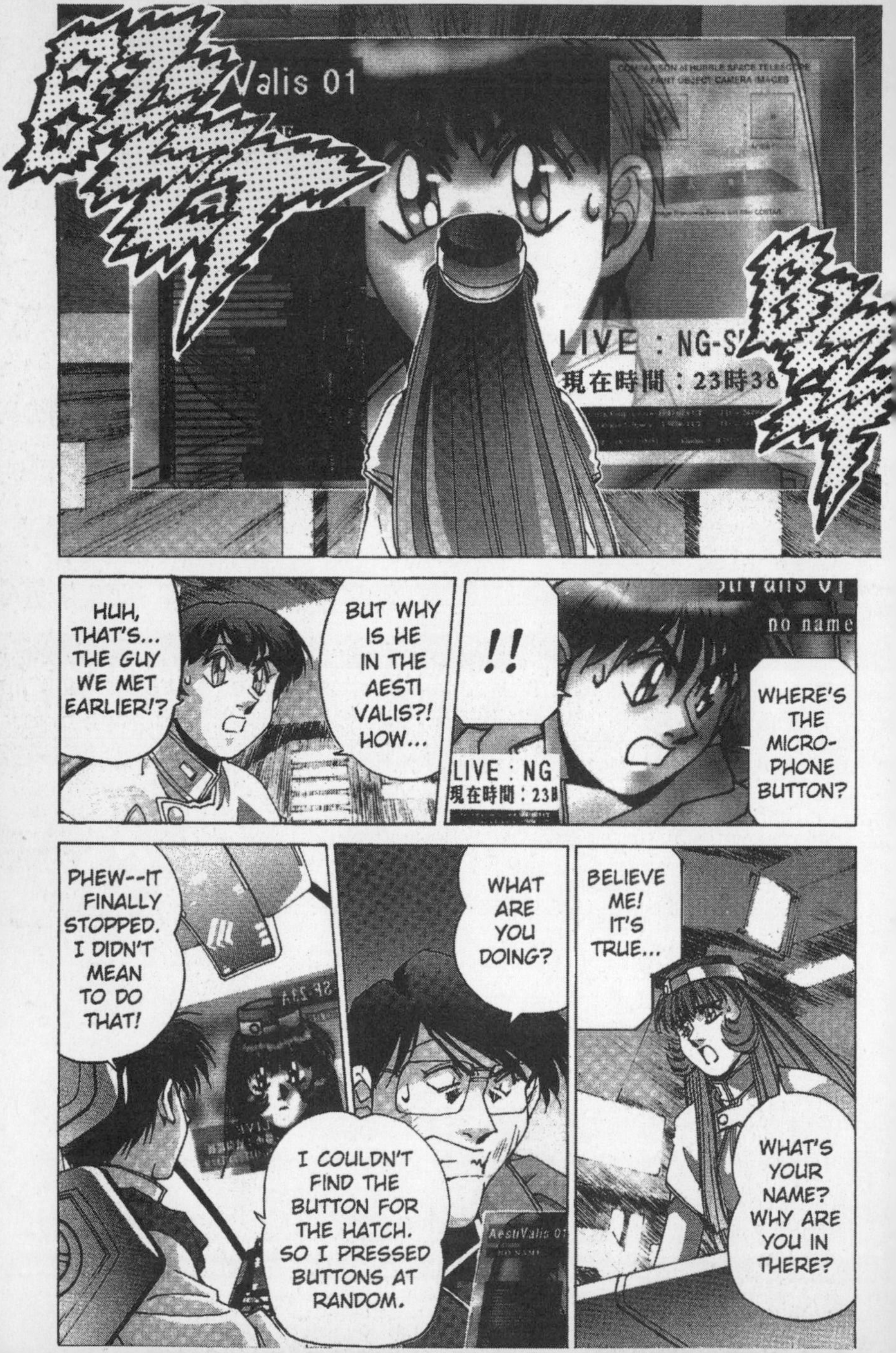
Valis 01
LIVE : NG-S
現在時間：23時38
HUH, THAT'S... THE GUY WE MET EARLIER!?
BUT WHY IS HE IN THE AESTI VALIS?! HOW...
!!
no name
WHERE'S THE MICROPHONE BUTTON?
LIVE : NG
PHEW--IT FINALLY STOPPED. I DIDN'T MEAN TO DO THAT!
WHAT ARE YOU DOING?
I COULDN'T FIND THE BUTTON FOR THE HATCH. SO I PRESSED BUTTONS AT RANDOM.
AestiValis 01
BELIEVE ME! IT'S TRUE...
WHAT'S YOUR NAME? WHY ARE YOU IN THERE?

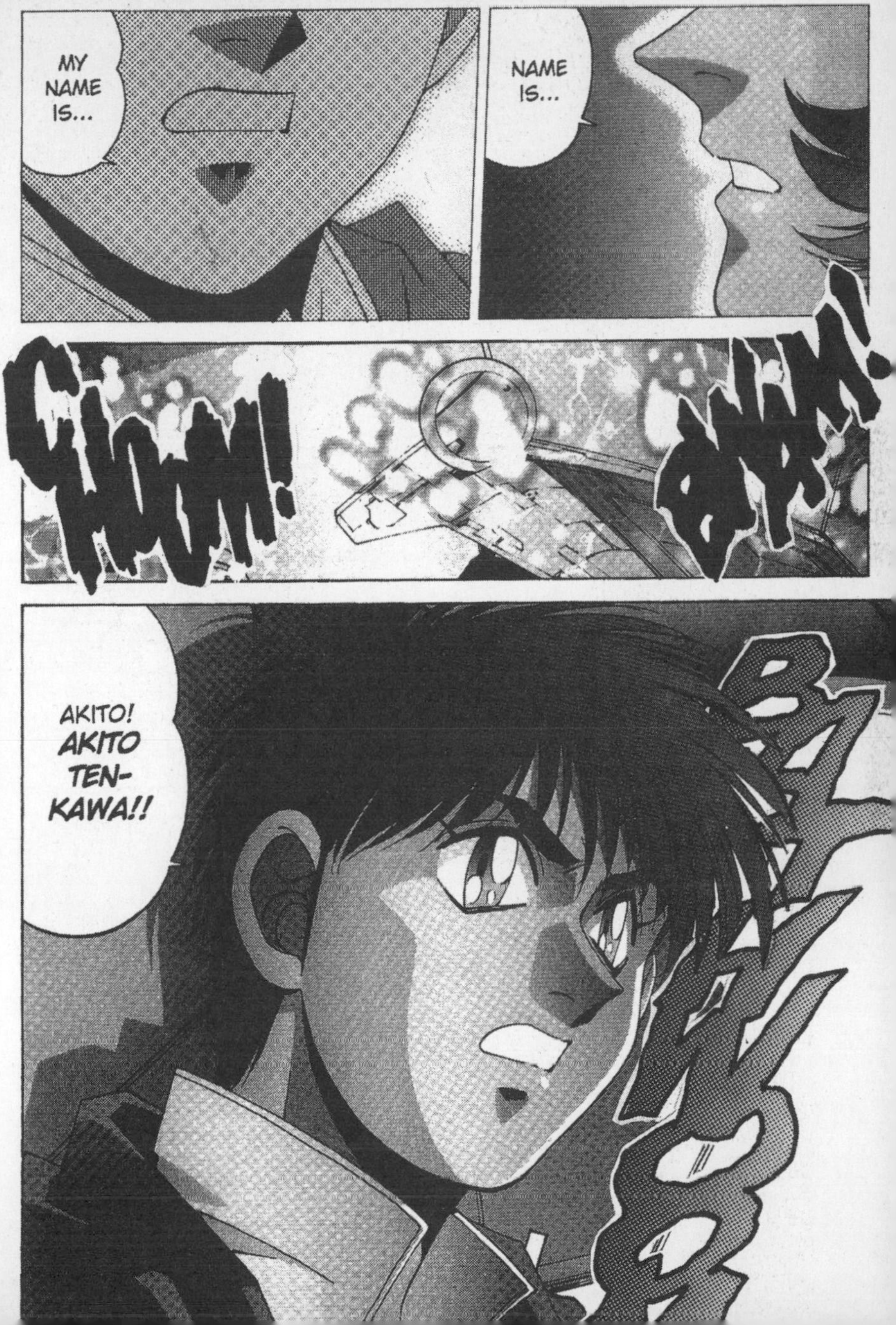
MY NAME IS...
NAME IS...
AKITO! AKITO TEN-KAWA!!

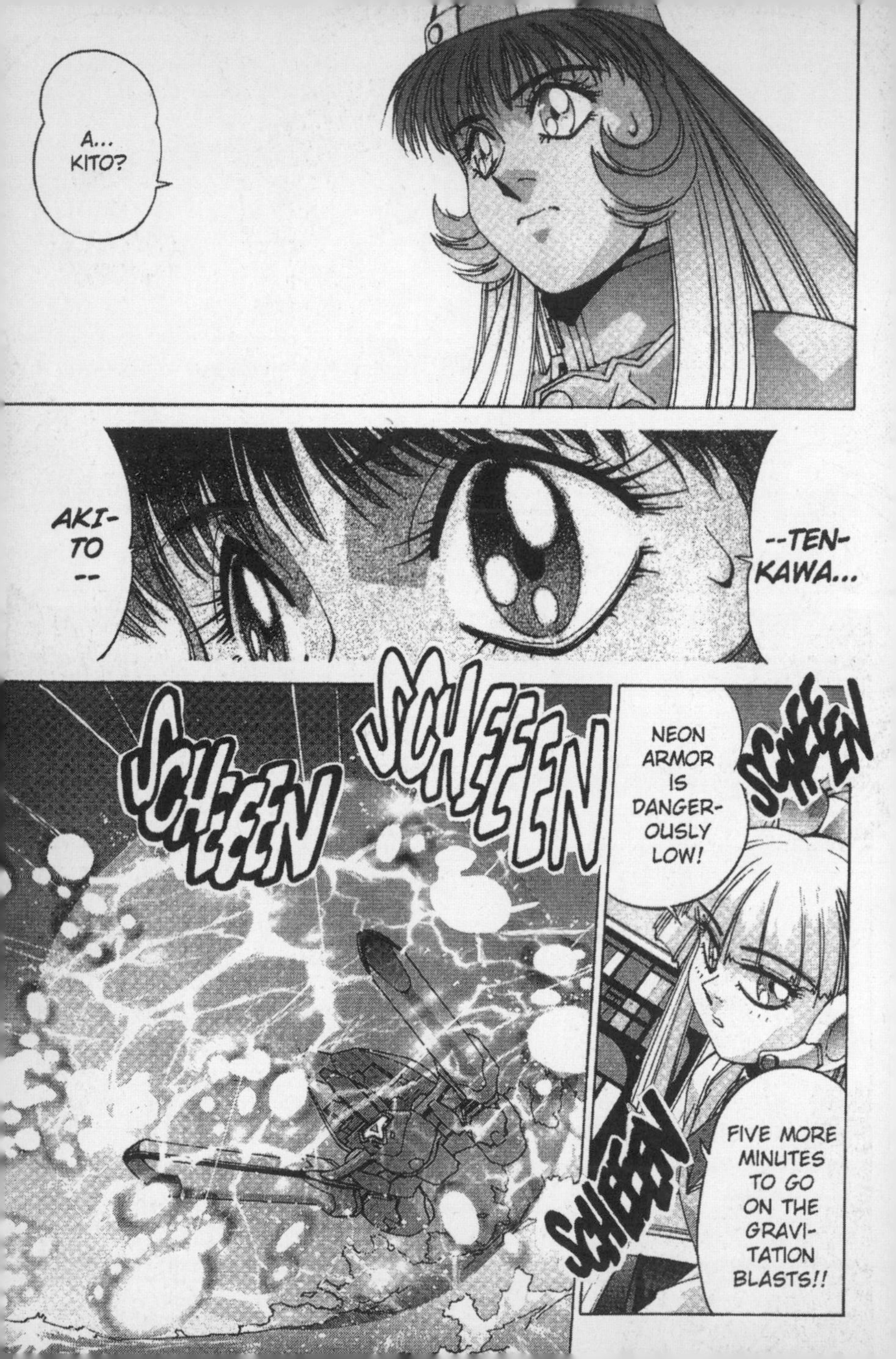
A... KITO?
AKI- TO --
--TEN- KAWA...
SCHEEEN
SCHEEEEN
NEON ARMOR IS DANGER- OUSLY LOW!
SCHEEEEN
SCHEEEN
FIVE MORE MINUTES TO GO ON THE GRAVI- TATION BLASTS!!

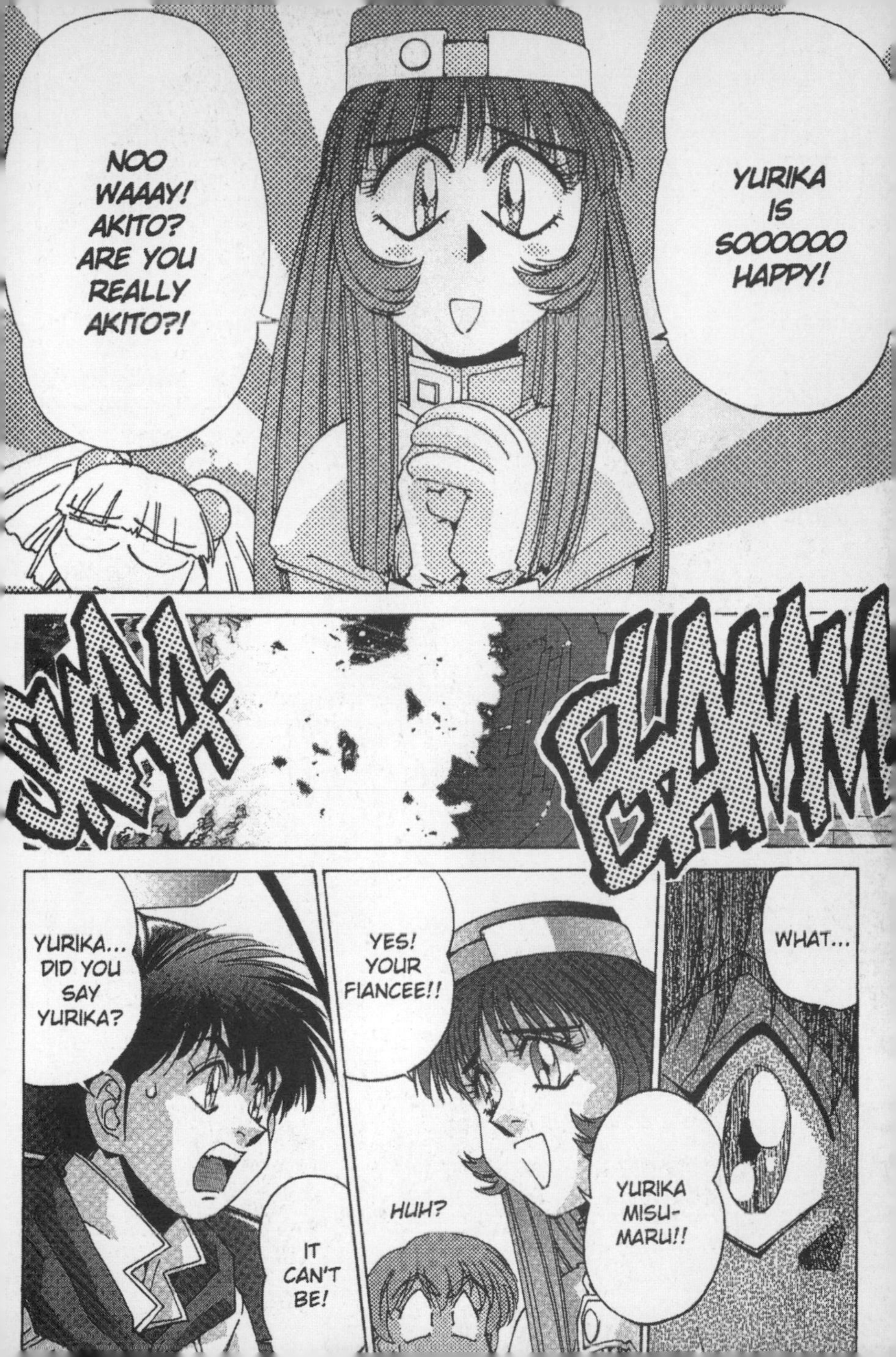
NOO WAAAY! AKITO? ARE YOU REALLY AKITO?!
YURIKA IS SOOOOOO HAPPY!
YURIKA... DID YOU SAY YURIKA?
IT CAN'T BE!
YES! YOUR FIANCEE!!
HUH?
YURIKA MISU-MARU!!
WHAT...

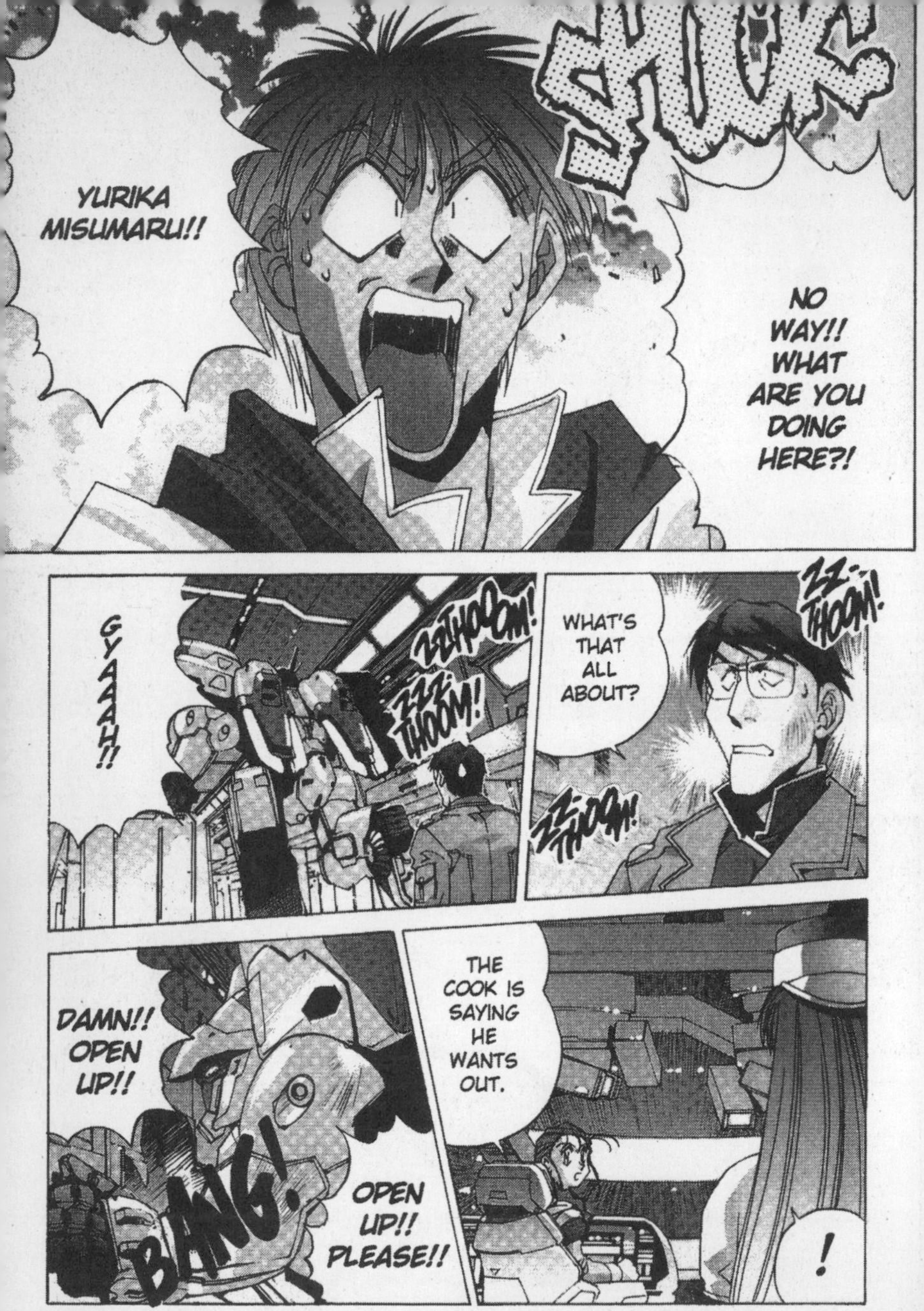
SHOCK!
YURIKA MISUMARU!!
NO WAY!! WHAT ARE YOU DOING HERE?!
GYAAAAH!!
ZZTHOOOOM!
ZZZ-THOOM!
WHAT'S THAT ALL ABOUT?
ZZ-THOOM!
ZZ-THOOM!
DAMN!! OPEN UP!!
BANG!
OPEN UP!! PLEASE!!
THE COOK IS SAYING HE WANTS OUT.
!

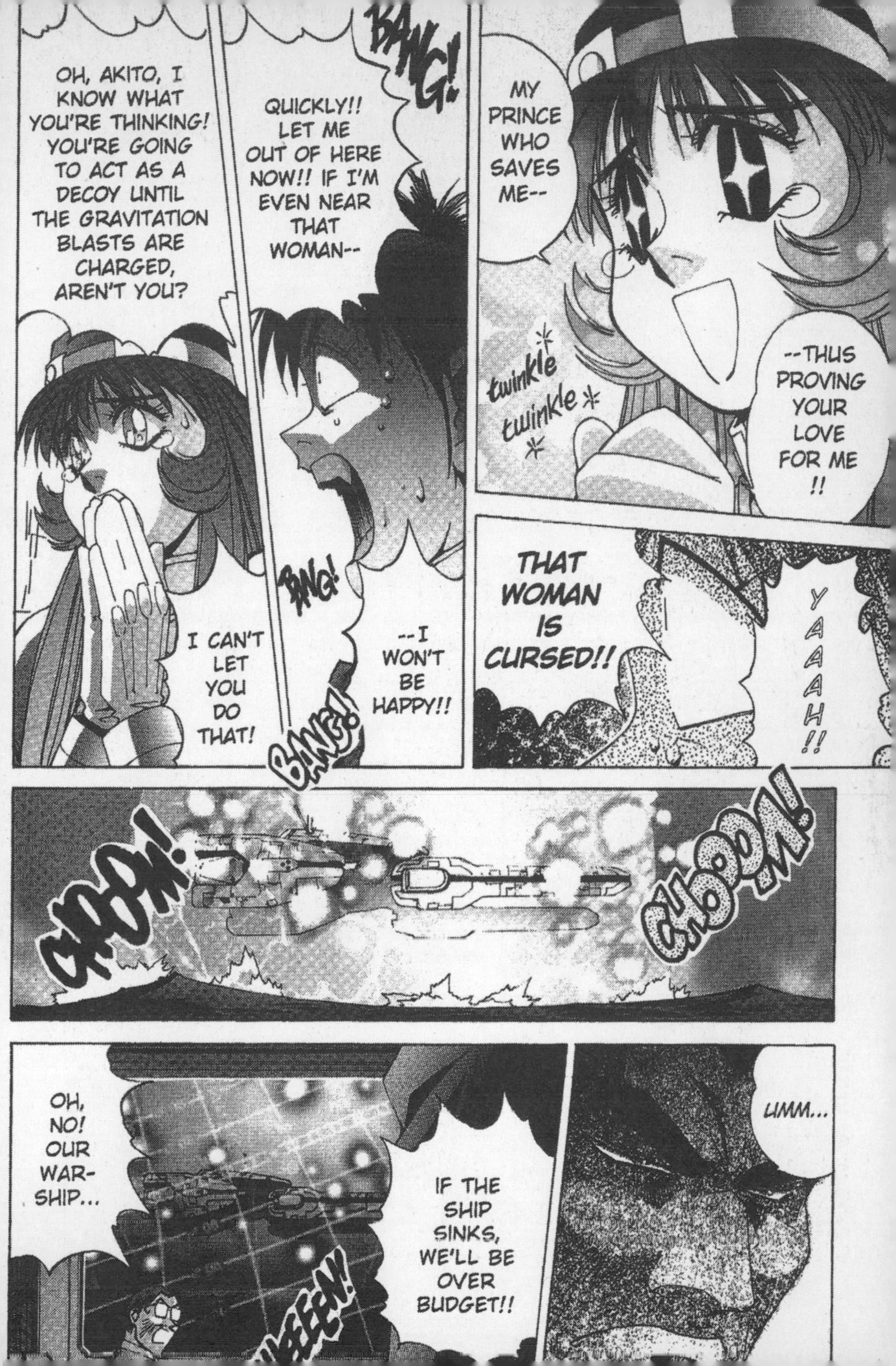
OH, AKITO, I KNOW WHAT YOU'RE THINKING! YOU'RE GOING TO ACT AS A DECOY UNTIL THE GRAVITATION BLASTS ARE CHARGED, AREN'T YOU?
I CAN'T LET YOU DO THAT!
BANG!
QUICKLY!! LET ME OUT OF HERE NOW!! IF I'M EVEN NEAR THAT WOMAN--
BANG!
--I WON'T BE HAPPY!!
BANG!
MY PRINCE WHO SAVES ME--
twinkle twinkle
--THUS PROVING YOUR LOVE FOR ME !!
THAT WOMAN IS CURSED!!
YAAAAH!!
CHOOM!
CHOOOM!
OH, NO! OUR WAR-SHIP...
IF THE SHIP SINKS, WE'LL BE OVER BUDGET!!
UMM...

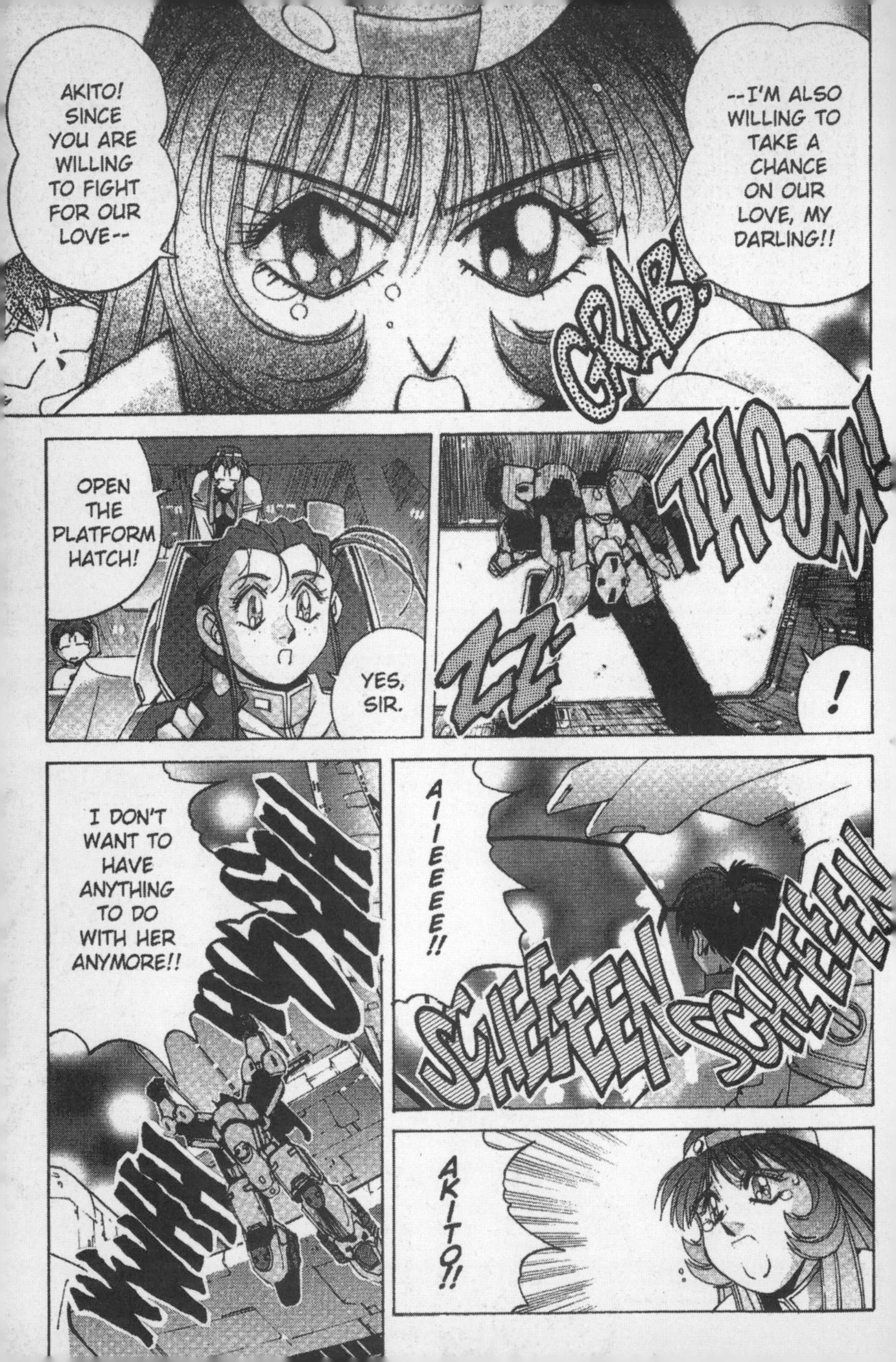
AKITO! SINCE YOU ARE WILLING TO FIGHT FOR OUR LOVE--
--I'M ALSO WILLING TO TAKE A CHANCE ON OUR LOVE, MY DARLING!!
GRAB!
OPEN THE PLATFORM HATCH!
YES, SIR.
THOOM!
ZZ
!
I DON'T WANT TO HAVE ANYTHING TO DO WITH HER ANYMORE!!
AIIEEEEE!!
AKITO!!

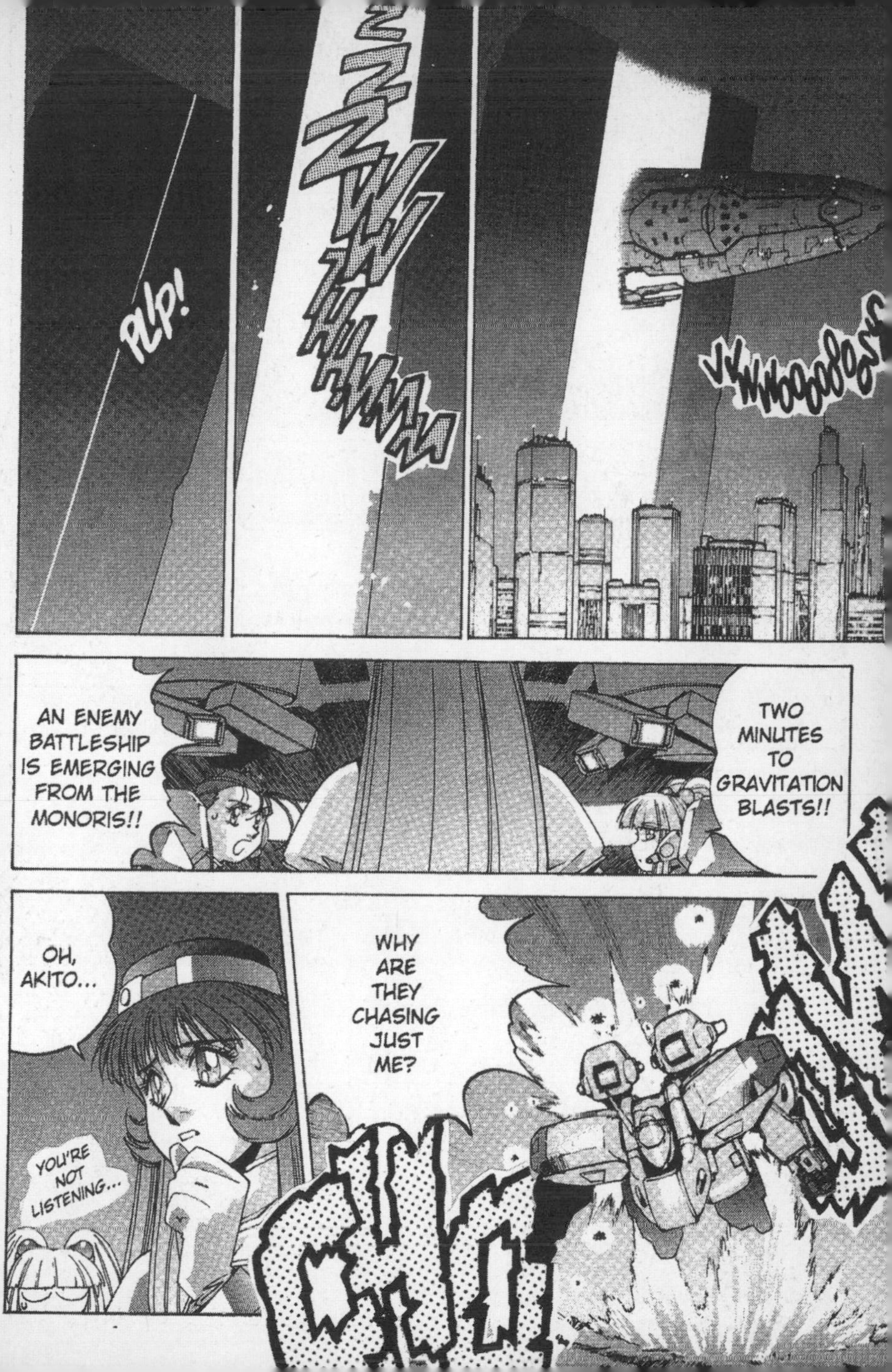
PLIP!
AN ENEMY BATTLESHIP IS EMERGING FROM THE MONORIS!!
TWO MINUTES TO GRAVITATION BLASTS!!
OH, AKITO...
YOU'RE NOT LISTENING...
WHY ARE THEY CHASING JUST ME?

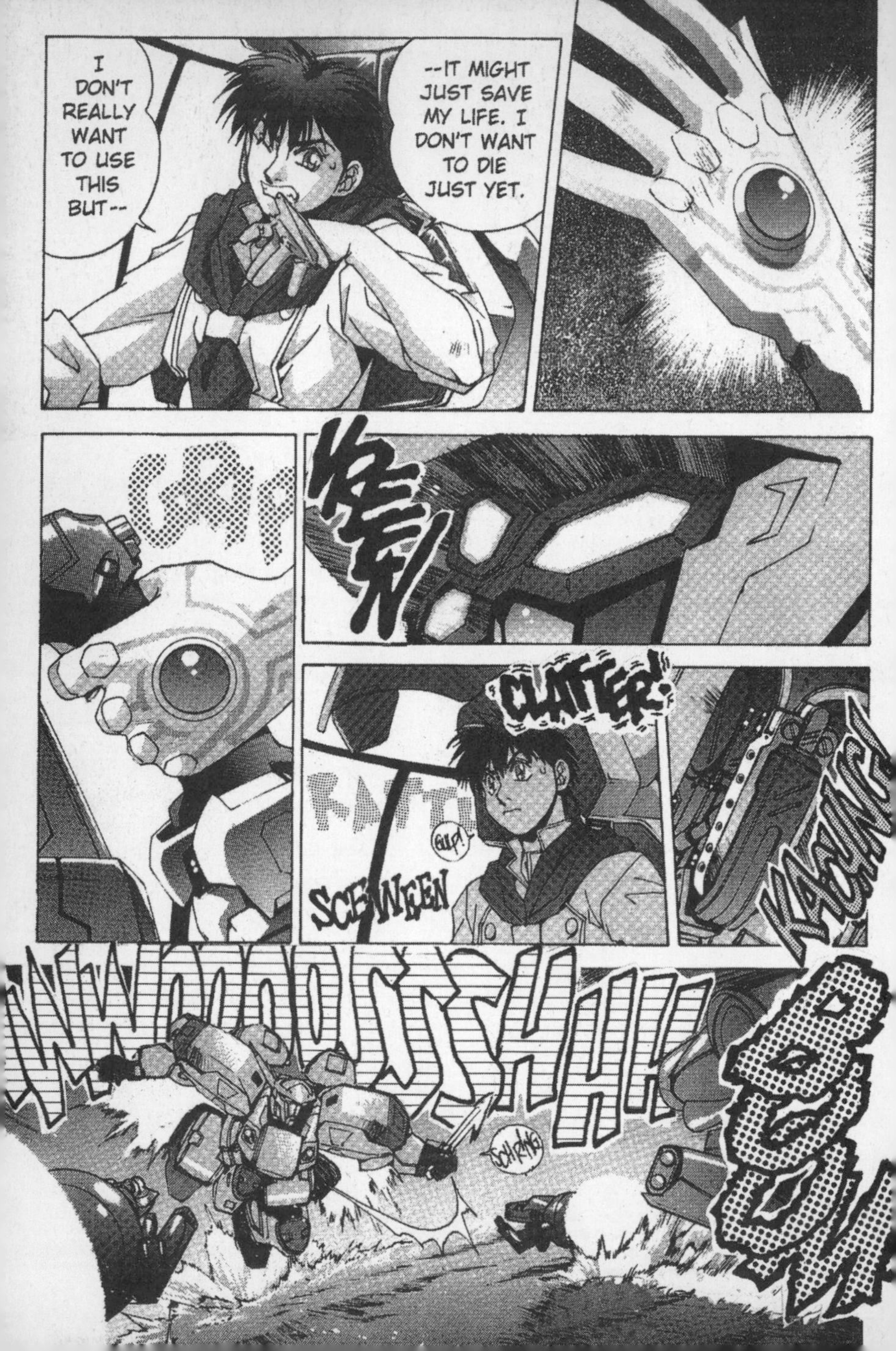
I DON'T REALLY WANT TO USE THIS BUT--
--IT MIGHT JUST SAVE MY LIFE. I DON'T WANT TO DIE JUST YET.
CLATTER!
GULP!
SCEWEEN
KACHUNG!

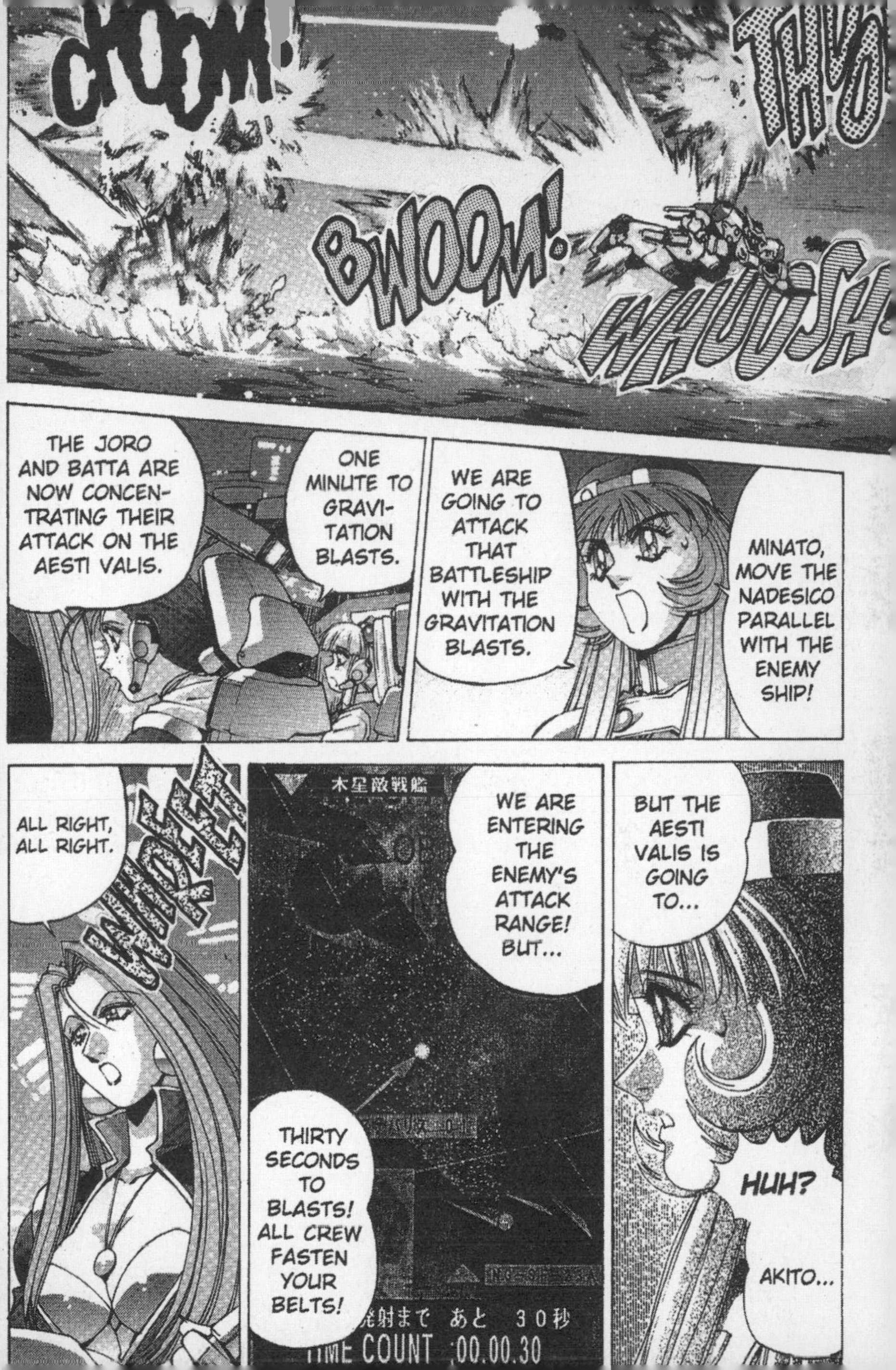
BWOOM!
THE JORO AND BATTA ARE NOW CONCENTRATING THEIR ATTACK ON THE AESTI VALIS.
ONE MINUTE TO GRAVITATION BLASTS.
WE ARE GOING TO ATTACK THAT BATTLESHIP WITH THE GRAVITATION BLASTS.
MINATO, MOVE THE NADESICO PARALLEL WITH THE ENEMY SHIP!
ALL RIGHT, ALL RIGHT.
木星敵戦艦
WE ARE ENTERING THE ENEMY'S ATTACK RANGE! BUT...
THIRTY SECONDS TO BLASTS! ALL CREW FASTEN YOUR BELTS!
射まで あと 30秒
ME COUNT :00.00.30
BUT THE AESTI VALIS IS GOING TO...
HUH?
AKITO...

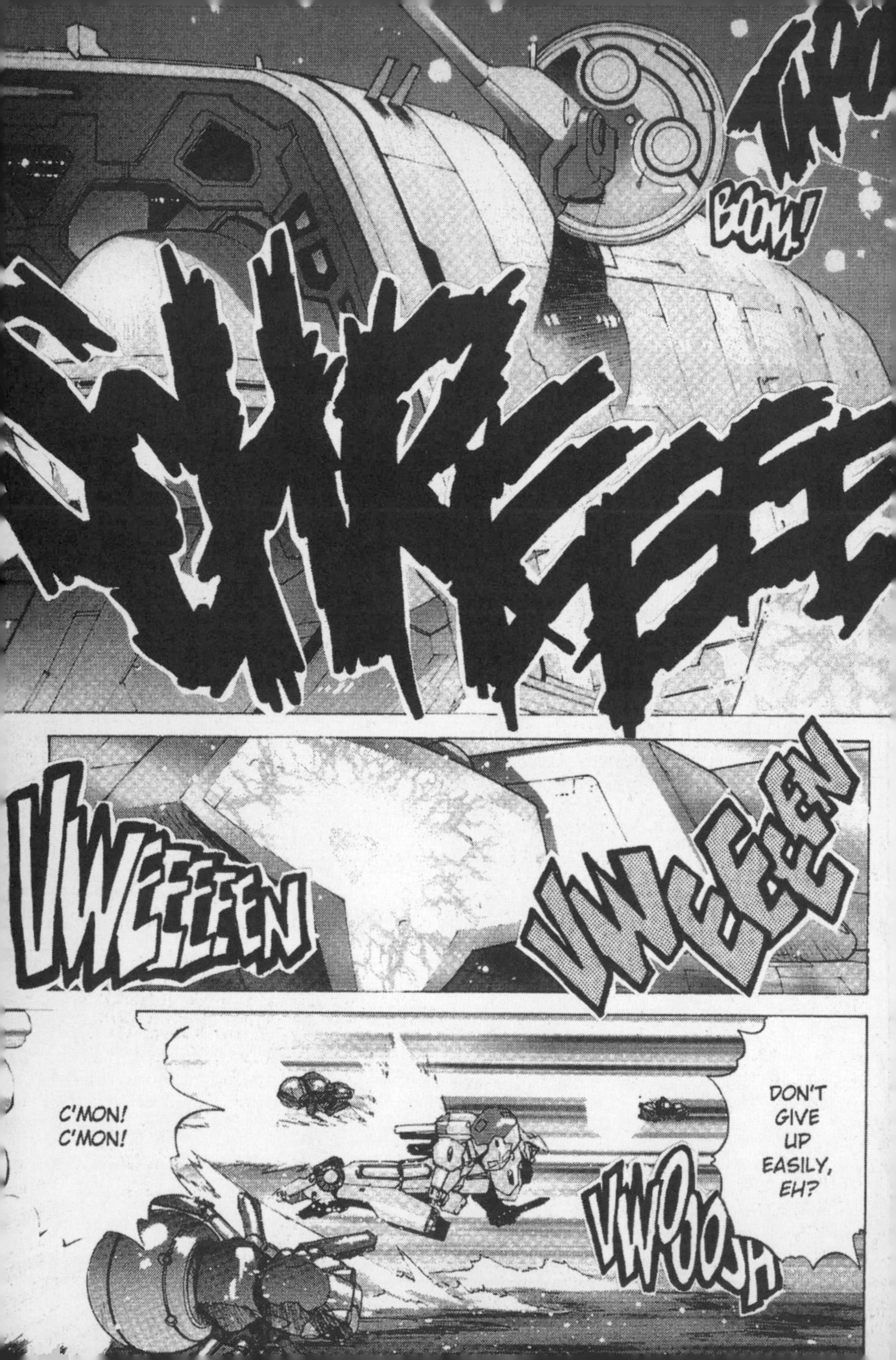
BOOM!
VWEEEEN
VWEEEEN
C'MON! C'MON!
DON'T GIVE UP EASILY, EH?
VWOOOSH

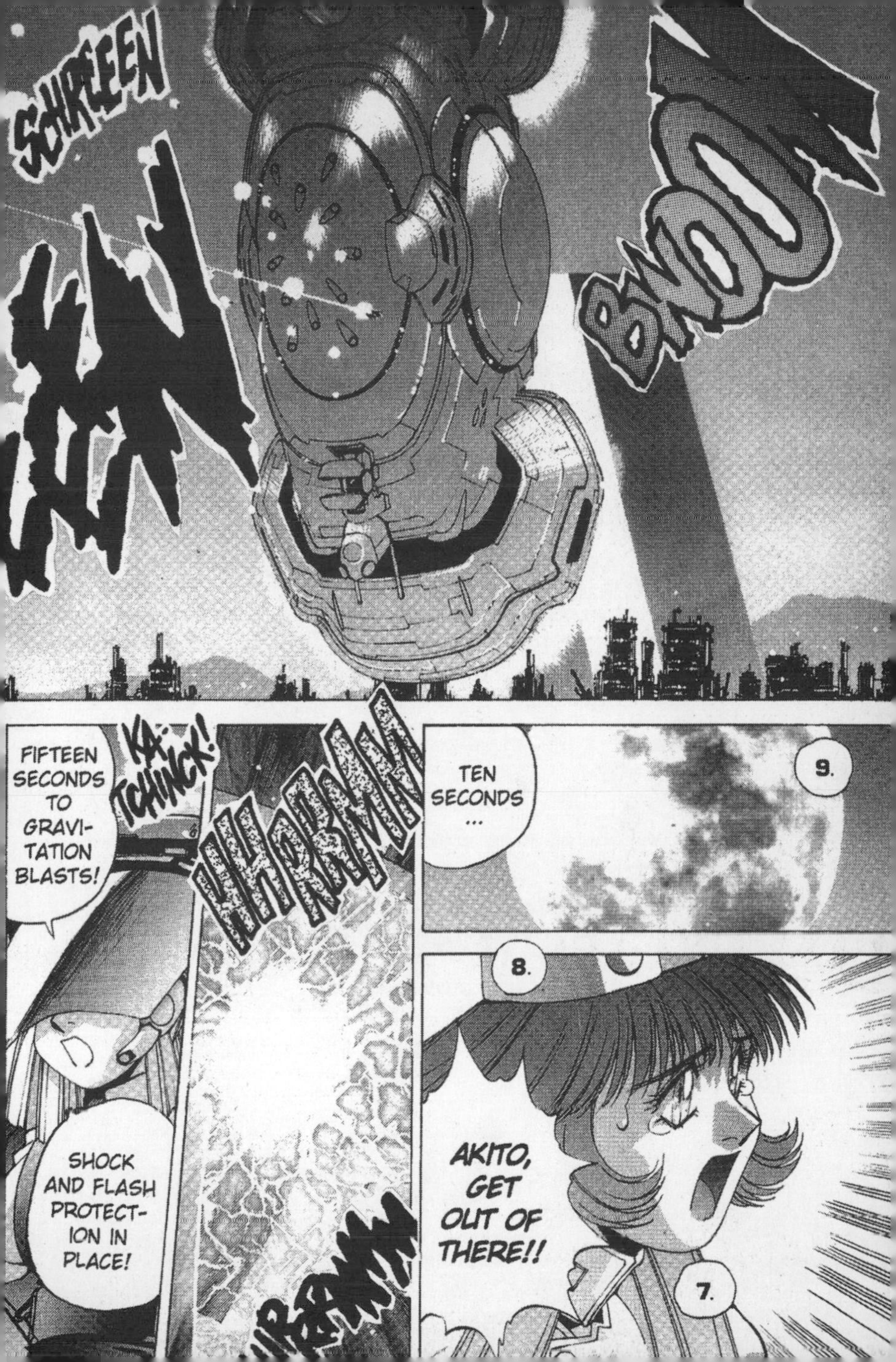
SCHREEN
FIFTEEN SECONDS TO GRAVITATION BLASTS!
KA-TCHINCK!
SHOCK AND FLASH PROTECTION IN PLACE!
TEN SECONDS ...
9.
8.
AKITO, GET OUT OF THERE!!
7.

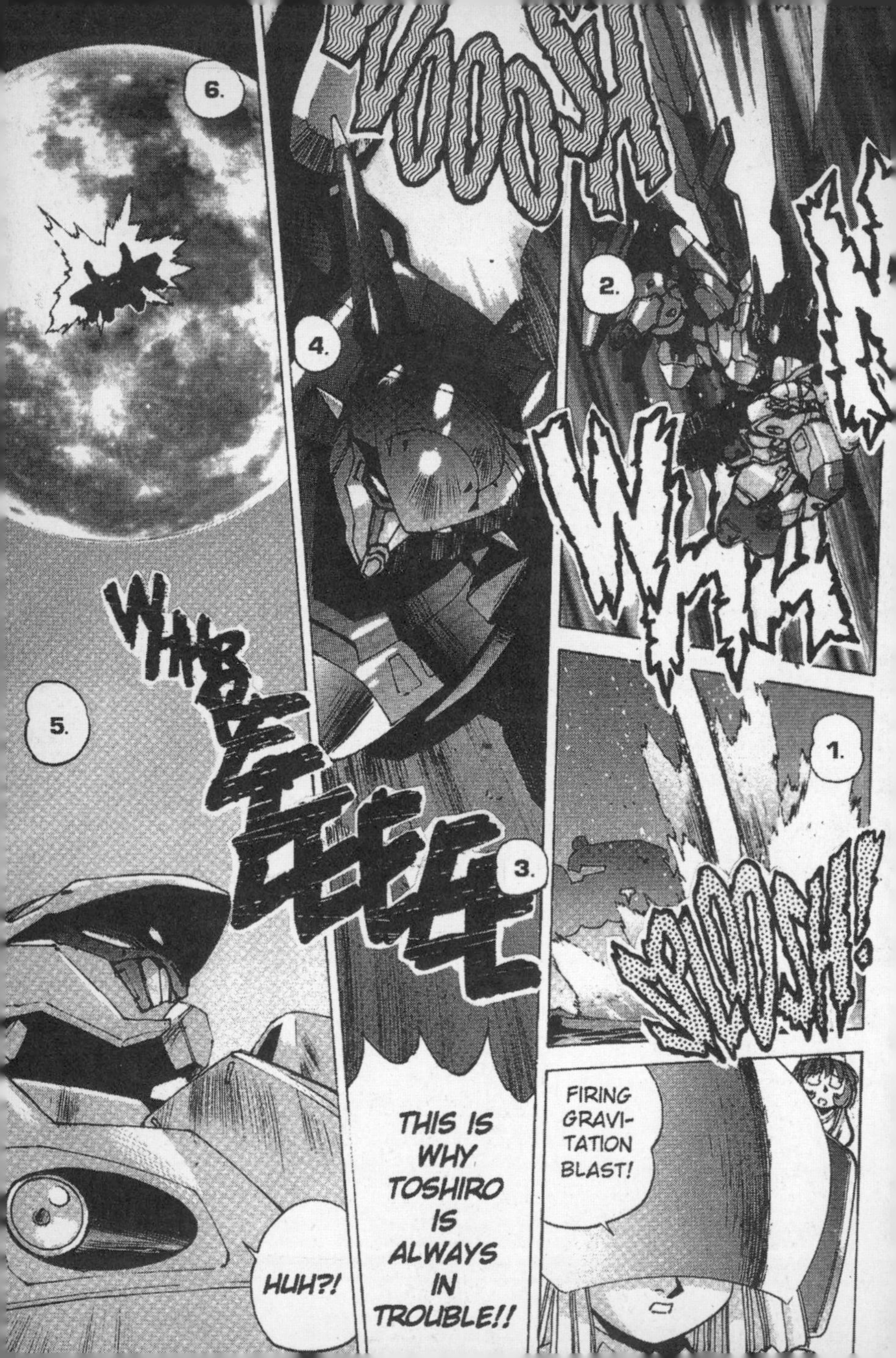

1.
BLOOSH!
2.
WHAM
3.
4.
WHOOSH
5.
6.
FIRING GRAVITATION BLAST!
THIS IS WHY TOSHIRO IS ALWAYS IN TROUBLE!!
HUH?!

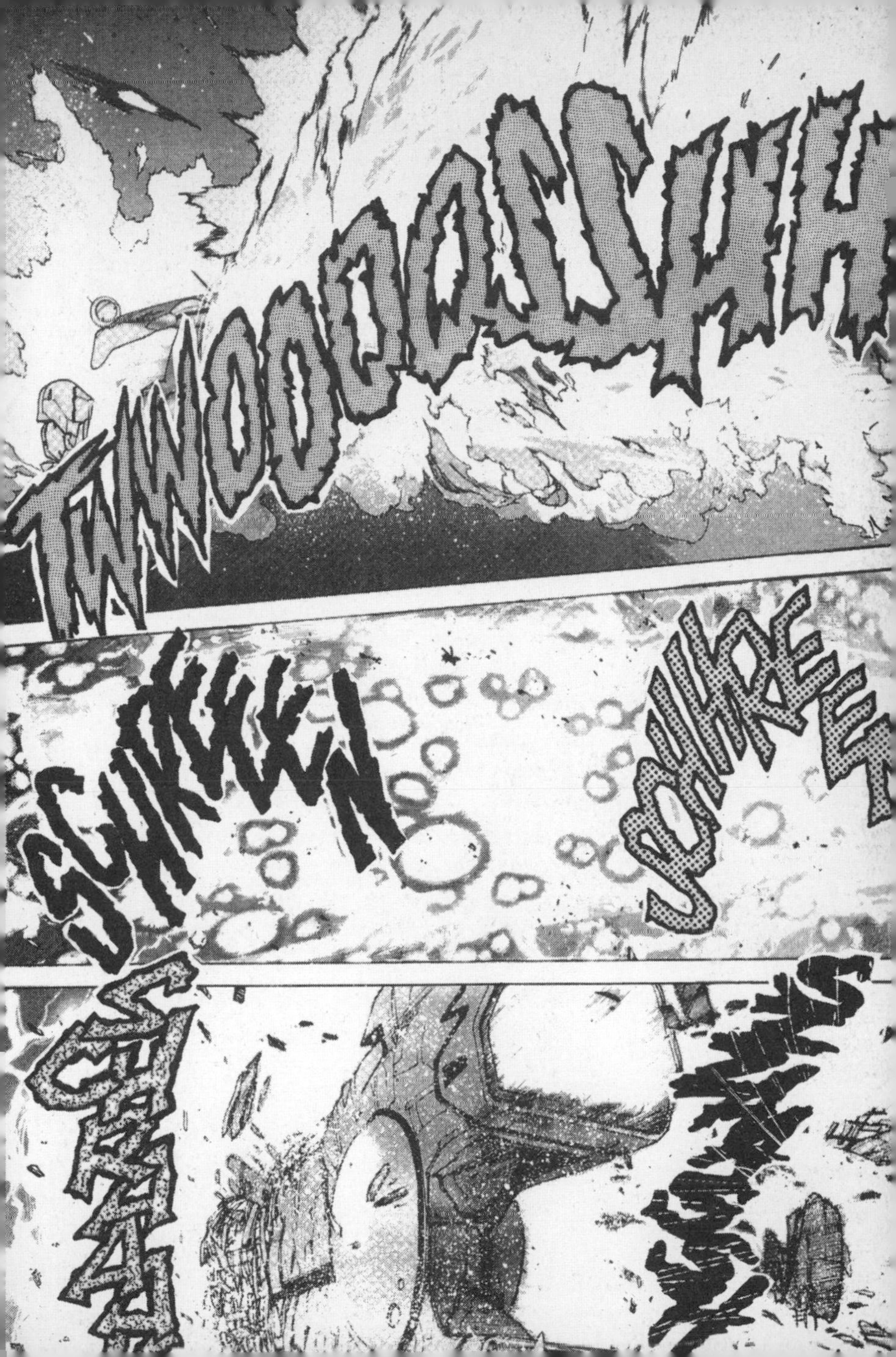

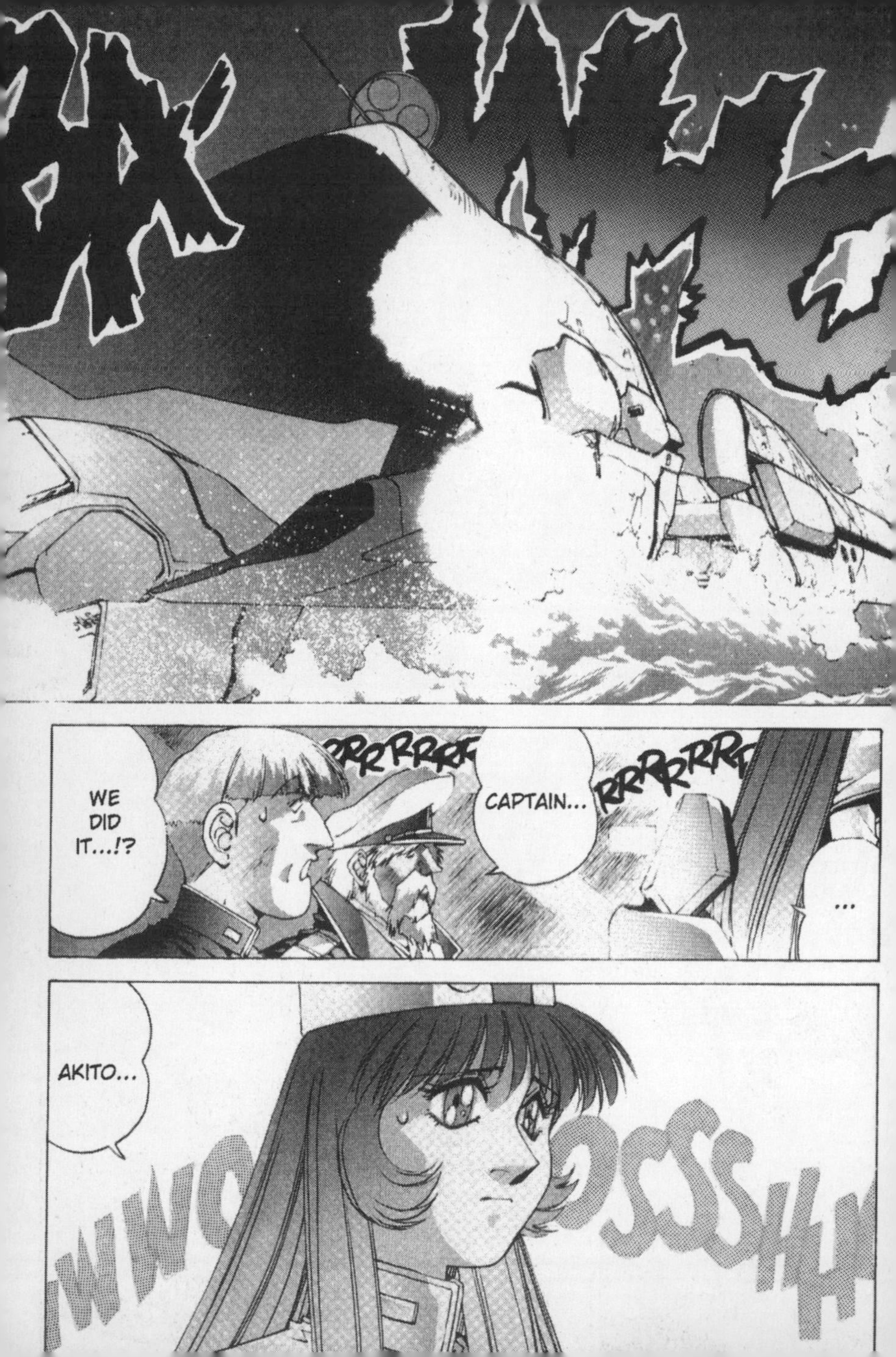

WE DID IT...!?
CAPTAIN...
...
AKITO...

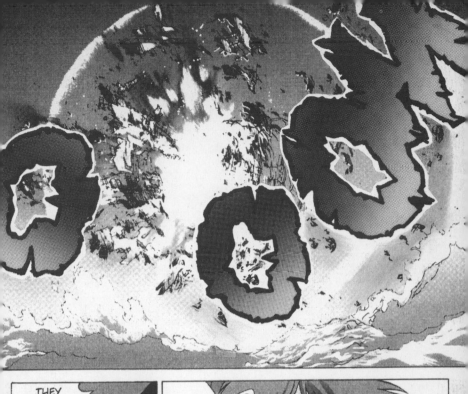

THEY CAN'T SHOOT THE GRAVITATION BLASTS IF YOU'RE IN THE LINE OF FIRE!

WHO... WHO ARE YOU?

GUY! I'M GUY DAIGOJI!!

GUY...

THANK YOU FOR SAVING ME. I'M AKITO... AKITO TENKAWA.

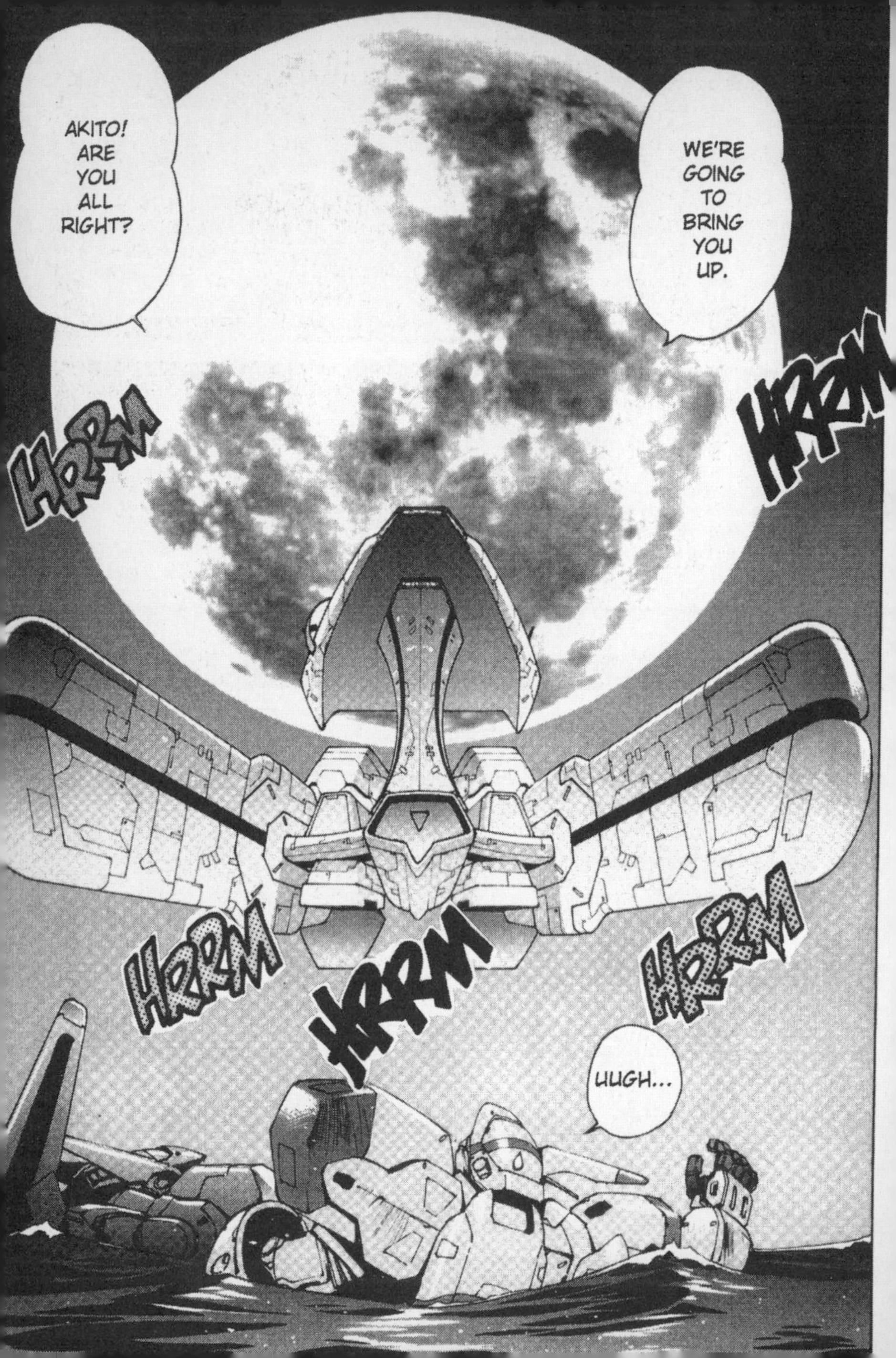
AKITO! ARE YOU ALL RIGHT?
WE'RE GOING TO BRING YOU UP.
HRRM
HRRM
HRRM
HRRM
HRRM
UUGH...

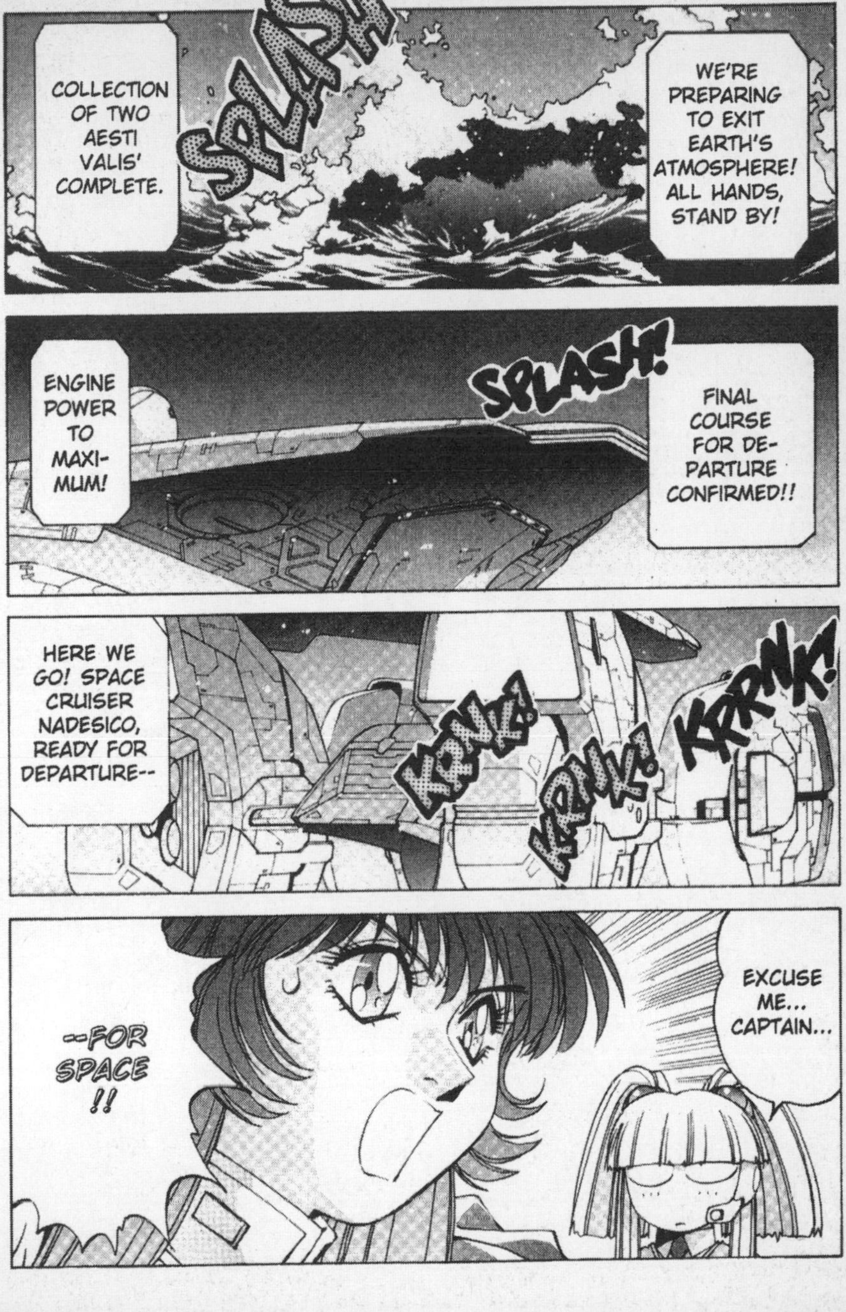
COLLECTION OF TWO AESTI VALIS' COMPLETE.
SPLASH!
WE'RE PREPARING TO EXIT EARTH'S ATMOSPHERE! ALL HANDS, STAND BY!
ENGINE POWER TO MAXI- MUM!
SPLASH!
FINAL COURSE FOR DE- PARTURE CONFIRMED!!
HERE WE GO! SPACE CRUISER NADESICO, READY FOR DEPARTURE--
KRNK!
KRRNK!
KRRNK!
--FOR SPACE !!
EXCUSE ME... CAPTAIN...

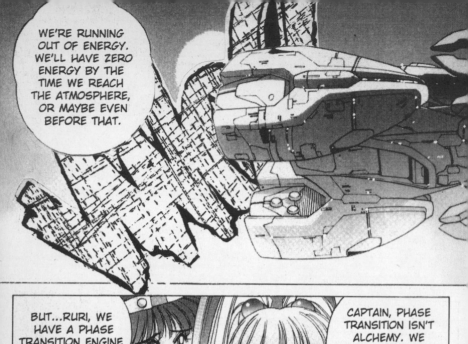

WE'RE RUNNING OUT OF ENERGY. WE'LL HAVE ZERO ENERGY BY THE TIME WE REACH THE ATMOSPHERE, OR MAYBE EVEN BEFORE THAT.

BUT...RURI, WE HAVE A PHASE TRANSITION ENGINE WHICH CAN CREATE AN INEXHAUSTIBLE SUPPLY OF ENERGY FROM WHAT I'VE HEARD.

CAPTAIN, PHASE TRANSITION ISN'T ALCHEMY. WE NEED ANOTHER SOURCE OF ENERGY TO POWER THE PHASE TRANSITION!

YOU MEAN WE'RE GOING TO BE LOST IN SPACE?

YES, WE ARE. BUT IF WE'RE LUCKY, WE'LL BE OK.

OH, NO... RURI, DON'T BE SO COLD.

WHRR!

CAPTAIN, PLEASE RETURN TO YOUR SEAT. I'M GOING TO POWER UP THE ENGINES.

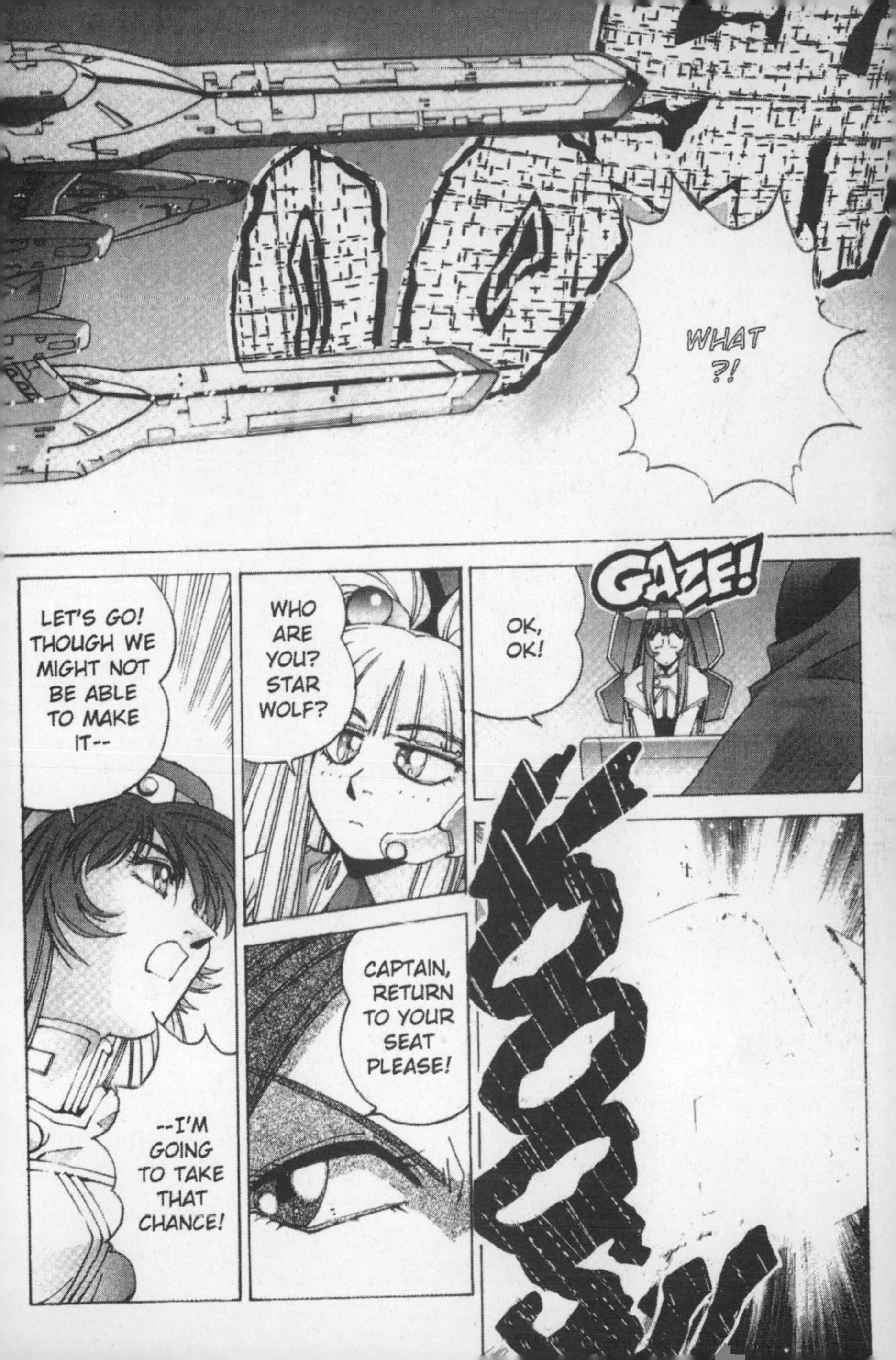
WHAT ?!
LET'S GO! THOUGH WE MIGHT NOT BE ABLE TO MAKE IT--
WHO ARE YOU? STAR WOLF?
GAZE!
OK, OK!
--I'M GOING TO TAKE THAT CHANCE!
CAPTAIN, RETURN TO YOUR SEAT PLEASE!

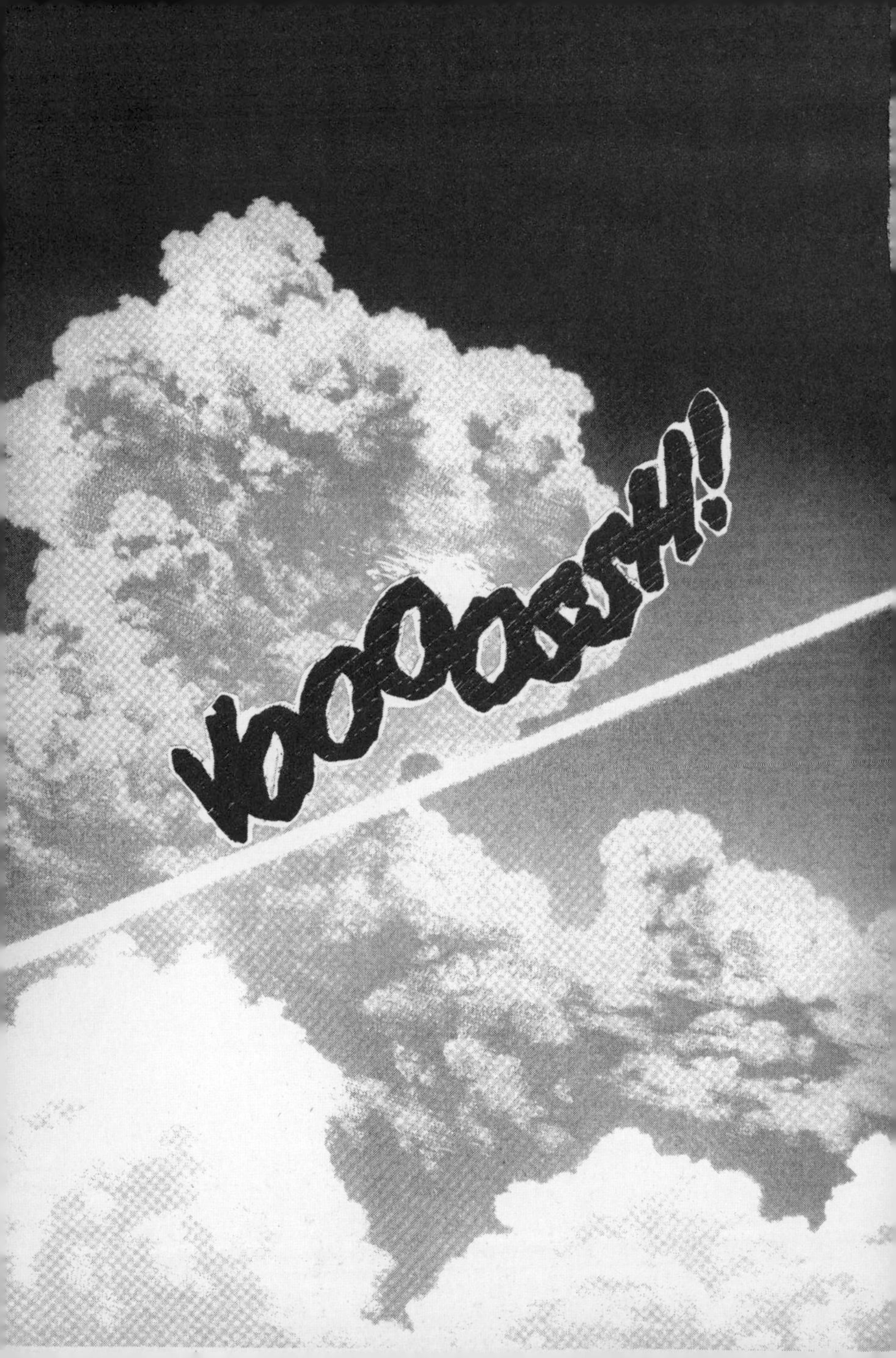
VOOOOSH!!

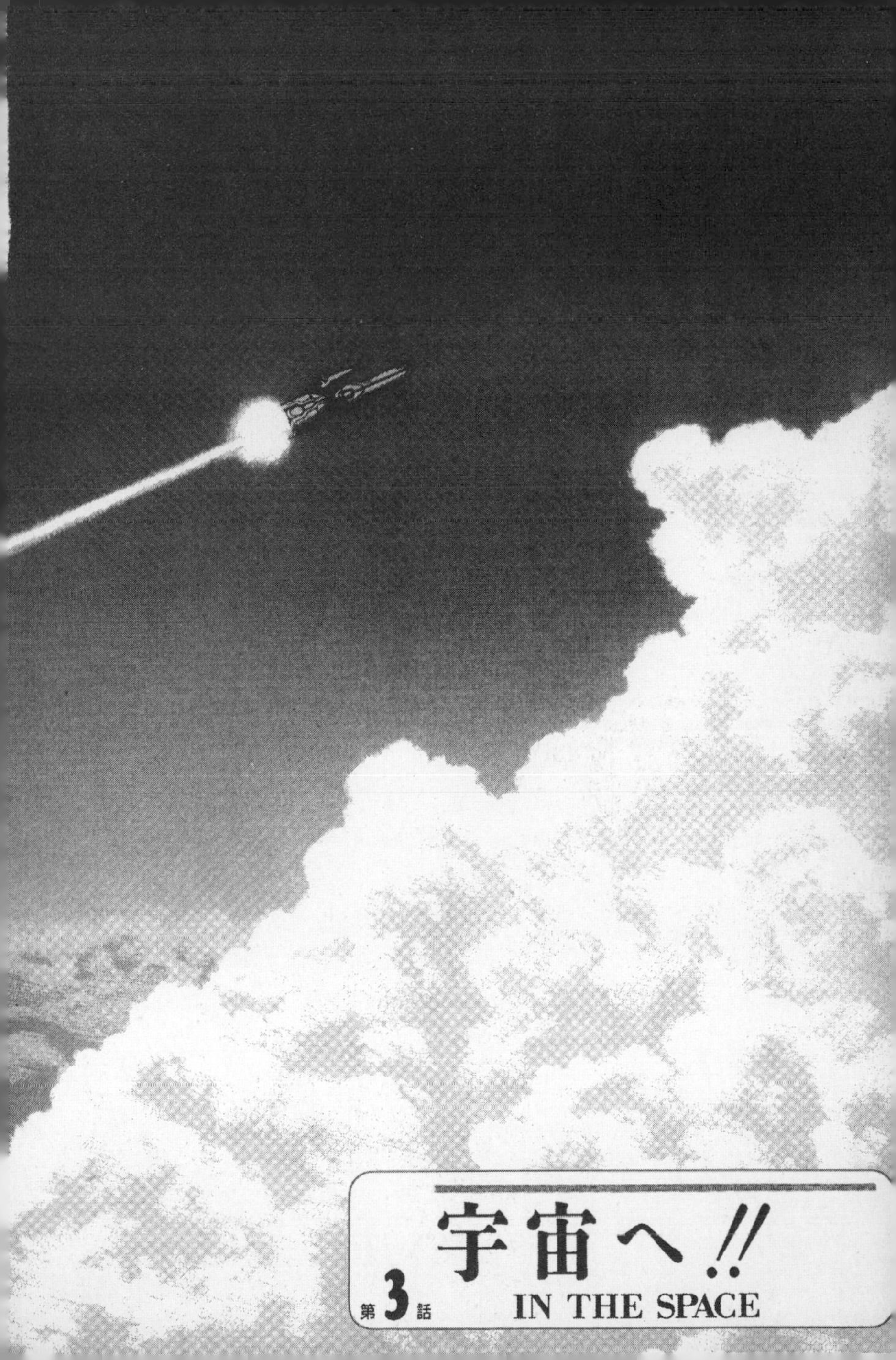
宇宙へ!!
第3話
IN THE SPACE

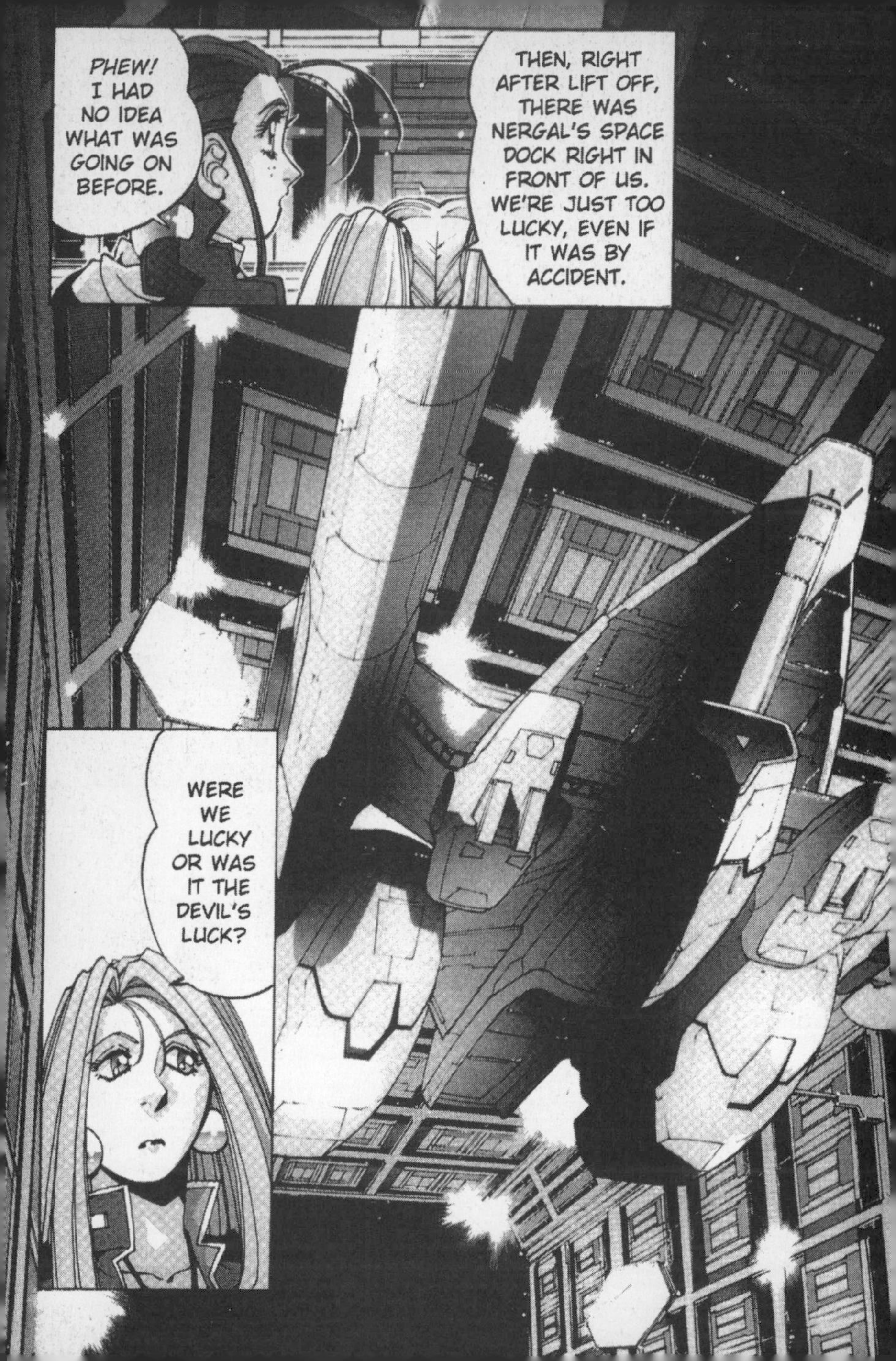
PHEW! I HAD NO IDEA WHAT WAS GOING ON BEFORE.
THEN, RIGHT AFTER LIFT OFF, THERE WAS NERGAL'S SPACE DOCK RIGHT IN FRONT OF US. WE'RE JUST TOO LUCKY, EVEN IF IT WAS BY ACCIDENT.
WERE WE LUCKY OR WAS IT THE DEVIL'S LUCK?

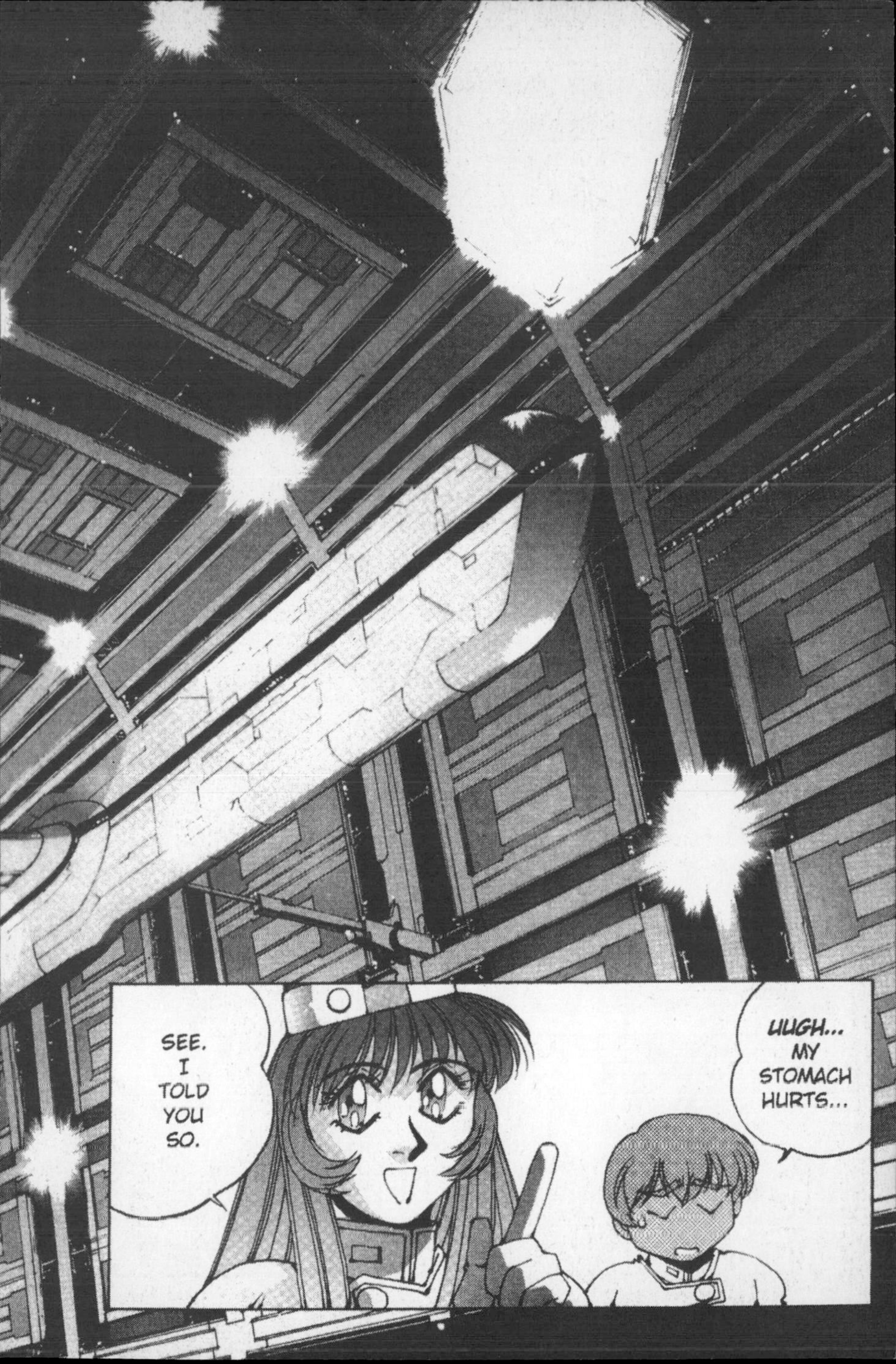
SEE. I TOLD YOU SO.
UUGH... MY STOMACH HURTS...

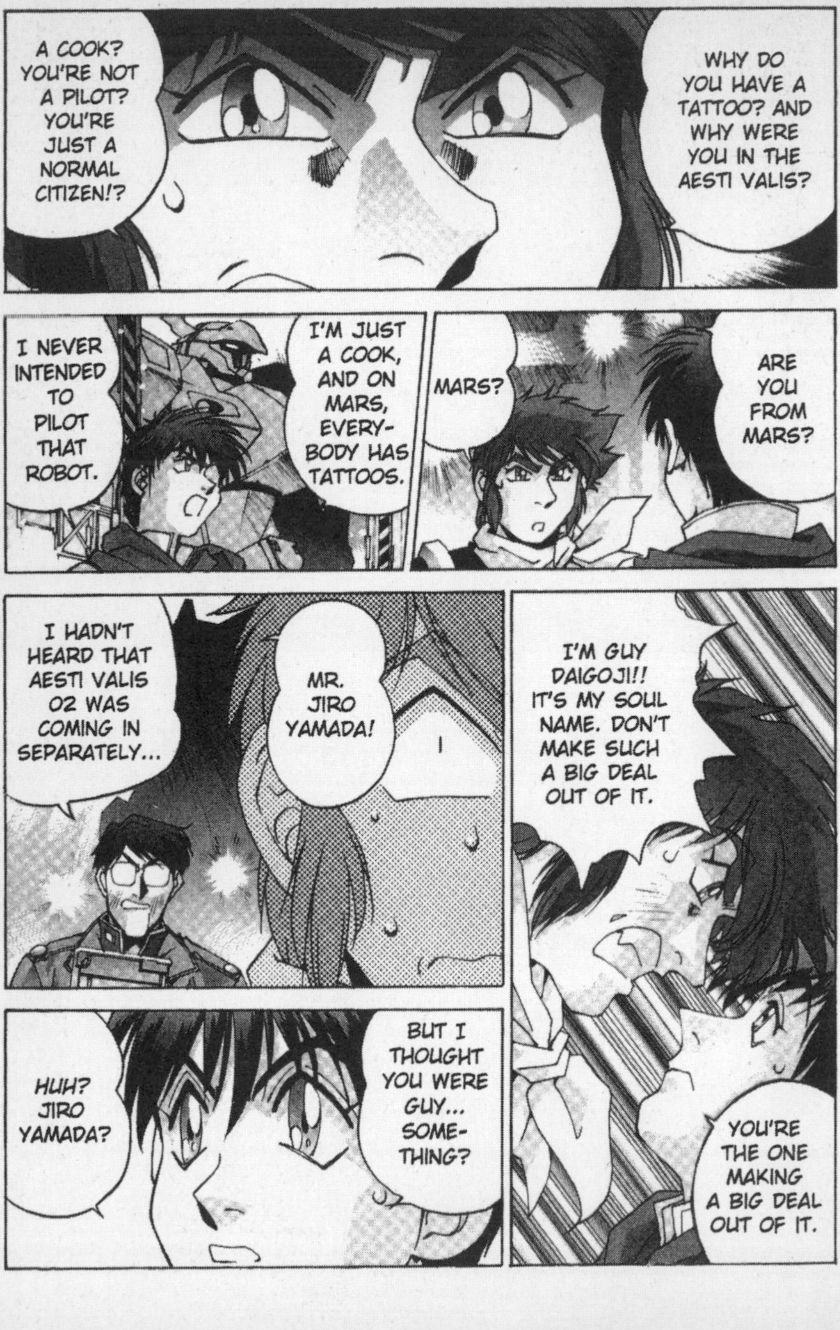
A COOK? YOU'RE NOT A PILOT? YOU'RE JUST A NORMAL CITIZEN!?
WHY DO YOU HAVE A TATTOO? AND WHY WERE YOU IN THE AESTI VALIS?
I NEVER INTENDED TO PILOT THAT ROBOT.
I'M JUST A COOK, AND ON MARS, EVERY-BODY HAS TATTOOS.
MARS?
ARE YOU FROM MARS?
I HADN'T HEARD THAT AESTI VALIS 02 WAS COMING IN SEPARATELY...
MR. JIRO YAMADA!
HUH? JIRO YAMADA?
BUT I THOUGHT YOU WERE GUY... SOME-THING?
I'M GUY DAIGOJI!! IT'S MY SOUL NAME. DON'T MAKE SUCH A BIG DEAL OUT OF IT.
YOU'RE THE ONE MAKING A BIG DEAL OUT OF IT.

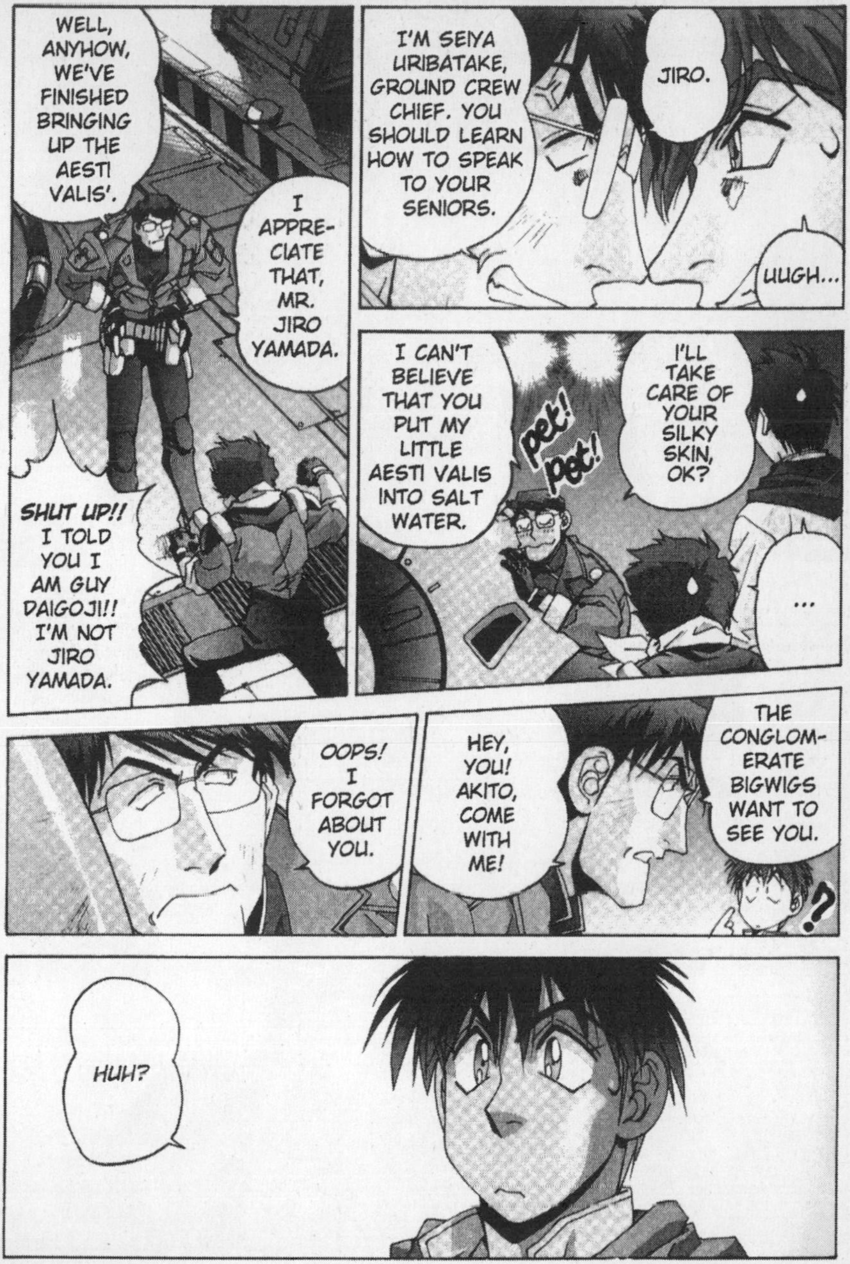
WELL, ANYHOW, WE'VE FINISHED BRINGING UP THE AESTI VALIS'.
I APPRECIATE THAT, MR. JIRO YAMADA.
SHUT UP!! I TOLD YOU I AM GUY DAIGOJI!! I'M NOT JIRO YAMADA.
I'M SEIYA URIBATAKE, GROUND CREW CHIEF. YOU SHOULD LEARN HOW TO SPEAK TO YOUR SENIORS.
JIRO.
UUGH...
I CAN'T BELIEVE THAT YOU PUT MY LITTLE AESTI VALIS INTO SALT WATER.
pet! pet!
I'LL TAKE CARE OF YOUR SILKY SKIN, OK?
...
OOPS! I FORGOT ABOUT YOU.
HEY, YOU! AKITO, COME WITH ME!
THE CONGLOMERATE BIGWIGS WANT TO SEE YOU.
?
HUH?

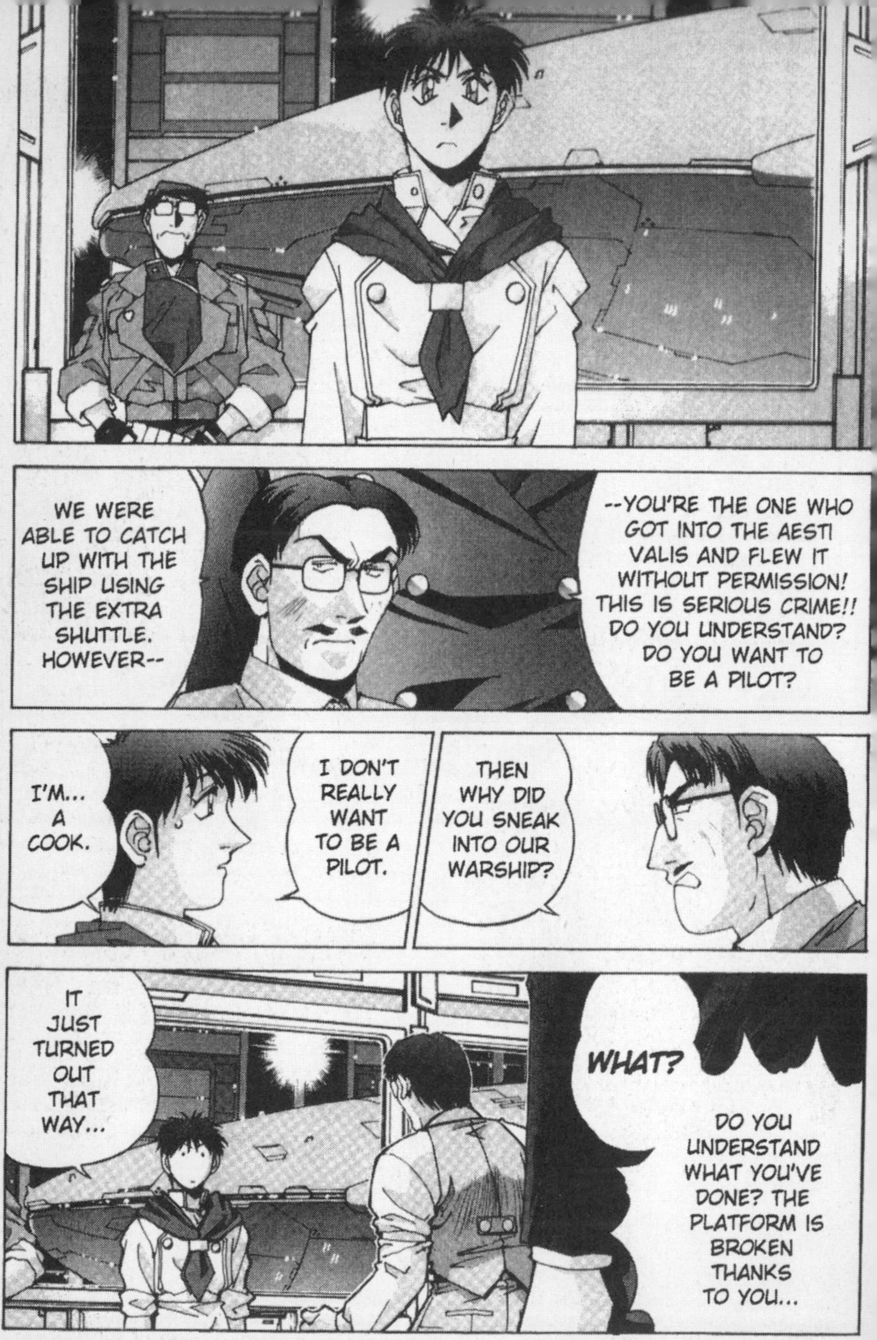
WE WERE ABLE TO CATCH UP WITH THE SHIP USING THE EXTRA SHUTTLE. HOWEVER--
--YOU'RE THE ONE WHO GOT INTO THE AESTI VALIS AND FLEW IT WITHOUT PERMISSION! THIS IS SERIOUS CRIME!! DO YOU UNDERSTAND? DO YOU WANT TO BE A PILOT?
I'M... A COOK.
I DON'T REALLY WANT TO BE A PILOT.
THEN WHY DID YOU SNEAK INTO OUR WARSHIP?
IT JUST TURNED OUT THAT WAY...
WHAT?
DO YOU UNDERSTAND WHAT YOU'VE DONE? THE PLATFORM IS BROKEN THANKS TO YOU...

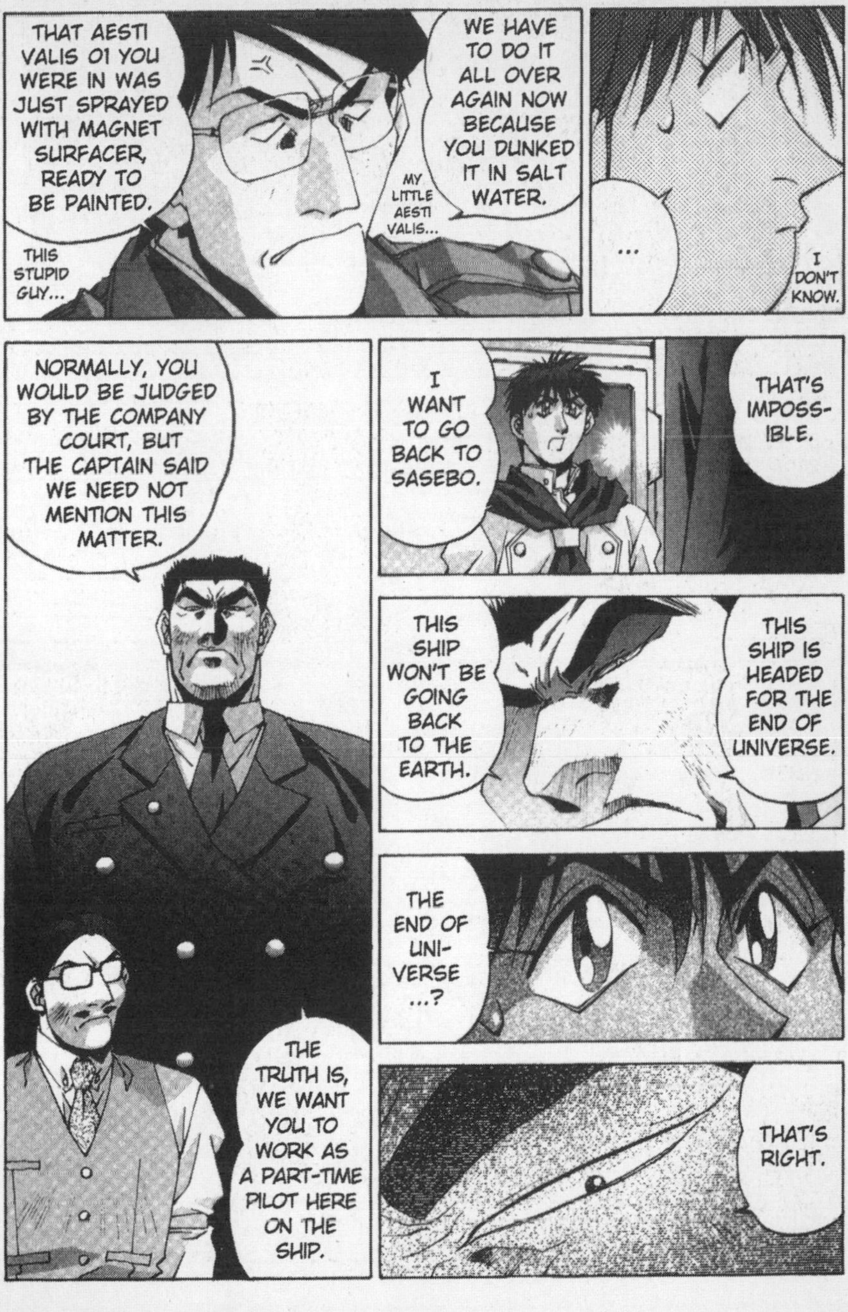
THAT AESTI VALIS 01 YOU WERE IN WAS JUST SPRAYED WITH MAGNET SURFACER, READY TO BE PAINTED.
THIS STUPID GUY...
MY LITTLE AESTI VALIS...
WE HAVE TO DO IT ALL OVER AGAIN NOW BECAUSE YOU DUNKED IT IN SALT WATER.
...
I DON'T KNOW.
NORMALLY, YOU WOULD BE JUDGED BY THE COMPANY COURT, BUT THE CAPTAIN SAID WE NEED NOT MENTION THIS MATTER.
THE TRUTH IS, WE WANT YOU TO WORK AS A PART-TIME PILOT HERE ON THE SHIP.
I WANT TO GO BACK TO SASEBO.
THAT'S IMPOSS-IBLE.
THIS SHIP WON'T BE GOING BACK TO THE EARTH.
THIS SHIP IS HEADED FOR THE END OF UNIVERSE.
THE END OF UNI-VERSE ...?
THAT'S RIGHT.

CAPTAIN, WHAT DO YOU MEAN, NADESICO?

I WANT TO KNOW WHEN THAT SHIP WAS NAMED THE NADESICO!?

JUST A LITTLE WHILE AGO. SIR, I HAVE PROOF THAT THIS SHIP IS THE NADESICO!!

WHAT!?

GGGRRRRR. I WANT TO SEE AKITO NOW, BUT THIS OLD FART WON'T SHUT UP!

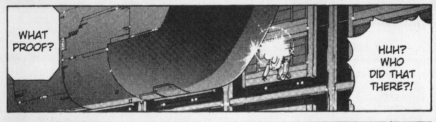

WHAT PROOF?

HUH? WHO DID THAT THERE?!

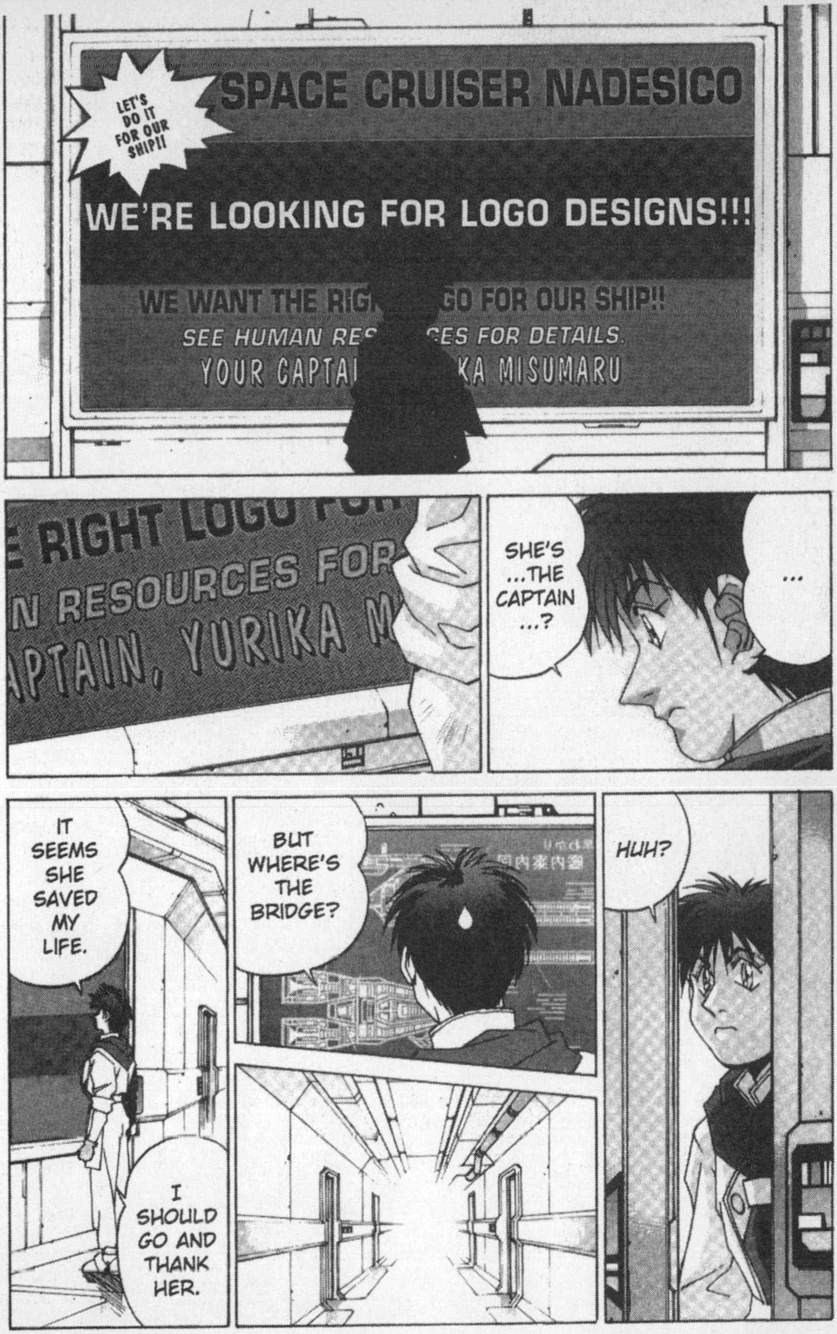
LET'S DO IT FOR OUR SHIP!!
SPACE CRUISER NADESICO
WE'RE LOOKING FOR LOGO DESIGNS!!!
WE WANT THE RIG GO FOR OUR SHIP!!
SEE HUMAN RES CES FOR DETAILS.
YOUR CAPTAI KA MISUMARU
E RIGHT LOGO FOR
N RESOURCES FOR
APTAIN, YURIKA M
SHE'S ...THE CAPTAIN ...?
...
IT SEEMS SHE SAVED MY LIFE.
I SHOULD GO AND THANK HER.
BUT WHERE'S THE BRIDGE?
HUH?

T--THIS IS AN ORIGINAL POSTER FOR THE GIANT ROBOT ANIME, "GEKIGANGER 3!!"

WHAT IS SUCH A RARE COLLECTIBLE DOING HERE!?

BOY, DOES THIS BRING ME BACK! I USED TO WATCH THIS ON MARS WHEN I WAS A KID.

WOW! KEN TENKU! JOE UMITSUBAME! COOL!!

OH, IT'S SUPER ALLOY GEKIGANGER!

*"GEKIGANGER 3" STARTS TUESDAY, OCTOBER 2, AT 7 PM

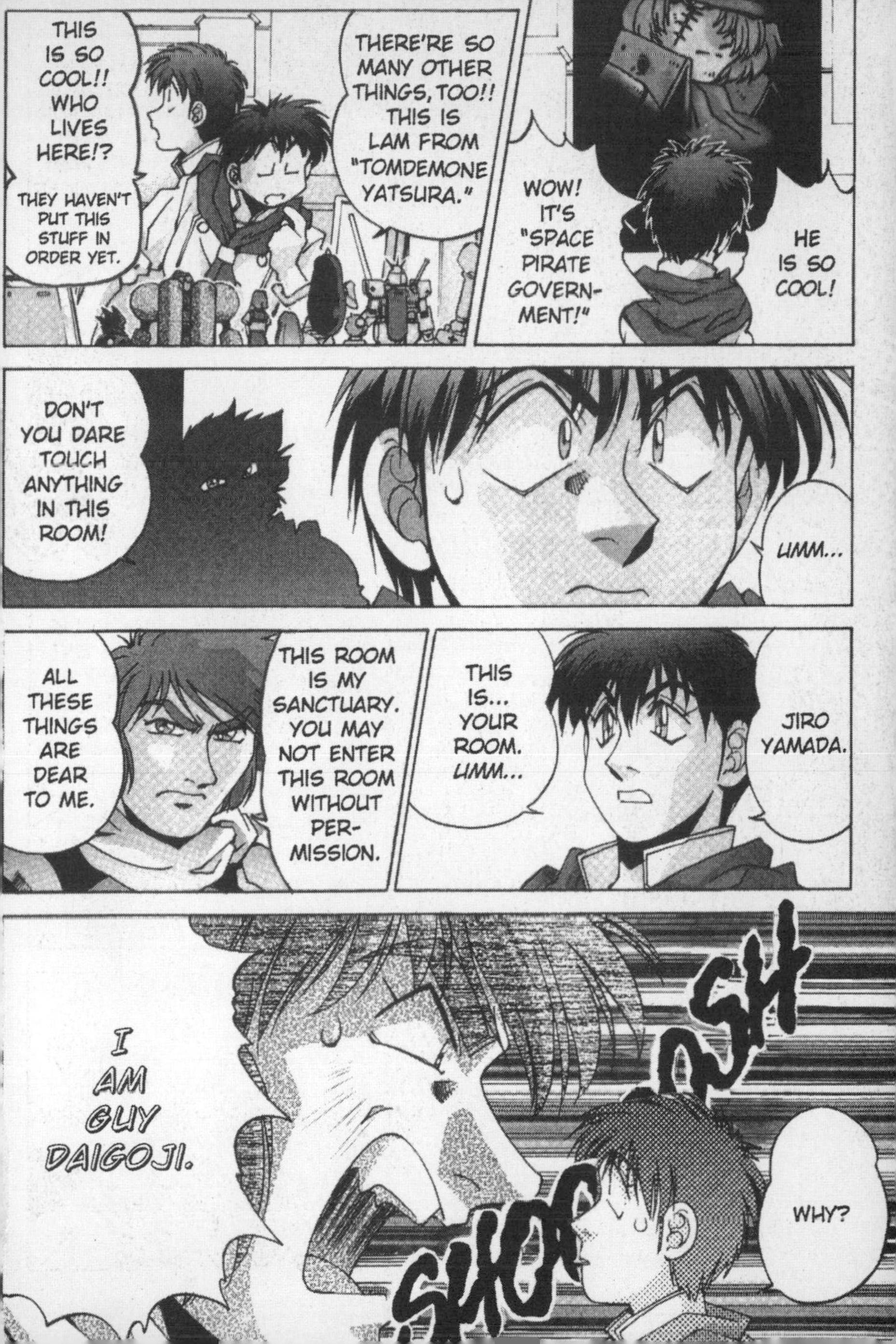
THIS IS SO COOL!! WHO LIVES HERE!?
THEY HAVEN'T PUT THIS STUFF IN ORDER YET.
THERE'RE SO MANY OTHER THINGS, TOO!! THIS IS LAM FROM "TOMDEMONE YATSURA."
WOW! IT'S "SPACE PIRATE GOVERN-MENT!"
HE IS SO COOL!
DON'T YOU DARE TOUCH ANYTHING IN THIS ROOM!
UMM...
ALL THESE THINGS ARE DEAR TO ME.
THIS ROOM IS MY SANCTUARY. YOU MAY NOT ENTER THIS ROOM WITHOUT PER-MISSION.
THIS IS... YOUR ROOM. UMM...
JIRO YAMADA.
I AM GUY DAIGOJI.
WHY?

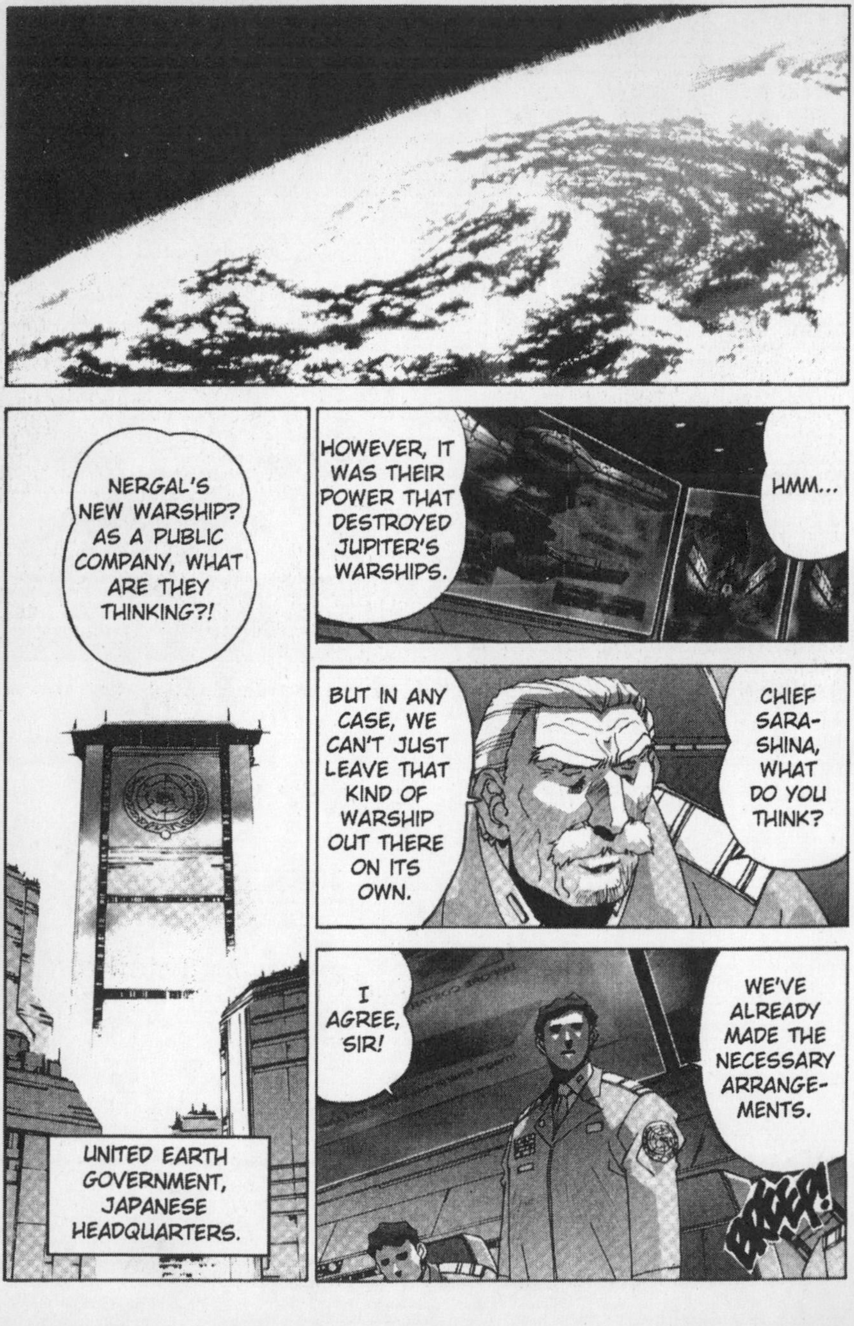
NERGAL'S NEW WARSHIP? AS A PUBLIC COMPANY, WHAT ARE THEY THINKING?!
UNITED EARTH GOVERNMENT, JAPANESE HEADQUARTERS.
HOWEVER, IT WAS THEIR POWER THAT DESTROYED JUPITER'S WARSHIPS.
HMM...
BUT IN ANY CASE, WE CAN'T JUST LEAVE THAT KIND OF WARSHIP OUT THERE ON ITS OWN.
CHIEF SARA-SHINA, WHAT DO YOU THINK?
I AGREE, SIR!
WE'VE ALREADY MADE THE NECESSARY ARRANGE-MENTS.
BREEP!

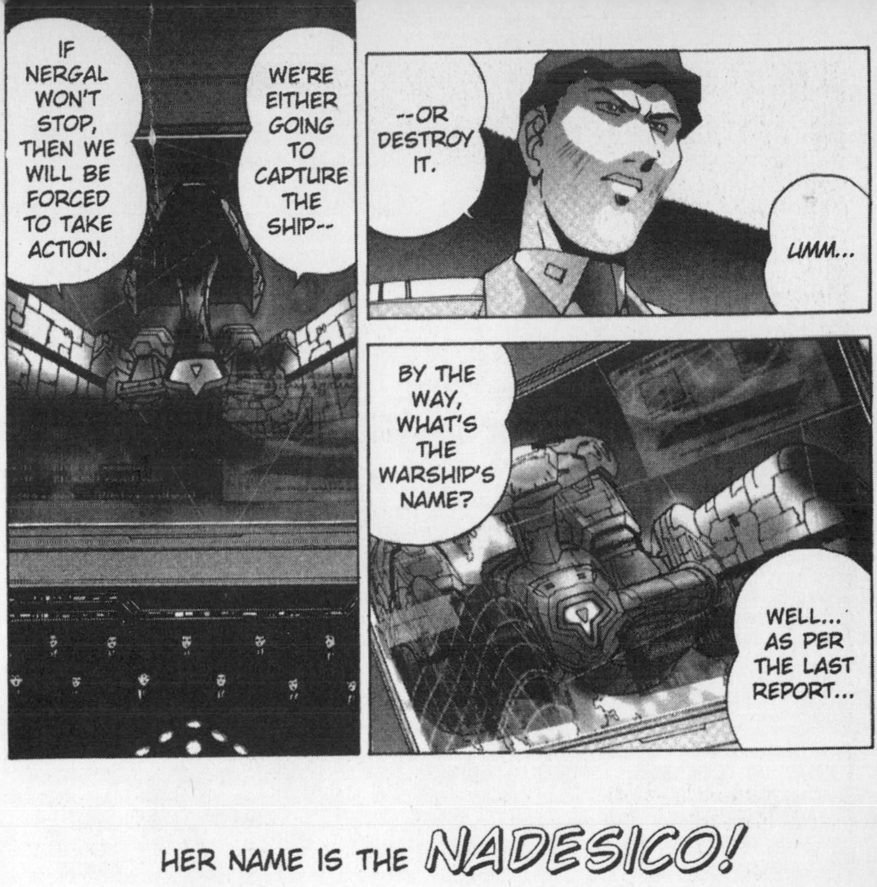
IF NERGAL WON'T STOP, THEN WE WILL BE FORCED TO TAKE ACTION.
WE'RE EITHER GOING TO CAPTURE THE SHIP--
--OR DESTROY IT.
UMM...
BY THE WAY, WHAT'S THE WARSHIP'S NAME?
WELL... AS PER THE LAST REPORT...

HER NAME IS THE *NADESICO!*

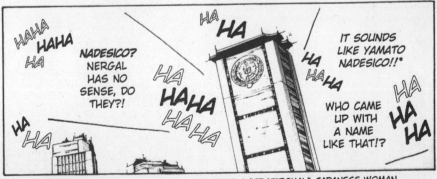

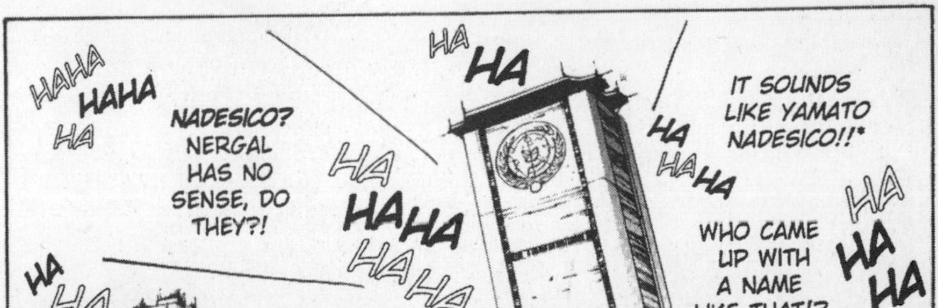
HAHA HAHA HA
NADESICO? NERGAL HAS NO SENSE, DO THEY?!
HA HA
HA HAHA HA HA
HA HA
HA HA
IT SOUNDS LIKE YAMATO NADESICO!!*
HA HAHA
WHO CAME UP WITH A NAME LIKE THAT!?
HA HA HA

* YAMATO NADESICO IS A TERM TO DESCRIBE A "TRADITIONAL" JAPANESE WOMAN. YAMATO IS ALSO THE NAME OF A FAMOUS BATTLESHIP.

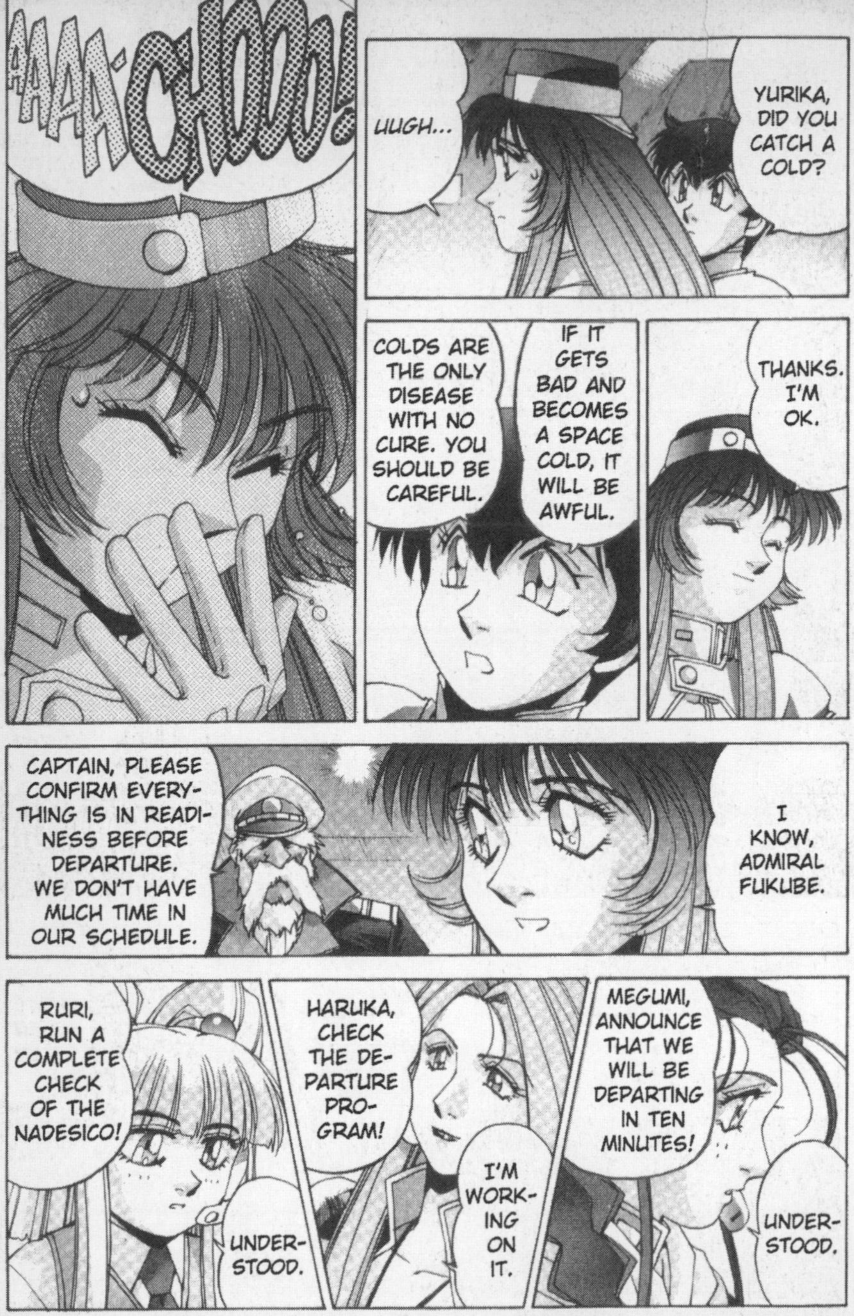
AAAA-CHOOO!
UUGH...
YURIKA, DID YOU CATCH A COLD?
COLDS ARE THE ONLY DISEASE WITH NO CURE. YOU SHOULD BE CAREFUL.
IF IT GETS BAD AND BECOMES A SPACE COLD, IT WILL BE AWFUL.
THANKS. I'M OK.
CAPTAIN, PLEASE CONFIRM EVERY-THING IS IN READI-NESS BEFORE DEPARTURE. WE DON'T HAVE MUCH TIME IN OUR SCHEDULE.
I KNOW, ADMIRAL FUKUBE.
RURI, RUN A COMPLETE CHECK OF THE NADESICO!
UNDER-STOOD.
HARUKA, CHECK THE DE-PARTURE PRO-GRAM!
I'M WORK-ING ON IT.
MEGUMI, ANNOUNCE THAT WE WILL BE DEPARTING IN TEN MINUTES!
UNDER-STOOD.

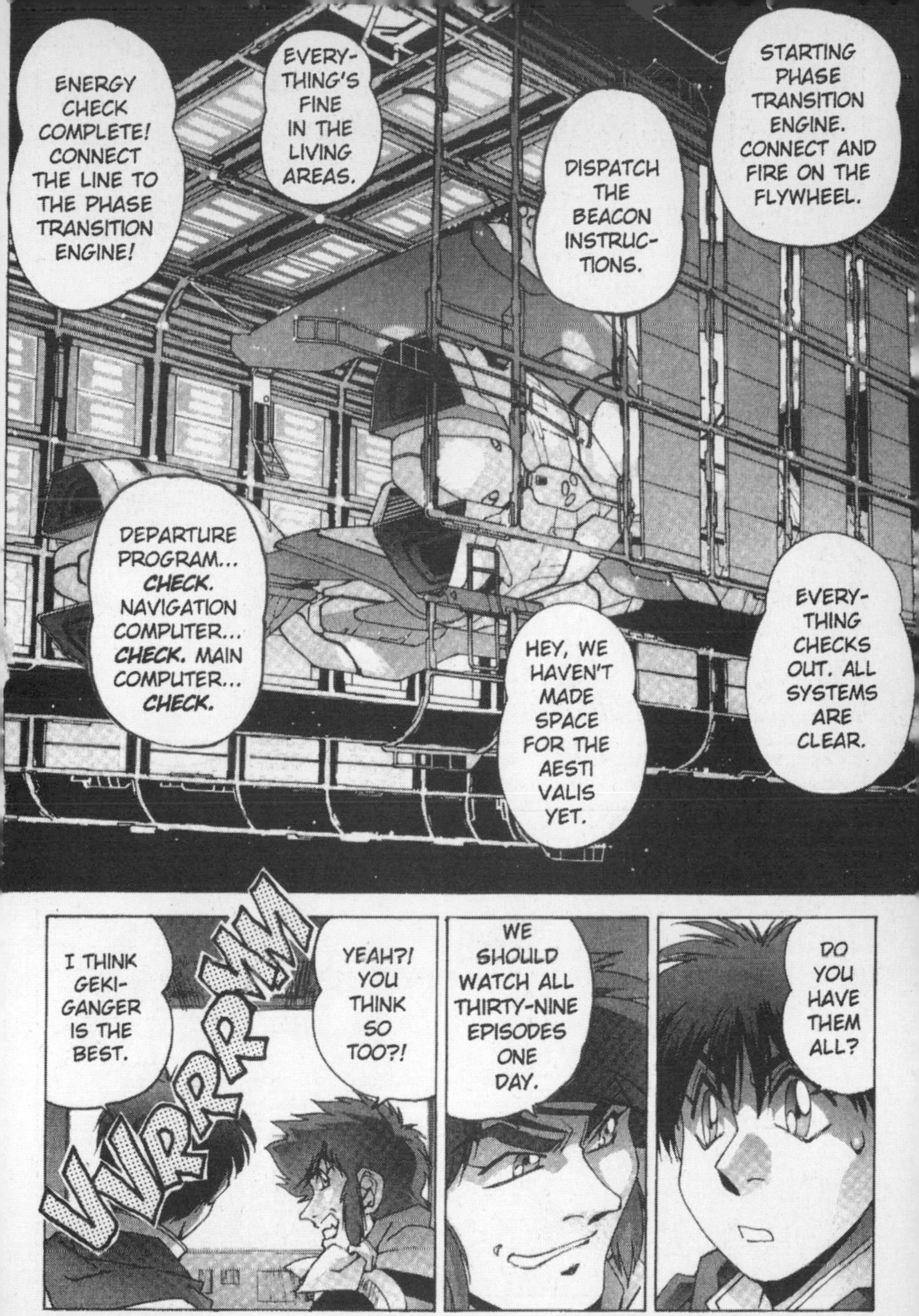

ENERGY CHECK COMPLETE! CONNECT THE LINE TO THE PHASE TRANSITION ENGINE!
EVERY-THING'S FINE IN THE LIVING AREAS.
DISPATCH THE BEACON INSTRUC-TIONS.
STARTING PHASE TRANSITION ENGINE. CONNECT AND FIRE ON THE FLYWHEEL.
DEPARTURE PROGRAM... **CHECK.** NAVIGATION COMPUTER... **CHECK.** MAIN COMPUTER... **CHECK.**
HEY, WE HAVEN'T MADE SPACE FOR THE AESTI VALIS YET.
EVERY-THING CHECKS OUT. ALL SYSTEMS ARE CLEAR.
I THINK GEKI-GANGER IS THE BEST.
VURRRM
YEAH?! YOU THINK SO TOO?!
WE SHOULD WATCH ALL THIRTY-NINE EPISODES ONE DAY.
DO YOU HAVE THEM ALL?

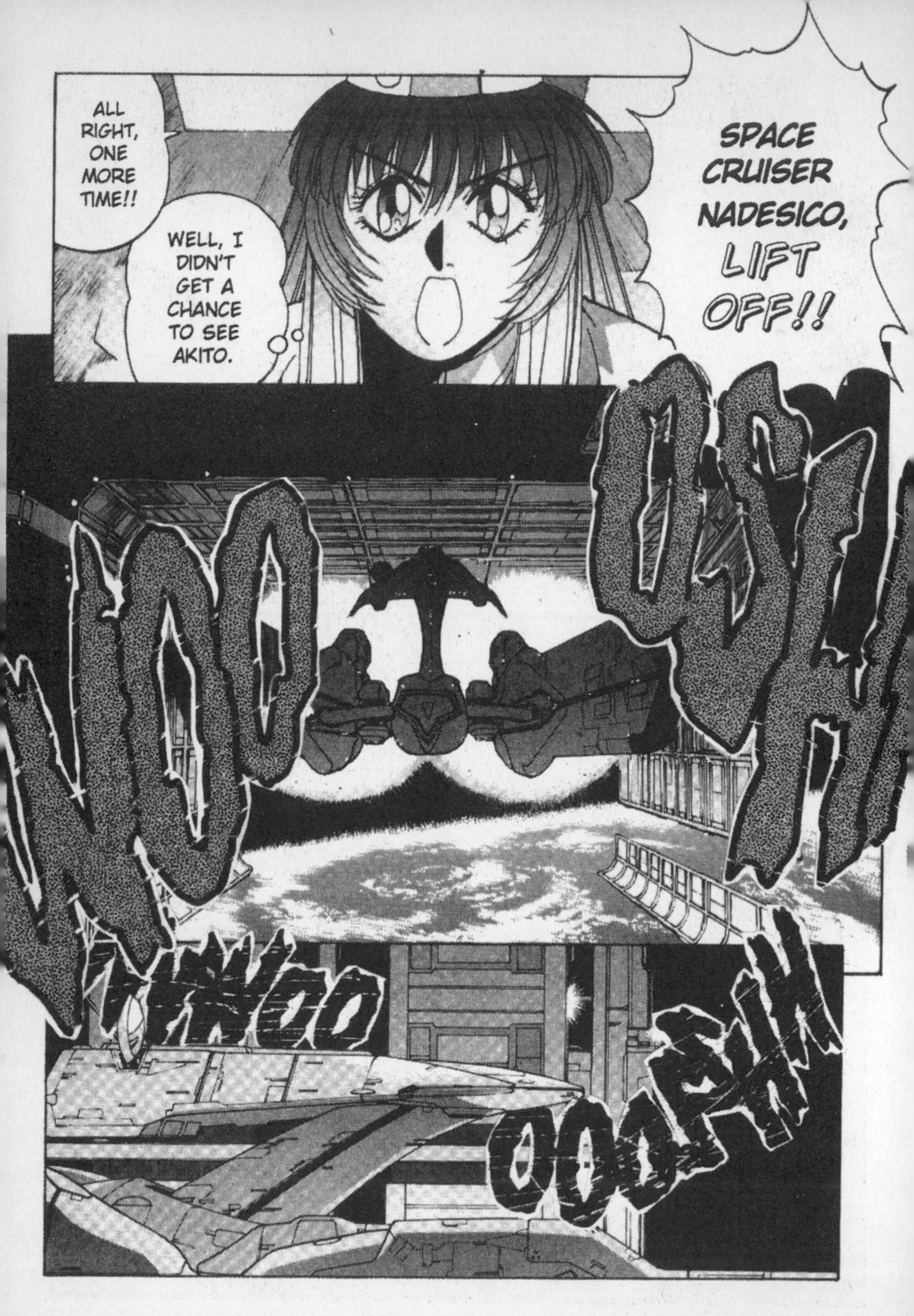
ALL RIGHT, ONE MORE TIME!!
WELL, I DIDN'T GET A CHANCE TO SEE AKITO.
SPACE CRUISER NADESICO, LIFT OFF!!

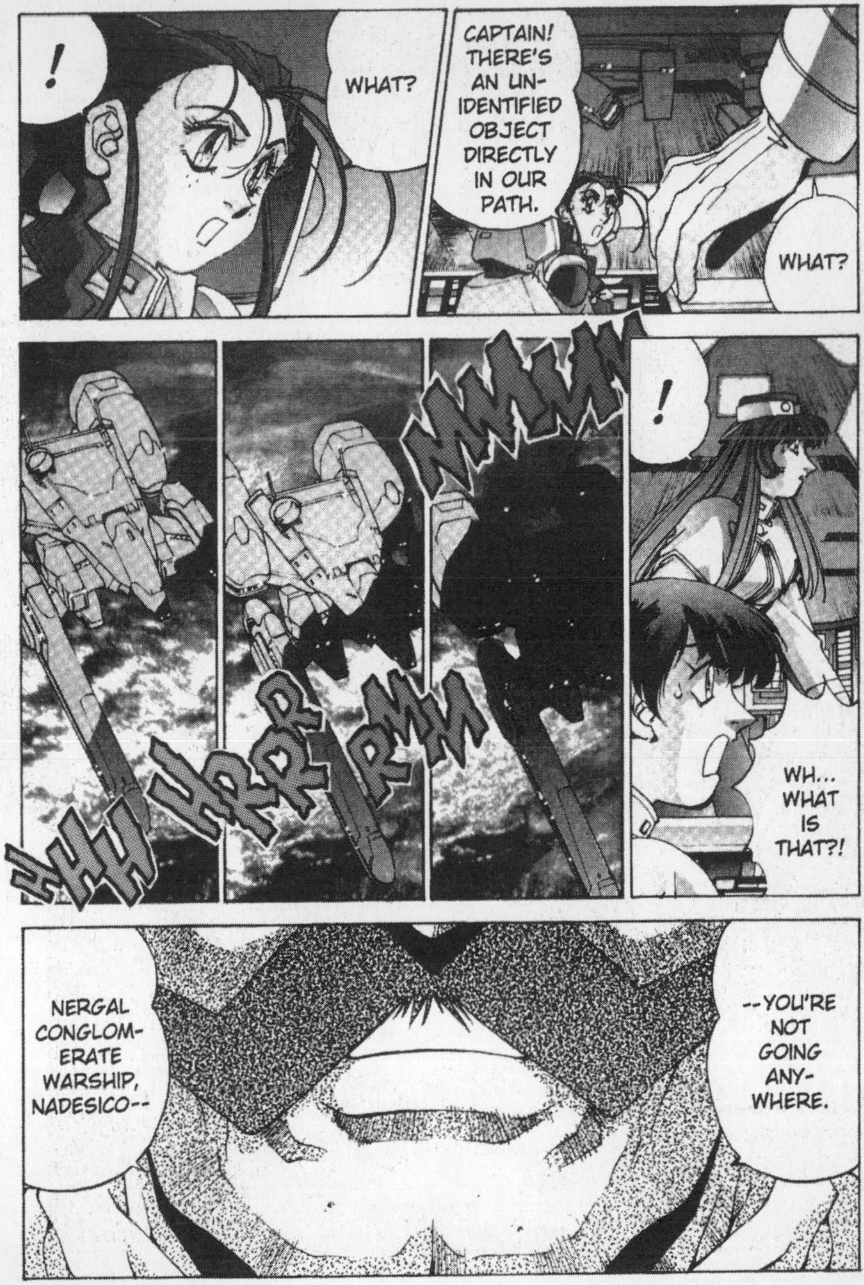
!
WHAT?
CAPTAIN! THERE'S AN UN-IDENTIFIED OBJECT DIRECTLY IN OUR PATH.
WHAT?
HHH HRR RRMM MMMM
!
WH... WHAT IS THAT?!
NERGAL CONGLOM-ERATE WARSHIP, NADESICO--
--YOU'RE NOT GOING ANY-WHERE.

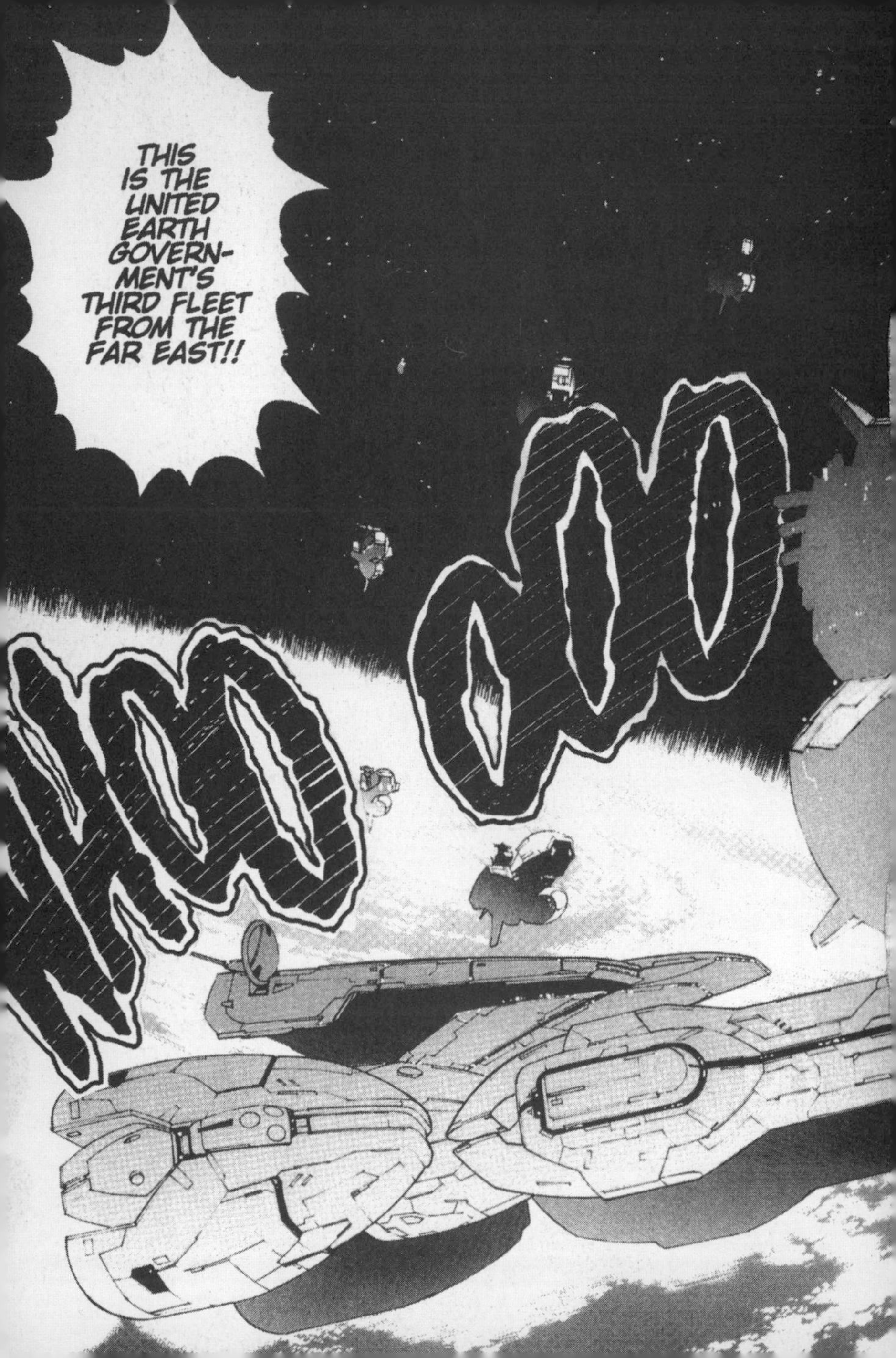
THIS IS THE UNITED EARTH GOVERNMENT'S THIRD FLEET FROM THE FAR EAST!!

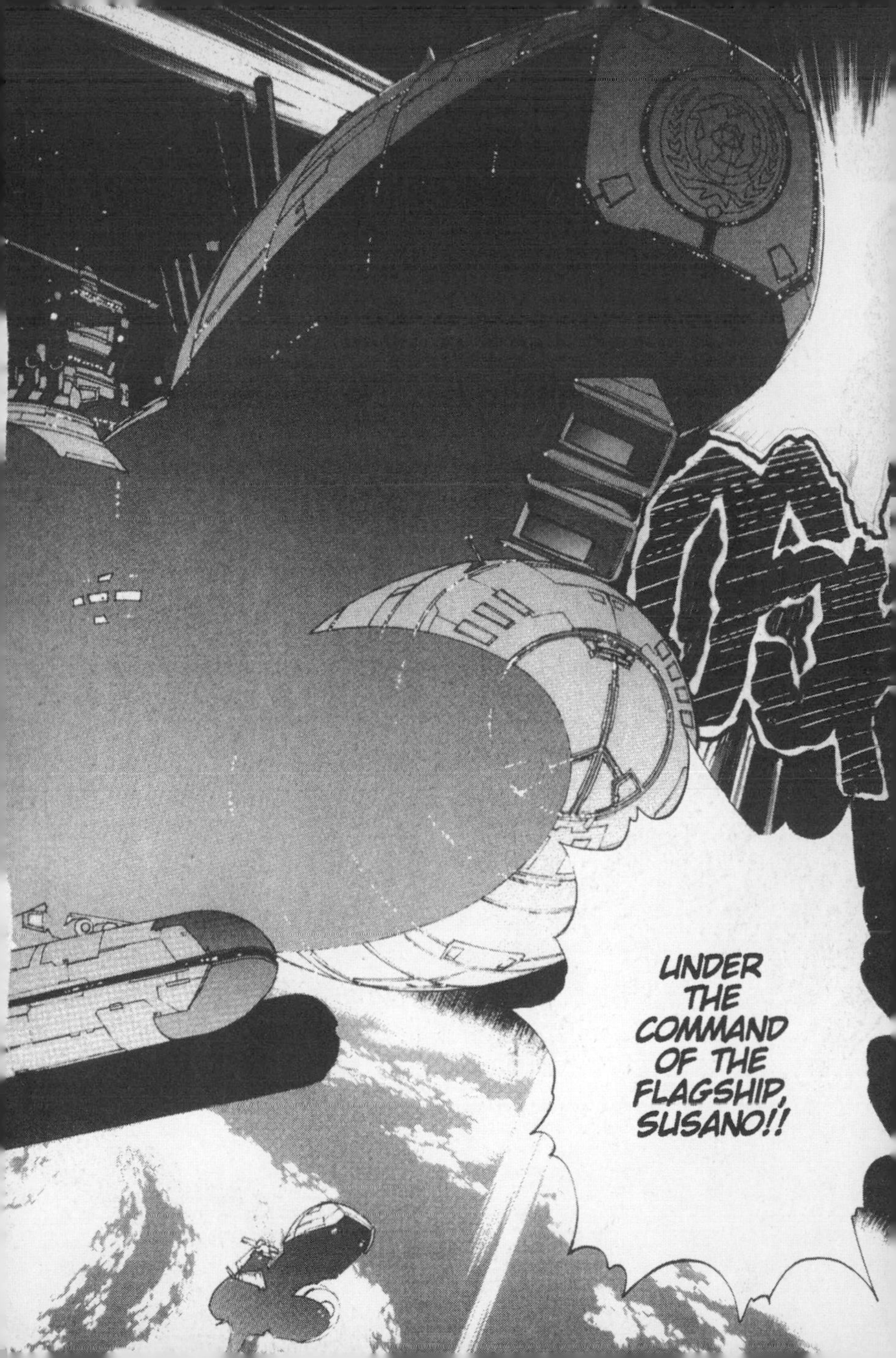
UNDER THE COMMAND OF THE FLAGSHIP, SUSANO!!

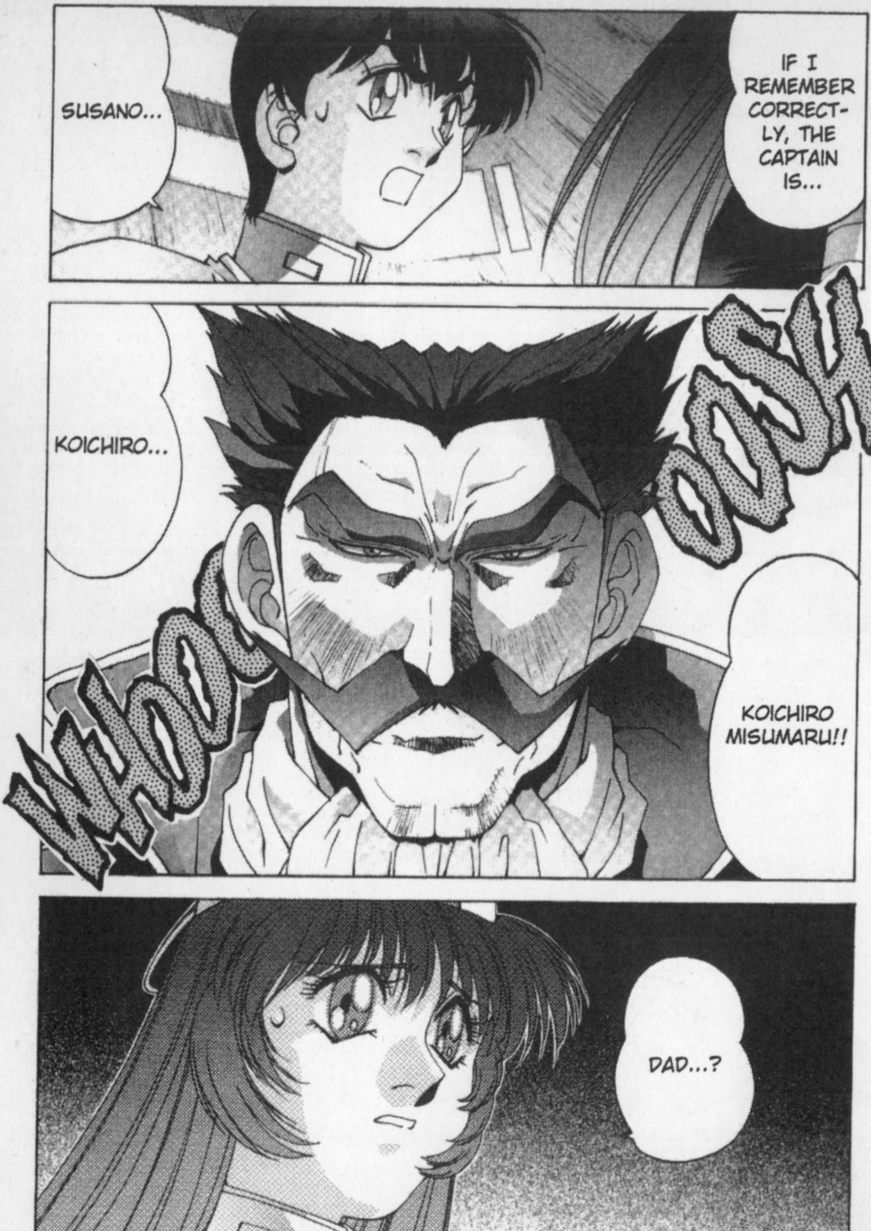
SUSANO...
IF I REMEMBER CORRECTLY, THE CAPTAIN IS...
KOICHIRO...
WHOOOOOSH
KOICHIRO MISUMARU!!
DAD...?

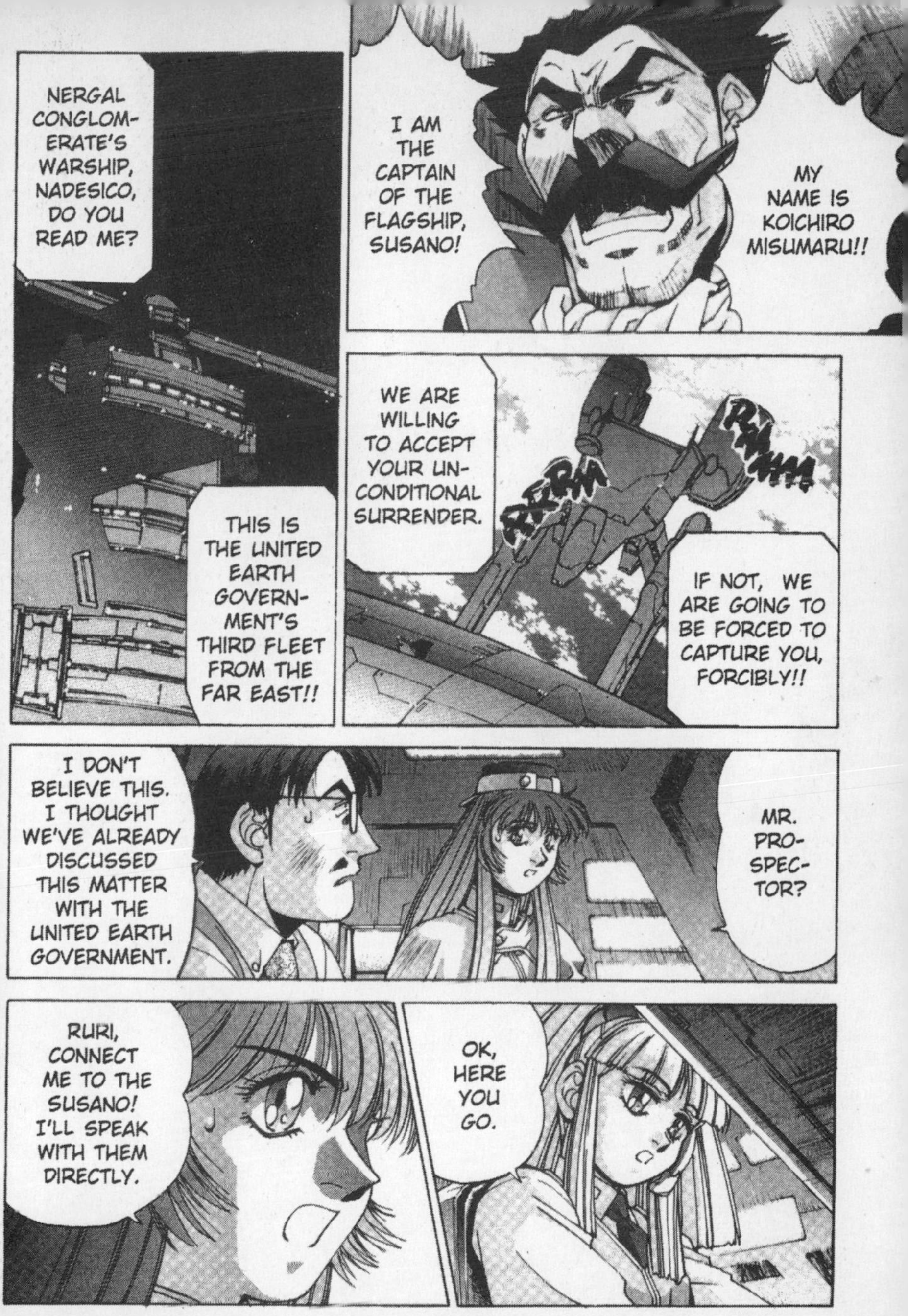
NERGAL CONGLOMERATE'S WARSHIP, NADESICO, DO YOU READ ME?
THIS IS THE UNITED EARTH GOVERNMENT'S THIRD FLEET FROM THE FAR EAST!!
I AM THE CAPTAIN OF THE FLAGSHIP, SUSANO!
MY NAME IS KOICHIRO MISUMARU!!
WE ARE WILLING TO ACCEPT YOUR UNCONDITIONAL SURRENDER.
IF NOT, WE ARE GOING TO BE FORCED TO CAPTURE YOU, FORCIBLY!!
I DON'T BELIEVE THIS. I THOUGHT WE'VE ALREADY DISCUSSED THIS MATTER WITH THE UNITED EARTH GOVERNMENT.
MR. PROSPECTOR?
RURI, CONNECT ME TO THE SUSANO! I'LL SPEAK WITH THEM DIRECTLY.
OK, HERE YOU GO.

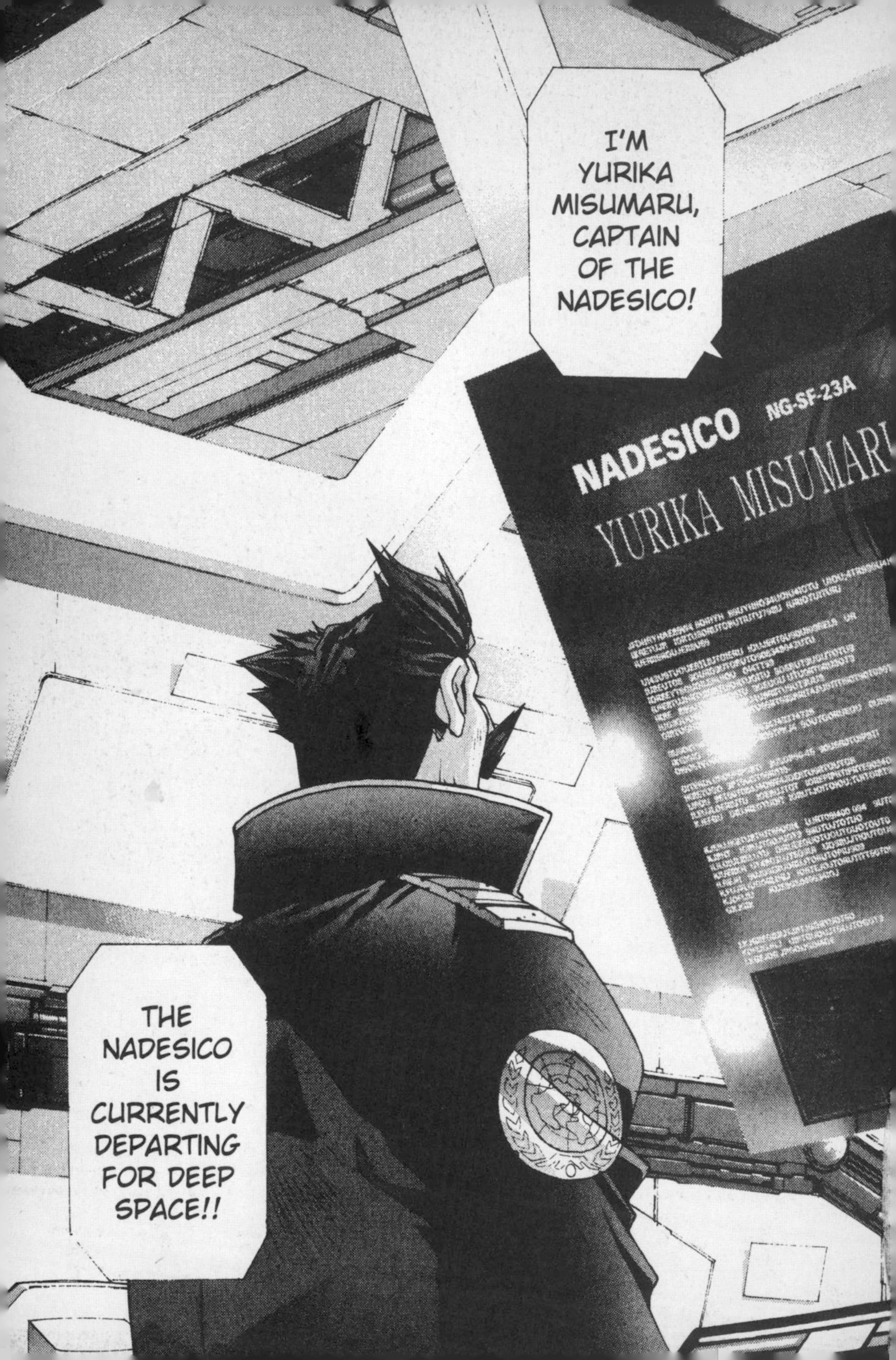
I'M YURIKA MISUMARU, CAPTAIN OF THE NADESICO!
NADESICO NG-SF-23A
YURIKA MISUMAR
THE NADESICO IS CURRENTLY DEPARTING FOR DEEP SPACE!!

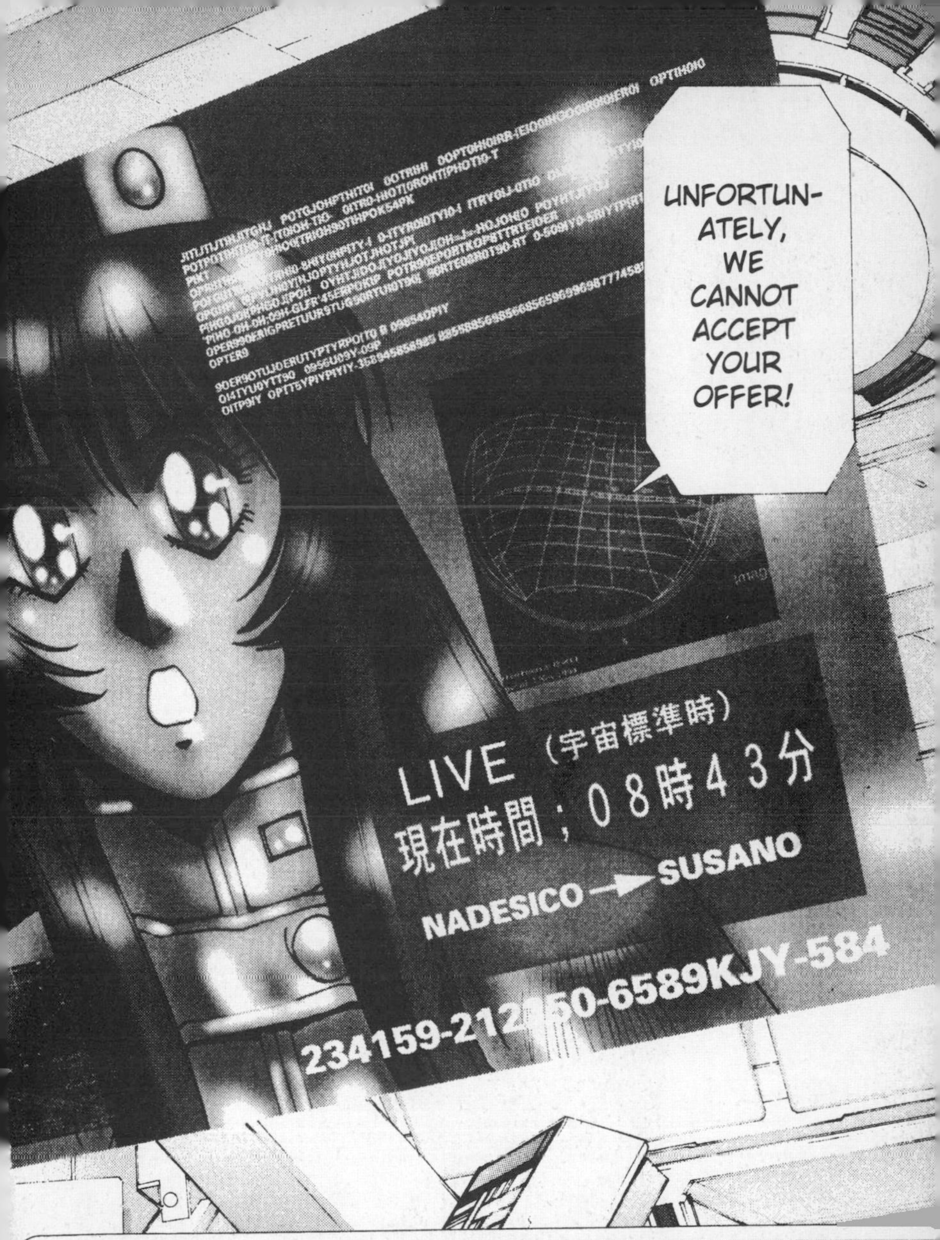
UNFORTUN-ATELY, WE CANNOT ACCEPT YOUR OFFER!
LIVE（宇宙標準時）
現在時間；０８時４３分
NADESICO → SUSANO

ナデシコ vs. スサノオ

第4話 NADESICO vs. SUSANO

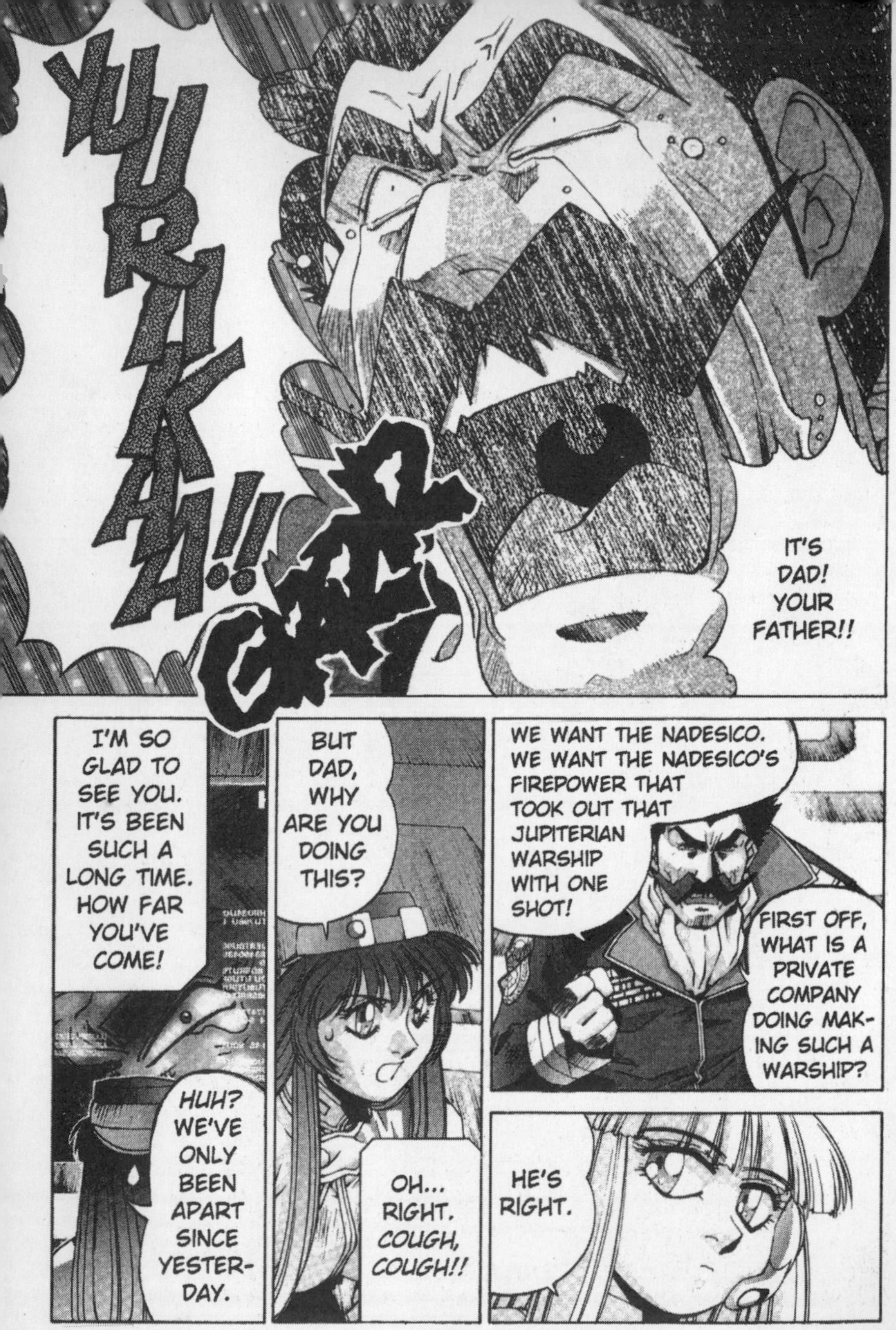
YUURIKAAA!!
IT'S DAD! YOUR FATHER!!
I'M SO GLAD TO SEE YOU. IT'S BEEN SUCH A LONG TIME. HOW FAR YOU'VE COME!
HUH? WE'VE ONLY BEEN APART SINCE YESTER-DAY.
BUT DAD, WHY ARE YOU DOING THIS?
OH... RIGHT. COUGH, COUGH!!
WE WANT THE NADESICO. WE WANT THE NADESICO'S FIREPOWER THAT TOOK OUT THAT JUPITERIAN WARSHIP WITH ONE SHOT!
FIRST OFF, WHAT IS A PRIVATE COMPANY DOING MAK-ING SUCH A WARSHIP?
HE'S RIGHT.

I CAN'T EXPLAIN IT ALL RIGHT NOW, BUT THE NADESICO HAS A GRAND PURPOSE.

IN ORDER TO ACCOMPLISH OUR GOAL, THE NADESICO HAS TREMENDOUS FIREPOWER SO THE JUPITERIANS CAN'T STOP US.

GRAND PUR-POSE?

WHAT?

AS THE CAPTAIN HAS STATED, WE AT NERGAL CAN USE THIS WAR-SHIP FOR PRIVATE REASONS...

WHO ARE YOU?

I AM CALLED PROS-PECTOR, IN CHARGE OF FINAN-CING THE NADESICO.

THAT'S EVEN BETTER.

BUT AS YOU MAY KNOW, THE MILITARY HELPED YOU MAKE THAT WARSHIP.

WE LET YOU USE THE DOCK AT SASEBO.

HOWEVER, THE SITUATION HERE HAS CHANGED!!

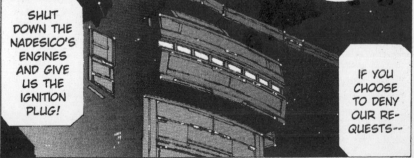

SHUT DOWN THE NADESICO'S ENGINES AND GIVE US THE IGNITION PLUG!

IF YOU CHOOSE TO DENY OUR RE-QUESTS--

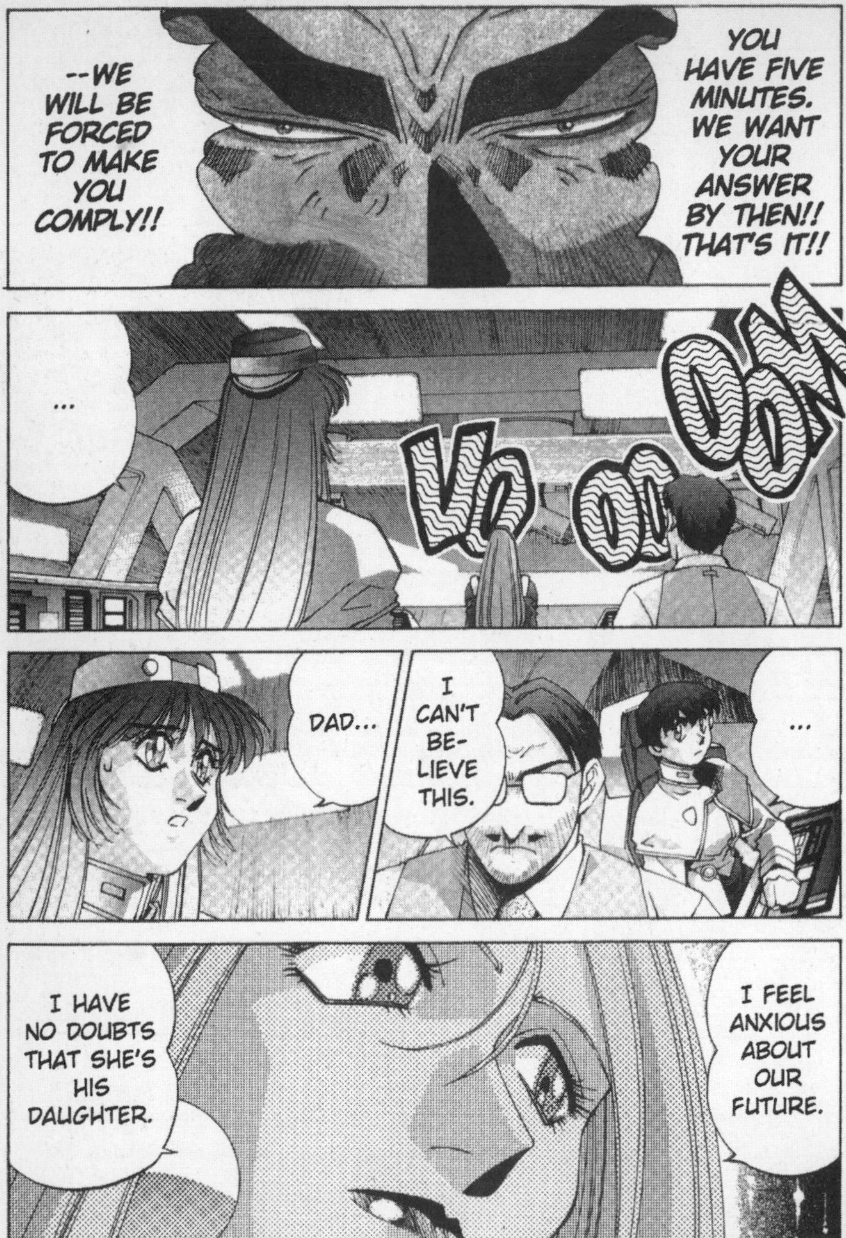
--WE WILL BE FORCED TO MAKE YOU COMPLY!!
YOU HAVE FIVE MINUTES. WE WANT YOUR ANSWER BY THEN!! THAT'S IT!!
...
VROOOOM
DAD...
I CAN'T BE-LIEVE THIS.
...
I HAVE NO DOUBTS THAT SHE'S HIS DAUGHTER.
I FEEL ANXIOUS ABOUT OUR FUTURE.

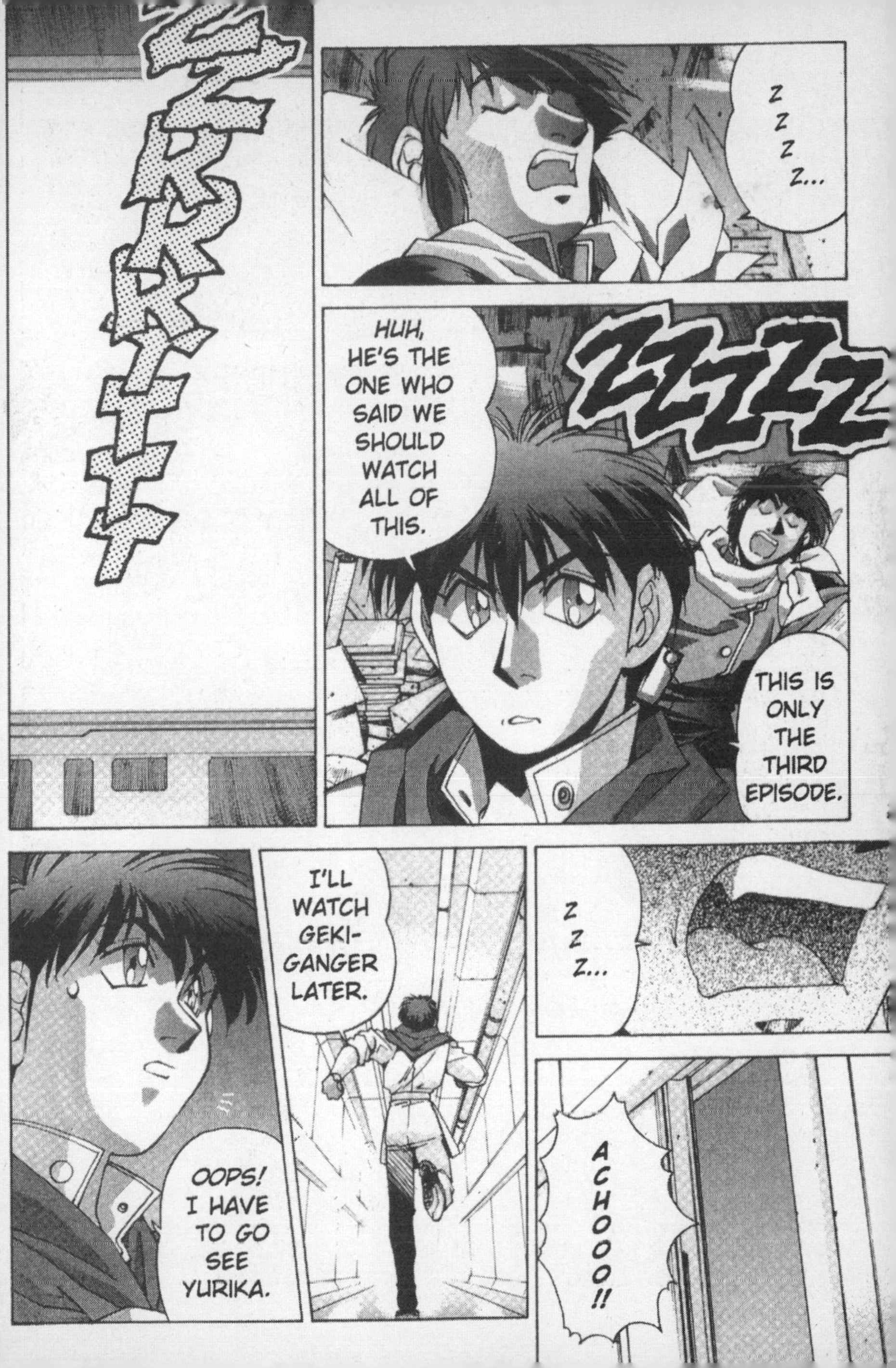
ZZRRRTTTT
Z Z Z Z...
HUH, HE'S THE ONE WHO SAID WE SHOULD WATCH ALL OF THIS.
ZZZZZ
THIS IS ONLY THE THIRD EPISODE.
OOPS! I HAVE TO GO SEE YURIKA.
I'LL WATCH GEKI-GANGER LATER.
Z Z Z...
ACHOOOO!!

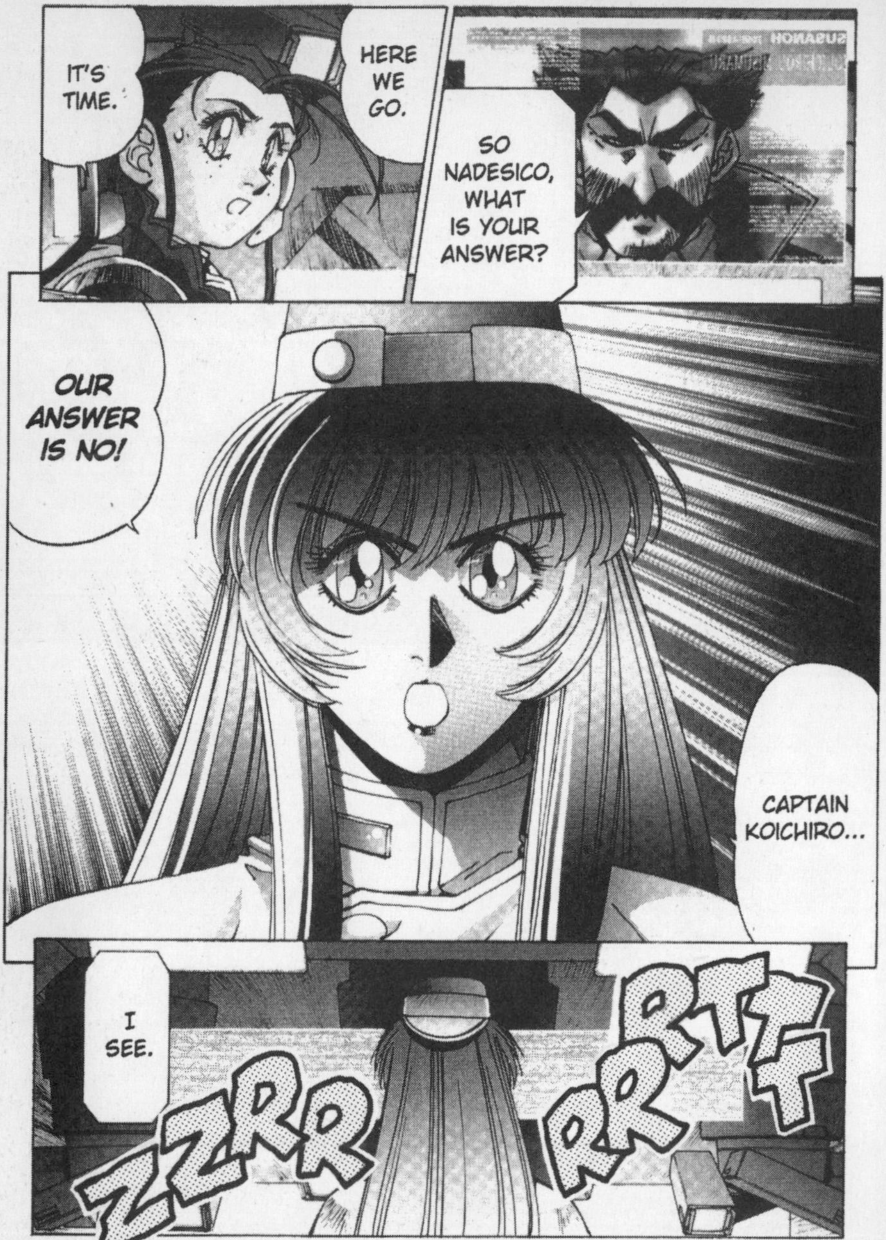
IT'S TIME.
HERE WE GO.
SO NADESICO, WHAT IS YOUR ANSWER?
OUR ANSWER IS NO!
CAPTAIN KOICHIRO...
I SEE.
ZZRR
RRRTT

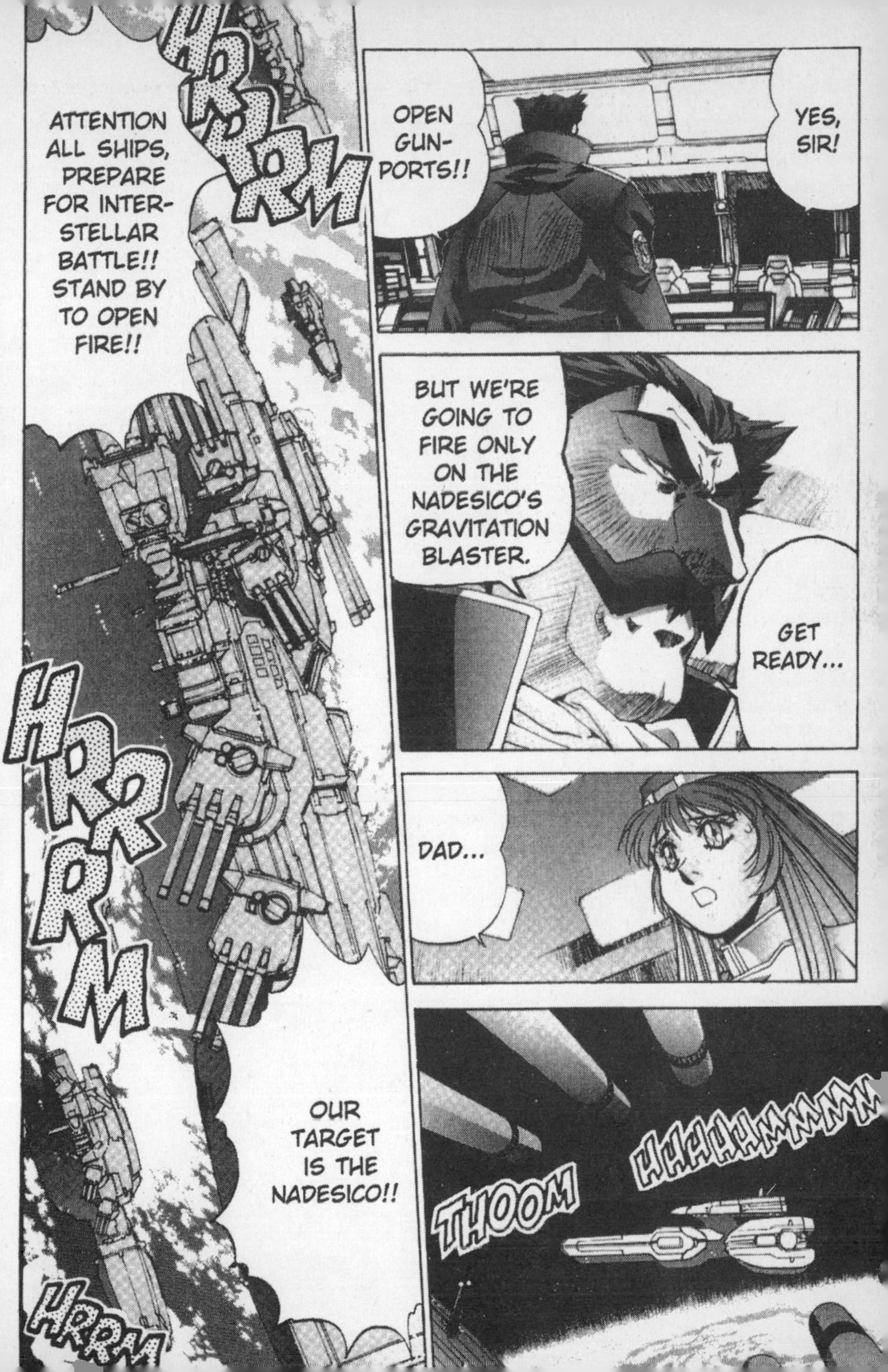
HRRRM
ATTENTION ALL SHIPS, PREPARE FOR INTER-STELLAR BATTLE!! STAND BY TO OPEN FIRE!!
HRRRRM
OUR TARGET IS THE NADESICO!!
HRRM
OPEN GUN-PORTS!!
YES, SIR!
BUT WE'RE GOING TO FIRE ONLY ON THE NADESICO'S GRAVITATION BLASTER.
GET READY...
DAD...
THOOM
HHHHHMMMMM

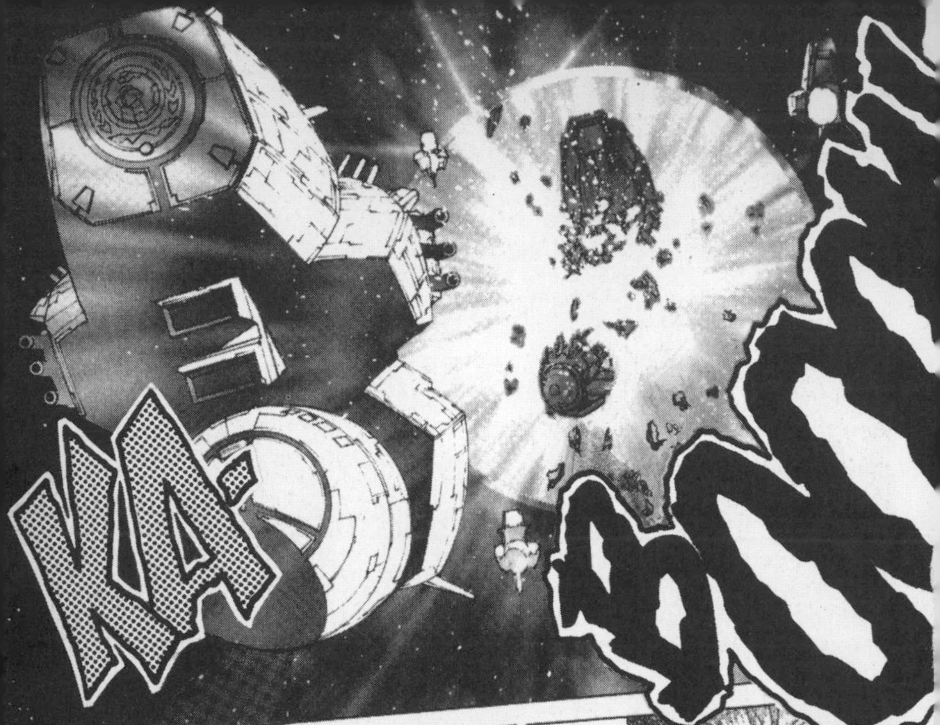
KA
BOOM
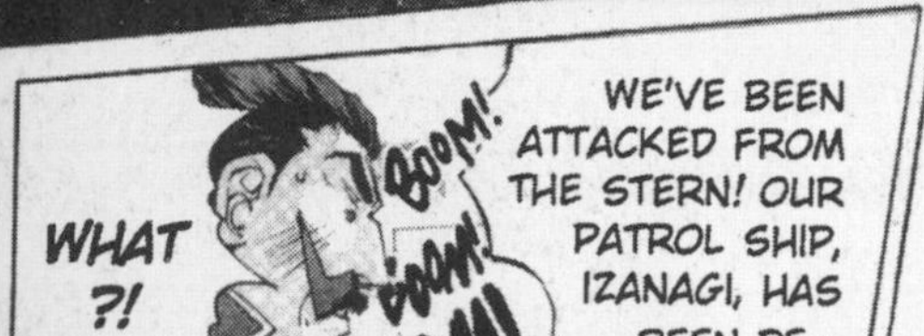
WHAT ?!
BOOM! BOOM! BOOM! BOOM!
WE'VE BEEN ATTACKED FROM THE STERN! OUR PATROL SHIP, IZANAGI, HAS BEEN DE-STROYED!!
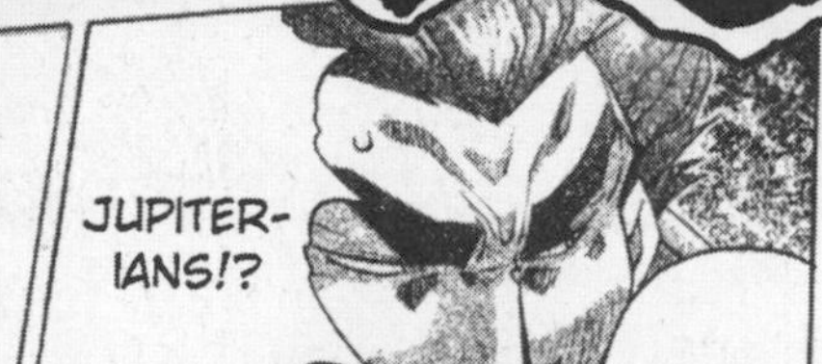
JUPITER-IANS!?
BUT HOW...
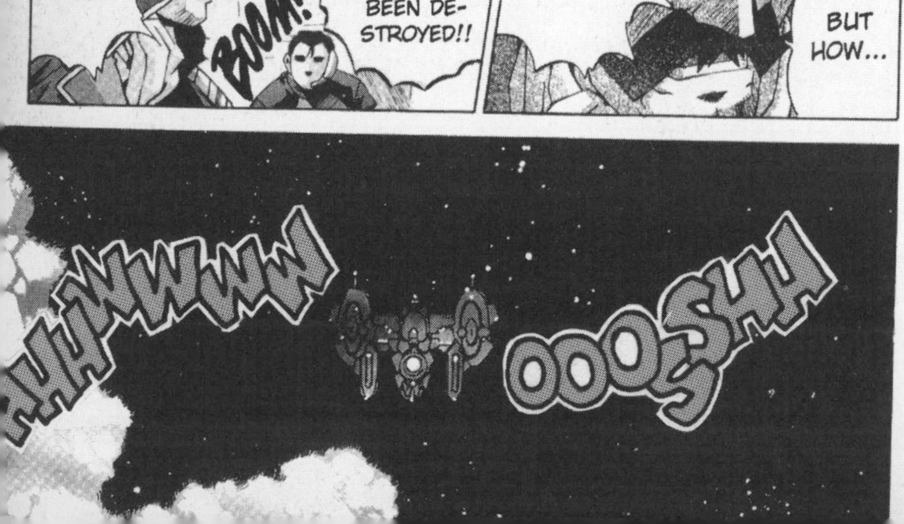

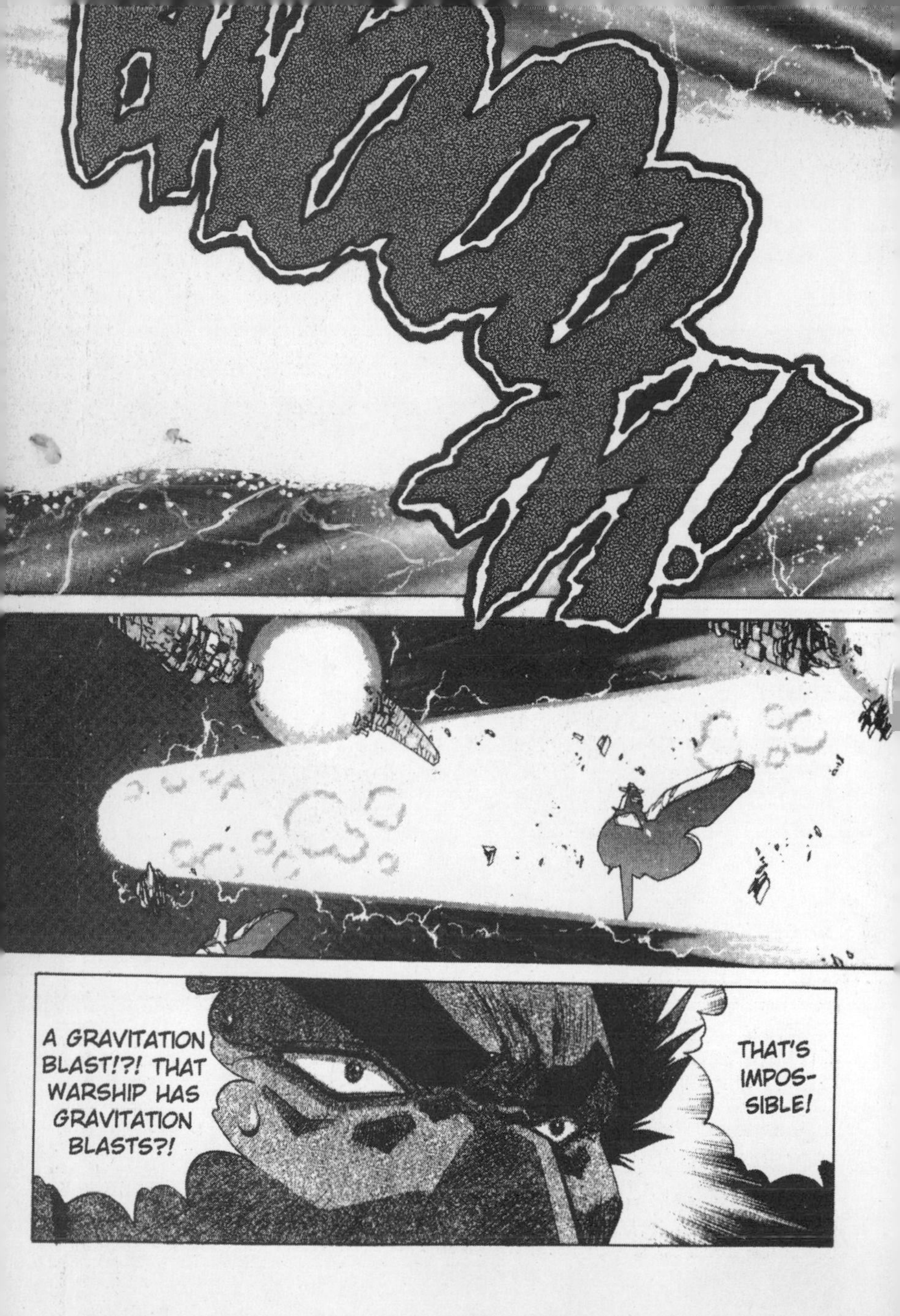
A GRAVITATION BLAST!?! THAT WARSHIP HAS GRAVITATION BLASTS?!
THAT'S IMPOS-SIBLE!

ALL SHIPS, FULL, REVERSE, TURN 180 DEGREES!! DESTROY ALL JUPITERIAN WARSHIPS!!

STAND BY ON-BOARD MACHINES FOR DEPARTURE AS SOON AS POSSIBLE!!

HHH

HRRR

RMMM

ENEMY WAR-SHIPS IDENTIFIED AS JORO AND BATTA.

HURRY UP ON BOARD MACHINES FOR DEPAR-TURE!!

FWA

ASH

OPEN ALL GUNPORTS!! BACK UP THE UNITED FEDERATION FORCES AND ATTACK THE JUPITERIAN WARSHIP!!

GRAVI-TATION BLASTS, STAND BY!! BEGIN POWERING UP!!

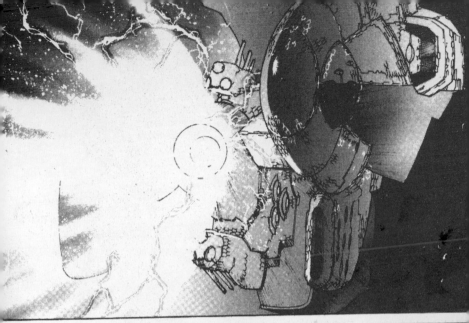

THEIR GRAVITATION BLAST WAS 85 PER- CENT AS POWERFUL AS OURS.

ACCORDING TO THIS DATA, OUR'S ARE STILL MORE POWERFUL.

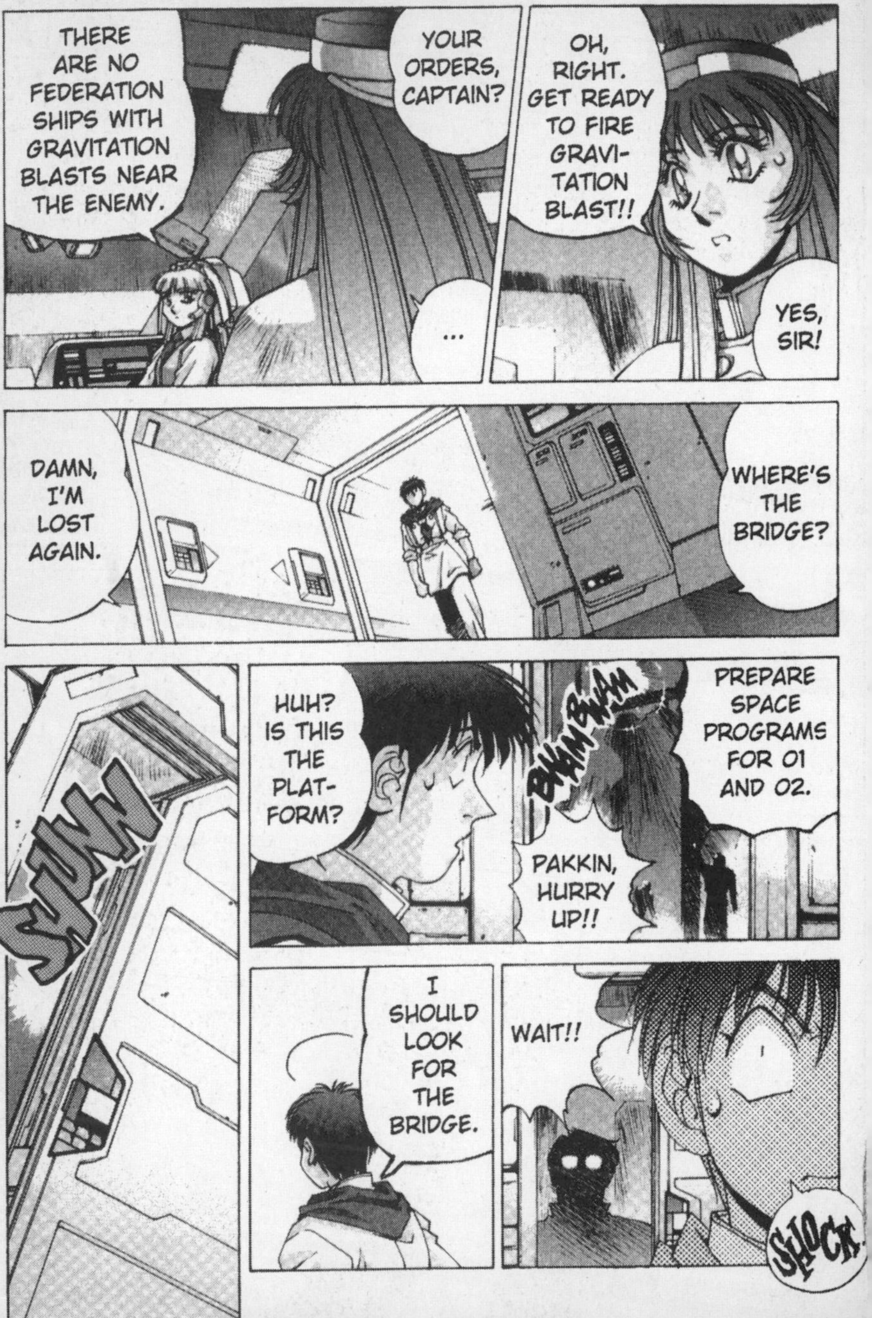
THERE ARE NO FEDERATION SHIPS WITH GRAVITATION BLASTS NEAR THE ENEMY.
YOUR ORDERS, CAPTAIN?
...
OH, RIGHT. GET READY TO FIRE GRAVI-TATION BLAST!!
YES, SIR!
DAMN, I'M LOST AGAIN.
WHERE'S THE BRIDGE?
SHUNN
HUH? IS THIS THE PLAT-FORM?
BWAM BWAM
PREPARE SPACE PROGRAMS FOR 01 AND 02.
PAKKIN, HURRY UP!!
I SHOULD LOOK FOR THE BRIDGE.
WAIT!!
SHOCK

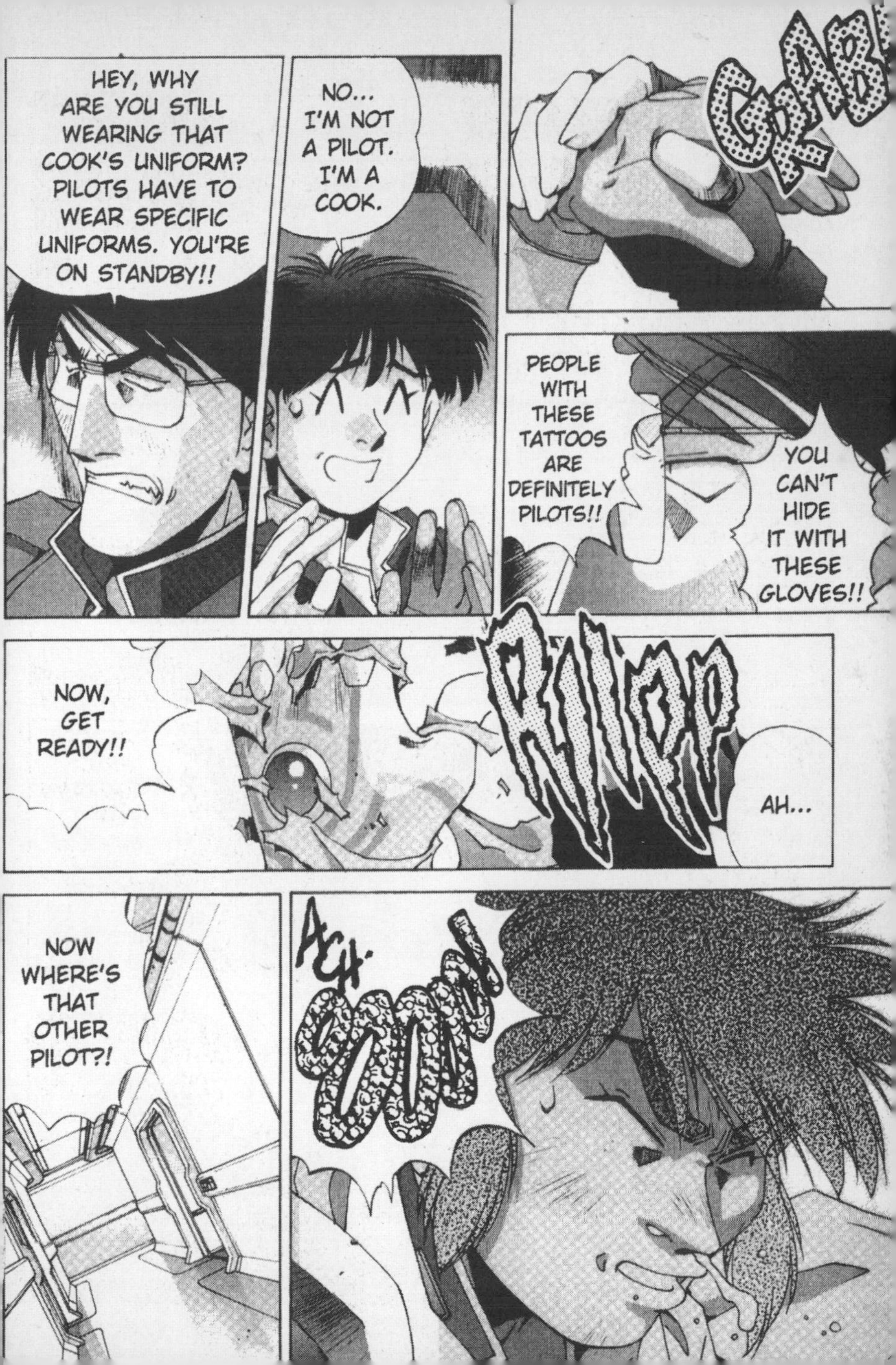
HEY, WHY ARE YOU STILL WEARING THAT COOK'S UNIFORM? PILOTS HAVE TO WEAR SPECIFIC UNIFORMS. YOU'RE ON STANDBY!!
NO... I'M NOT A PILOT. I'M A COOK.
GRAB!
PEOPLE WITH THESE TATTOOS ARE DEFINITELY PILOTS!!
YOU CAN'T HIDE IT WITH THESE GLOVES!!
NOW, GET READY!!
AH...
NOW WHERE'S THAT OTHER PILOT?!
ACH-

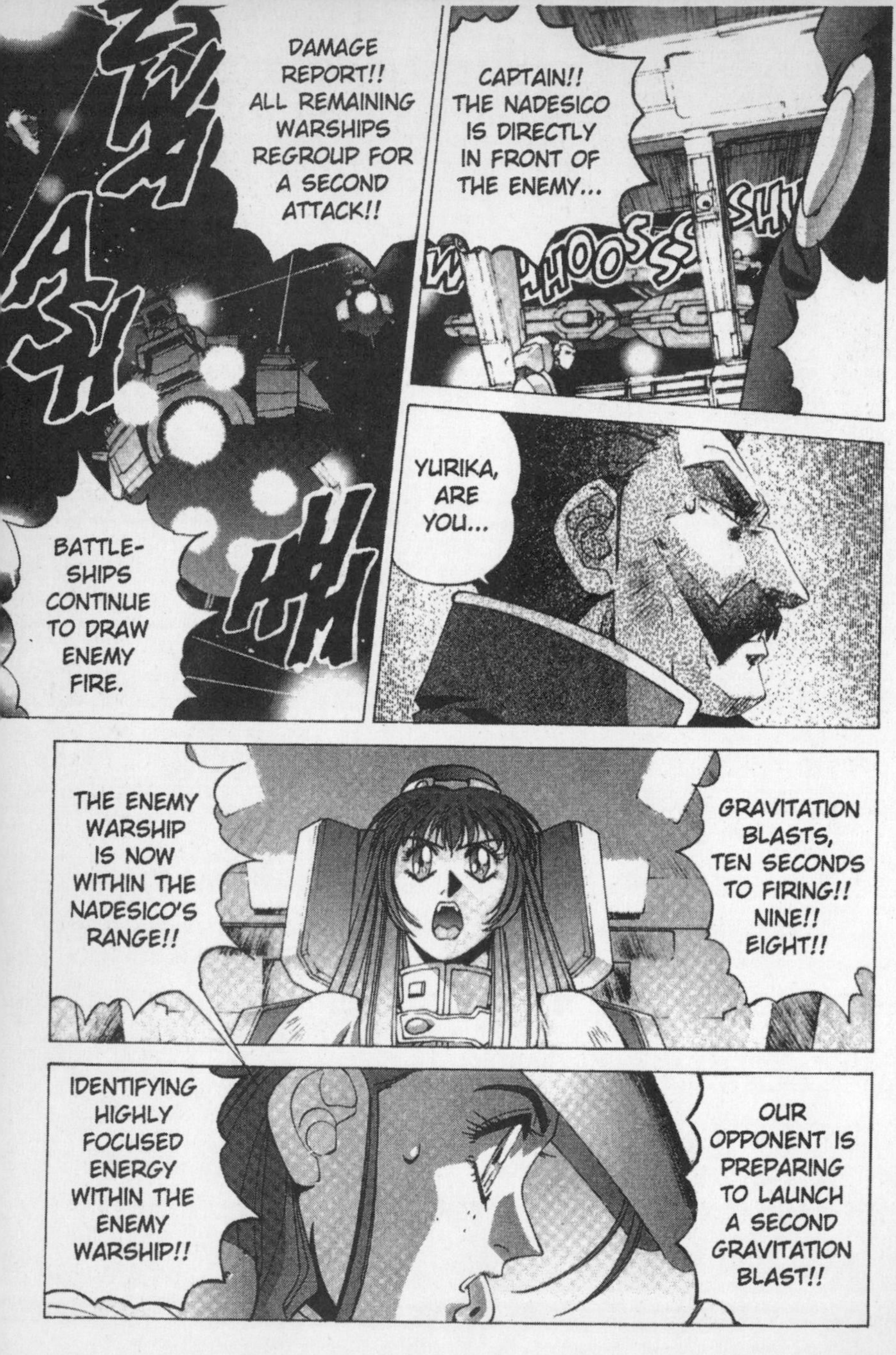
DAMAGE REPORT!! ALL REMAINING WARSHIPS REGROUP FOR A SECOND ATTACK!!
BATTLE-SHIPS CONTINUE TO DRAW ENEMY FIRE.
CAPTAIN!! THE NADESICO IS DIRECTLY IN FRONT OF THE ENEMY...
YURIKA, ARE YOU...
THE ENEMY WARSHIP IS NOW WITHIN THE NADESICO'S RANGE!!
GRAVITATION BLASTS, TEN SECONDS TO FIRING!! NINE!! EIGHT!!
IDENTIFYING HIGHLY FOCUSED ENERGY WITHIN THE ENEMY WARSHIP!!
OUR OPPONENT IS PREPARING TO LAUNCH A SECOND GRAVITATION BLAST!!

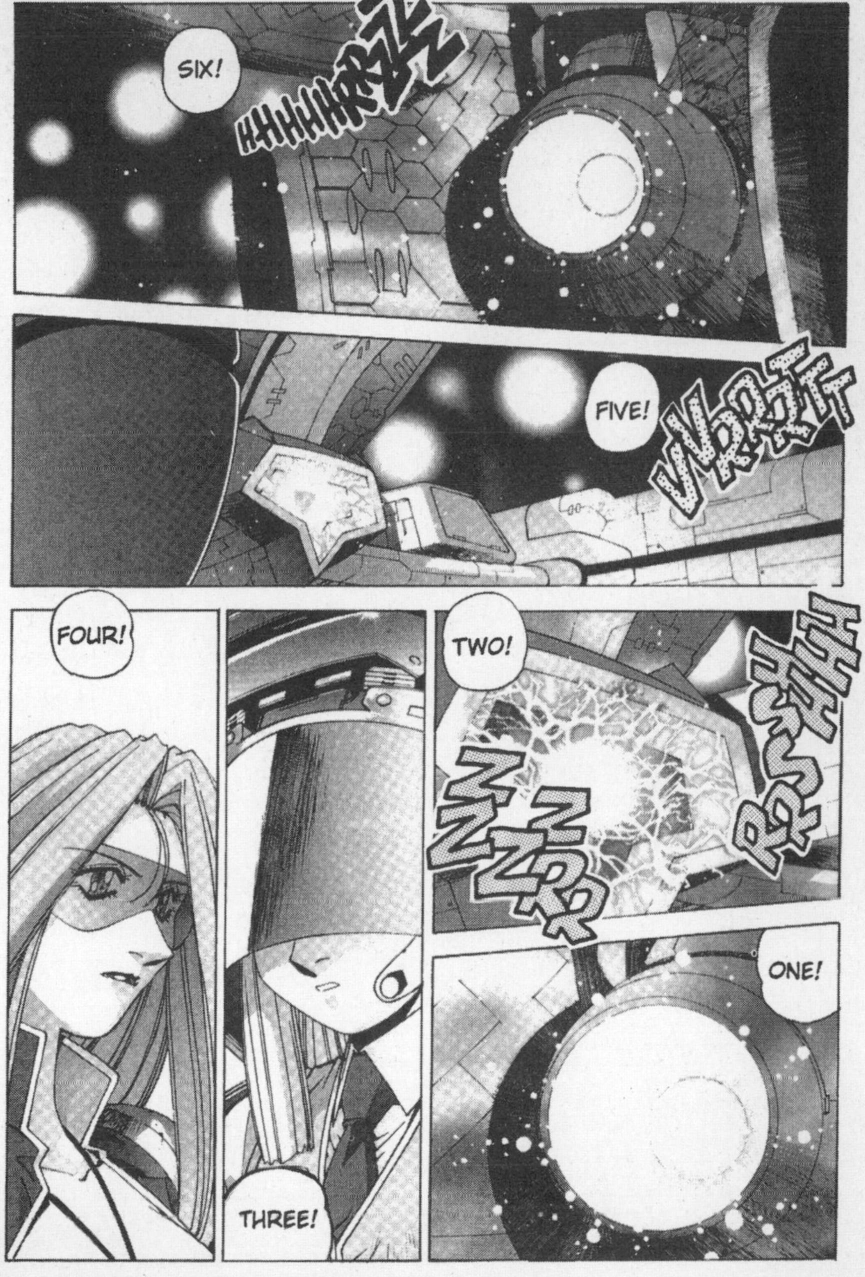
SIX!
FIVE!
FOUR!
THREE!
TWO!
ONE!

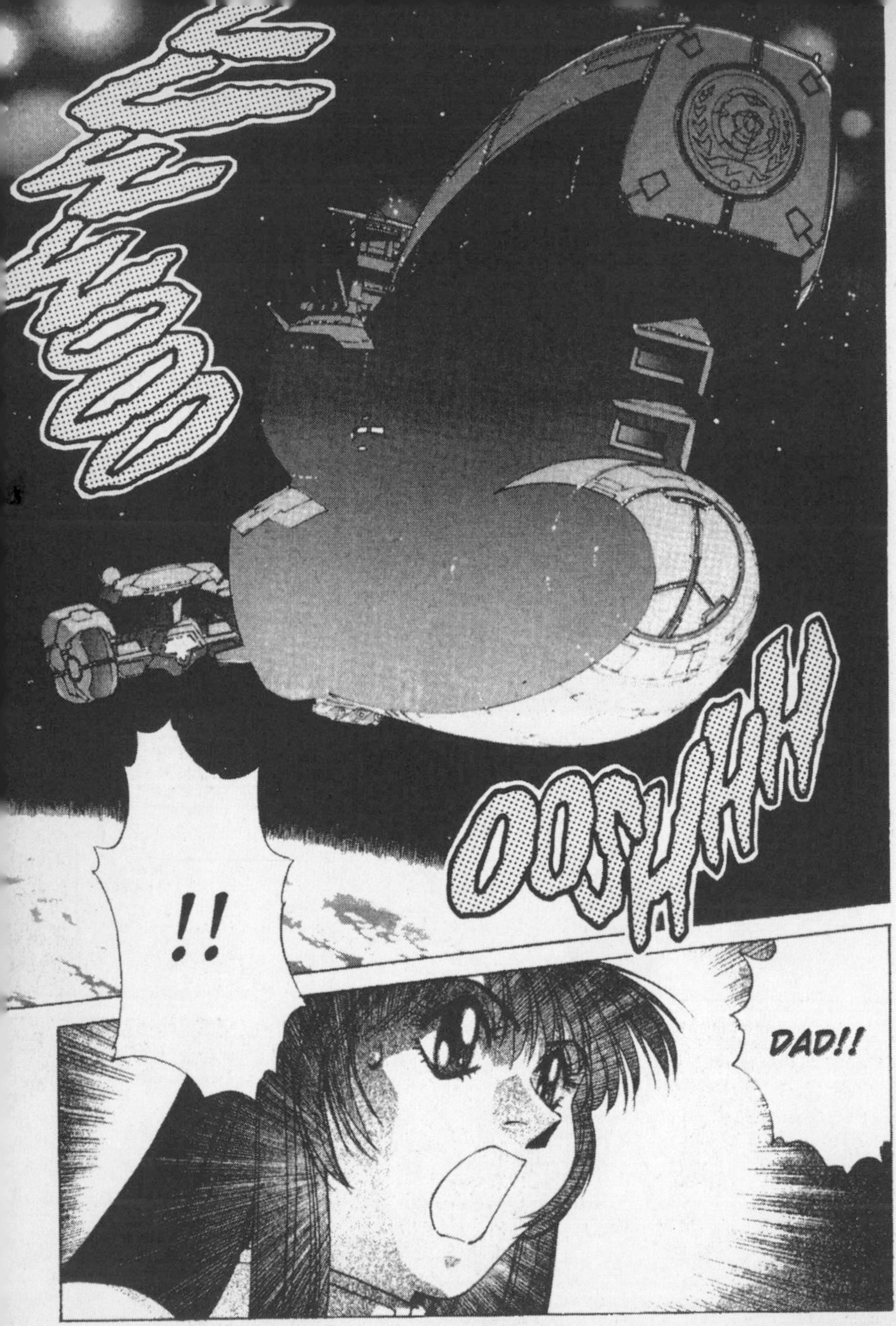
VWOOOO
OOSHHH
!!
DAD!!

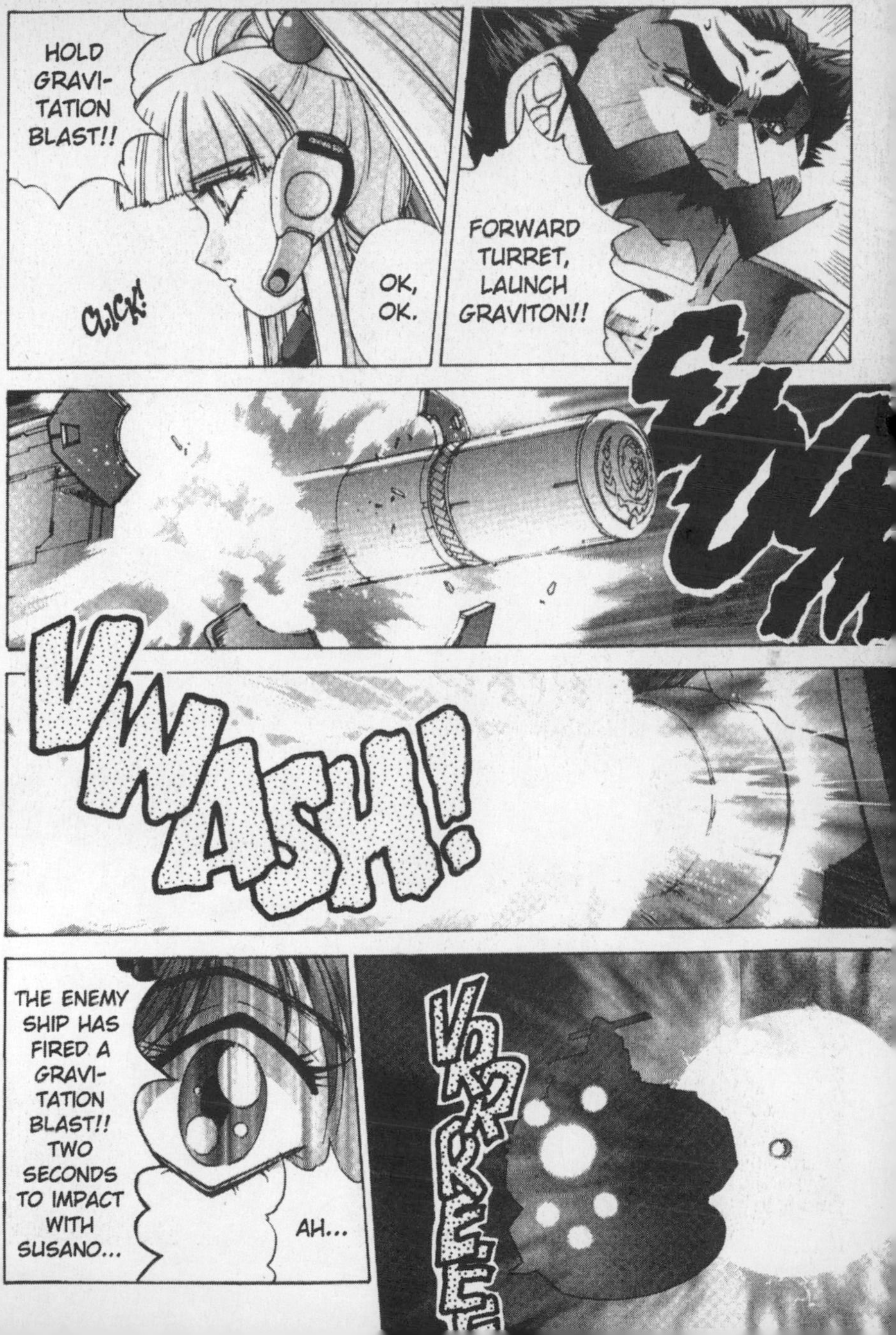
HOLD GRAVITATION BLAST!!
CLICK!
OK, OK.
FORWARD TURRET, LAUNCH GRAVITON!!
VWASH!
THE ENEMY SHIP HAS FIRED A GRAVITATION BLAST!! TWO SECONDS TO IMPACT WITH SUSANO...
AH...

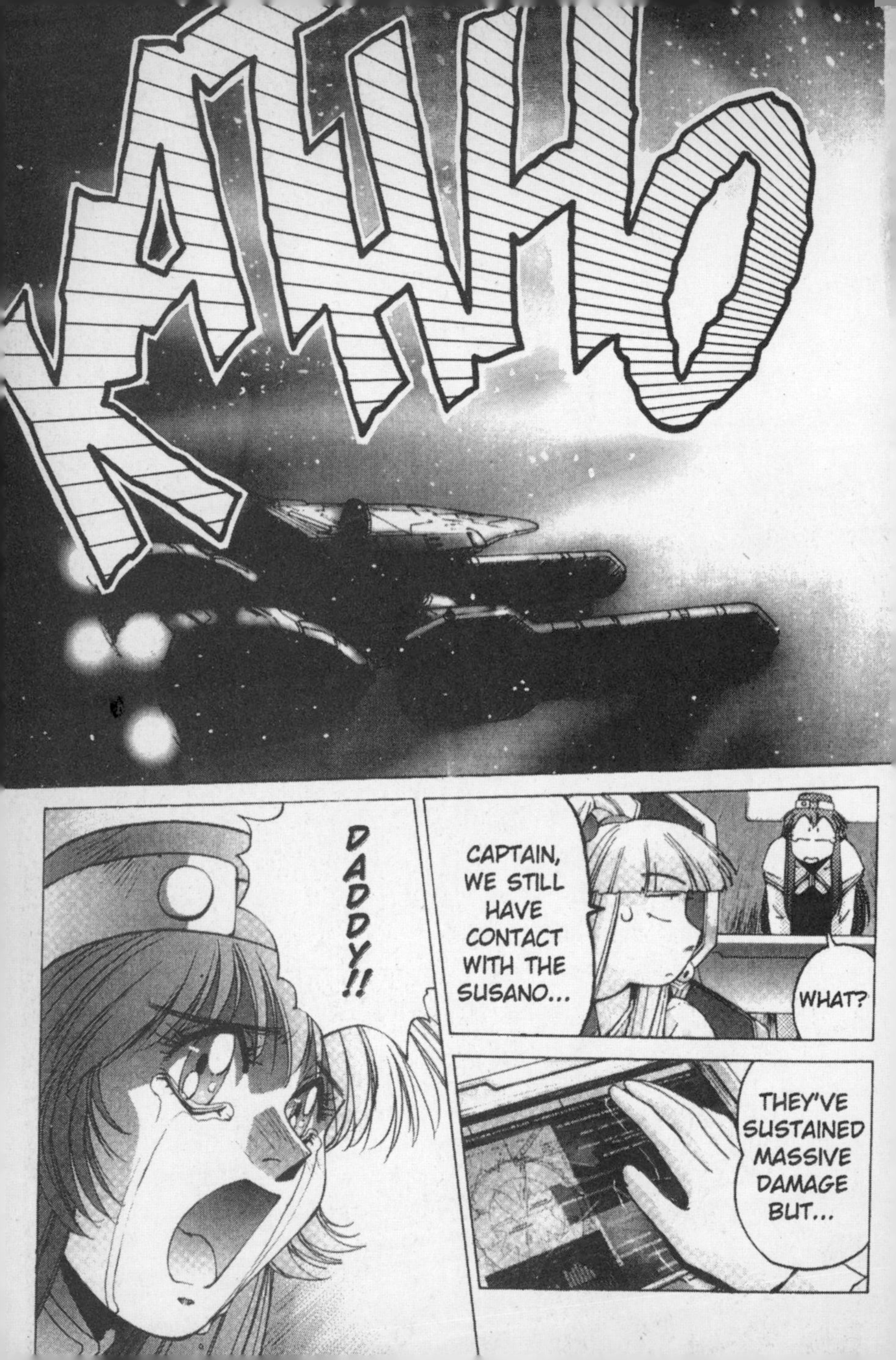
DADDY!!
CAPTAIN, WE STILL HAVE CONTACT WITH THE SUSANO...
WHAT?
THEY'VE SUSTAINED MASSIVE DAMAGE BUT...

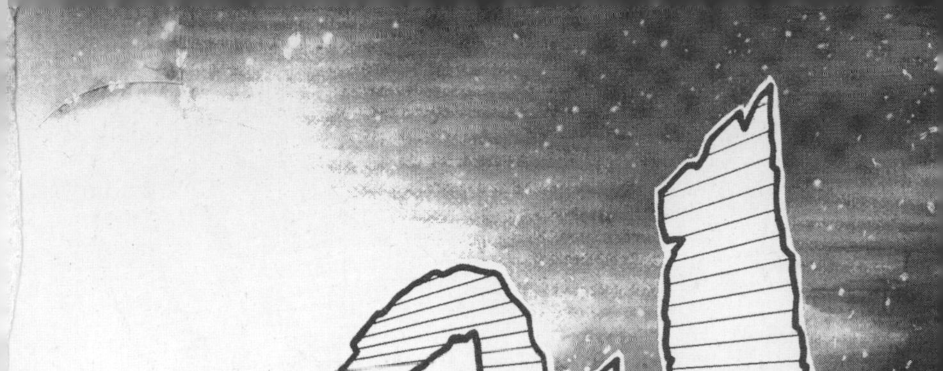
OOM

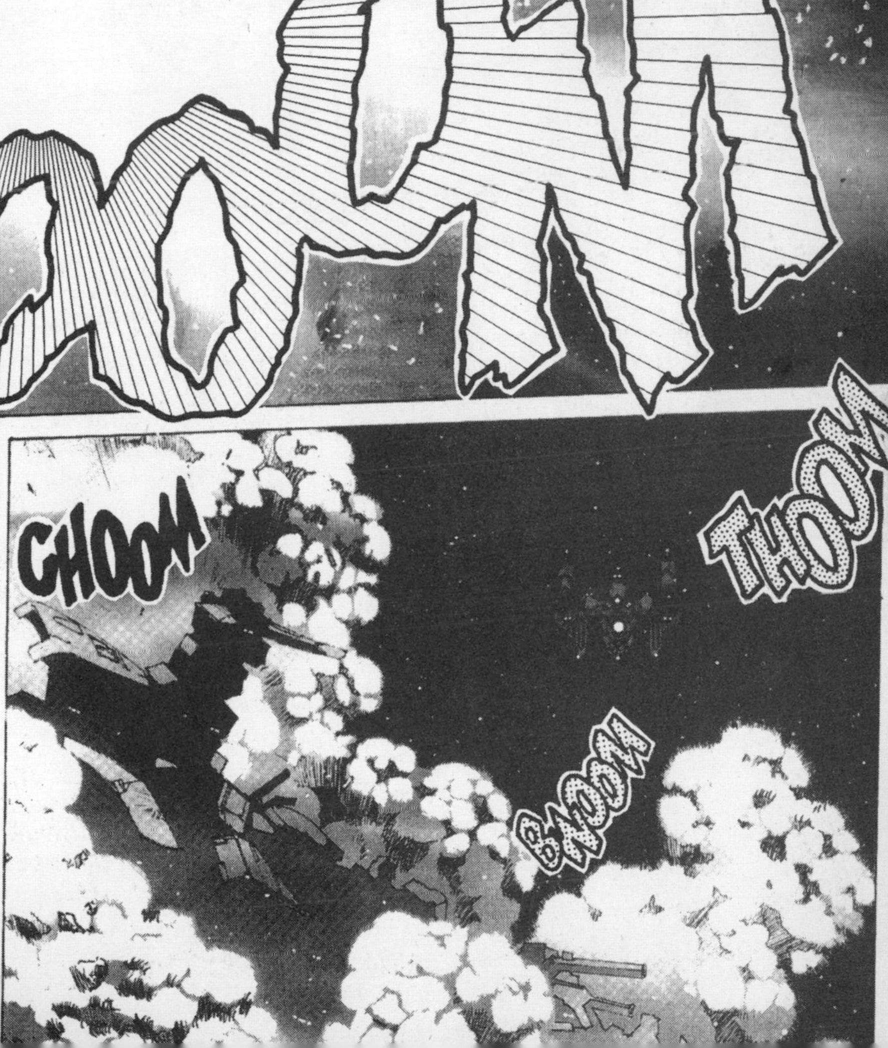
CHOOM
THOOM
BVOOM

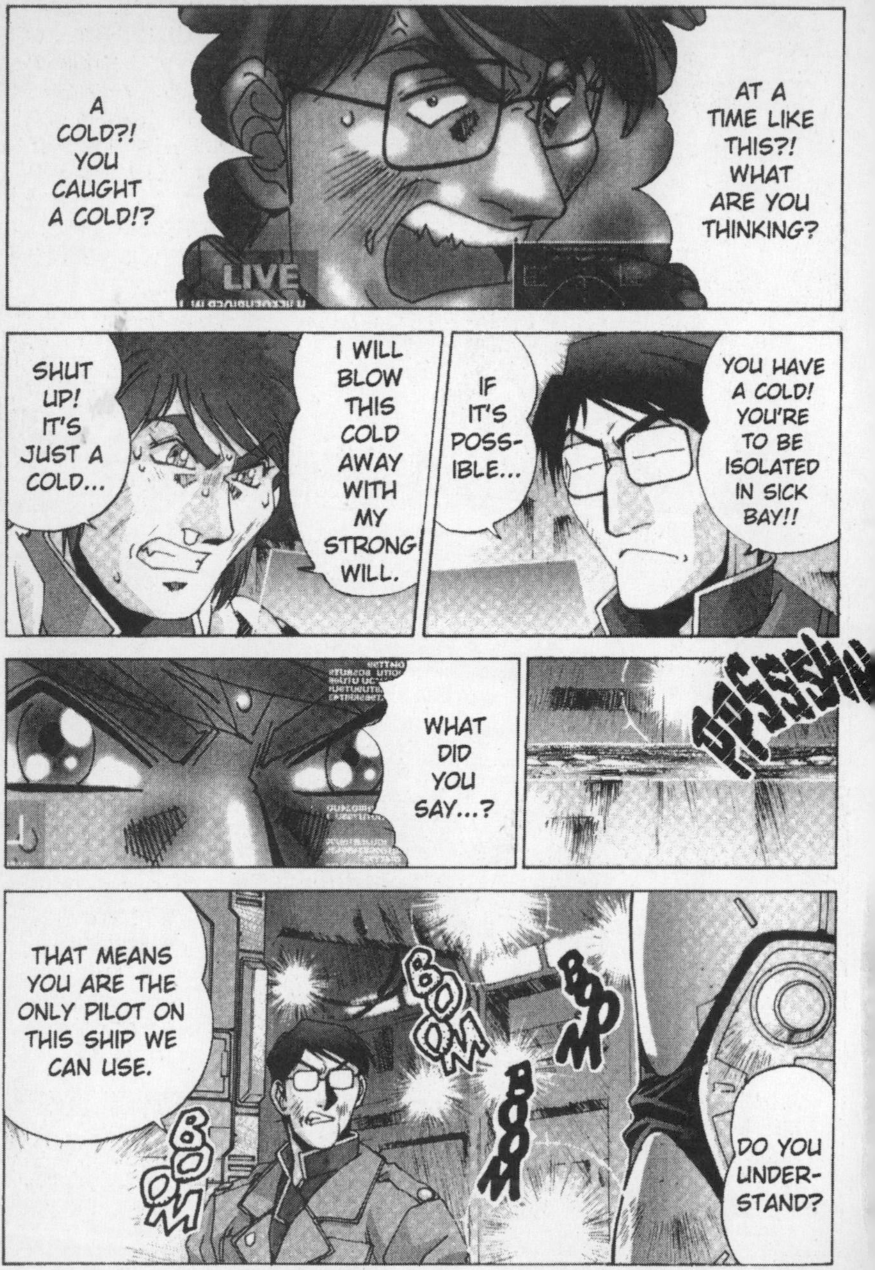
A COLD?! YOU CAUGHT A COLD!?
LIVE
AT A TIME LIKE THIS?! WHAT ARE YOU THINKING?
SHUT UP! IT'S JUST A COLD...
I WILL BLOW THIS COLD AWAY WITH MY STRONG WILL.
IF IT'S POSS-IBLE...
YOU HAVE A COLD! YOU'RE TO BE ISOLATED IN SICK BAY!!
WHAT DID YOU SAY...?
PSSSH
THAT MEANS YOU ARE THE ONLY PILOT ON THIS SHIP WE CAN USE.
BOOM
BOOM
BOOM
BOOM
DO YOU UNDER-STAND?

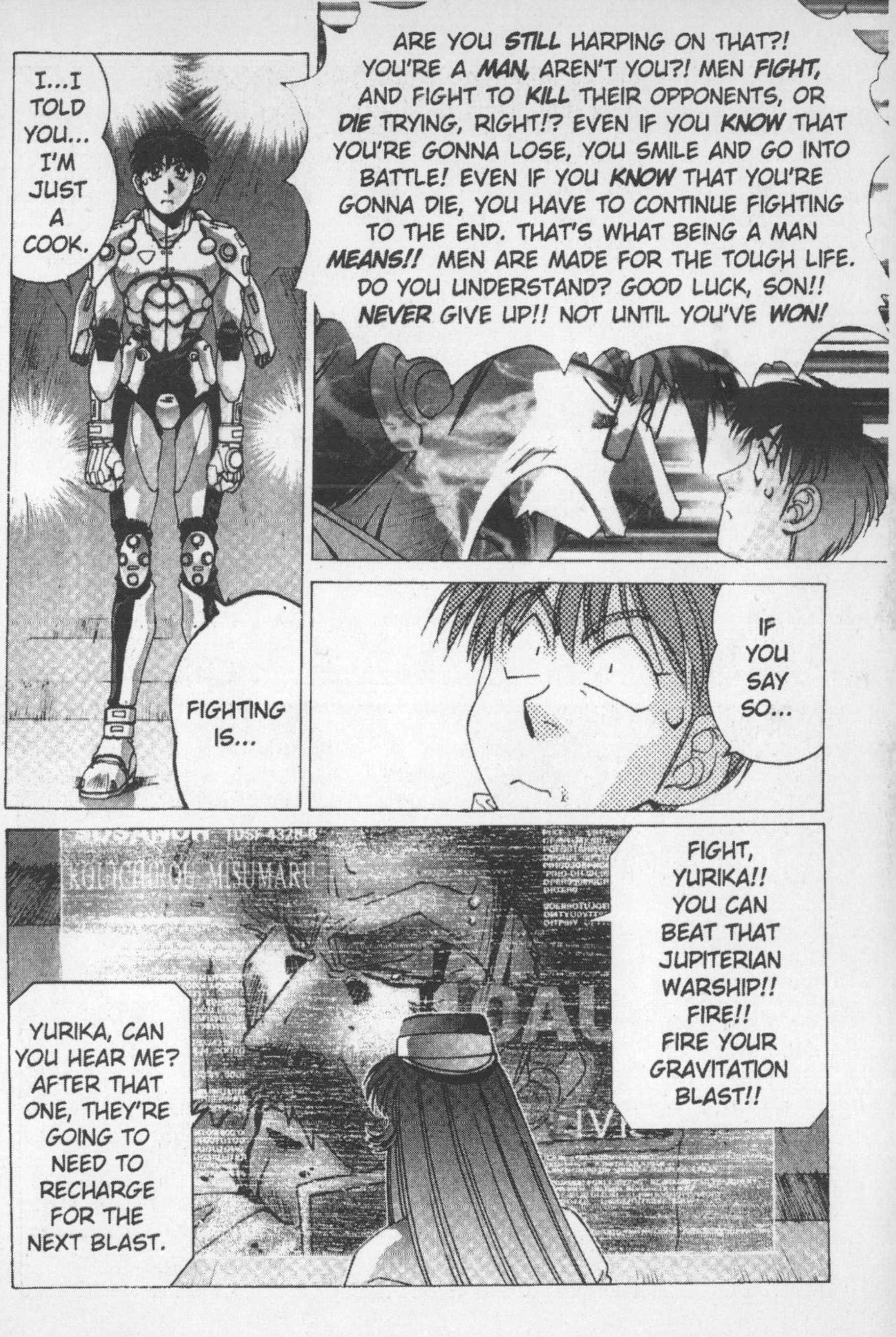
I...I TOLD YOU... I'M JUST A COOK.
FIGHTING IS...
ARE YOU STILL HARPING ON THAT?! YOU'RE A MAN, AREN'T YOU?! MEN FIGHT, AND FIGHT TO KILL THEIR OPPONENTS, OR DIE TRYING, RIGHT!? EVEN IF YOU KNOW THAT YOU'RE GONNA LOSE, YOU SMILE AND GO INTO BATTLE! EVEN IF YOU KNOW THAT YOU'RE GONNA DIE, YOU HAVE TO CONTINUE FIGHTING TO THE END. THAT'S WHAT BEING A MAN MEANS!! MEN ARE MADE FOR THE TOUGH LIFE. DO YOU UNDERSTAND? GOOD LUCK, SON!! NEVER GIVE UP!! NOT UNTIL YOU'VE WON!
IF YOU SAY SO...
FIGHT, YURIKA!! YOU CAN BEAT THAT JUPITERIAN WARSHIP!! FIRE!! FIRE YOUR GRAVITATION BLAST!!
YURIKA, CAN YOU HEAR ME? AFTER THAT ONE, THEY'RE GOING TO NEED TO RECHARGE FOR THE NEXT BLAST.

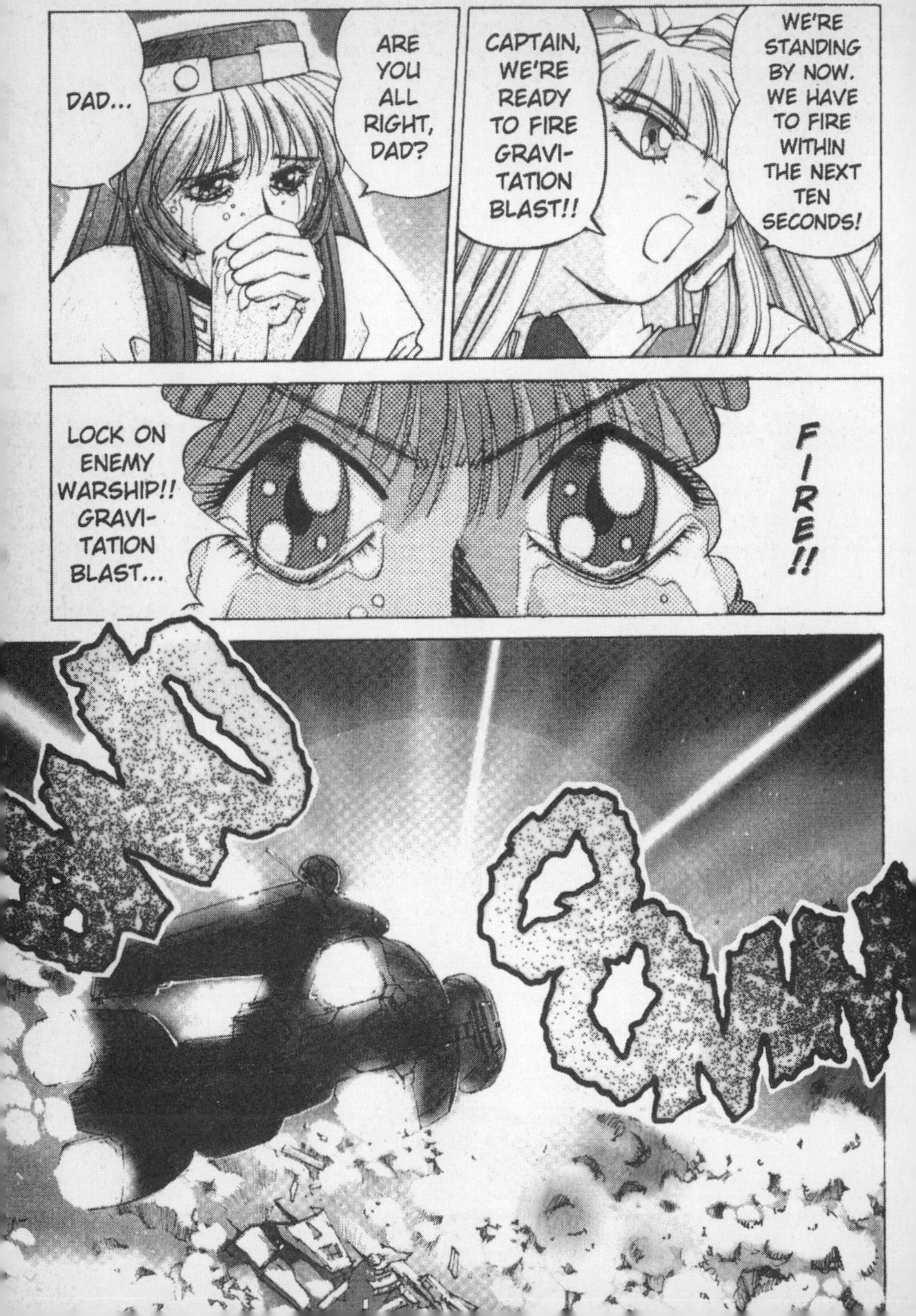
DAD...
ARE YOU ALL RIGHT, DAD?
CAPTAIN, WE'RE READY TO FIRE GRAVI-TATION BLAST!!
WE'RE STANDING BY NOW. WE HAVE TO FIRE WITHIN THE NEXT TEN SECONDS!
LOCK ON ENEMY WARSHIP!! GRAVI-TATION BLAST...
FIRE!!

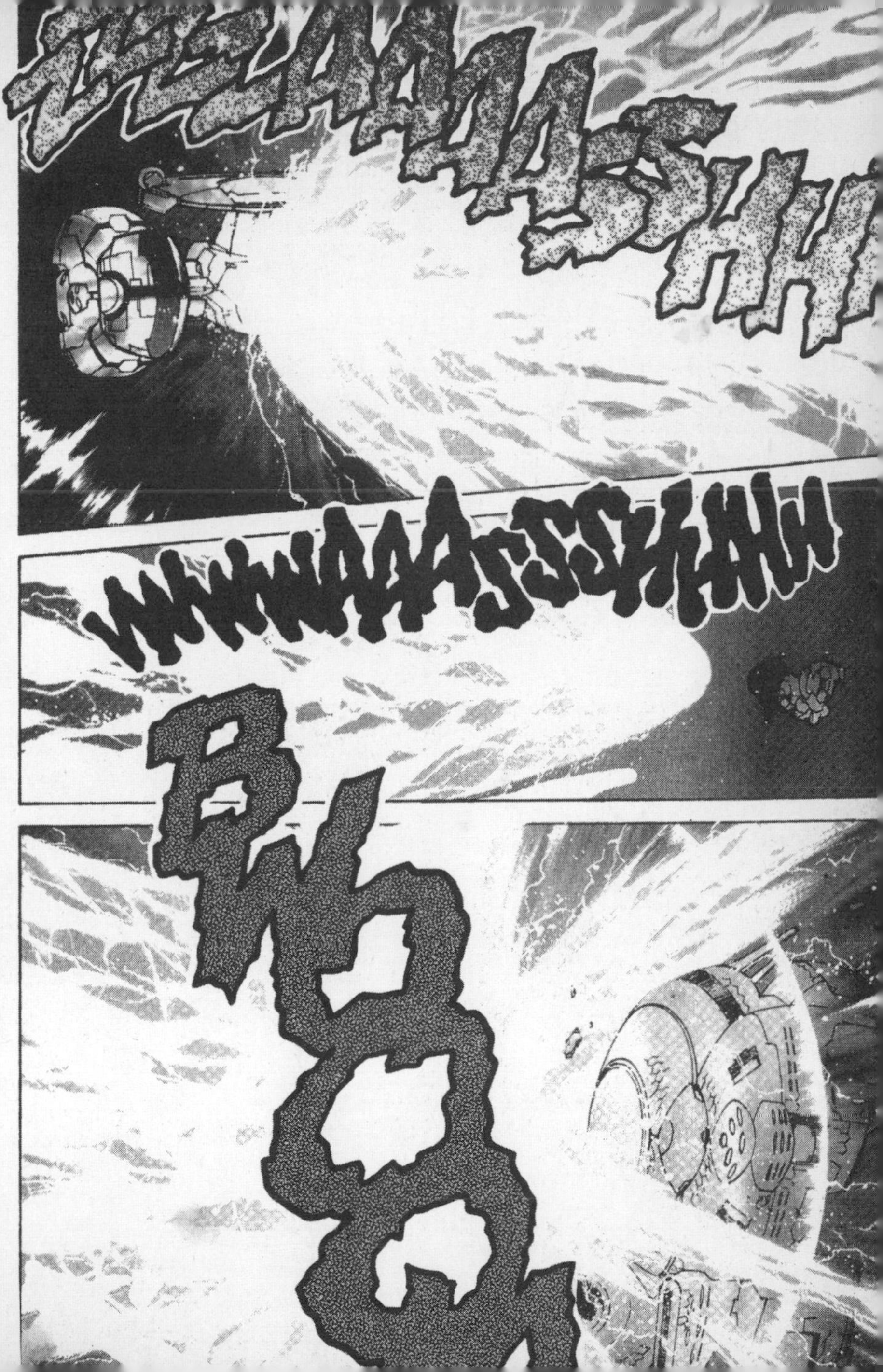

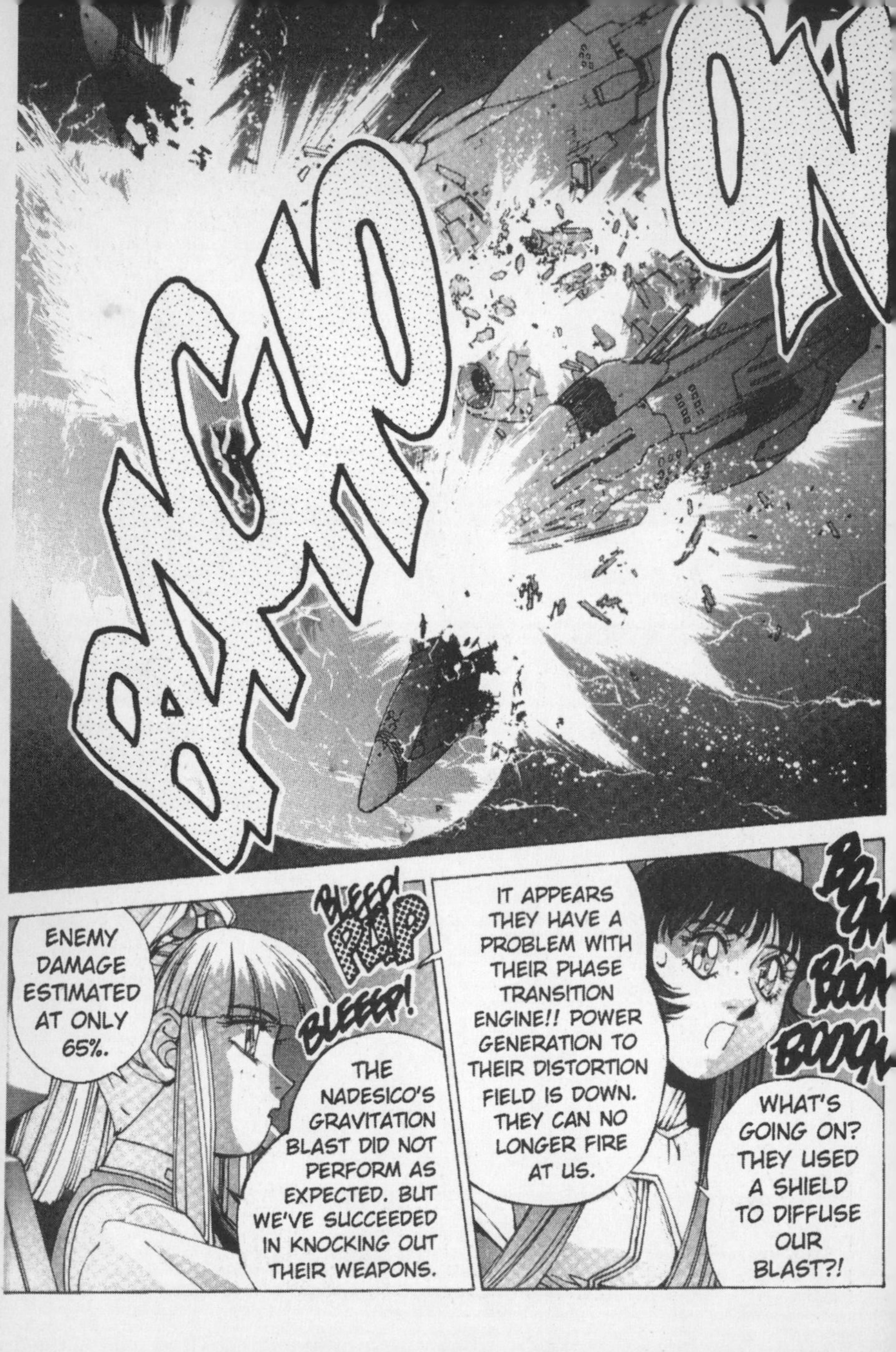
ENEMY DAMAGE ESTIMATED AT ONLY 65%.
BLEEP!
BLEEEP!
THE NADESICO'S GRAVITATION BLAST DID NOT PERFORM AS EXPECTED. BUT WE'VE SUCCEEDED IN KNOCKING OUT THEIR WEAPONS.
IT APPEARS THEY HAVE A PROBLEM WITH THEIR PHASE TRANSITION ENGINE!! POWER GENERATION TO THEIR DISTORTION FIELD IS DOWN. THEY CAN NO LONGER FIRE AT US.
WHAT'S GOING ON? THEY USED A SHIELD TO DIFFUSE OUR BLAST?!

I HAVE CONFIRMED IT IS INDEED A DISTORTION FIELD.

OUR OPPONENT HAS THE SAME SYSTEM THE NADESICO DOES.

JORO AND BATTA ARE APPROACHING THE NADESICO'S BOW AT TEN O'CLOCK.

THE ENEMY WARSHIP IS REMAINING STATIONARY. WE SHOULD TRY TO BREAK THROUGH THE CENTER OF THE ENEMY FORMATION. THE FEDERATION FORCES HAVE BROKEN FORMATION ALREADY.

UNDER-STOOD. FULL SPEED AHEAD!

OPEN EVERY GUN TURRET! WE'RE GOING TO BREAK RIGHT THROUGH THE MIDDLE!

YES, SIR.

FULL SPEED AHEAD!

OUR SCOUT SHIP DECOY--

--WILL DRAW THEIR FIRE.

AESTI VALIS 01, PREPARE TO LAUNCH!!

KICK THEIR BUTTS AND CLEAN UP THIS MESS!!

第5話 宇宙に死す

—DEATH IN OUTER SPACE—

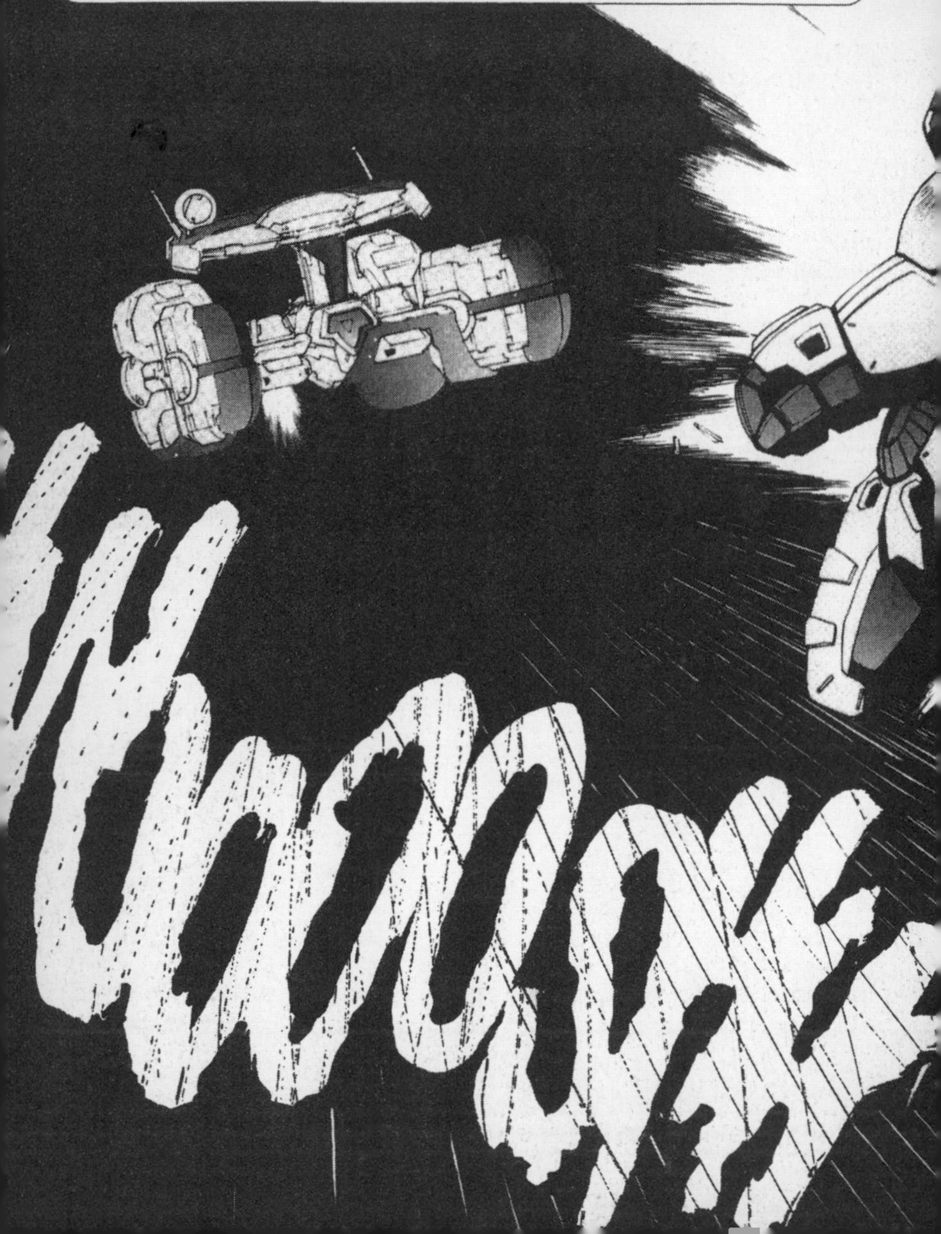

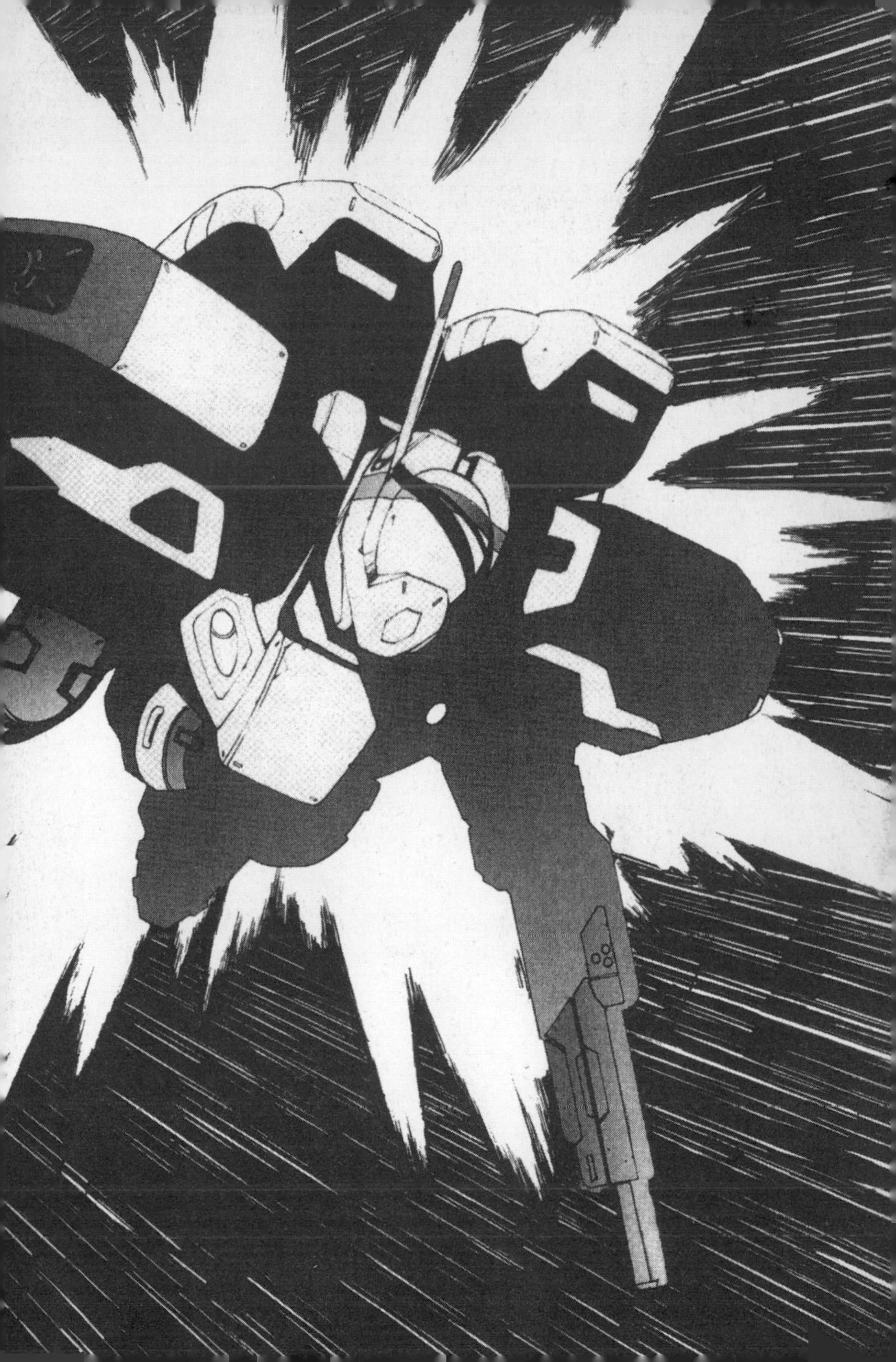

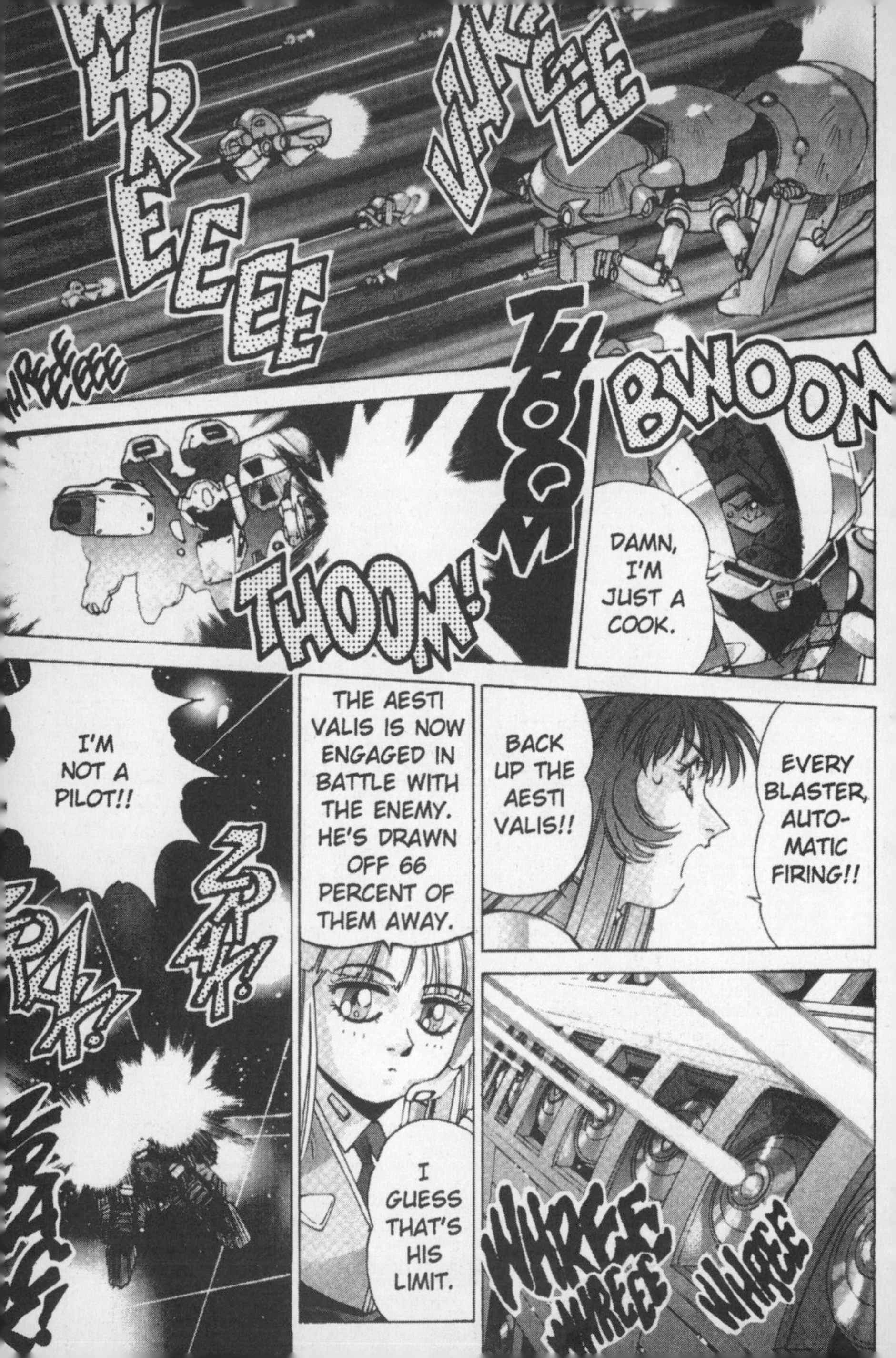

WHREEEE
THOOM
BWOOM
THOOM!
DAMN, I'M JUST A COOK.
I'M NOT A PILOT!!
THE AESTI VALIS IS NOW ENGAGED IN BATTLE WITH THE ENEMY. HE'S DRAWN OFF 66 PERCENT OF THEM AWAY.
I GUESS THAT'S HIS LIMIT.
BACK UP THE AESTI VALIS!!
EVERY BLASTER, AUTO-MATIC FIRING!!
WHREEE
WHREEE
WHREEE

MEDICAL ROOM

Visitors must have an appointment with the doctor.

Visiting Hours
(Ship standard time)
13:00 - 17:00

UMM...

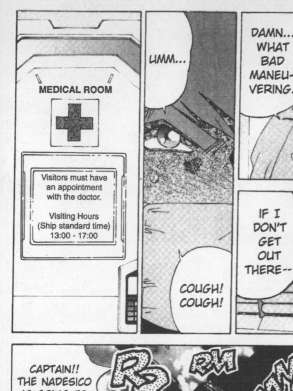

COUGH!
COUGH!

DAMN... WHAT BAD MANEUVERING.

IF I DON'T GET OUT THERE--

--THE NADESICO IS GOING DOWN.

CAPTAIN!! THE NADESICO IS GOING TO TRY TO BREAK THROUGH THE ENEMY RANKS!

IF THEY CAN BREAK THROUGH, LET THEM GO. WE CAN'T DO ANYTHING FOR THEM AT THIS POINT.

MY DAUGHTER IS ON HER OWN.

THAT'S RIGHT.

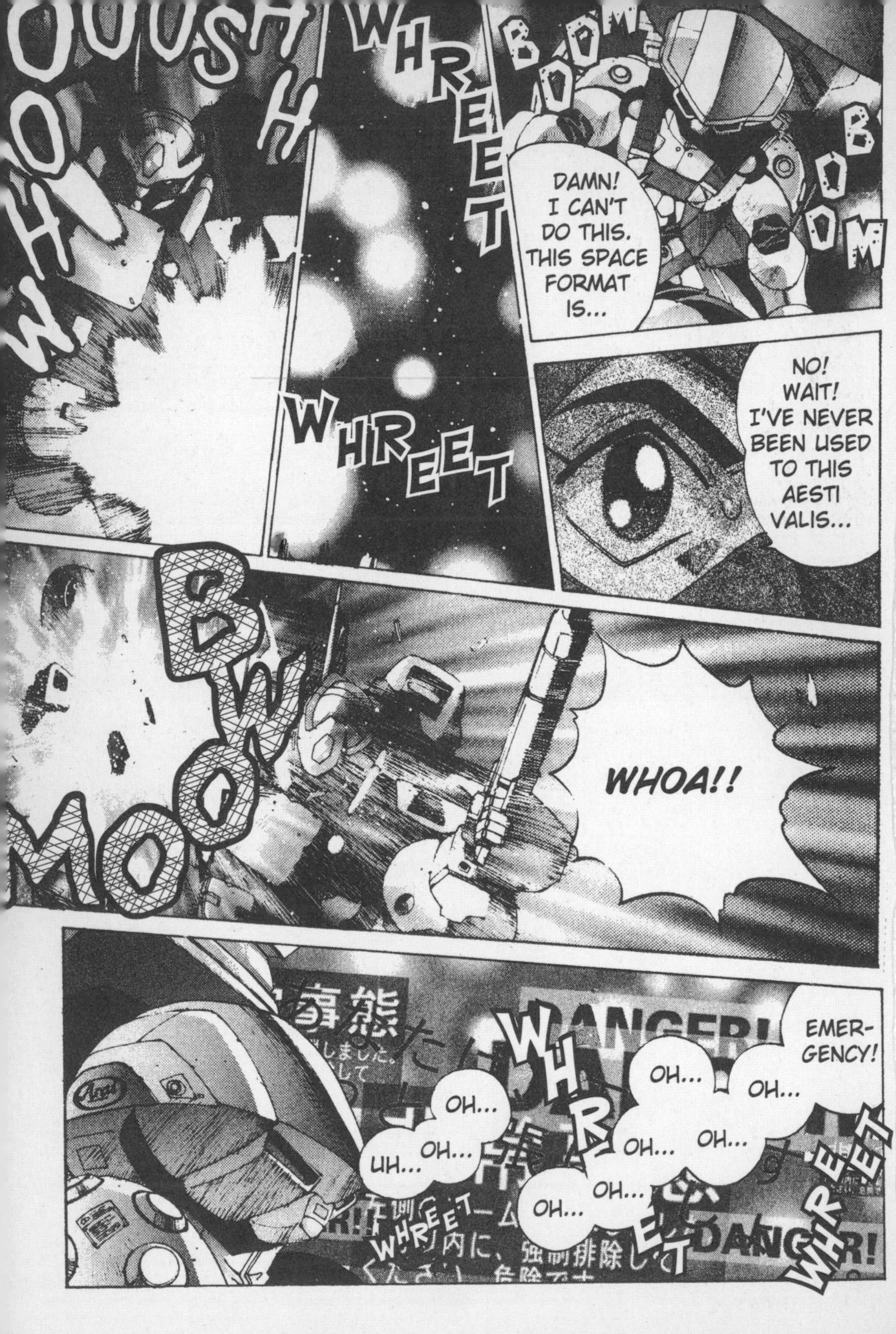
WHOOSH
WHREET
WHREET
BOOM
BOOM
DAMN! I CAN'T DO THIS. THIS SPACE FORMAT IS...
NO! WAIT! I'VE NEVER BEEN USED TO THIS AESTI VALIS...
BWOOOM
WHOA!!
DANGER!
WHREET
EMER-GENCY!
UH...
OH...
OH...
OH...
OH...
OH...
OH...
OH...
OH...
WHREET
WHREET
DANGER!

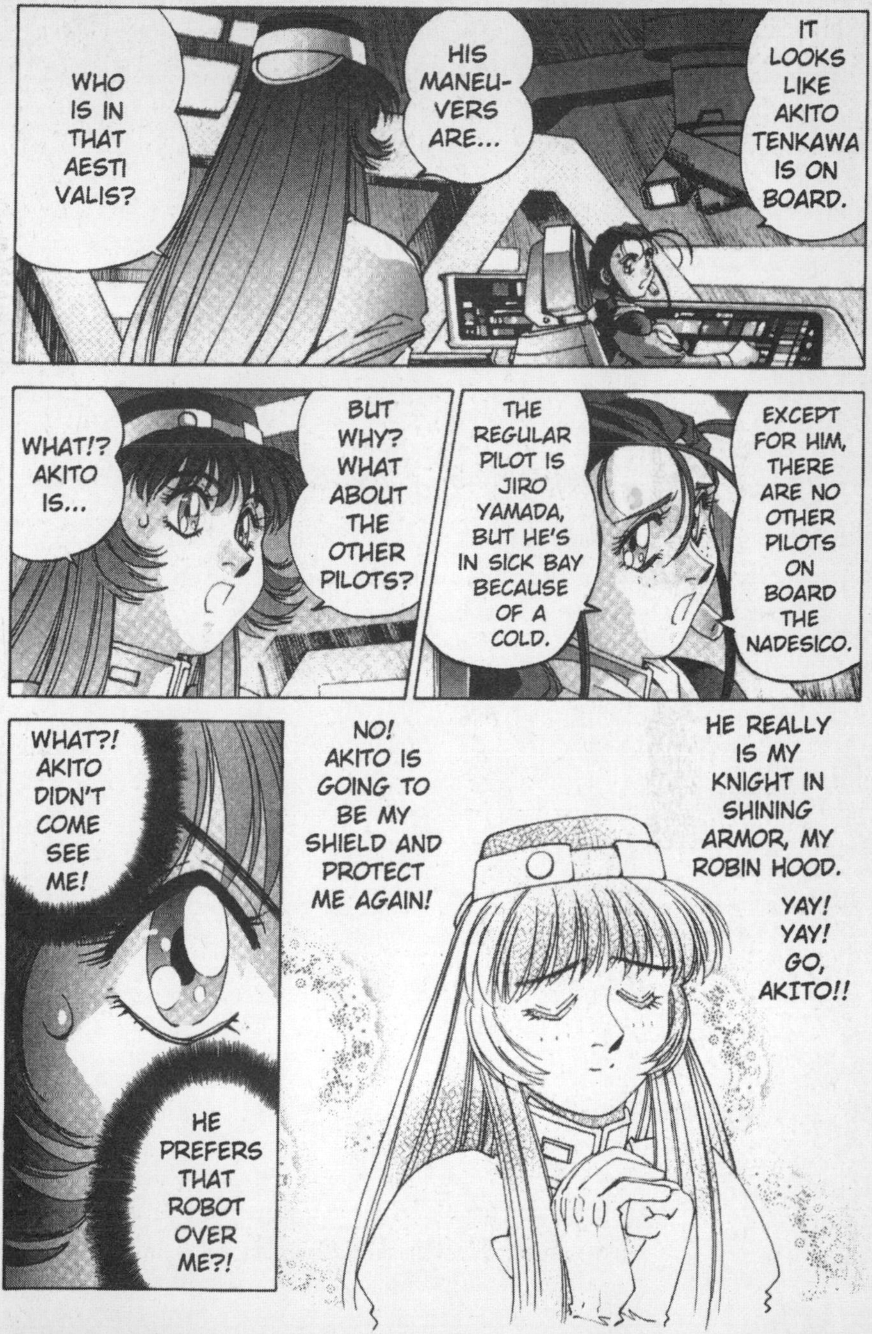
WHO IS IN THAT AESTI VALIS?
HIS MANEU-VERS ARE...
IT LOOKS LIKE AKITO TENKAWA IS ON BOARD.
WHAT!? AKITO IS...
BUT WHY? WHAT ABOUT THE OTHER PILOTS?
THE REGULAR PILOT IS JIRO YAMADA, BUT HE'S IN SICK BAY BECAUSE OF A COLD.
EXCEPT FOR HIM, THERE ARE NO OTHER PILOTS ON BOARD THE NADESICO.
WHAT?! AKITO DIDN'T COME SEE ME!
HE PREFERS THAT ROBOT OVER ME?!
NO! AKITO IS GOING TO BE MY SHIELD AND PROTECT ME AGAIN!
HE REALLY IS MY KNIGHT IN SHINING ARMOR, MY ROBIN HOOD.
YAY! YAY! GO, AKITO!!

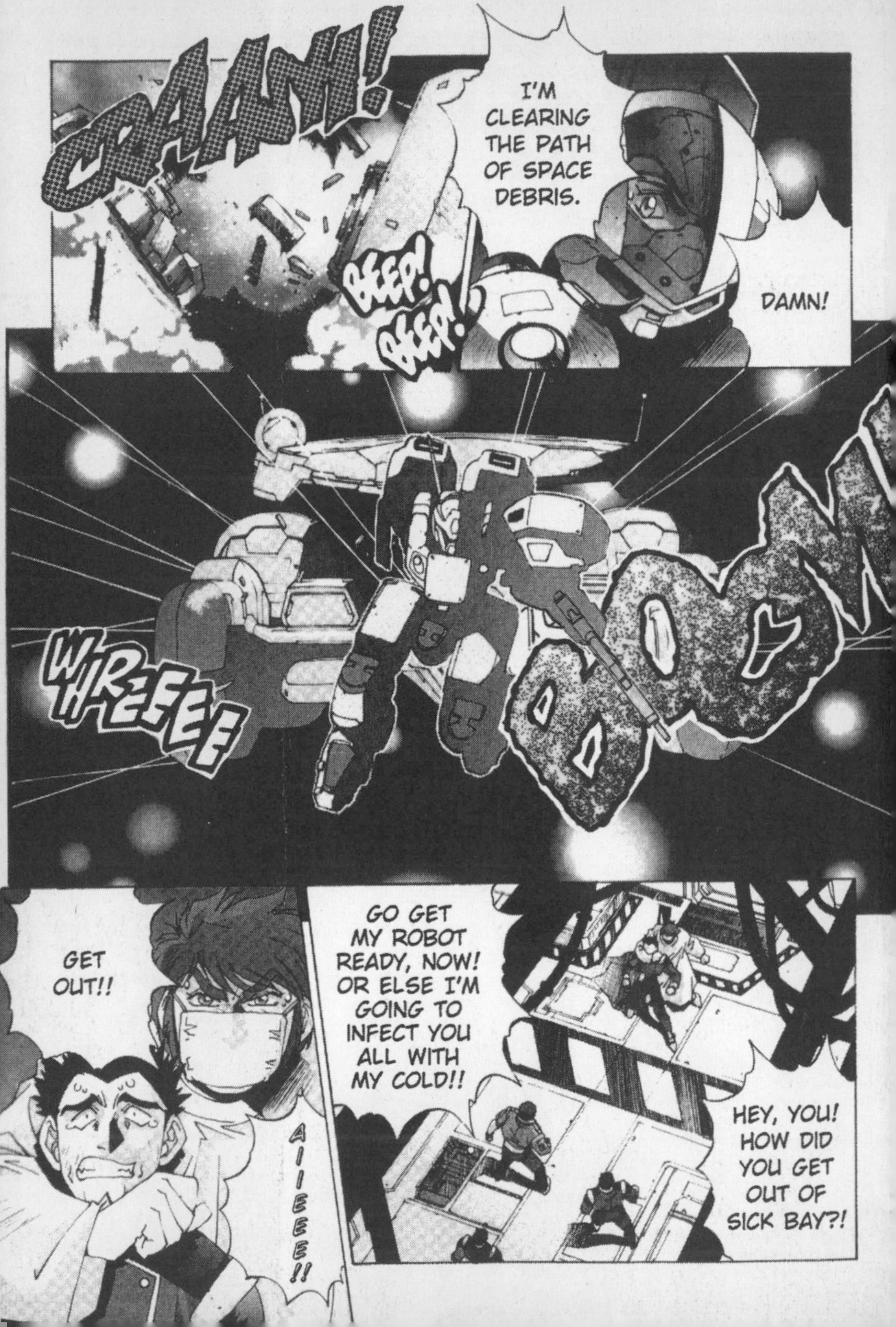
CRAAM!
I'M CLEARING THE PATH OF SPACE DEBRIS.
BEEP! BEEP!
DAMN!
BOOM
GET OUT!!
AIIEEEE!!
GO GET MY ROBOT READY, NOW! OR ELSE I'M GOING TO INFECT YOU ALL WITH MY COLD!!
HEY, YOU! HOW DID YOU GET OUT OF SICK BAY?!

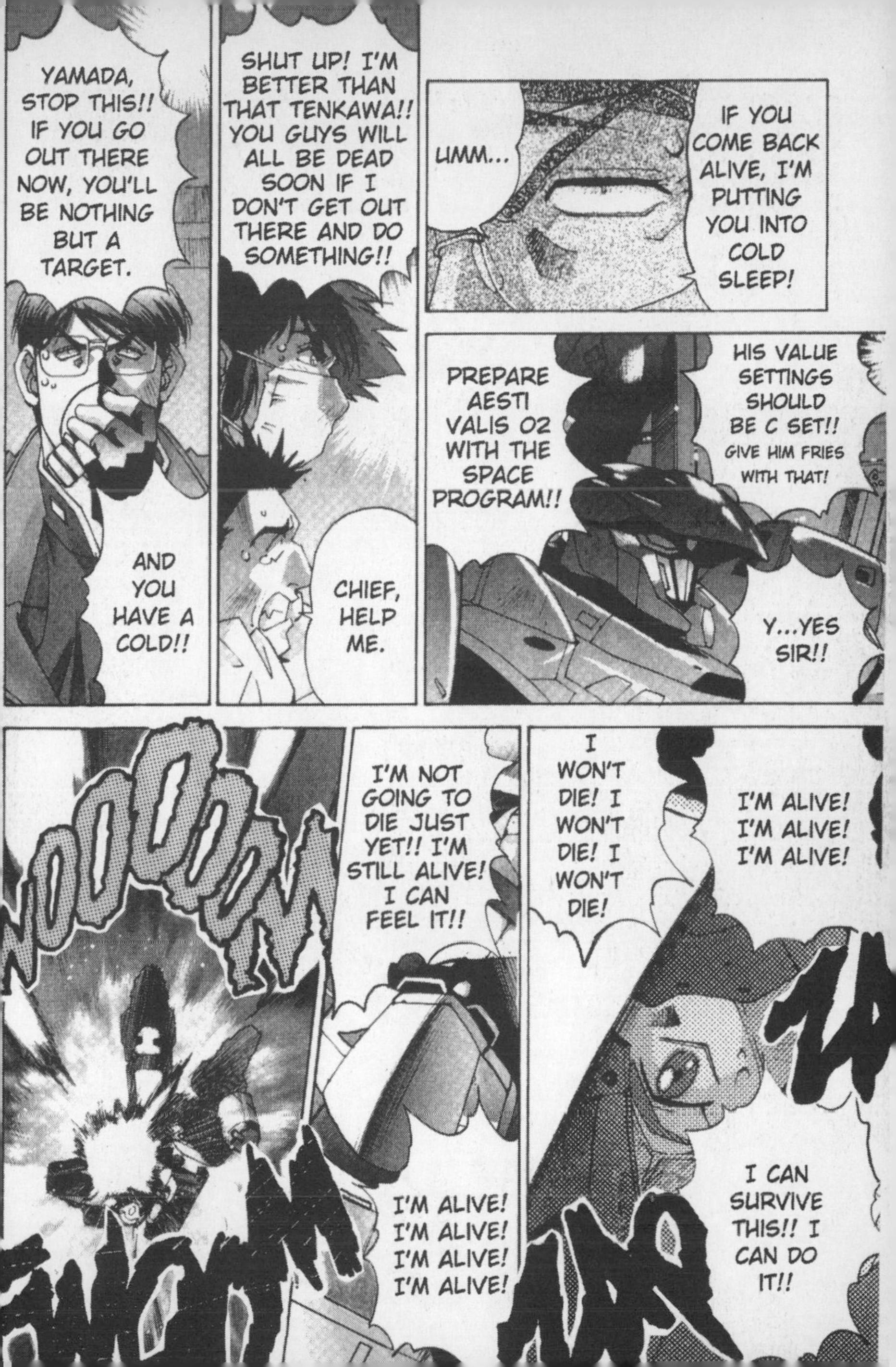
YAMADA, STOP THIS!! IF YOU GO OUT THERE NOW, YOU'LL BE NOTHING BUT A TARGET.
AND YOU HAVE A COLD!!
SHUT UP! I'M BETTER THAN THAT TENKAWA!! YOU GUYS WILL ALL BE DEAD SOON IF I DON'T GET OUT THERE AND DO SOMETHING!!
CHIEF, HELP ME.
UMM...
IF YOU COME BACK ALIVE, I'M PUTTING YOU INTO COLD SLEEP!
PREPARE AESTI VALIS 02 WITH THE SPACE PROGRAM!!
HIS VALUE SETTINGS SHOULD BE C SET!! GIVE HIM FRIES WITH THAT!
Y...YES SIR!!
I'M NOT GOING TO DIE JUST YET!! I'M STILL ALIVE! I CAN FEEL IT!!
I'M ALIVE! I'M ALIVE! I'M ALIVE! I'M ALIVE!
I WON'T DIE! I WON'T DIE! I WON'T DIE!
I'M ALIVE! I'M ALIVE! I'M ALIVE!
I CAN SURVIVE THIS!! I CAN DO IT!!

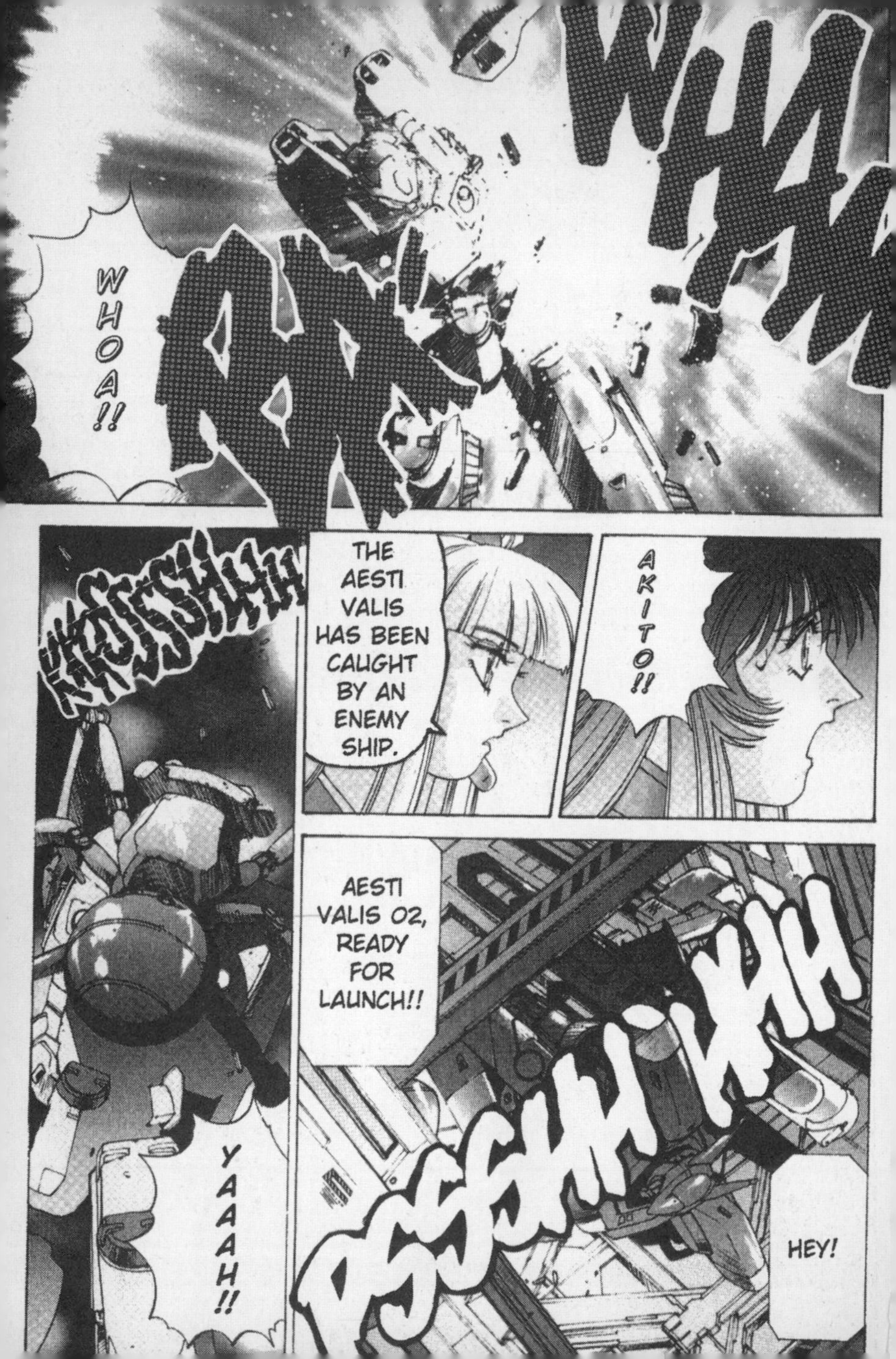
WHOA!!
YAAAAH!!
THE AESTI VALIS HAS BEEN CAUGHT BY AN ENEMY SHIP.
AKITO!!
AESTI VALIS 02, READY FOR LAUNCH!!
HEY!

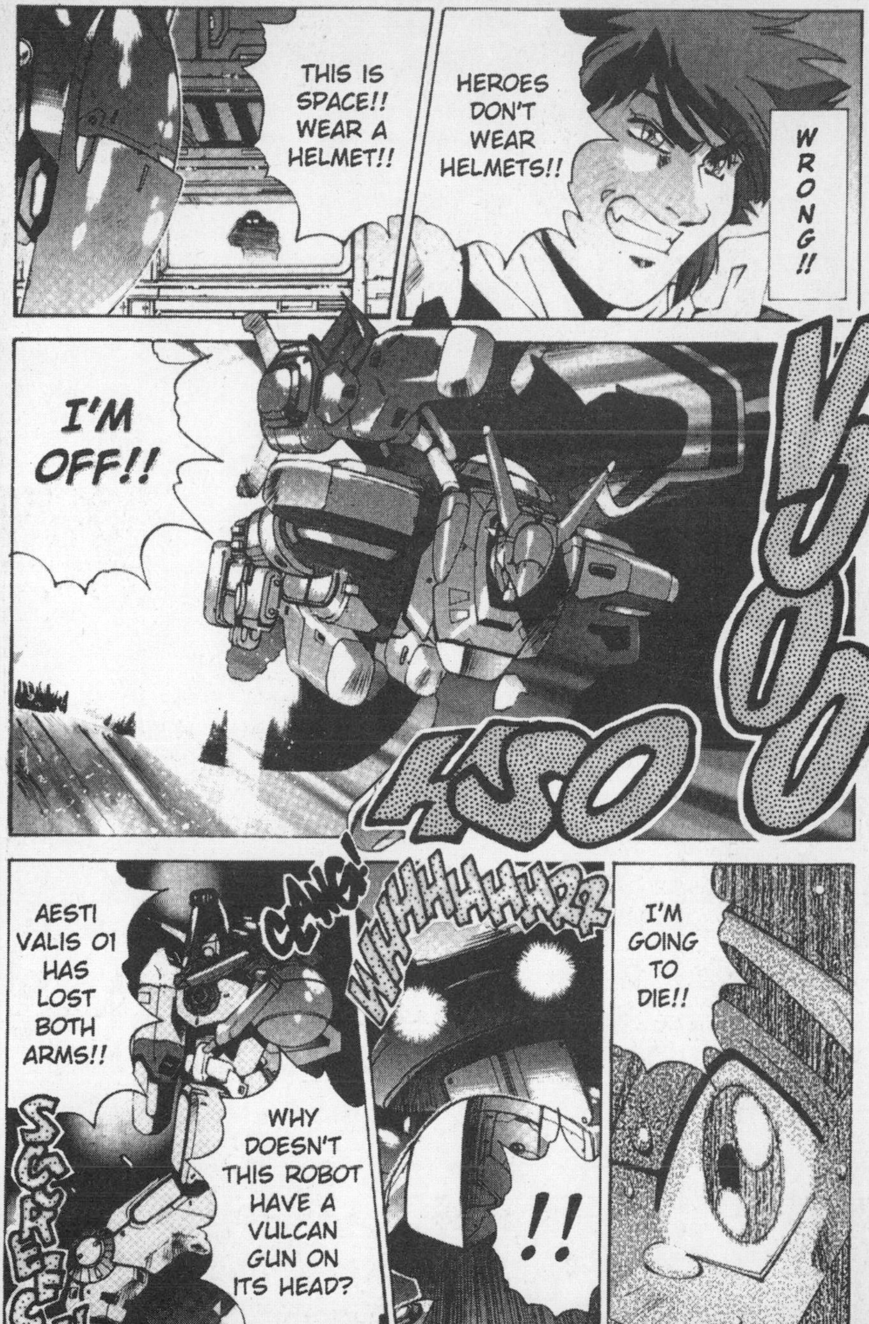
THIS IS SPACE!! WEAR A HELMET!!
HEROES DON'T WEAR HELMETS!!
WRONG!!
I'M OFF!!
AESTI VALIS 01 HAS LOST BOTH ARMS!!
WHY DOESN'T THIS ROBOT HAVE A VULCAN GUN ON ITS HEAD?
!!
I'M GOING TO DIE!!

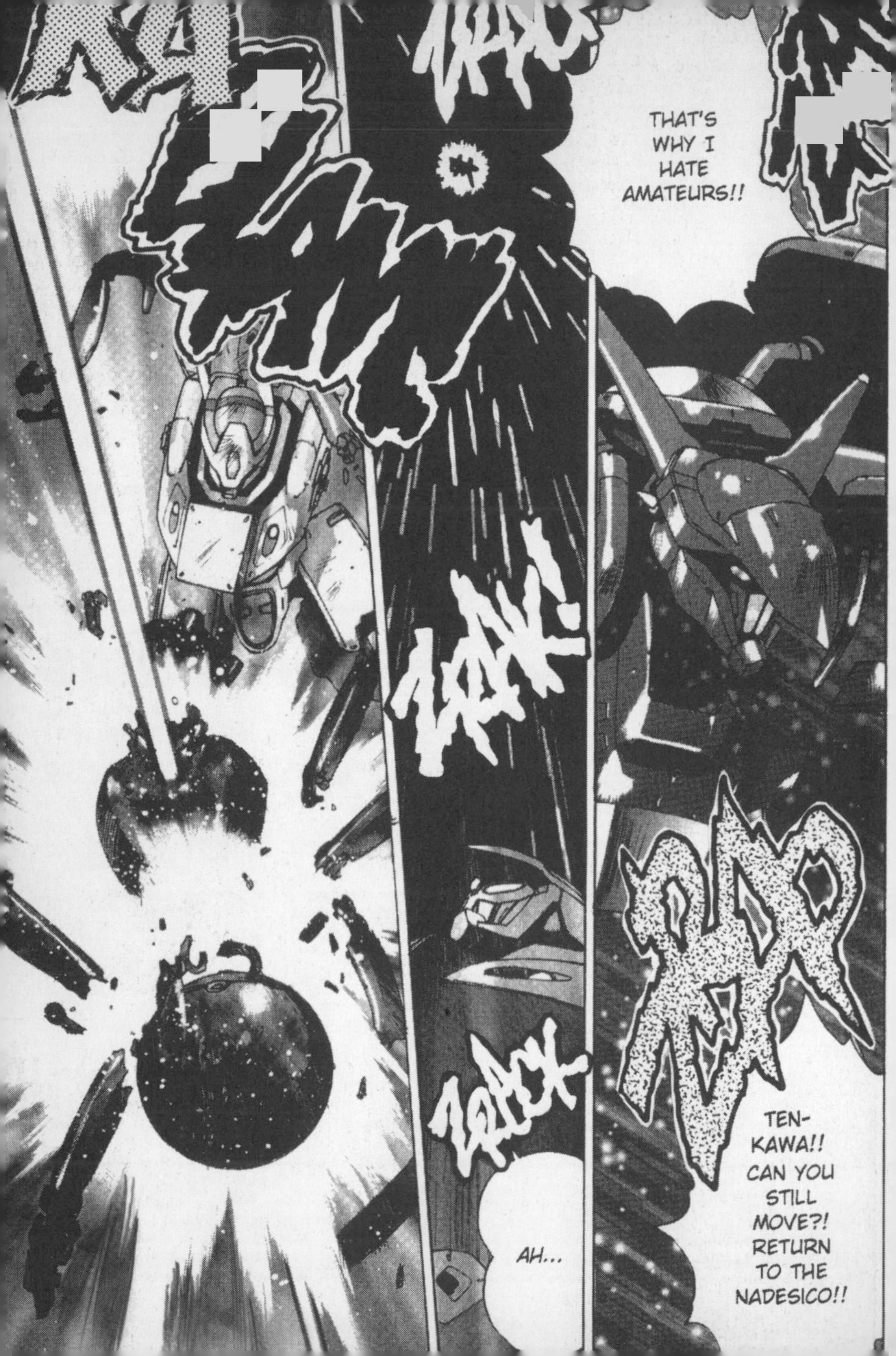
AH...
THAT'S WHY I HATE AMATEURS!!
TEN-KAWA!! CAN YOU STILL MOVE?! RETURN TO THE NADESICO!!

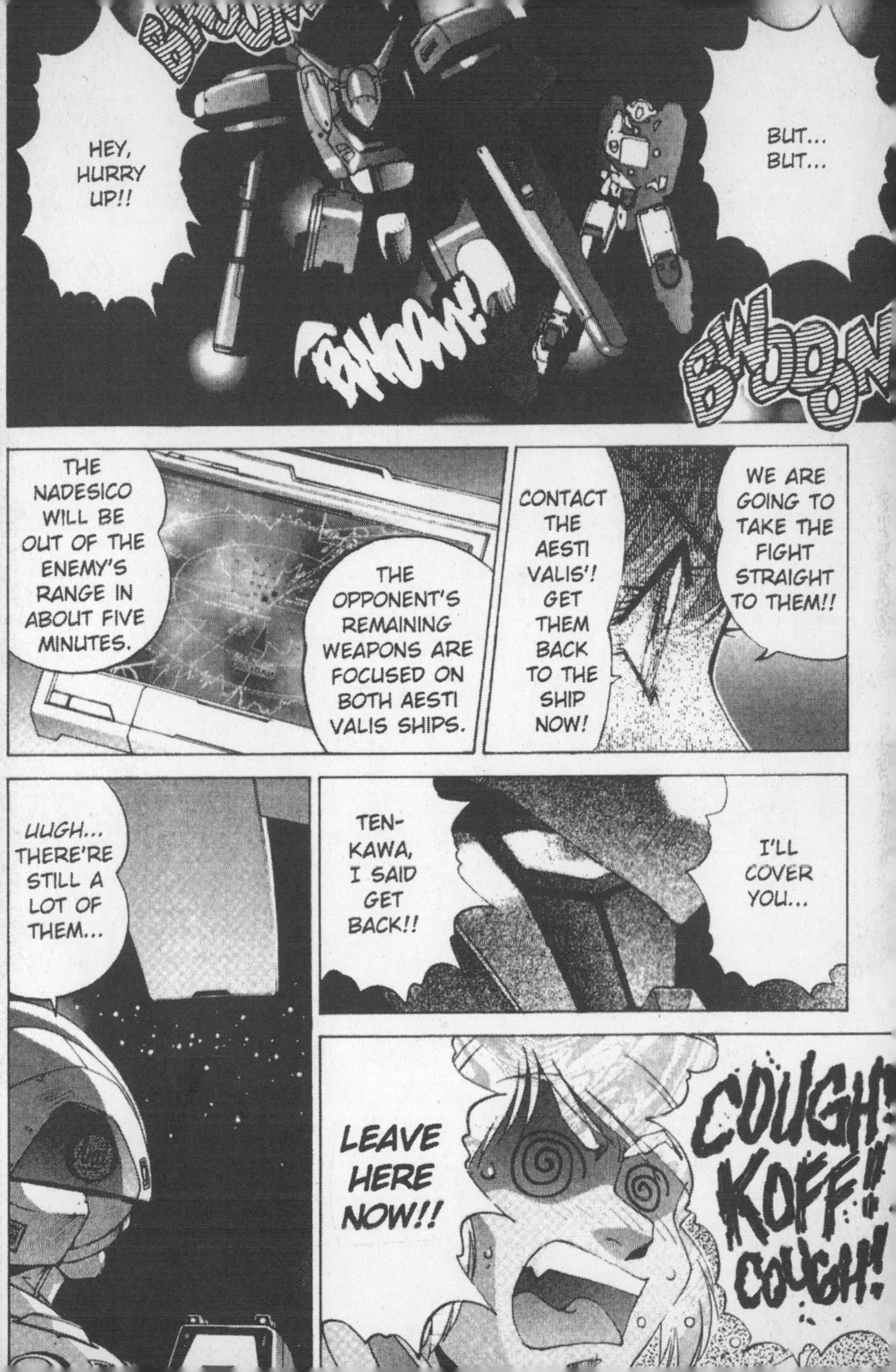
HEY, HURRY UP!!
BUT... BUT...
BWOOM!
BWOOOM
THE NADESICO WILL BE OUT OF THE ENEMY'S RANGE IN ABOUT FIVE MINUTES.
THE OPPONENT'S REMAINING WEAPONS ARE FOCUSED ON BOTH AESTI VALIS SHIPS.
CONTACT THE AESTI VALIS'! GET THEM BACK TO THE SHIP NOW!
WE ARE GOING TO TAKE THE FIGHT STRAIGHT TO THEM!!
UUGH... THERE'RE STILL A LOT OF THEM...
TEN-KAWA, I SAID GET BACK!!
I'LL COVER YOU...
LEAVE HERE NOW!!
COUGH! KOFF!! COUGH!

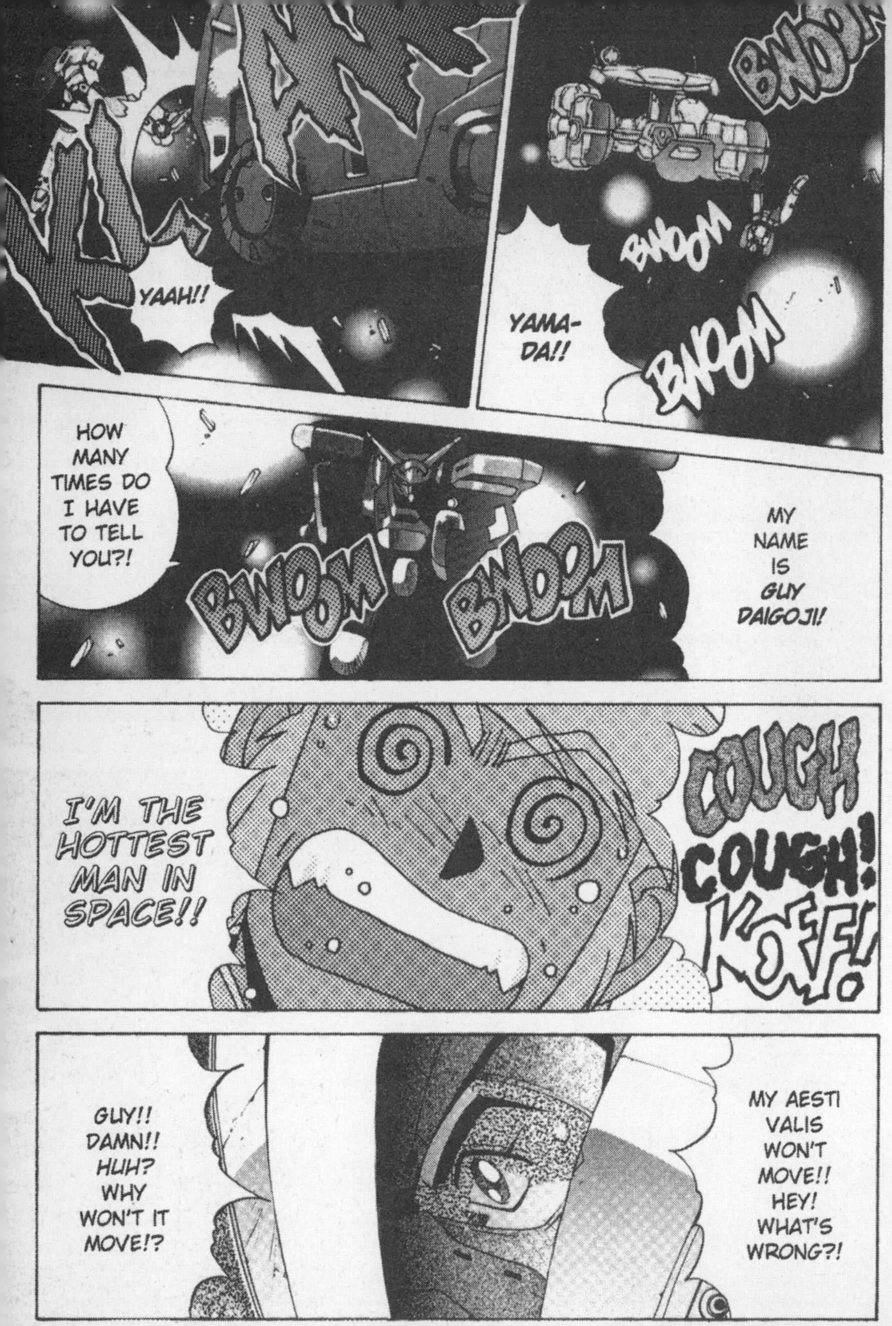
YAAH!!
BWOOM
YAMA-DA!!
BWOOM
HOW MANY TIMES DO I HAVE TO TELL YOU?!
BWOOM
BWOOM
MY NAME IS GUY DAIGOJI!
I'M THE HOTTEST MAN IN SPACE!!
COUGH COUGH! KOFF!
GUY!! DAMN!! HUH? WHY WON'T IT MOVE!?
MY AESTI VALIS WON'T MOVE!! HEY! WHAT'S WRONG?!

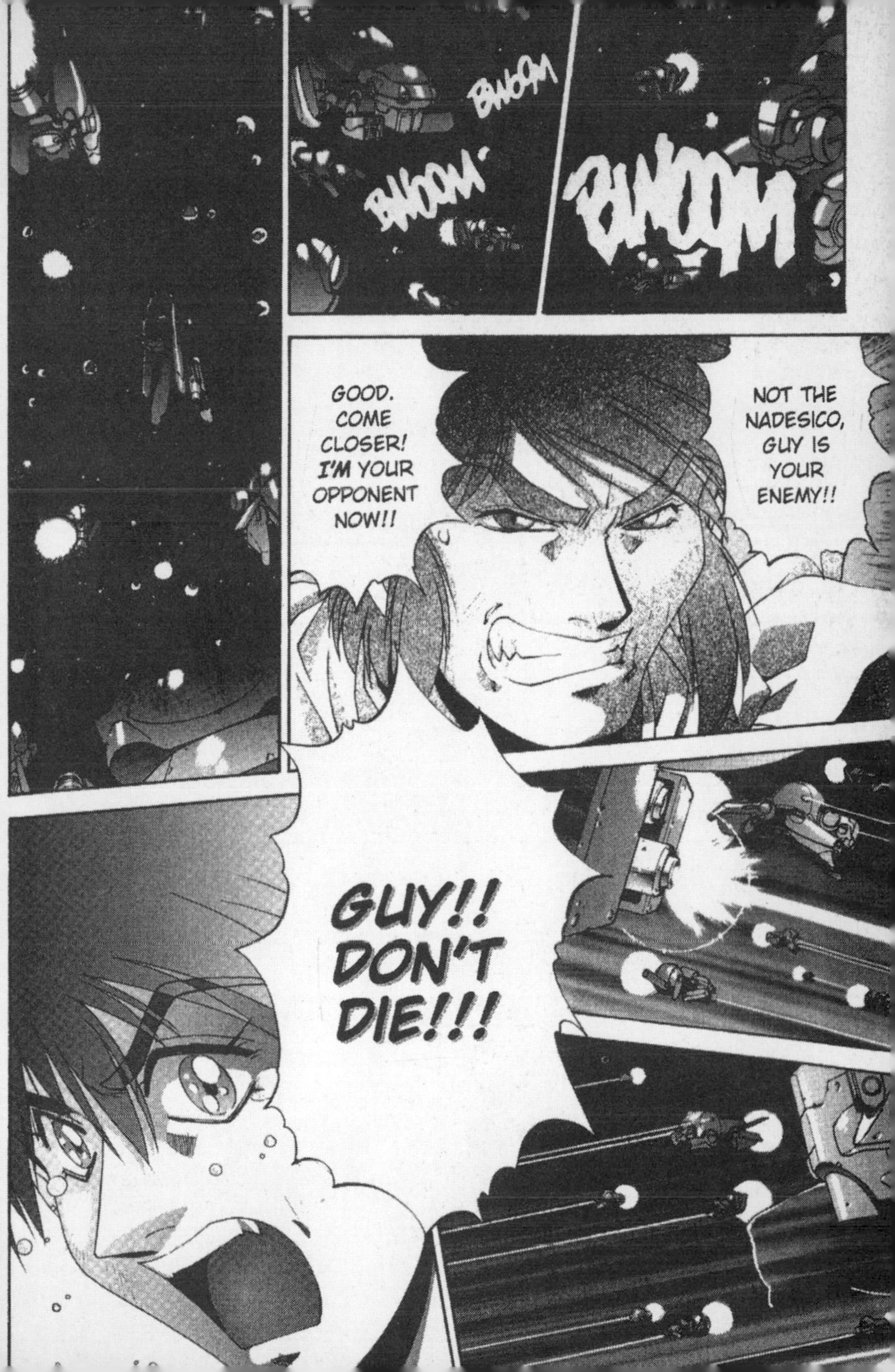
BWOOM
BWOOM
BWOOM
GOOD. COME CLOSER! I'M YOUR OPPONENT NOW!!
NOT THE NADESICO, GUY IS YOUR ENEMY!!
GUY!! DON'T DIE!!!

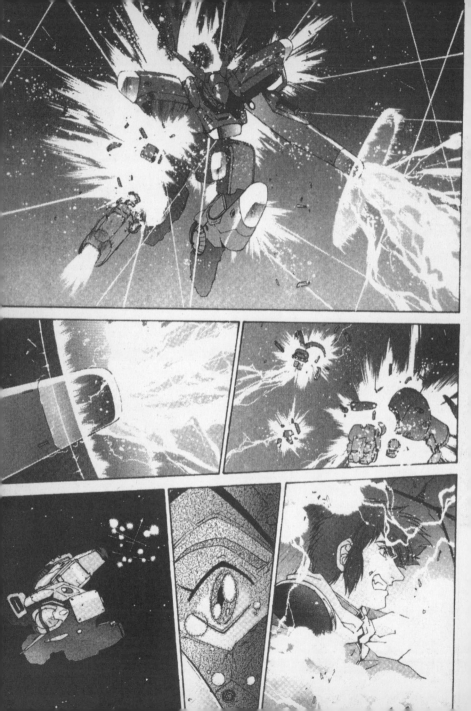

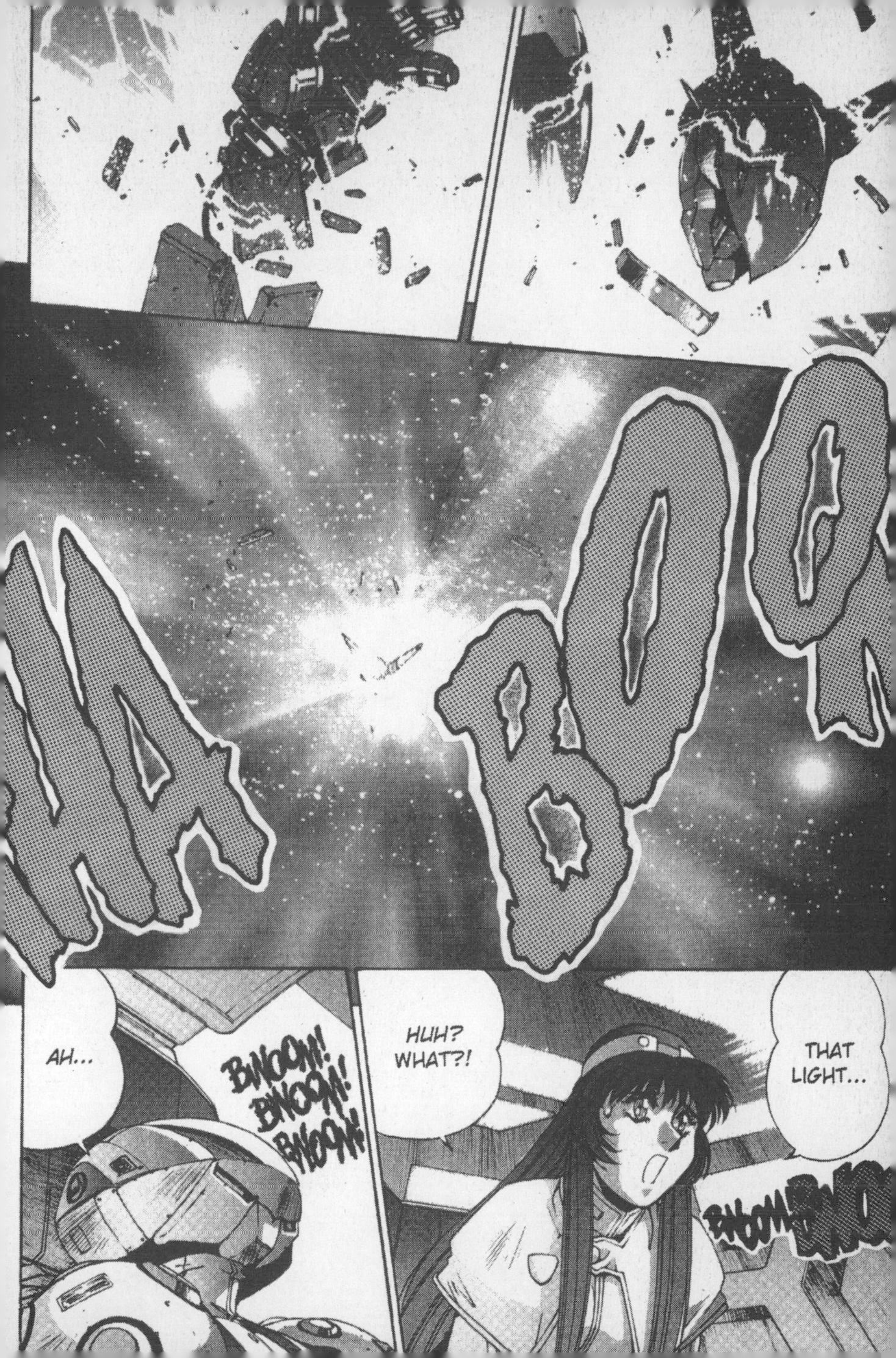
AH...
BWOOM! BWOOM! BWOOM!
HUH? WHAT?!
THAT LIGHT...
BWOOM

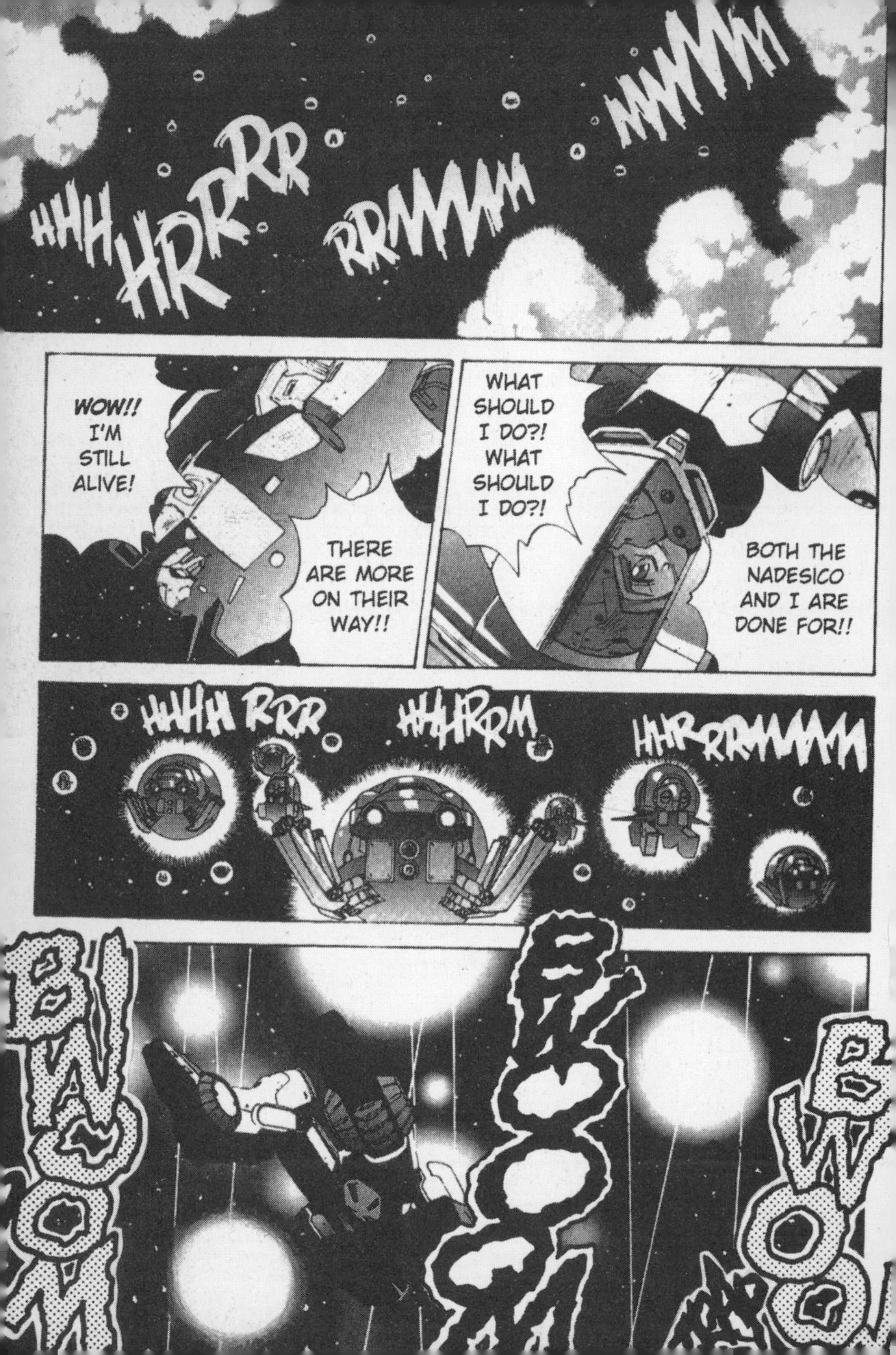
HHH HRRRR
RRMMMM
MMMMM
WOW!! I'M STILL ALIVE!
THERE ARE MORE ON THEIR WAY!!
WHAT SHOULD I DO?! WHAT SHOULD I DO?!
BOTH THE NADESICO AND I ARE DONE FOR!!
HHHH RRR
HHHRRM
HHRRRMMMMM
BOOM
BOOM
BOOM

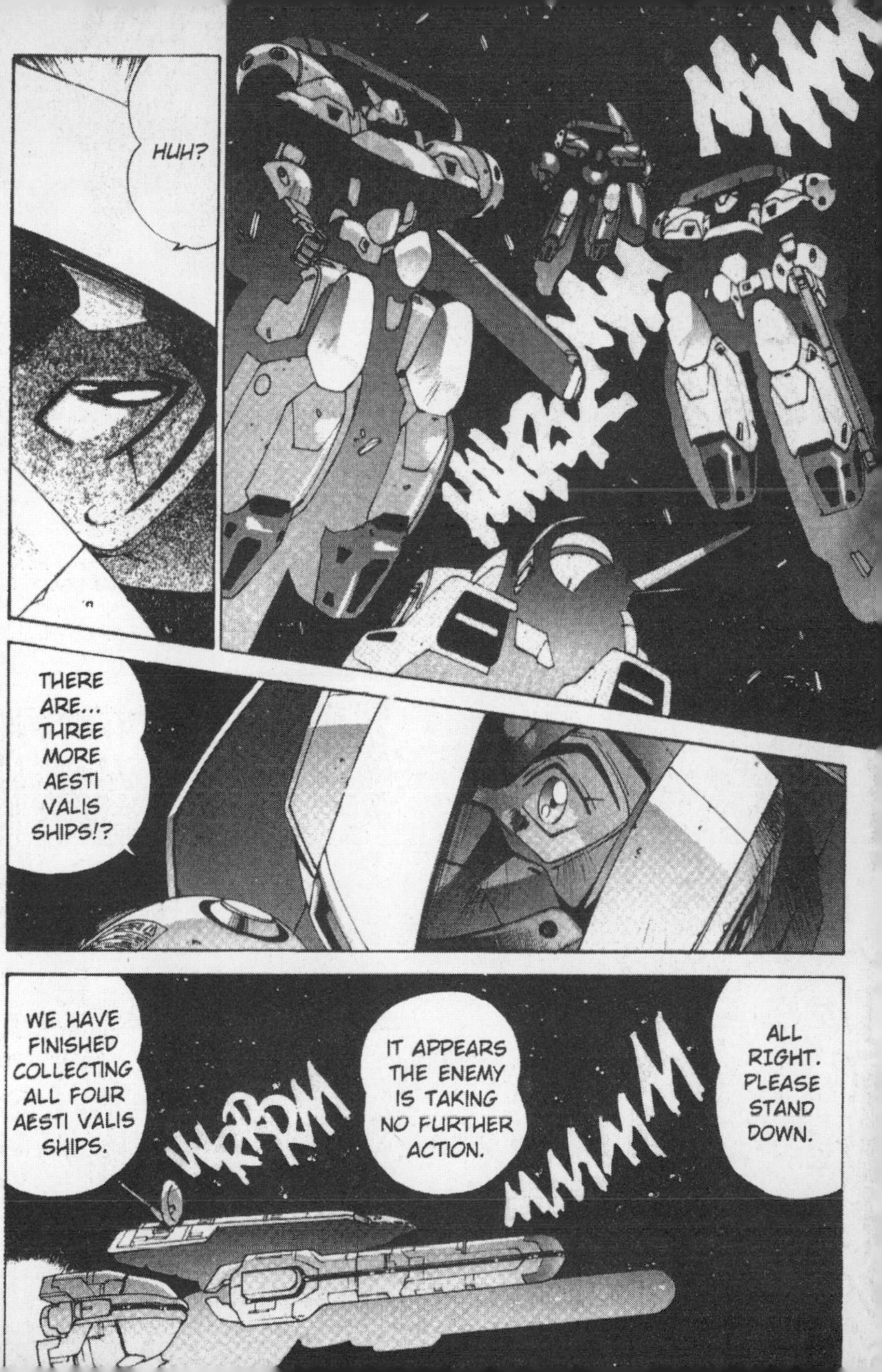
HUH?
THERE ARE... THREE MORE AESTI VALIS SHIPS!?
WE HAVE FINISHED COLLECTING ALL FOUR AESTI VALIS SHIPS.
IT APPEARS THE ENEMY IS TAKING NO FURTHER ACTION.
ALL RIGHT. PLEASE STAND DOWN.

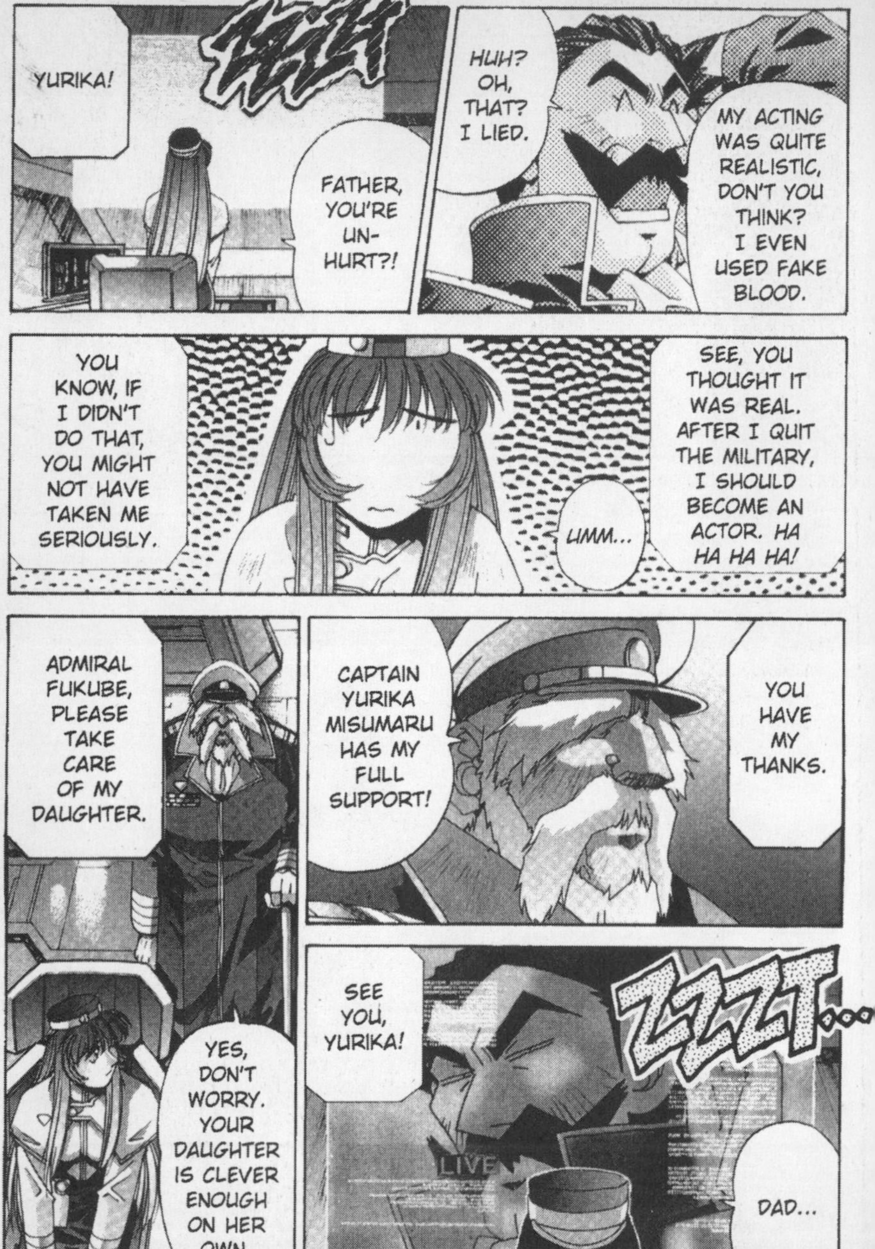
YURIKA!
FATHER, YOU'RE UN-HURT?!
HUH? OH, THAT? I LIED.
MY ACTING WAS QUITE REALISTIC, DON'T YOU THINK? I EVEN USED FAKE BLOOD.
YOU KNOW, IF I DIDN'T DO THAT, YOU MIGHT NOT HAVE TAKEN ME SERIOUSLY.
UMM...
SEE, YOU THOUGHT IT WAS REAL. AFTER I QUIT THE MILITARY, I SHOULD BECOME AN ACTOR. HA HA HA HA!
ADMIRAL FUKUBE, PLEASE TAKE CARE OF MY DAUGHTER.
YES, DON'T WORRY. YOUR DAUGHTER IS CLEVER ENOUGH ON HER OWN.
CAPTAIN YURIKA MISUMARU HAS MY FULL SUPPORT!
YOU HAVE MY THANKS.
SEE YOU, YURIKA!
ZZZZT...
LIVE
DAD...

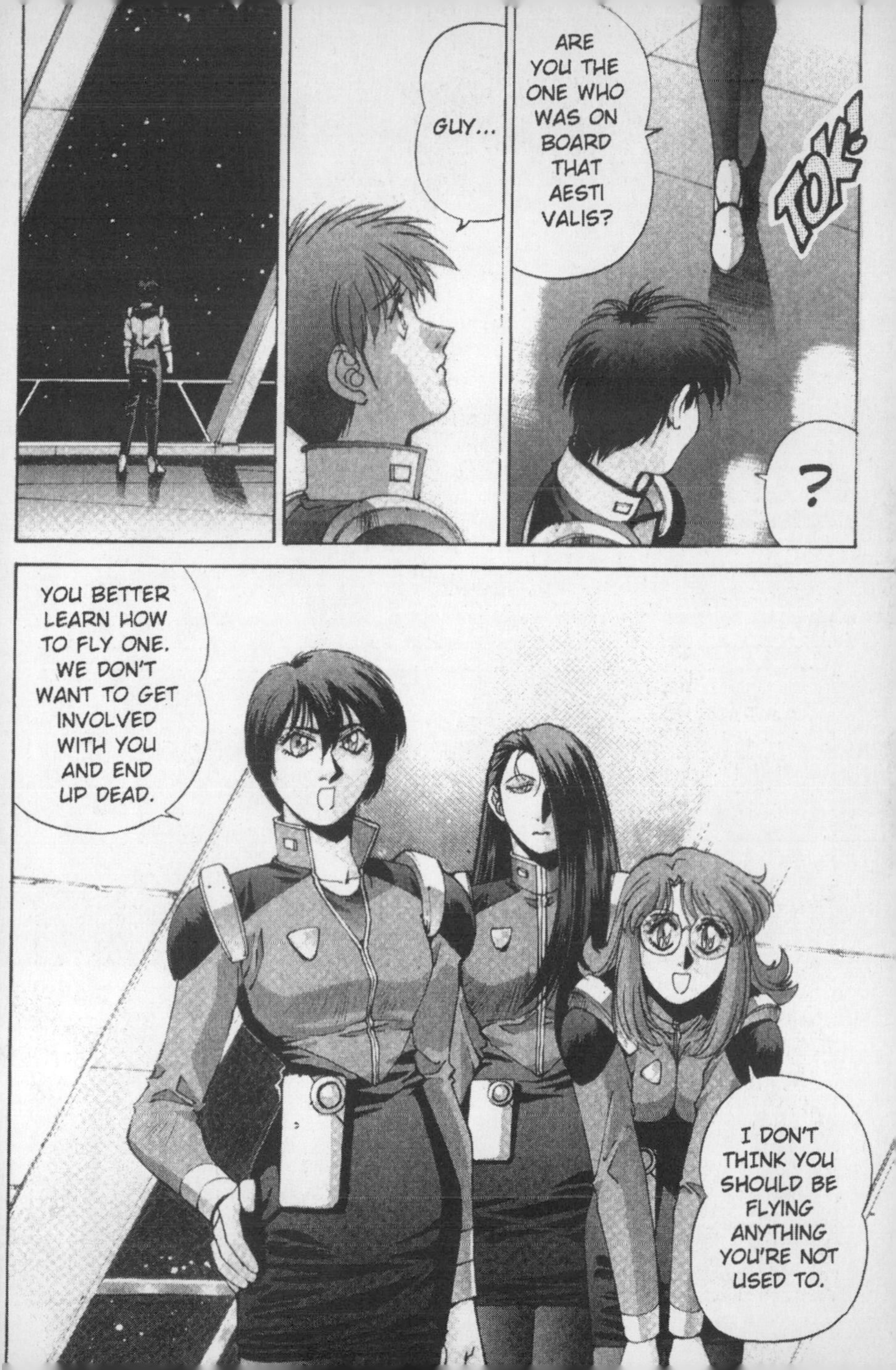
GUY...
ARE YOU THE ONE WHO WAS ON BOARD THAT AESTI VALIS?
TOK!
?
YOU BETTER LEARN HOW TO FLY ONE. WE DON'T WANT TO GET INVOLVED WITH YOU AND END UP DEAD.
I DON'T THINK YOU SHOULD BE FLYING ANYTHING YOU'RE NOT USED TO.

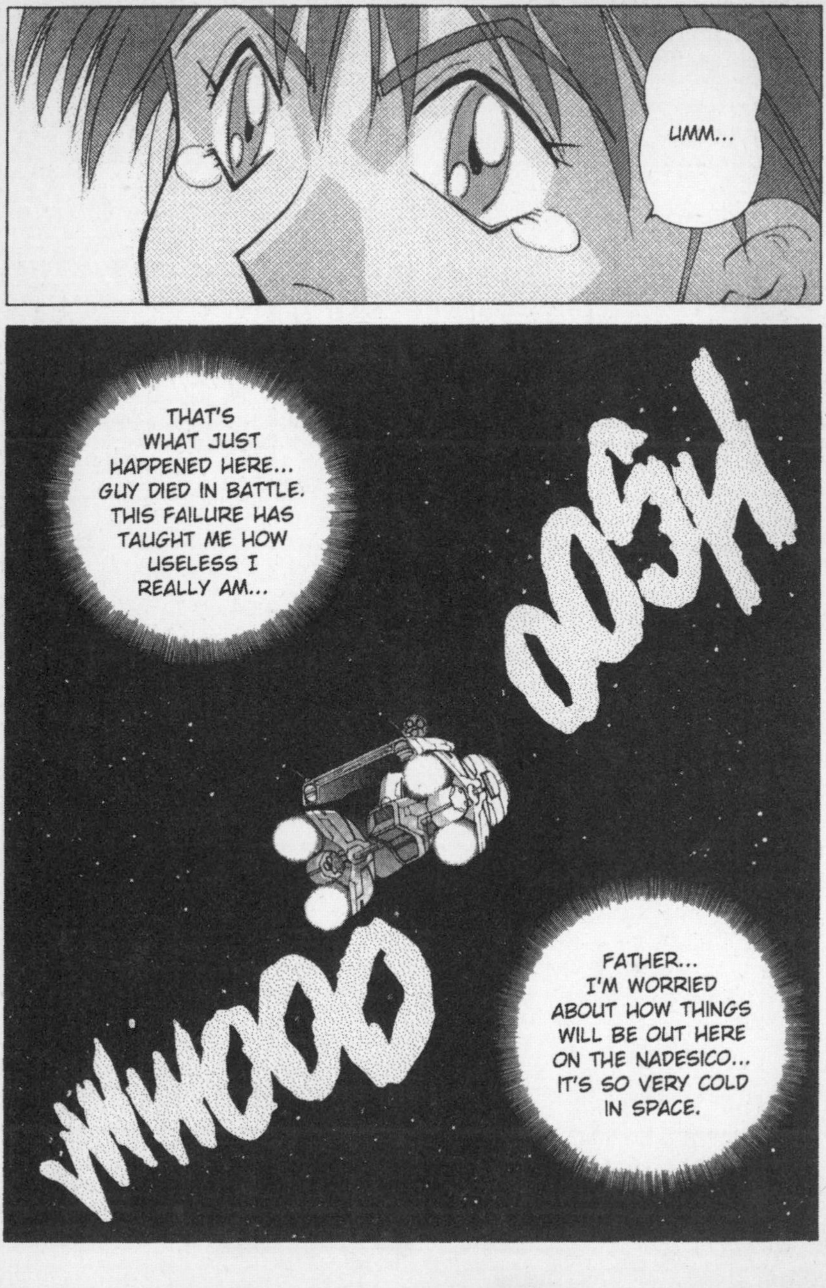
UMM...
THAT'S WHAT JUST HAPPENED HERE... GUY DIED IN BATTLE. THIS FAILURE HAS TAUGHT ME HOW USELESS I REALLY AM...
WHOOO OOSH
FATHER... I'M WORRIED ABOUT HOW THINGS WILL BE OUT HERE ON THE NADESICO... IT'S SO VERY COLD IN SPACE.

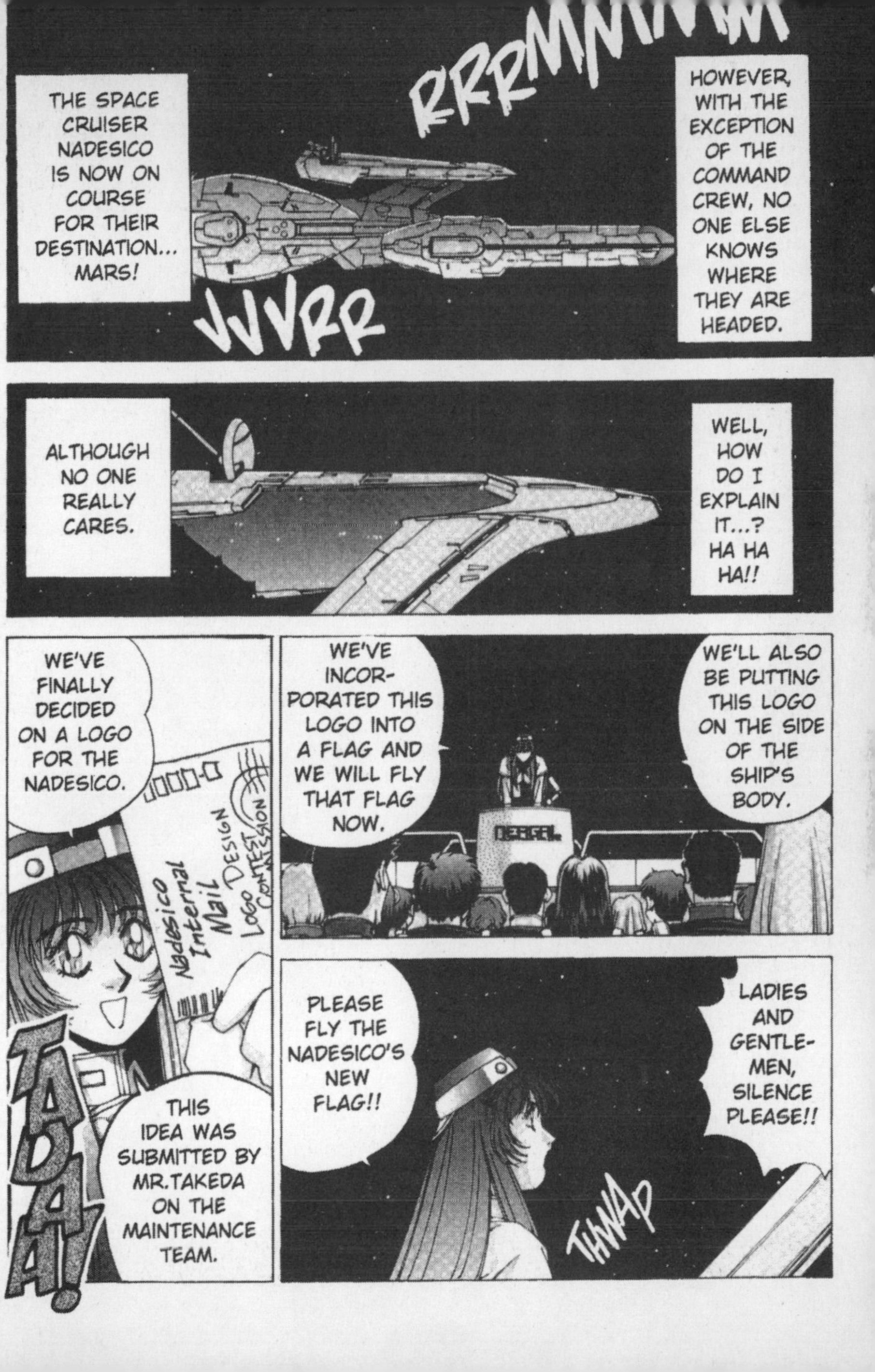
THE SPACE CRUISER NADESICO IS NOW ON COURSE FOR THEIR DESTINATION... MARS!
RRRMMMM
HOWEVER, WITH THE EXCEPTION OF THE COMMAND CREW, NO ONE ELSE KNOWS WHERE THEY ARE HEADED.
VVVRR
ALTHOUGH NO ONE REALLY CARES.
WELL, HOW DO I EXPLAIN IT...? HA HA HA!!
WE'VE FINALLY DECIDED ON A LOGO FOR THE NADESICO.
Nadesico Internal Mail
TADA!
THIS IDEA WAS SUBMITTED BY MR.TAKEDA ON THE MAINTENANCE TEAM.
WE'VE INCORPORATED THIS LOGO INTO A FLAG AND WE WILL FLY THAT FLAG NOW.
WE'LL ALSO BE PUTTING THIS LOGO ON THE SIDE OF THE SHIP'S BODY.
PLEASE FLY THE NADESICO'S NEW FLAG!!
LADIES AND GENTLEMEN, SILENCE PLEASE!!
THWAP

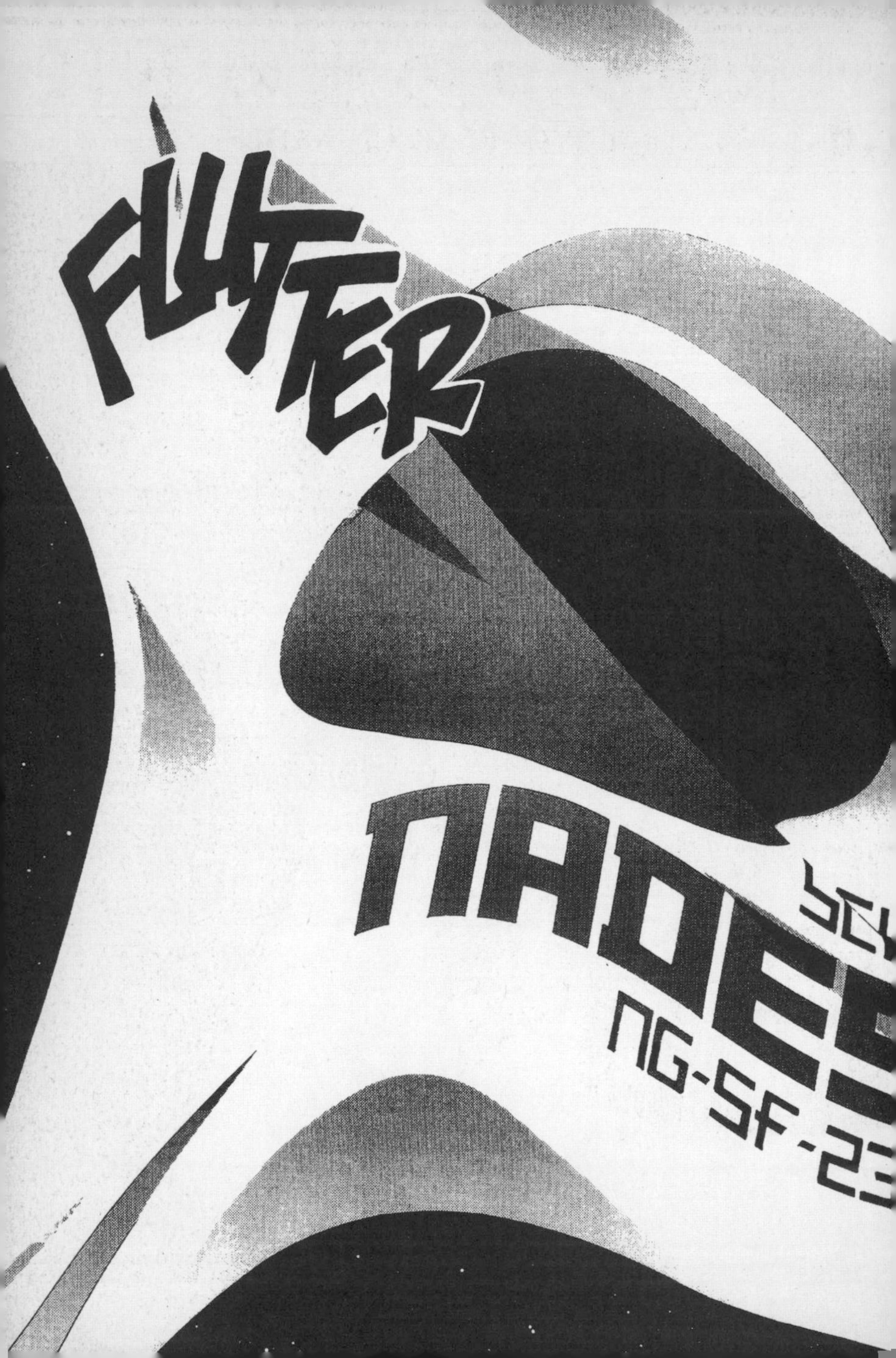
FLUTTER
NADE
NG-SF-23

ナデシコの旗の下に

第6話——UNDER THE FLAG OF NADESICO——

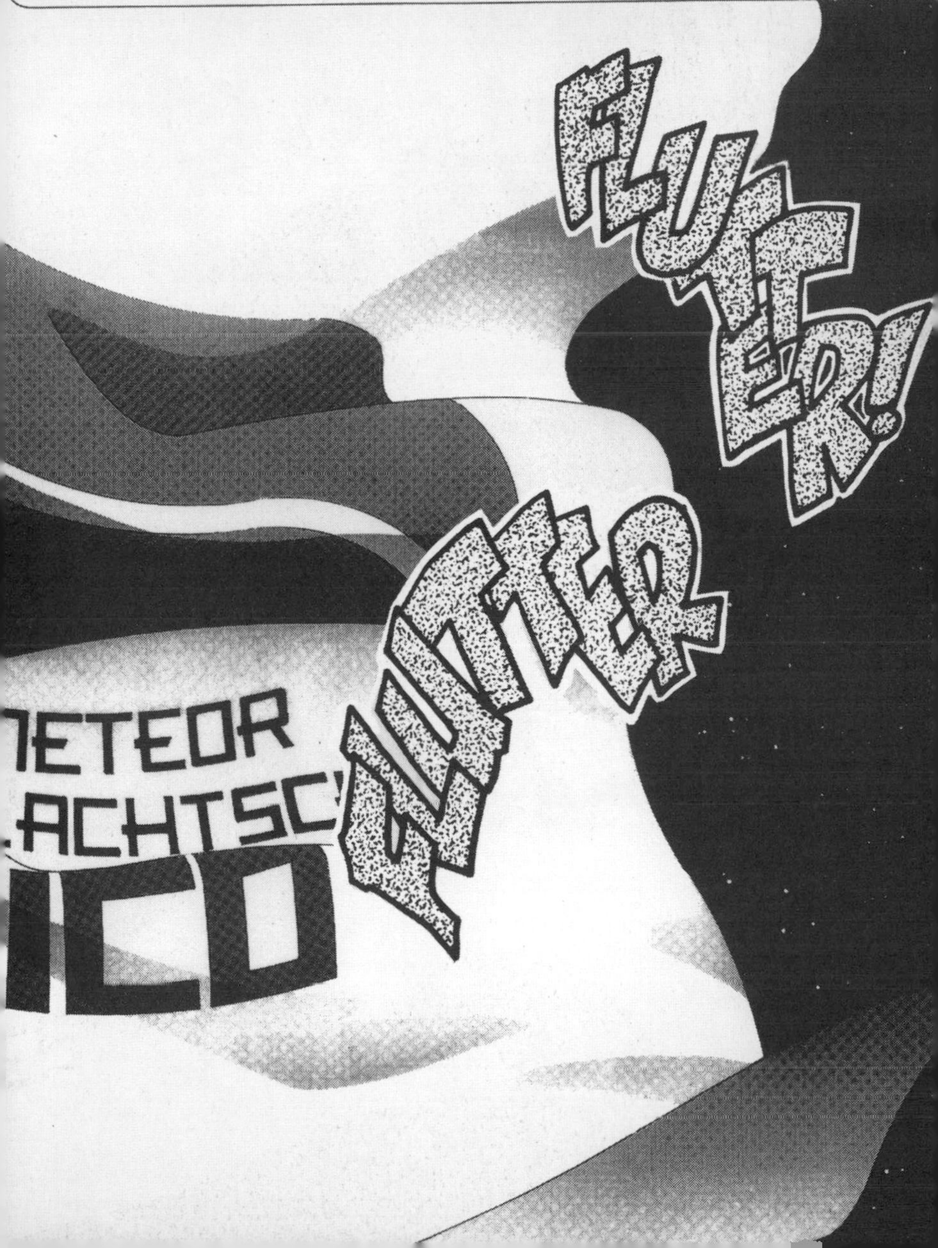
FLUTTER!
FLUTTER

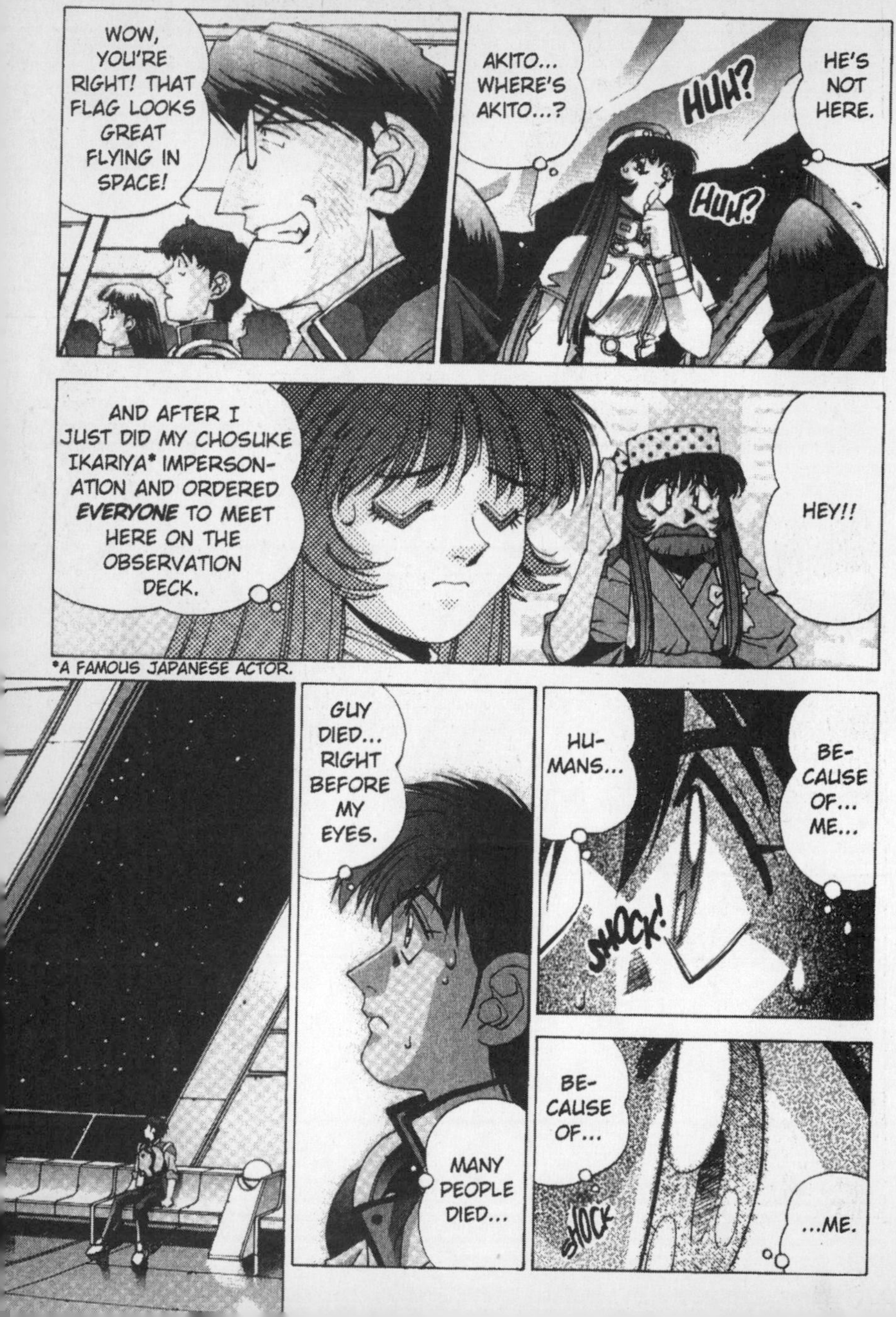
WOW, YOU'RE RIGHT! THAT FLAG LOOKS GREAT FLYING IN SPACE!
AKITO... WHERE'S AKITO...?
HUH?
HE'S NOT HERE.
HUH?
AND AFTER I JUST DID MY CHOSUKE IKARIYA* IMPERSON-ATION AND ORDERED ***EVERYONE*** TO MEET HERE ON THE OBSERVATION DECK.
HEY!!
*A FAMOUS JAPANESE ACTOR.
GUY DIED... RIGHT BEFORE MY EYES.
MANY PEOPLE DIED...
HU-MANS...
BE-CAUSE OF... ME...
SHOCK!
BE-CAUSE OF...
SHOCK
...ME.

HOW GLOOMY!

LITTLE BOY, WHAT'RE YOU DOING HERE ALL BY YOURSELF?

WHAT? AH... I... I...

THUMP!

I SEE YOU SKIPPED THE MEETING, EH?

EVER SINCE I WAS A KID I NEVER LIKED LARGE GATHERINGS.

UMP

THW

SIGH.

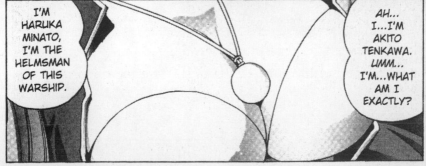

I'M HARUKA MINATO, I'M THE HELMSMAN OF THIS WARSHIP.

AH... I...I'M AKITO TENKAWA. UMM... I'M...WHAT AM I EXACTLY?

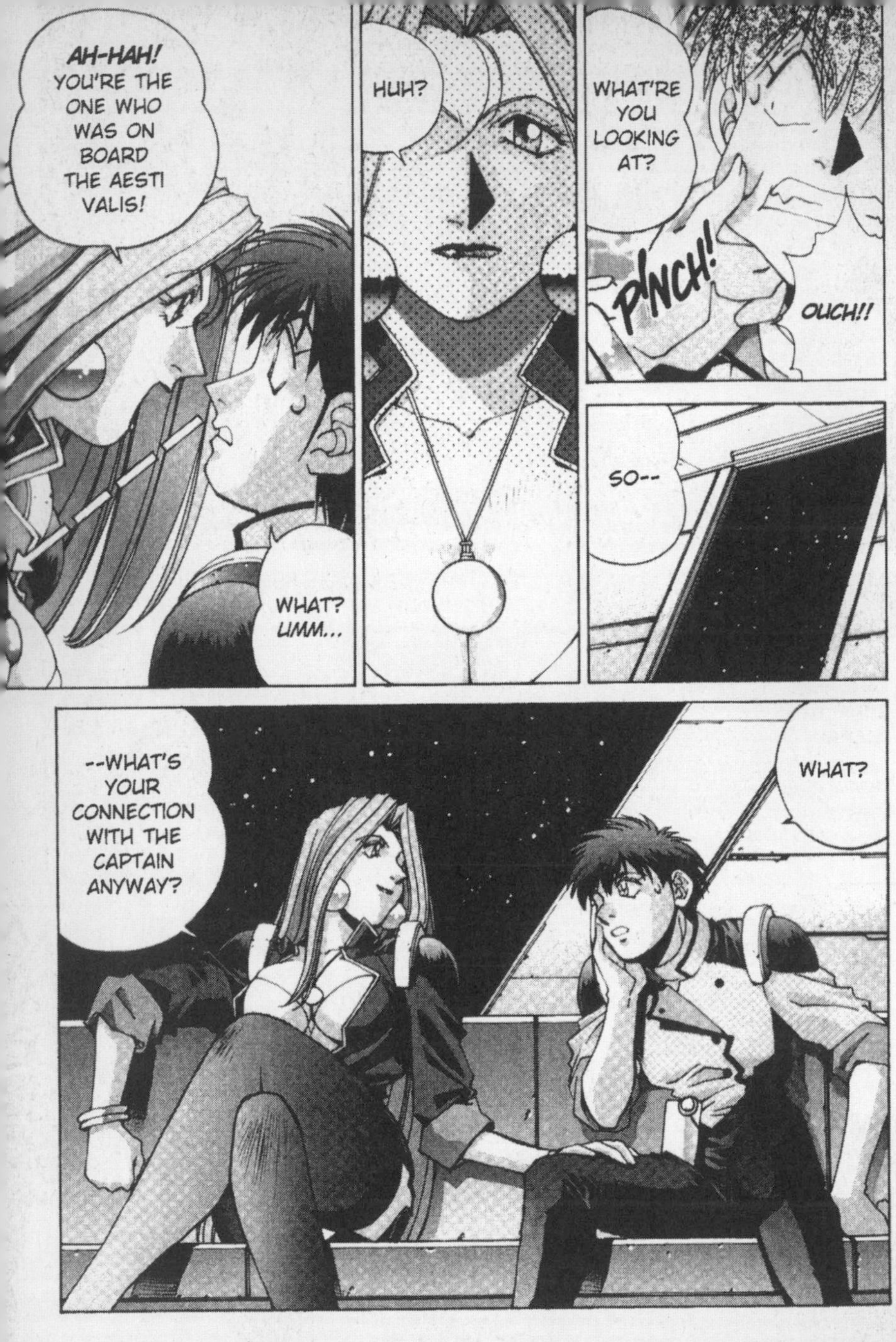
AH-HAH! YOU'RE THE ONE WHO WAS ON BOARD THE AESTI VALIS!
WHAT? UMM...
HUH?
WHAT'RE YOU LOOKING AT?
PINCH!
OUCH!!
SO--
--WHAT'S YOUR CONNECTION WITH THE CAPTAIN ANYWAY?
WHAT?

HHHHHRR RRRMMMM

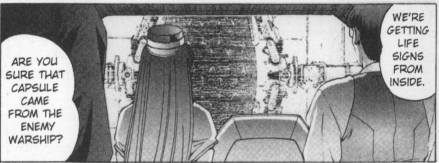

ARE YOU SURE THAT CAPSULE CAME FROM THE ENEMY WARSHIP?

WE'RE GETTING LIFE SIGNS FROM INSIDE.

THAT MEANS IT'S AN ESCAPE POD?!

SIGH!

THEY MAY COME POURING OUT OF THERE...

IT'S OPEN-ING!

IT'S BECAUSE THE CAPTAIN OPENED HER MOUTH!

KRAA

OH, NO!!

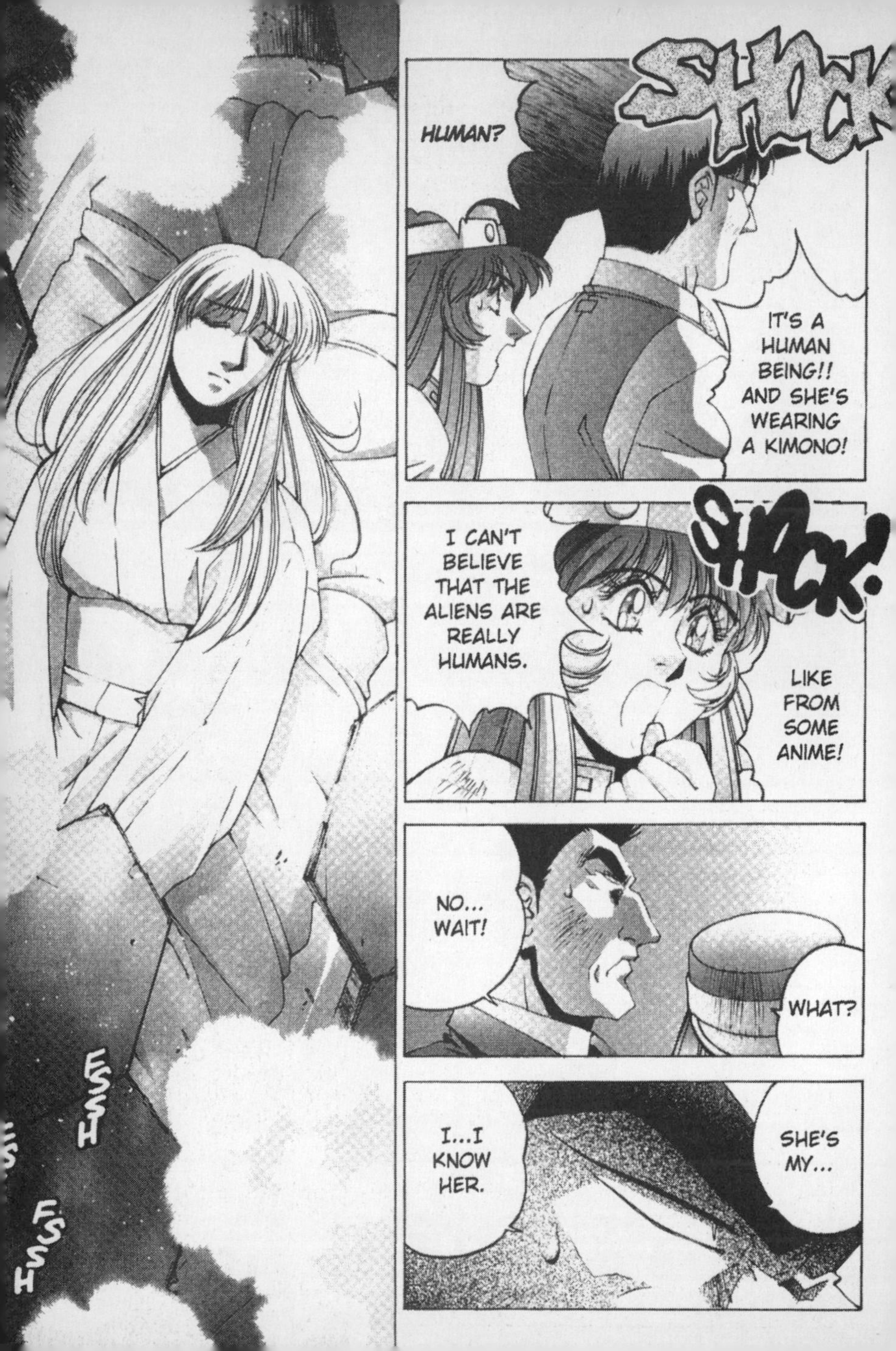
FSSH
FSSH
SHOCK
HUMAN?
IT'S A HUMAN BEING!! AND SHE'S WEARING A KIMONO!
I CAN'T BELIEVE THAT THE ALIENS ARE REALLY HUMANS.
SHOCK!
LIKE FROM SOME ANIME!
NO... WAIT!
WHAT?
I...I KNOW HER.
SHE'S MY...

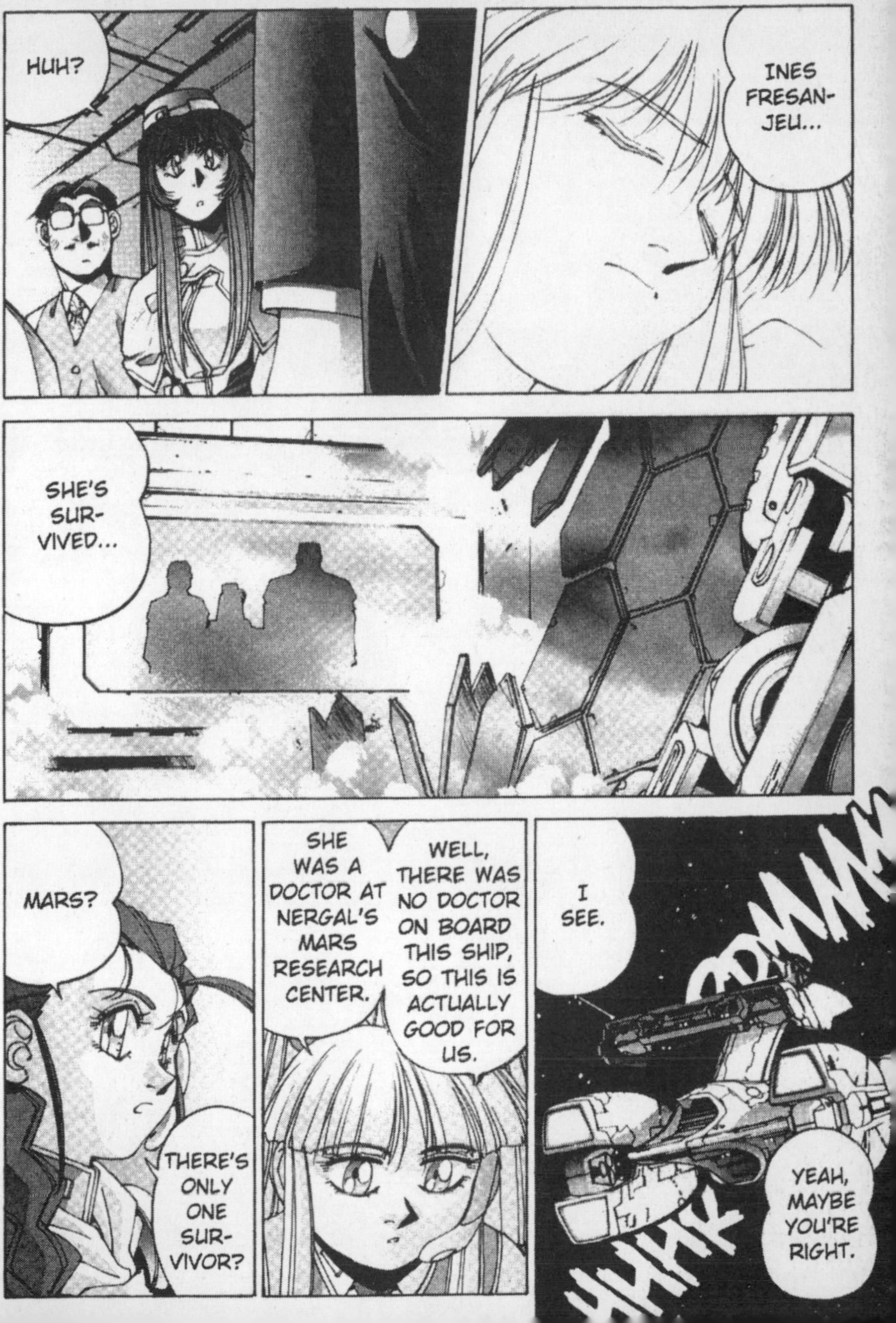
HUH?
INES FRESAN-JEU...
SHE'S SUR-VIVED...
MARS?
THERE'S ONLY ONE SUR-VIVOR?
SHE WAS A DOCTOR AT NERGAL'S MARS RESEARCH CENTER.
WELL, THERE WAS NO DOCTOR ON BOARD THIS SHIP, SO THIS IS ACTUALLY GOOD FOR US.
I SEE.
YEAH, MAYBE YOU'RE RIGHT.

UNITED EARTH GOVERNMENT MOON DOCK 377.

CLUNK!

ARE YOU READY TO GO?

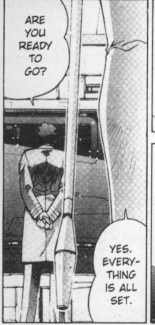

YES. EVERY-THING IS ALL SET.

WELL, YOU AND THAT WARSHIP OF YOURS ARE OUR TRUMP CARD.

I DO NOT WANT YOU TO DESTROY THE NADESICO. I WANT HER INTACT.

YES, SIR! I'LL DO MY BEST TO MEET YOUR EVERY EXPECTATION--

--STAFF OFFICER SARA-SHINA.

WE BEGAN BUILDING THIS WARSHIP TO BE JUST LIKE THE NADESICO, BUT IT'S IMPOSSIBLE TO COMPLETE A WARSHIP LIKE THAT IN A WEEK.

WE NEED SOMETHING WE CAN USE NOW.

IT'S FOR THE GOOD OF THE UNITED EARTH GOVERNMENT.

I UNDERSTAND.

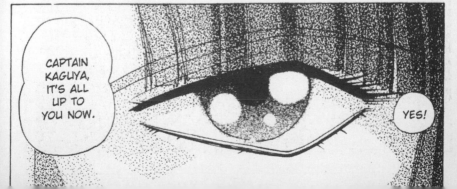

CAPTAIN KAGUYA, IT'S ALL UP TO YOU NOW.

YES!

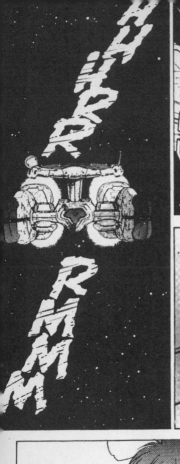

EXCUSE ME? UMM...IS THIS THE BRIDGE?

YAAAYY!! AKITO! AKITO! AKITO!! AKITO!! AKITO!!

WE FINALLY MEET!! I'M SO ULTRA HAPPY!!

HUH? HEY!!

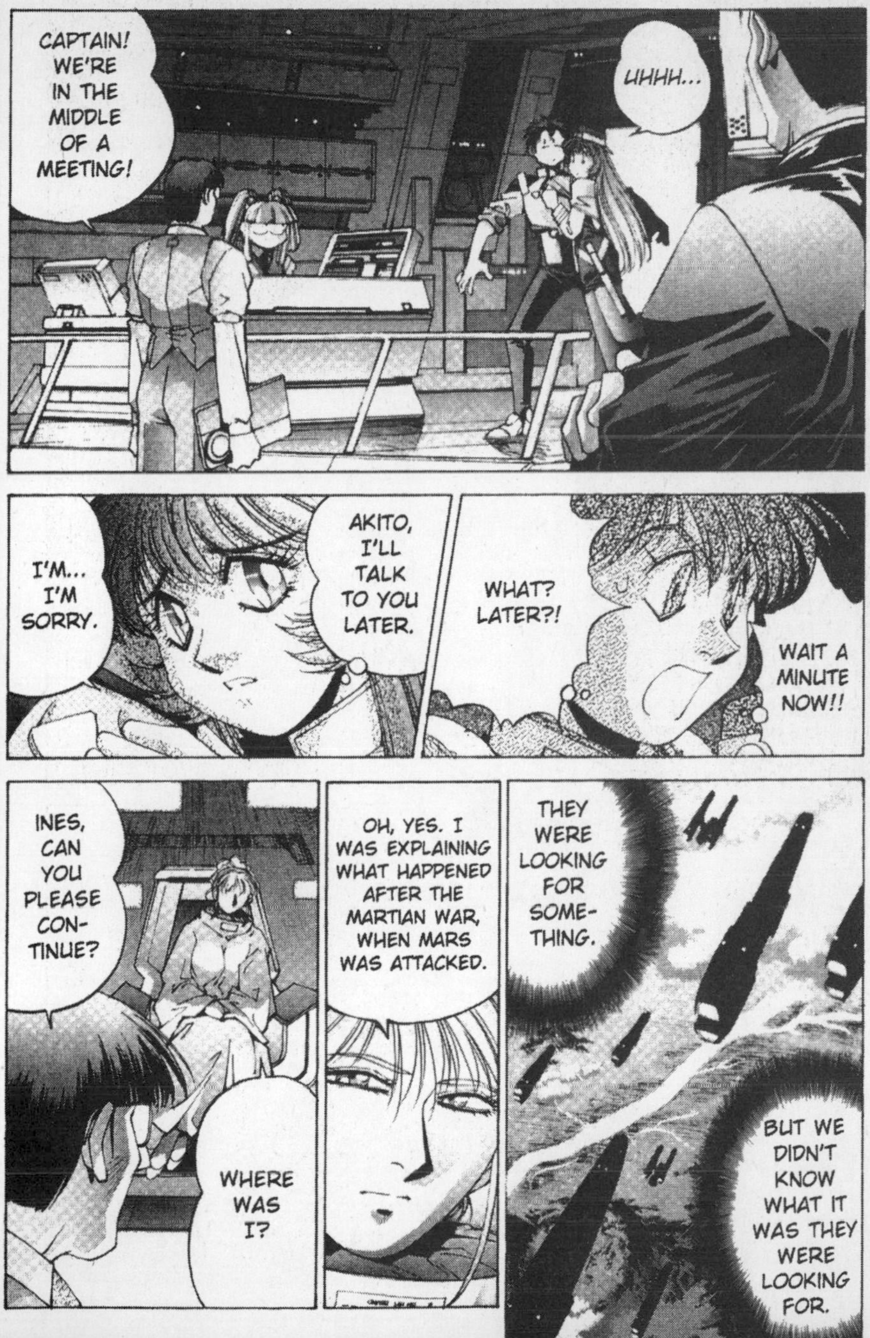
CAPTAIN! WE'RE IN THE MIDDLE OF A MEETING!
UHHH...
I'M... I'M SORRY.
AKITO, I'LL TALK TO YOU LATER.
WHAT? LATER?!
WAIT A MINUTE NOW!!
INES, CAN YOU PLEASE CON- TINUE?
WHERE WAS I?
OH, YES. I WAS EXPLAINING WHAT HAPPENED AFTER THE MARTIAN WAR, WHEN MARS WAS ATTACKED.
THEY WERE LOOKING FOR SOME- THING.
BUT WE DIDN'T KNOW WHAT IT WAS THEY WERE LOOKING FOR.

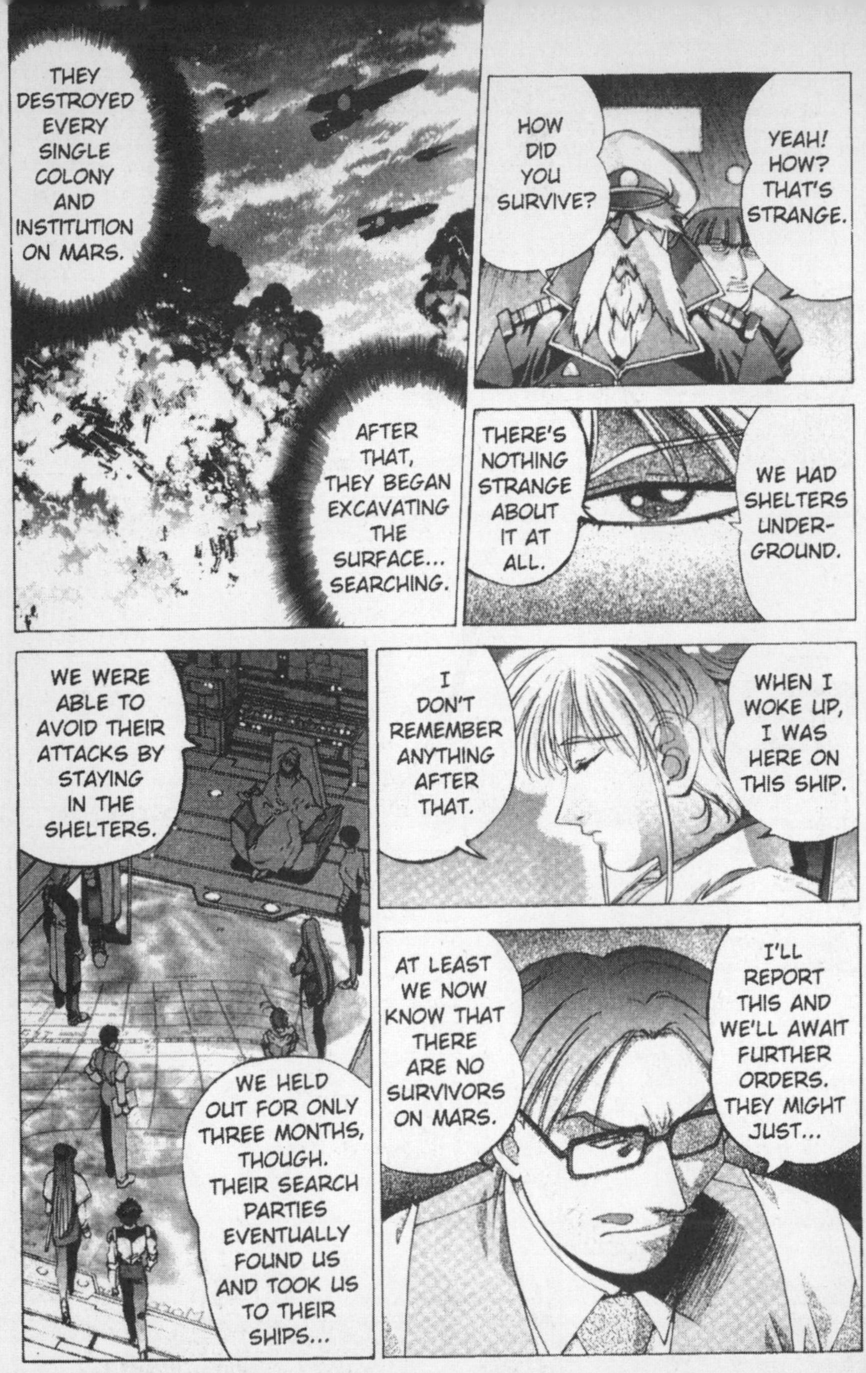
THEY DESTROYED EVERY SINGLE COLONY AND INSTITUTION ON MARS.
AFTER THAT, THEY BEGAN EXCAVATING THE SURFACE... SEARCHING.
HOW DID YOU SURVIVE?
YEAH! HOW? THAT'S STRANGE.
THERE'S NOTHING STRANGE ABOUT IT AT ALL.
WE HAD SHELTERS UNDER-GROUND.
WE WERE ABLE TO AVOID THEIR ATTACKS BY STAYING IN THE SHELTERS.
WE HELD OUT FOR ONLY THREE MONTHS, THOUGH. THEIR SEARCH PARTIES EVENTUALLY FOUND US AND TOOK US TO THEIR SHIPS...
I DON'T REMEMBER ANYTHING AFTER THAT.
WHEN I WOKE UP, I WAS HERE ON THIS SHIP.
AT LEAST WE NOW KNOW THAT THERE ARE NO SURVIVORS ON MARS.
I'LL REPORT THIS AND WE'LL AWAIT FURTHER ORDERS. THEY MIGHT JUST...

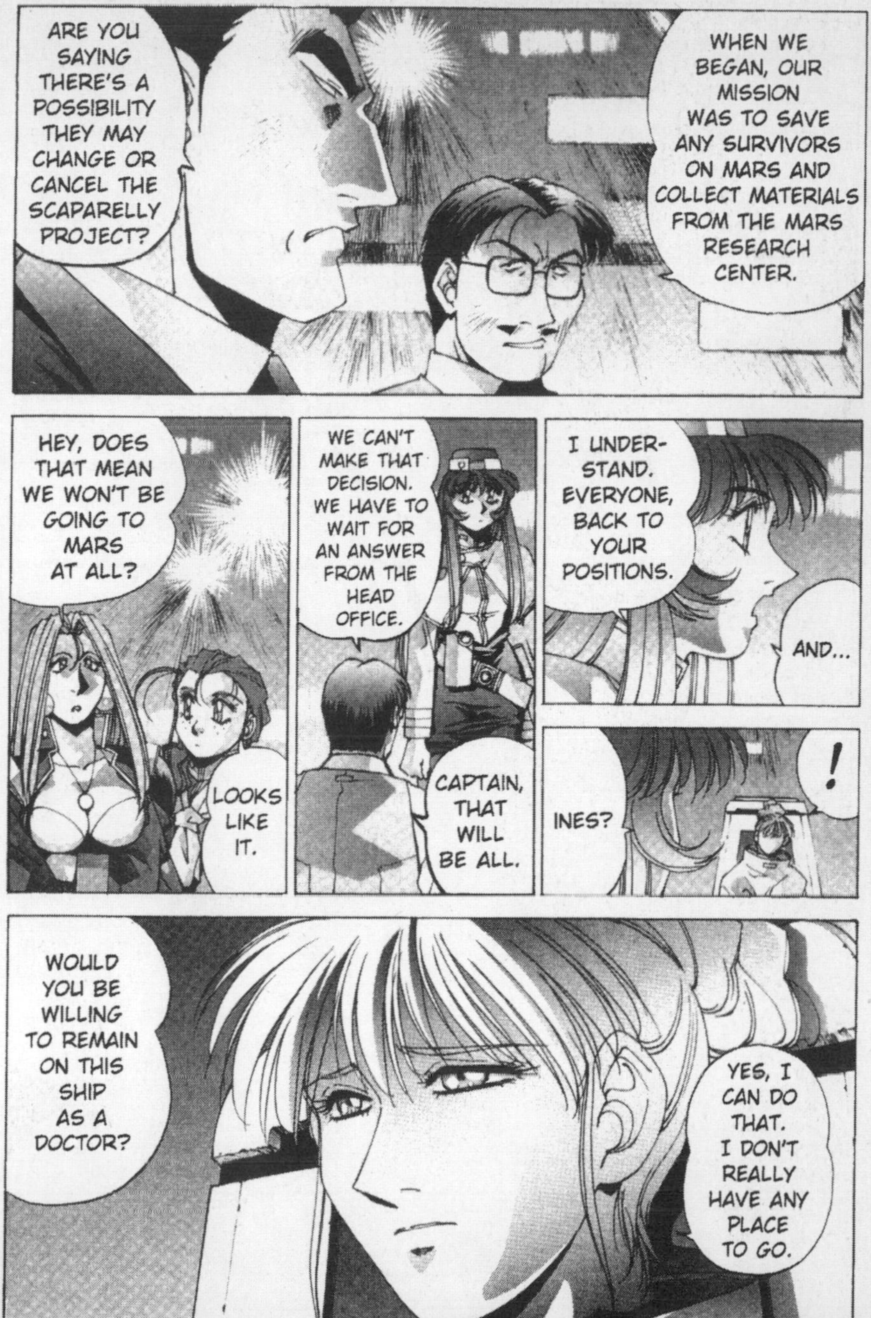
ARE YOU SAYING THERE'S A POSSIBILITY THEY MAY CHANGE OR CANCEL THE SCAPARELLY PROJECT?
WHEN WE BEGAN, OUR MISSION WAS TO SAVE ANY SURVIVORS ON MARS AND COLLECT MATERIALS FROM THE MARS RESEARCH CENTER.
HEY, DOES THAT MEAN WE WON'T BE GOING TO MARS AT ALL?
LOOKS LIKE IT.
WE CAN'T MAKE THAT DECISION. WE HAVE TO WAIT FOR AN ANSWER FROM THE HEAD OFFICE.
CAPTAIN, THAT WILL BE ALL.
I UNDER-STAND. EVERYONE, BACK TO YOUR POSITIONS.
AND...
INES?
!
WOULD YOU BE WILLING TO REMAIN ON THIS SHIP AS A DOCTOR?
YES, I CAN DO THAT. I DON'T REALLY HAVE ANY PLACE TO GO.

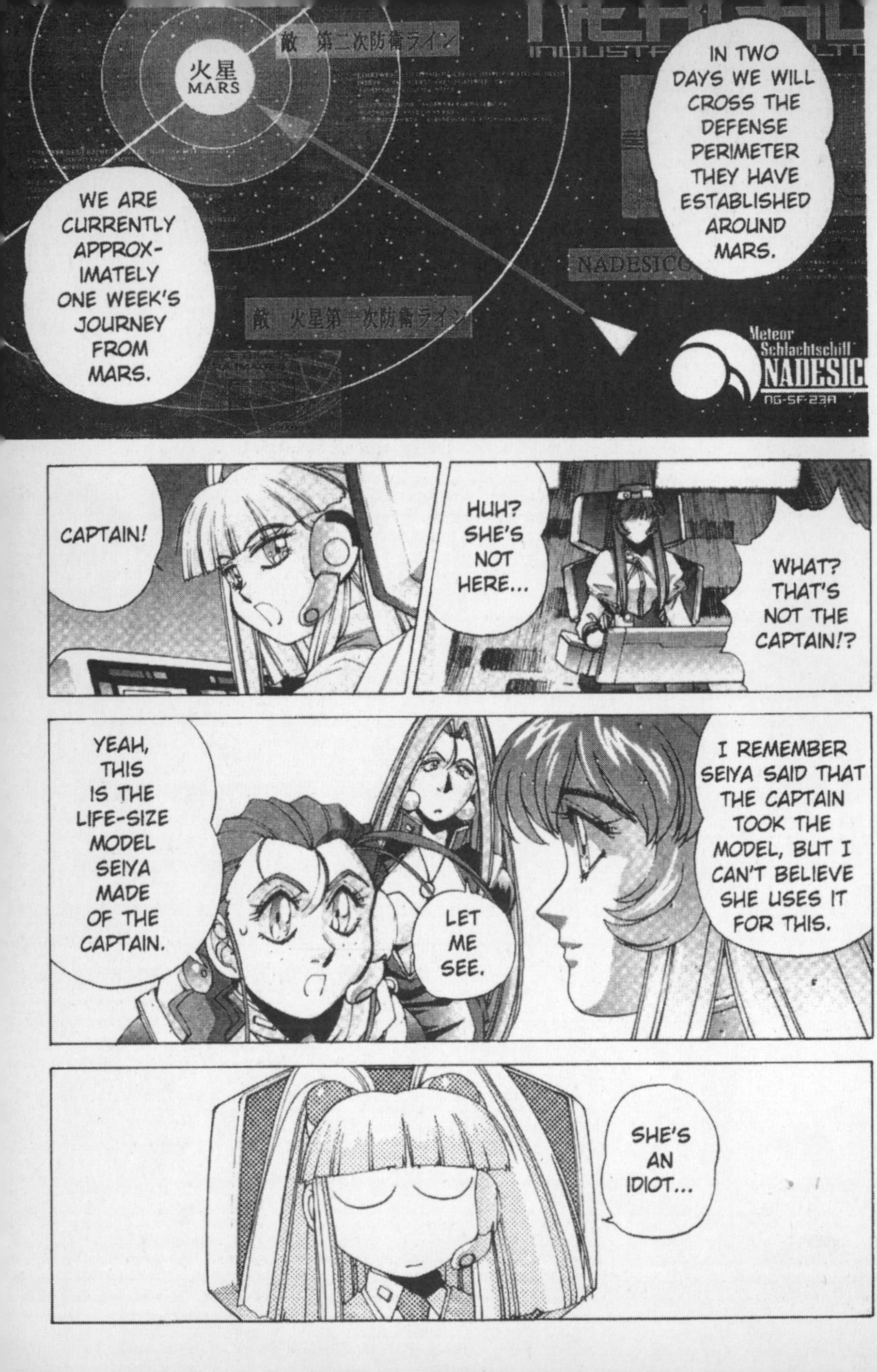
火星
MARS
敵 第二次防衛ライン
WE ARE CURRENTLY APPROX-IMATELY ONE WEEK'S JOURNEY FROM MARS.
IN TWO DAYS WE WILL CROSS THE DEFENSE PERIMETER THEY HAVE ESTABLISHED AROUND MARS.
NADESICO
敵 火星第一次防衛ライン
Meteor Schlachtschiff
NADESIC
NG-SF-23A
CAPTAIN!
HUH? SHE'S NOT HERE...
WHAT? THAT'S NOT THE CAPTAIN!?
YEAH, THIS IS THE LIFE-SIZE MODEL SEIYA MADE OF THE CAPTAIN.
LET ME SEE.
I REMEMBER SEIYA SAID THAT THE CAPTAIN TOOK THE MODEL, BUT I CAN'T BELIEVE SHE USES IT FOR THIS.
SHE'S AN IDIOT...

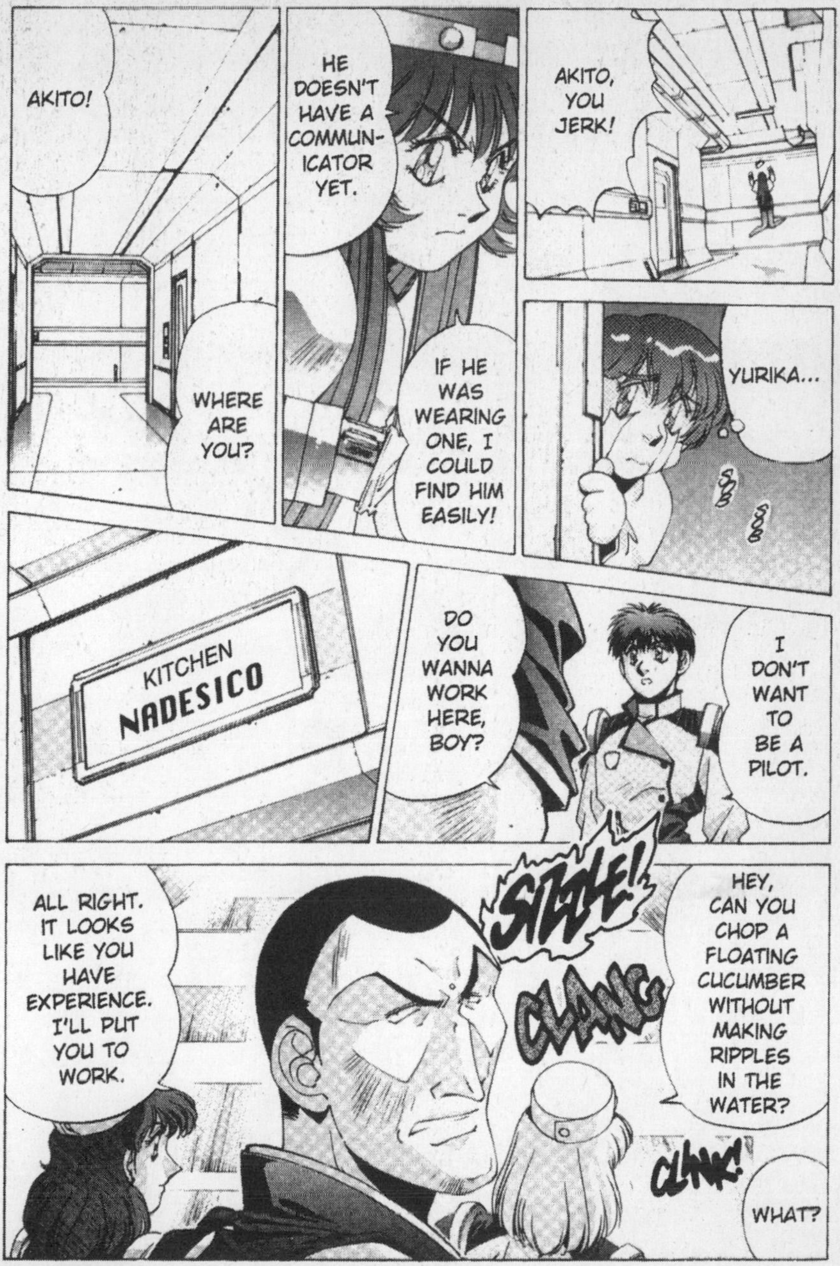
AKITO!
WHERE ARE YOU?
HE DOESN'T HAVE A COMMUNICATOR YET.
IF HE WAS WEARING ONE, I COULD FIND HIM EASILY!
AKITO, YOU JERK!
YURIKA...
SOB
SOB
KITCHEN
NADESICO
DO YOU WANNA WORK HERE, BOY?
I DON'T WANT TO BE A PILOT.
ALL RIGHT. IT LOOKS LIKE YOU HAVE EXPERIENCE. I'LL PUT YOU TO WORK.
SIZZLE!
CLANG
HEY, CAN YOU CHOP A FLOATING CUCUMBER WITHOUT MAKING RIPPLES IN THE WATER?
CLINK!
WHAT?

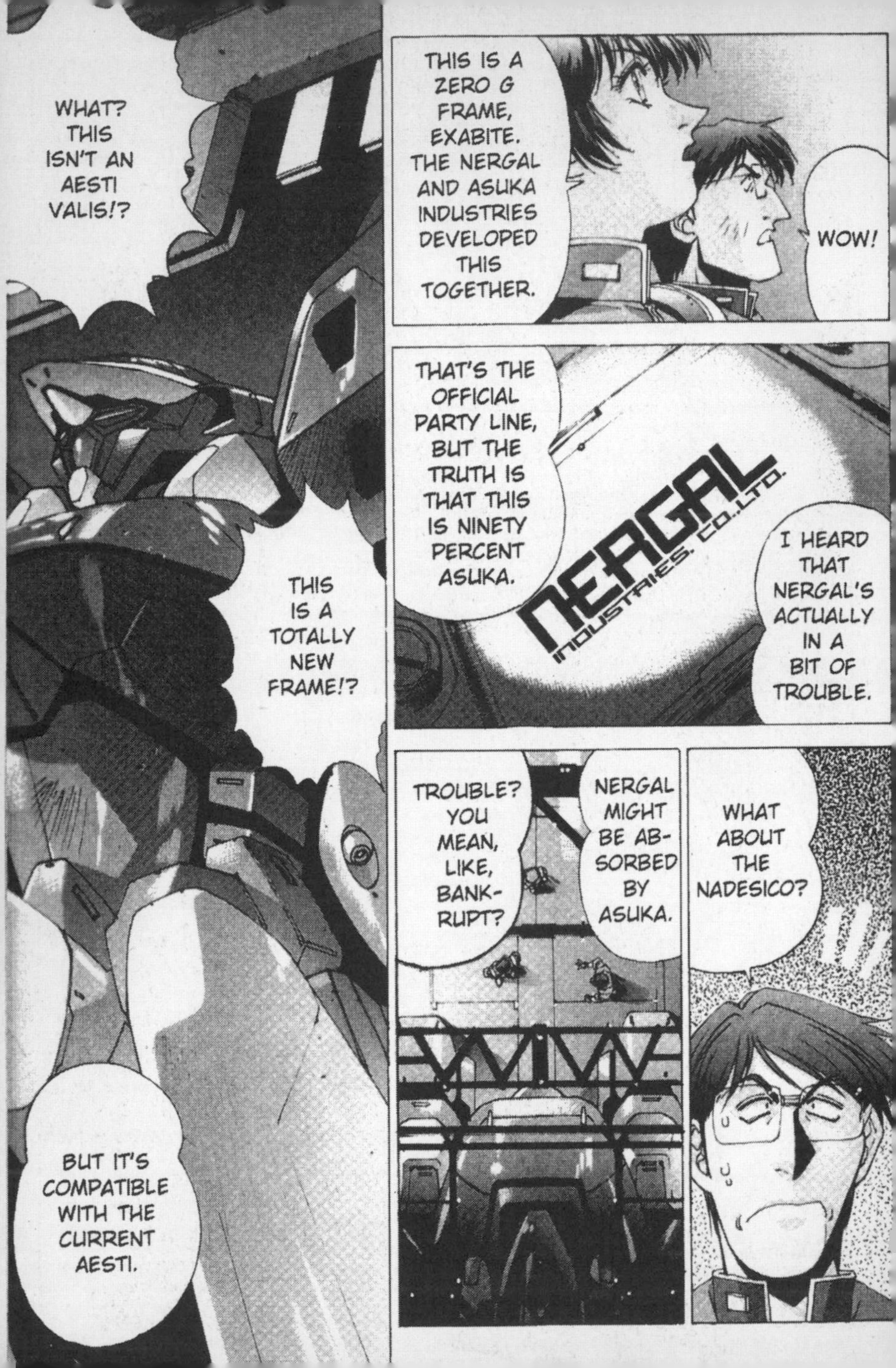
WHAT? THIS ISN'T AN AESTI VALIS!?
THIS IS A TOTALLY NEW FRAME!?
BUT IT'S COMPATIBLE WITH THE CURRENT AESTI.
THIS IS A ZERO G FRAME, EXABITE. THE NERGAL AND ASUKA INDUSTRIES DEVELOPED THIS TOGETHER.
WOW!
THAT'S THE OFFICIAL PARTY LINE, BUT THE TRUTH IS THAT THIS IS NINETY PERCENT ASUKA.
NERGAL INDUSTRIES. CO.,LTD.
I HEARD THAT NERGAL'S ACTUALLY IN A BIT OF TROUBLE.
TROUBLE? YOU MEAN, LIKE, BANK-RUPT?
NERGAL MIGHT BE AB-SORBED BY ASUKA.
WHAT ABOUT THE NADESICO?

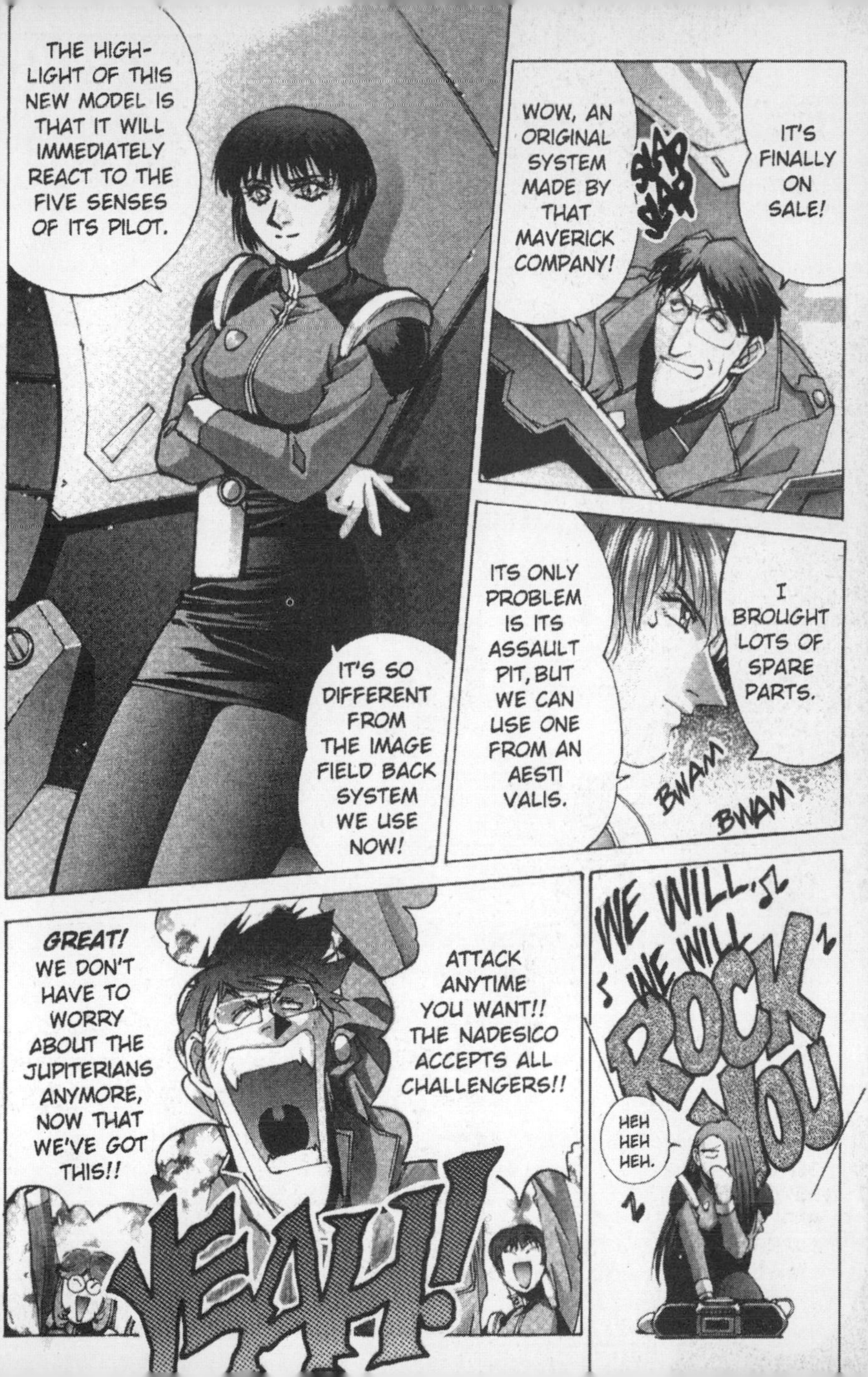
THE HIGHLIGHT OF THIS NEW MODEL IS THAT IT WILL IMMEDIATELY REACT TO THE FIVE SENSES OF ITS PILOT.
IT'S SO DIFFERENT FROM THE IMAGE FIELD BACK SYSTEM WE USE NOW!
WOW, AN ORIGINAL SYSTEM MADE BY THAT MAVERICK COMPANY!
SLAP SLAP
IT'S FINALLY ON SALE!
ITS ONLY PROBLEM IS ITS ASSAULT PIT, BUT WE CAN USE ONE FROM AN AESTI VALIS.
I BROUGHT LOTS OF SPARE PARTS.
BWAM BWAM
GREAT! WE DON'T HAVE TO WORRY ABOUT THE JUPITERIANS ANYMORE, NOW THAT WE'VE GOT THIS!!
ATTACK ANYTIME YOU WANT!! THE NADESICO ACCEPTS ALL CHALLENGERS!!
YEAH!
WE WILL, WE WILL ROCK YOU
HEH HEH HEH.

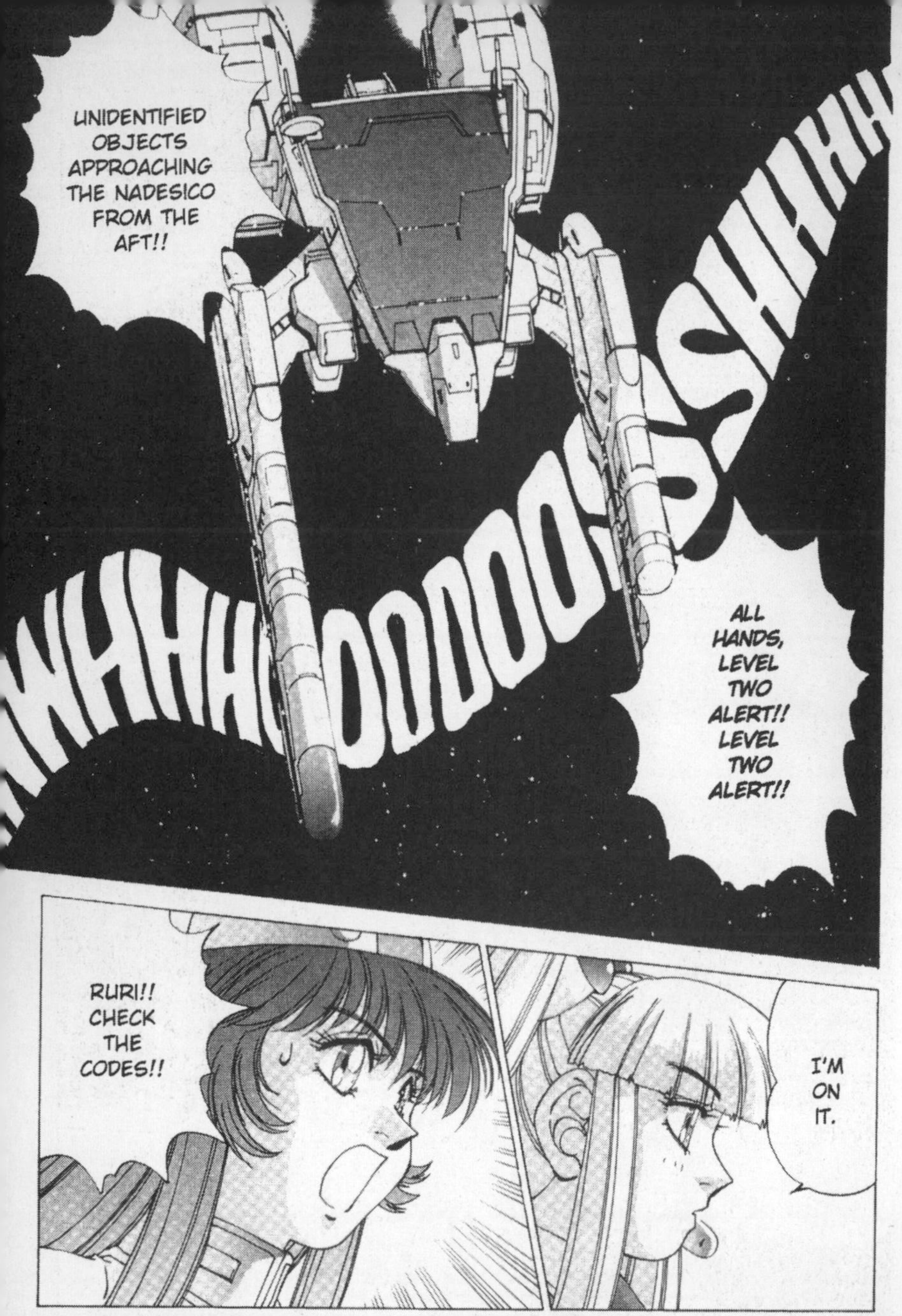
UNIDENTIFIED OBJECTS APPROACHING THE NADESICO FROM THE AFT!!
WHHHOOOOOOSHHHH
ALL HANDS, LEVEL TWO ALERT!! LEVEL TWO ALERT!!
RURI!! CHECK THE CODES!!
I'M ON IT.

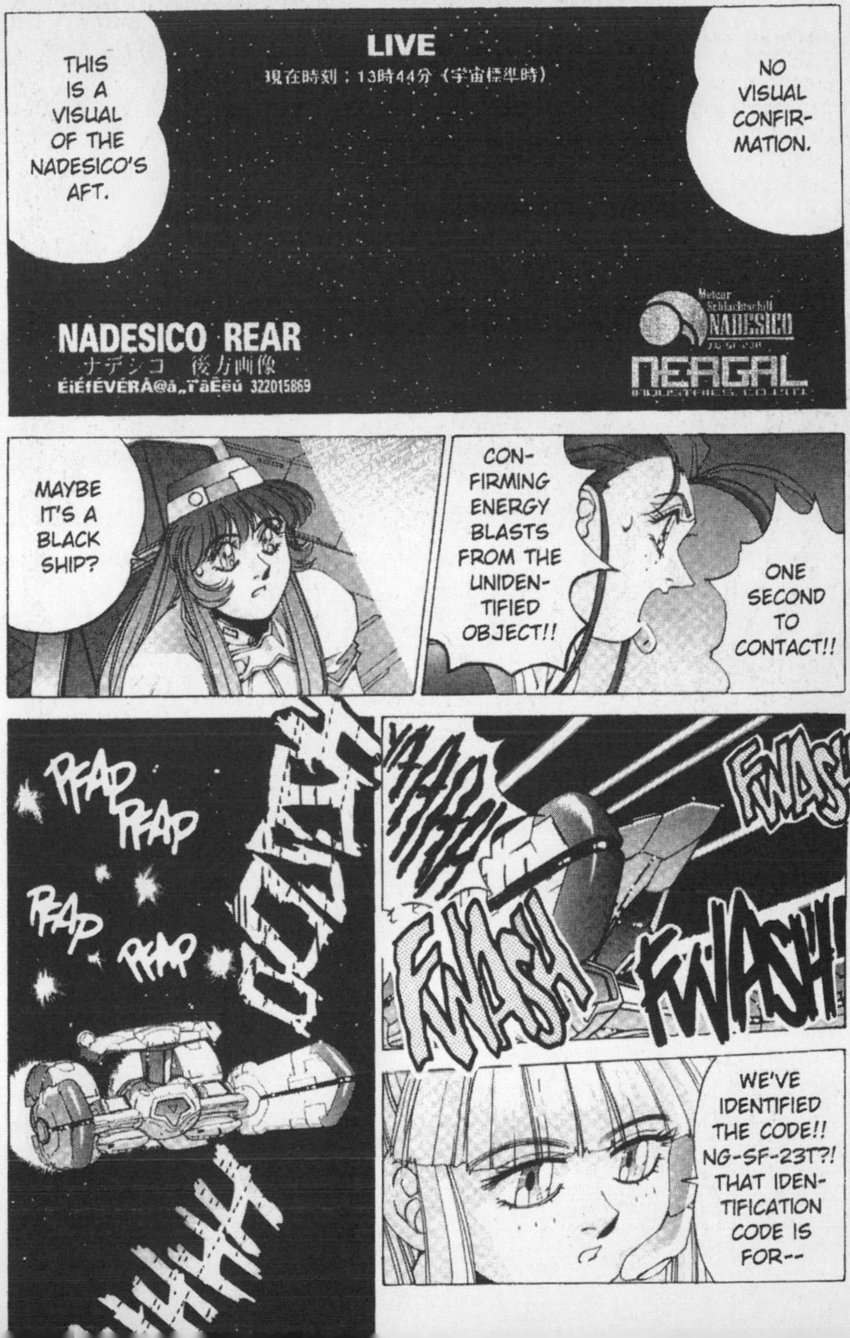
LIVE
現在時刻：13時44分（宇宙標準時）
THIS IS A VISUAL OF THE NADESICO'S AFT.
NO VISUAL CONFIR-MATION.
NADESICO REAR
ナデシコ 後方画像
ÉiÉfÉVÉRÁ@ã„TâÊú 322015869
NADESICO
NERGAL
MAYBE IT'S A BLACK SHIP?
CON-FIRMING ENERGY BLASTS FROM THE UNIDEN-TIFIED OBJECT!!
ONE SECOND TO CONTACT!!
PFAP
PFAP
PFAP
PFAP
FWASH
FWASH
FWASH!
WE'VE IDENTIFIED THE CODE!! NG-SF-23T?! THAT IDEN-TIFICATION CODE IS FOR--

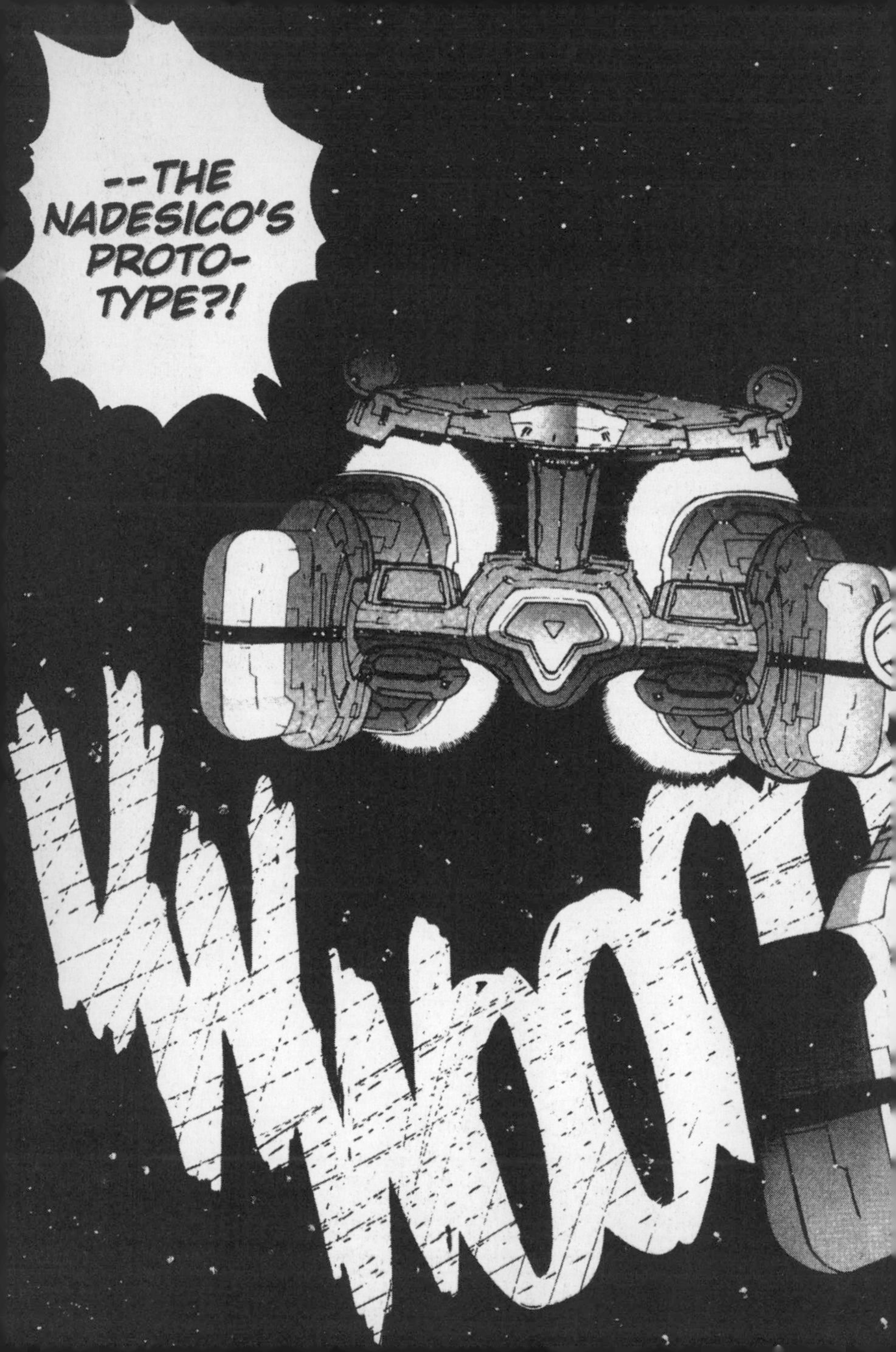
--THE NADESICO'S PROTO-TYPE?!
WHOOO

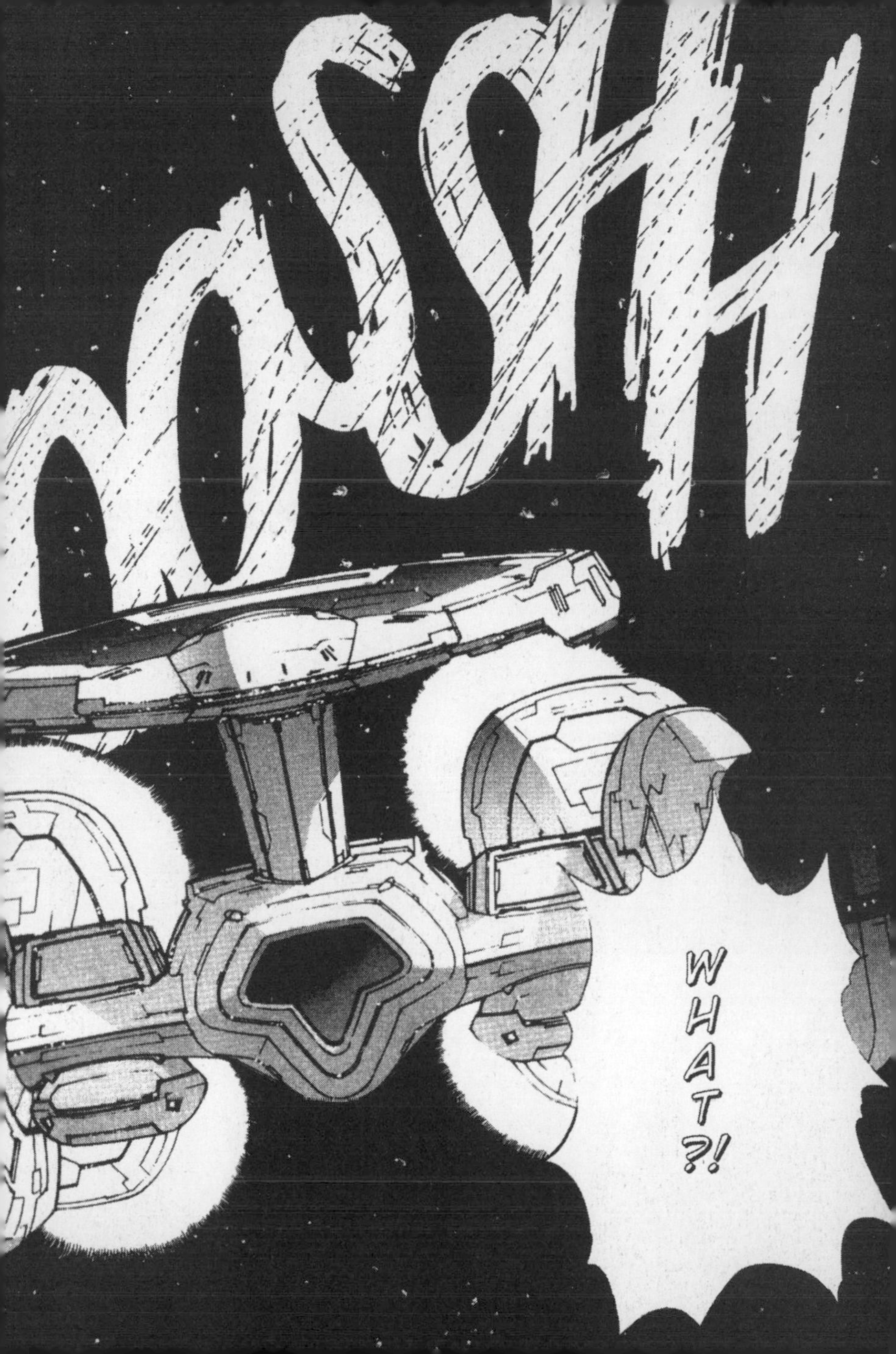
OOSH
WHAT?!

UN-FORTUNATELY, YOU'RE WRONG!

WHAT?!

THAT'S OUR OLD CODE!!

THIS SHIP IS NOW UN-SF-444A, THE KAGUYA, OF THE UNITED EARTH GOVERNMENT. SPACE CRUISER KAGUYA!

I AM THE CAPTAIN, KAGUYA ONIKIRIMARU! YURIKA, HOW HAVE YOU BEEN?

KAGUYA   UN-SF-444A
KAGUYA ONIKIRIMARU

LIVE （宇宙標準時）
現在時間；13時46分
KAGUYA → NADESICO
1258984-5896

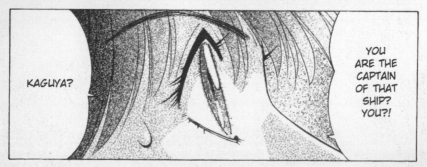

KAGUYA?

YOU ARE THE CAPTAIN OF THAT SHIP? YOU?!

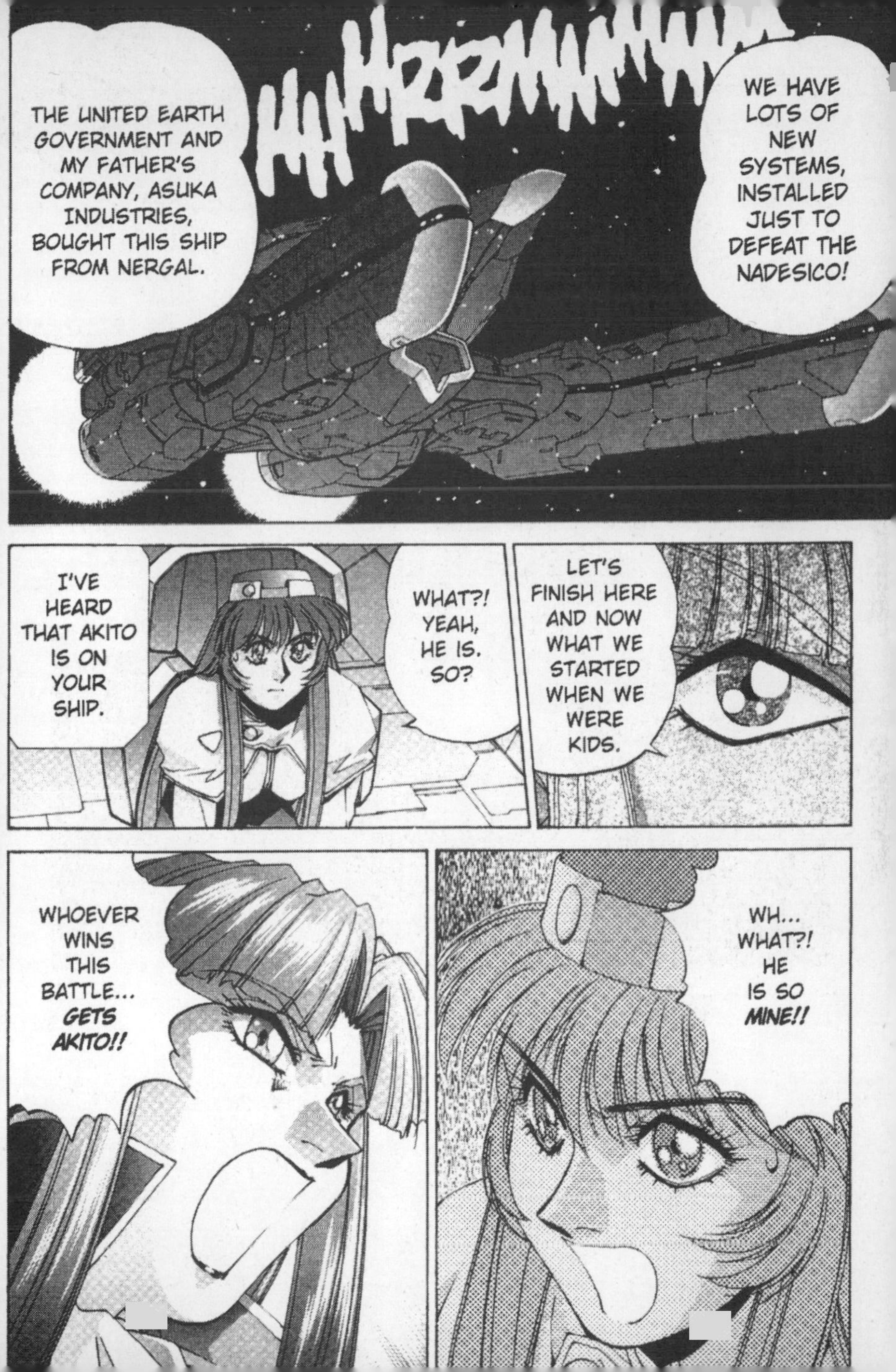
THE UNITED EARTH GOVERNMENT AND MY FATHER'S COMPANY, ASUKA INDUSTRIES, BOUGHT THIS SHIP FROM NERGAL.
WE HAVE LOTS OF NEW SYSTEMS, INSTALLED JUST TO DEFEAT THE NADESICO!
I'VE HEARD THAT AKITO IS ON YOUR SHIP.
WHAT?! YEAH, HE IS. SO?
LET'S FINISH HERE AND NOW WHAT WE STARTED WHEN WE WERE KIDS.
WHOEVER WINS THIS BATTLE... ***GETS AKITO!!***
WH... WHAT?! HE IS SO ***MINE!!***

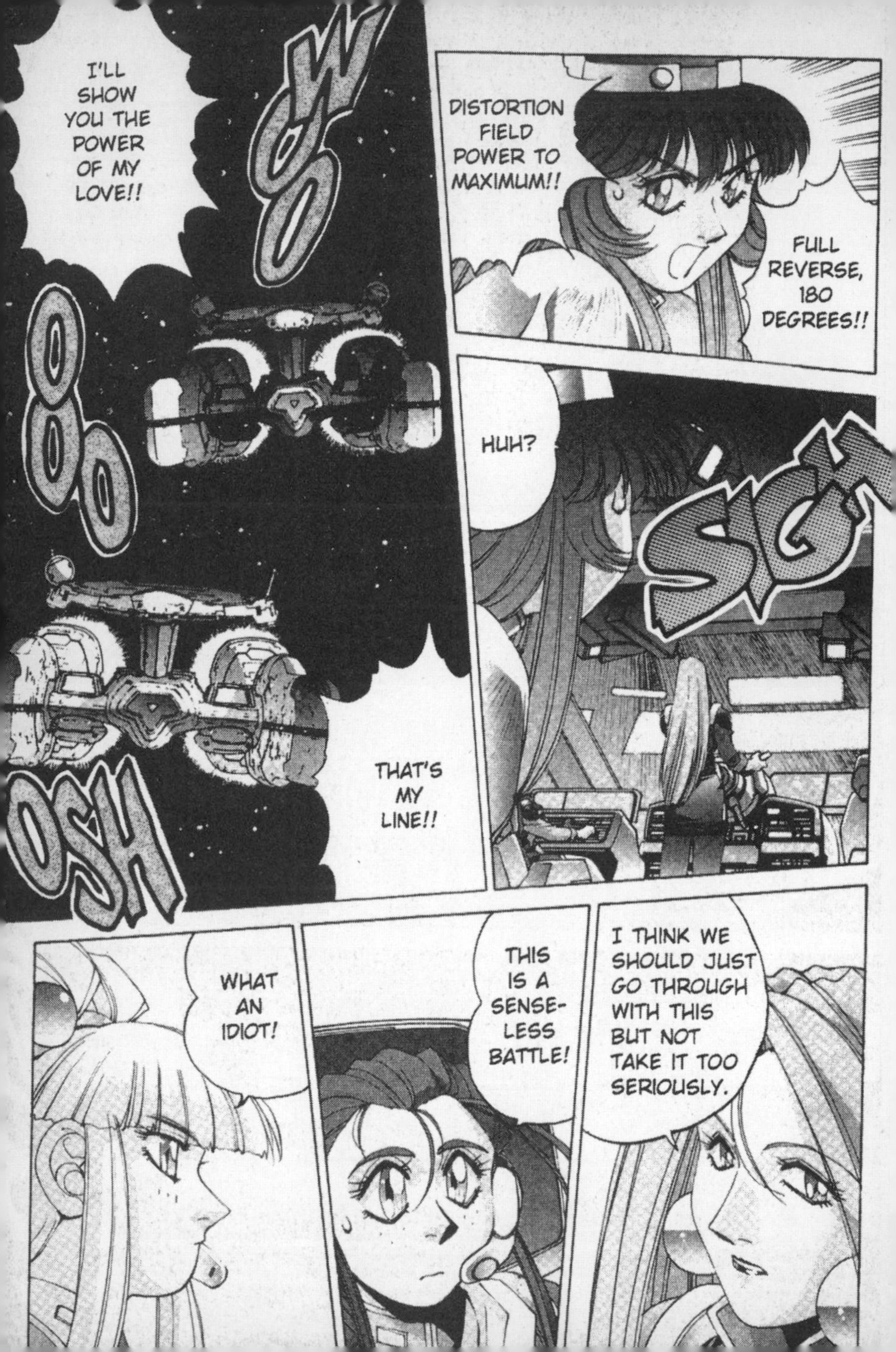
I'LL SHOW YOU THE POWER OF MY LOVE!!
WOOOOSH
THAT'S MY LINE!!
DISTORTION FIELD POWER TO MAXIMUM!!
FULL REVERSE, 180 DEGREES!!
HUH?
SIGH
WHAT AN IDIOT!
THIS IS A SENSE-LESS BATTLE!
I THINK WE SHOULD JUST GO THROUGH WITH THIS BUT NOT TAKE IT TOO SERIOUSLY.

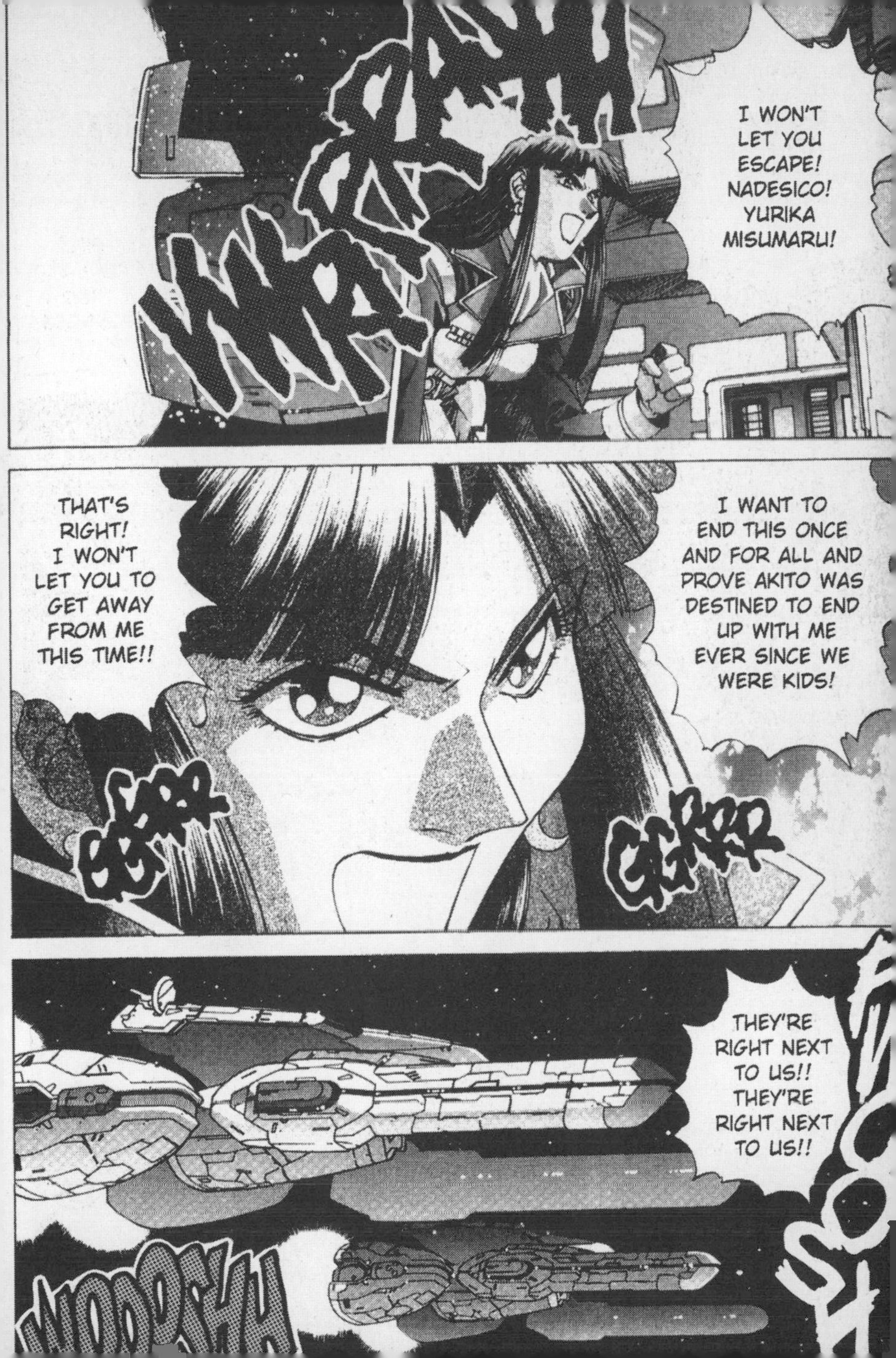
I WON'T LET YOU ESCAPE! NADESICO! YURIKA MISUMARU!
THAT'S RIGHT! I WON'T LET YOU TO GET AWAY FROM ME THIS TIME!!
I WANT TO END THIS ONCE AND FOR ALL AND PROVE AKITO WAS DESTINED TO END UP WITH ME EVER SINCE WE WERE KIDS!
THEY'RE RIGHT NEXT TO US!! THEY'RE RIGHT NEXT TO US!!

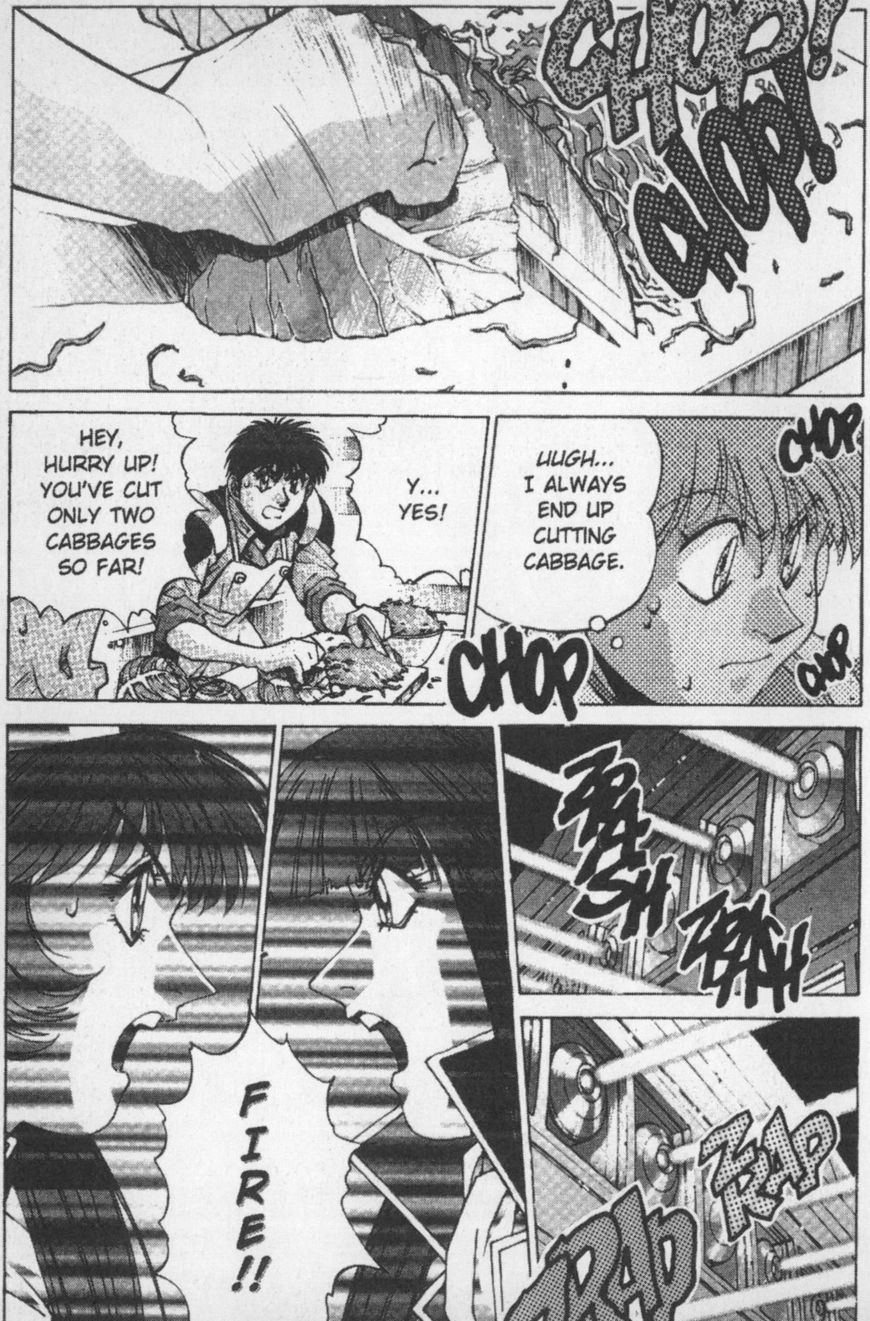
CHOP! CHOP!
HEY, HURRY UP! YOU'VE CUT ONLY TWO CABBAGES SO FAR!
Y... YES!
UUGH... I ALWAYS END UP CUTTING CABBAGE.
CHOP
CHOP
CHOP
ZBASH
ZBASH
FIRE!!
ZBAP
ZBAP

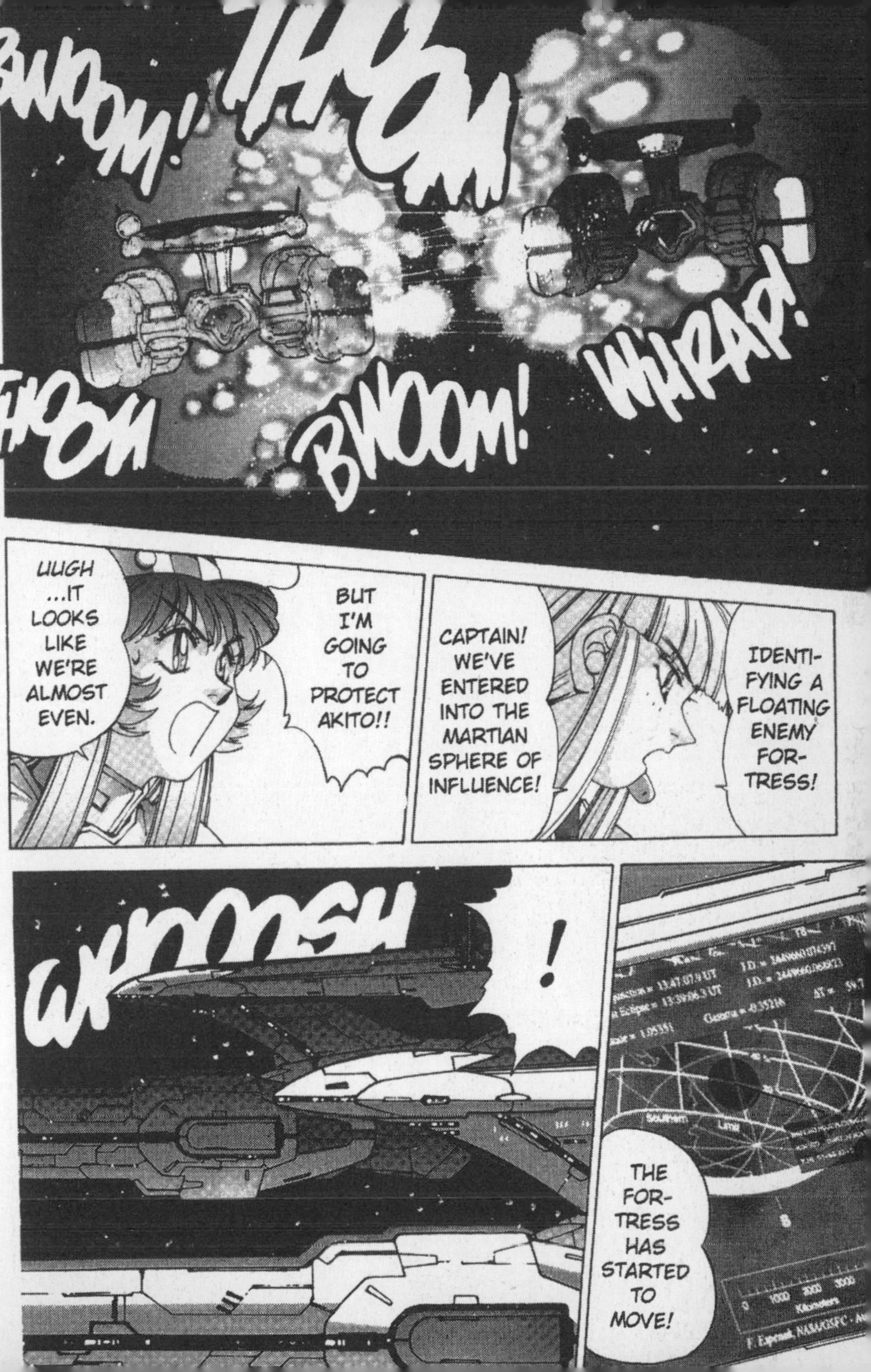
BWOOM!
THOOM
THOOM
BWOOM!
WHRAP!
UUGH ...IT LOOKS LIKE WE'RE ALMOST EVEN.
BUT I'M GOING TO PROTECT AKITO!!
CAPTAIN! WE'VE ENTERED INTO THE MARTIAN SPHERE OF INFLUENCE!
IDENTI-FYING A FLOATING ENEMY FOR-TRESS!
WOOOSH
!
THE FOR-TRESS HAS STARTED TO MOVE!

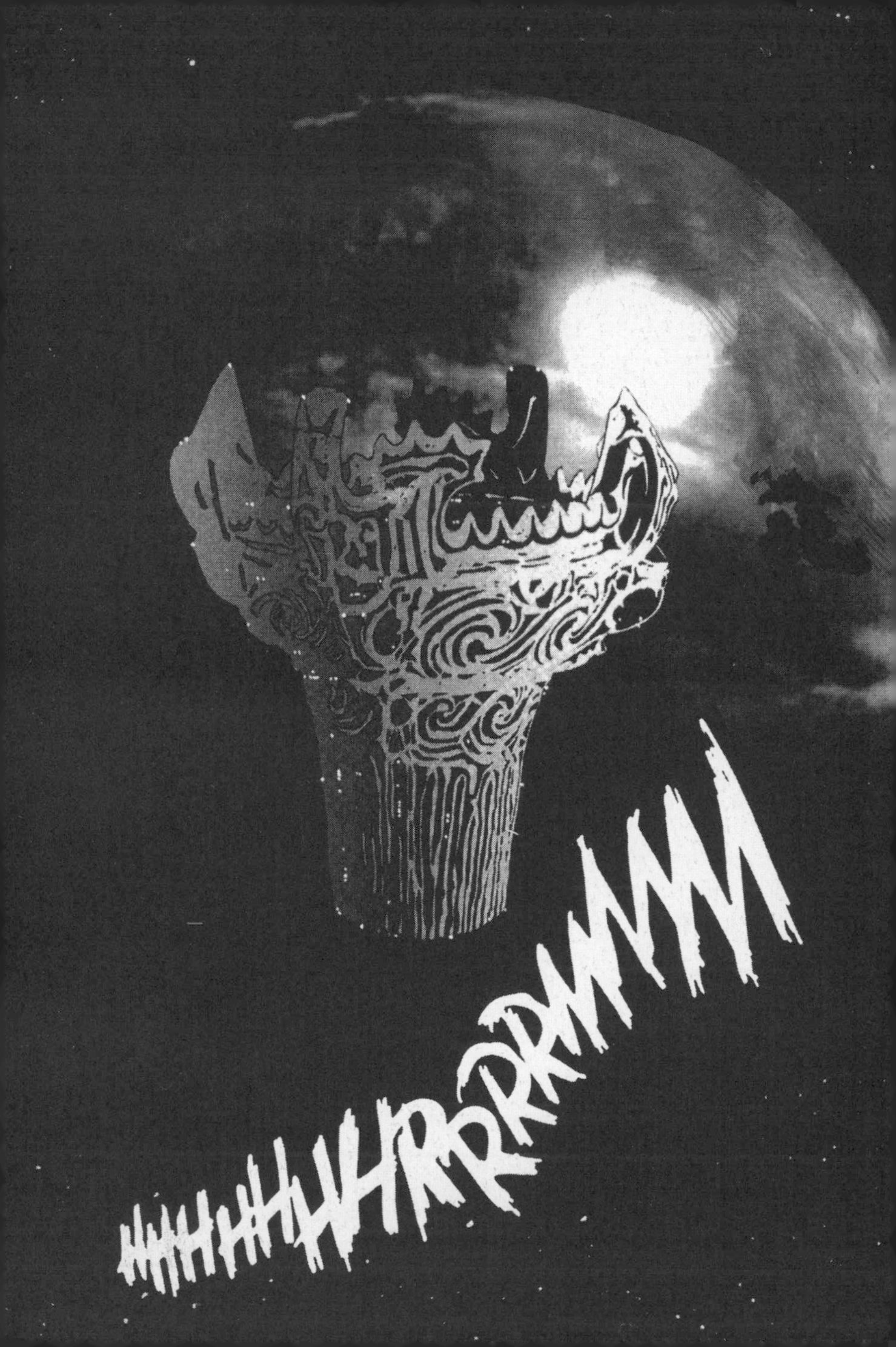
HHHHHHRRRRMMM

KIA ASAMIYA is a world-famous master of manga. He has created several series, including *Silent Möbius, Dark Angel, Gunhed* and *Nadesico*, which have been the basis for many popular motion pictures and anime. His titles define entire genres within Japanese popular culture and he is respected by fans and creators alike.

A fan of American comic books, he has done a manga adaptation of *Star Wars,* and was the artist for *Uncanny X-Men* and *Batman: Child of Dreams.*

A frequent visitor to the United States and a popular American convention guest, he is the founder of his own manga workshop, Studio Tron.

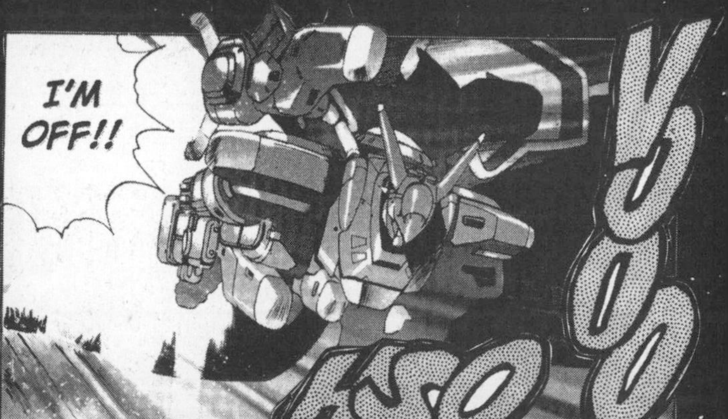
I'M OFF!!
WHOOOSH

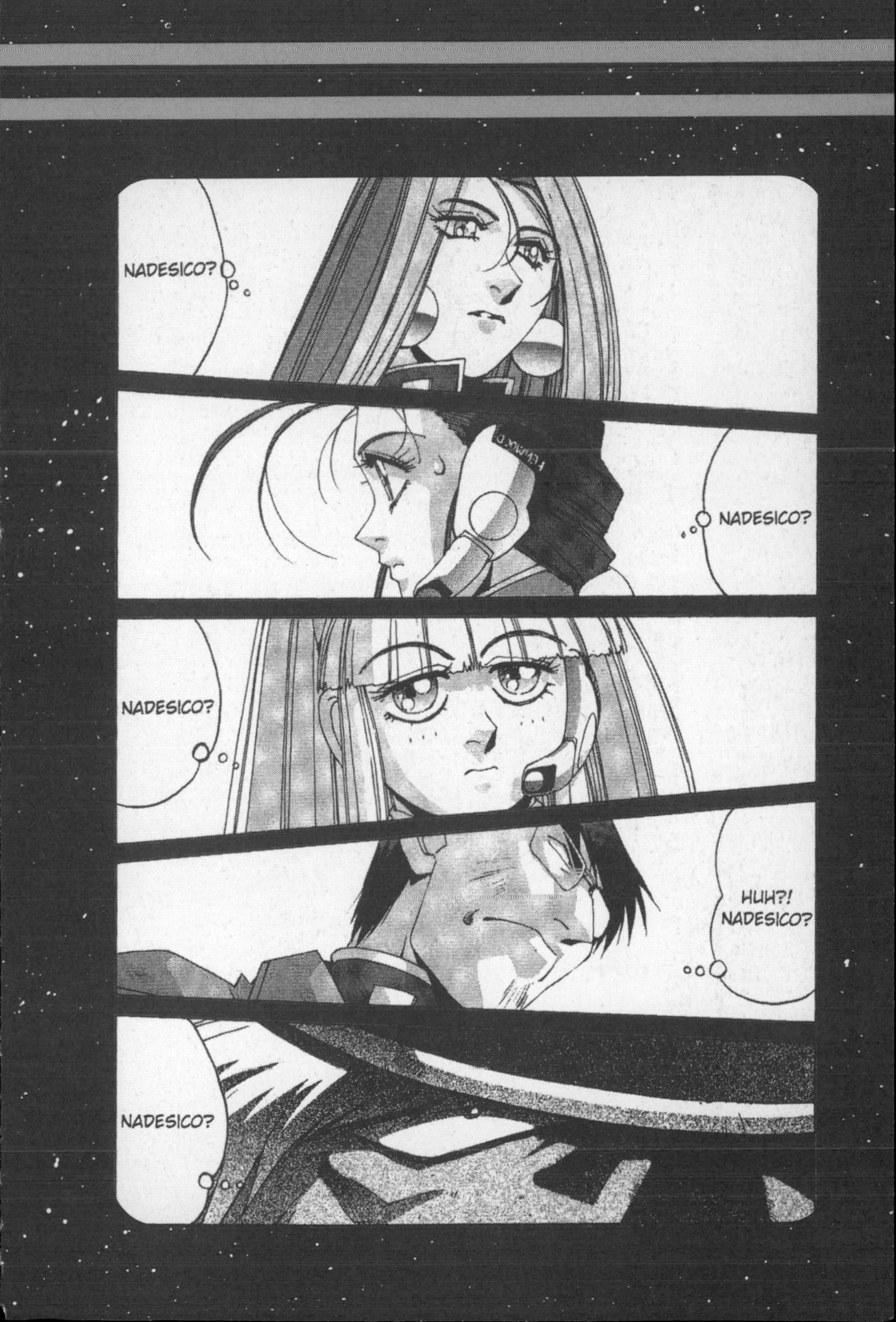
NADESICO?
NADESICO?
NADESICO?
HUH?! NADESICO?
NADESICO?

Classic Manga
The Right Size, The Right Price

$9.99 each

Call Me Princess
Available now

Popcorn Romance
All new romance from
Tomoko Taniguchi
Available now

Aquarium
Available
November 2003

Nadesico
Book 1
As seen on
Cartoon Network!
Available now

Dark Angel
Book 1: The Path To Destiny
By **Kia Asamiya**
*Batman Child of Dreams,
Uncanny X-Men*

Available
November 2003

CPM® MANGA

The Manga Zone™
To order call:
Mangamania® Club of America
1-800-626-4277
www.cpmmanga.com

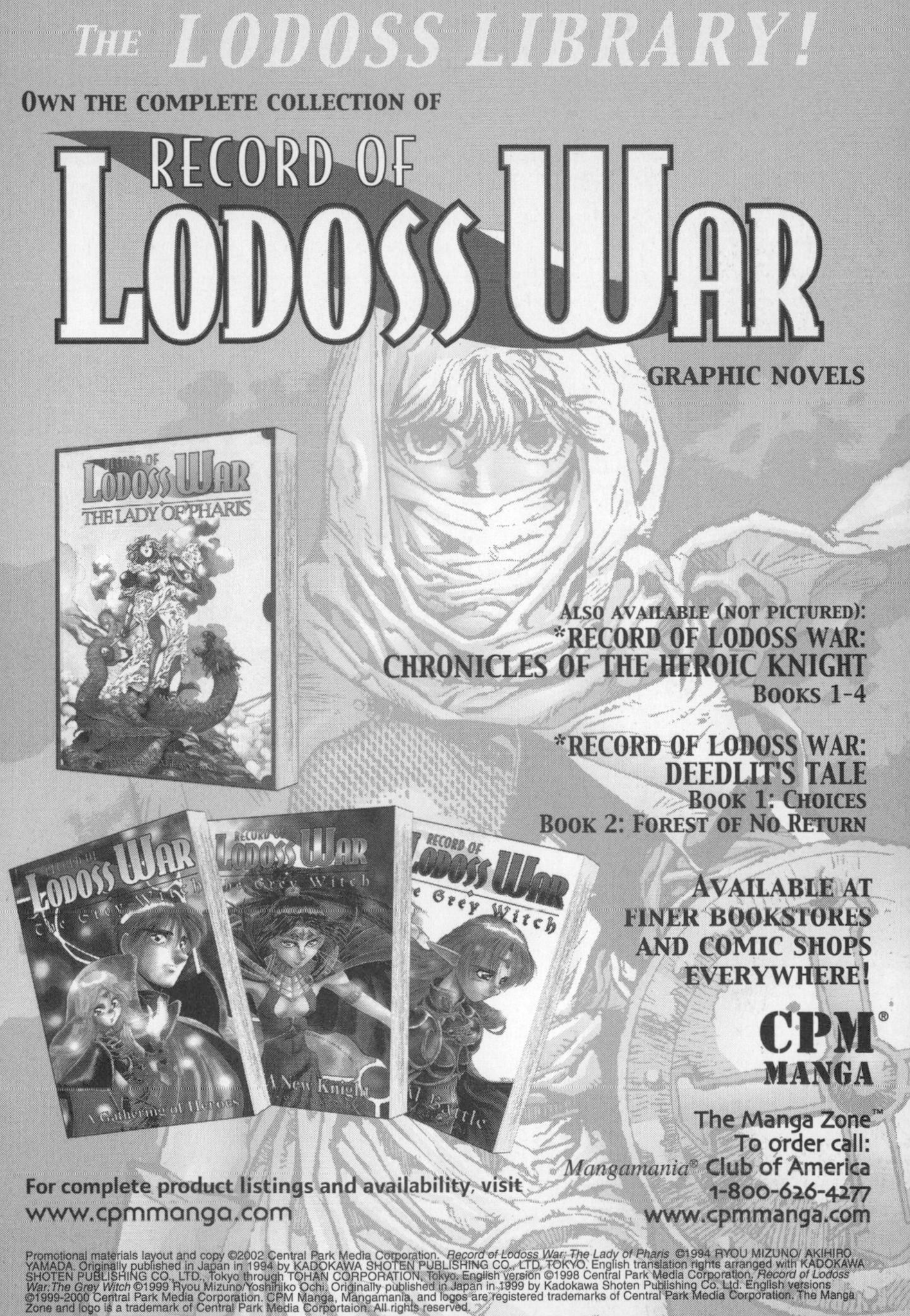

THE LODOSS LIBRARY!
OWN THE COMPLETE COLLECTION OF
RECORD OF LODOSS WAR
GRAPHIC NOVELS
RECORD OF LODOSS WAR
THE LADY OF PHARIS
ALSO AVAILABLE (NOT PICTURED):
*RECORD OF LODOSS WAR:
CHRONICLES OF THE HEROIC KNIGHT
BOOKS 1-4
*RECORD OF LODOSS WAR:
DEEDLIT'S TALE
BOOK 1: CHOICES
BOOK 2: FOREST OF NO RETURN
LODOSS WAR
The Grey Witch
A Gathering of Heroes
RECORD OF LODOSS WAR
The Grey Witch
A New Knight
RECORD OF LODOSS WAR
The Grey Witch
AVAILABLE AT
FINER BOOKSTORES
AND COMIC SHOPS
EVERYWHERE!
CPM®
MANGA
The Manga Zone™
To order call:
Mangamania® Club of America
1-800-626-4277
www.cpmmanga.com
For complete product listings and availability, visit
www.cpmmanga.com
Promotional materials layout and copy ©2002 Central Park Media Corporation. Record of Lodoss War: The Lady of Pharis ©1994 RYOU MIZUNO/ AKIHIRO YAMADA. Originally published in Japan in 1994 by KADOKAWA SHOTEN PUBLISHING CO., LTD, TOKYO. English translation rights arranged with KADOKAWA SHOTEN PUBLISHING CO., LTD., Tokyo through TOHAN CORPORATION, Tokyo. English version ©1998 Central Park Media Corporation. Record of Lodoss War: The Grey Witch ©1999 Ryou Mizuno/Yoshihiko Ochi. Originally published in Japan in 1999 by Kadokawa Shoten Publishing Co. Ltd. English versions ©1999-2000 Central Park Media Corporation. CPM Manga, Mangamania, and logos are registered trademarks of Central Park Media Corporation. The Manga Zone and logo is a trademark of Central Park Media Corportaion. All rights reserved.

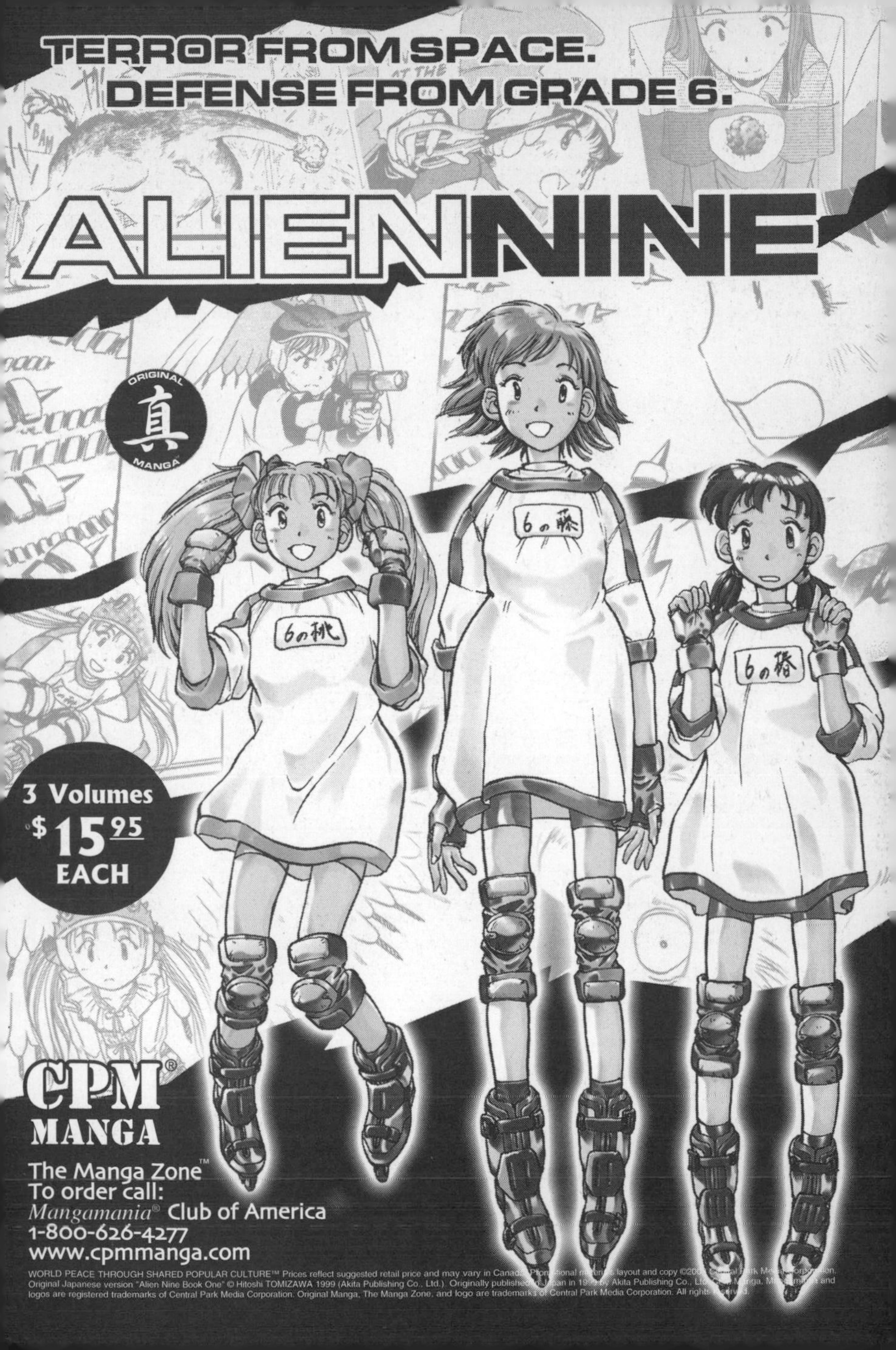

TERROR FROM SPACE.
DEFENSE FROM GRADE 6.
ALIEN NINE
ORIGINAL 真 MANGA
3 Volumes
$15.95
EACH
CPM®
MANGA
The Manga Zone™
To order call:
Mangamania® Club of America
1-800-626-4277
www.cpmmanga.com
WORLD PEACE THROUGH SHARED POPULAR CULTURE™ Prices reflect suggested retail price and may vary in Canada. Promotional material layout and copy ©200 Central Park Media Corporation. Original Japanese version "Alien Nine Book One" © Hitoshi TOMIZAWA 1999 (Akita Publishing Co., Ltd.) Originally published in Japan in 19 by Akita Publishing Co., Ltd. CPM Manga, Mangamania and logos are registered trademarks of Central Park Media Corporation. Original Manga, The Manga Zone, and logo are trademarks of Central Park Media Corporation. All rights reserved.

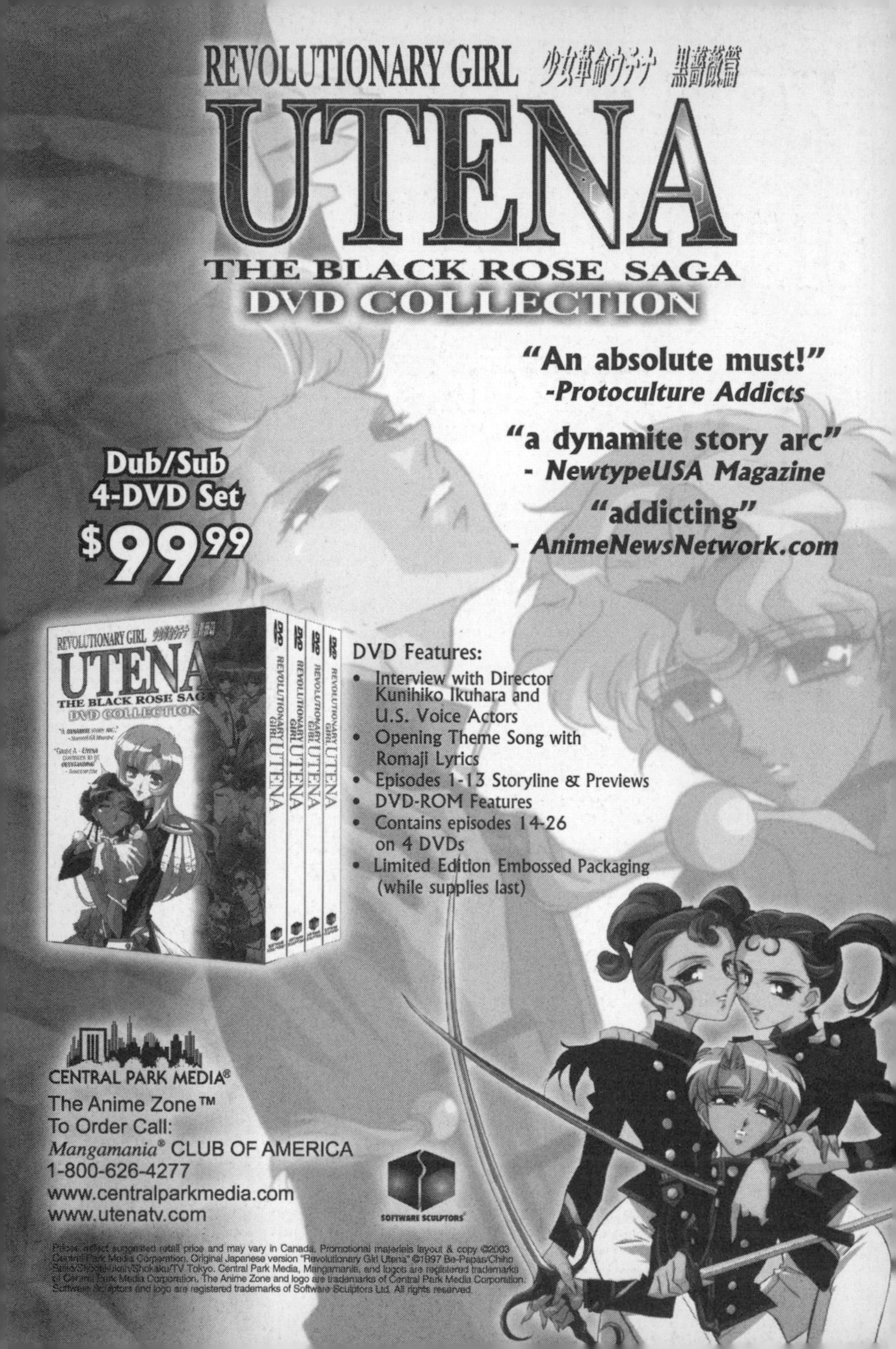

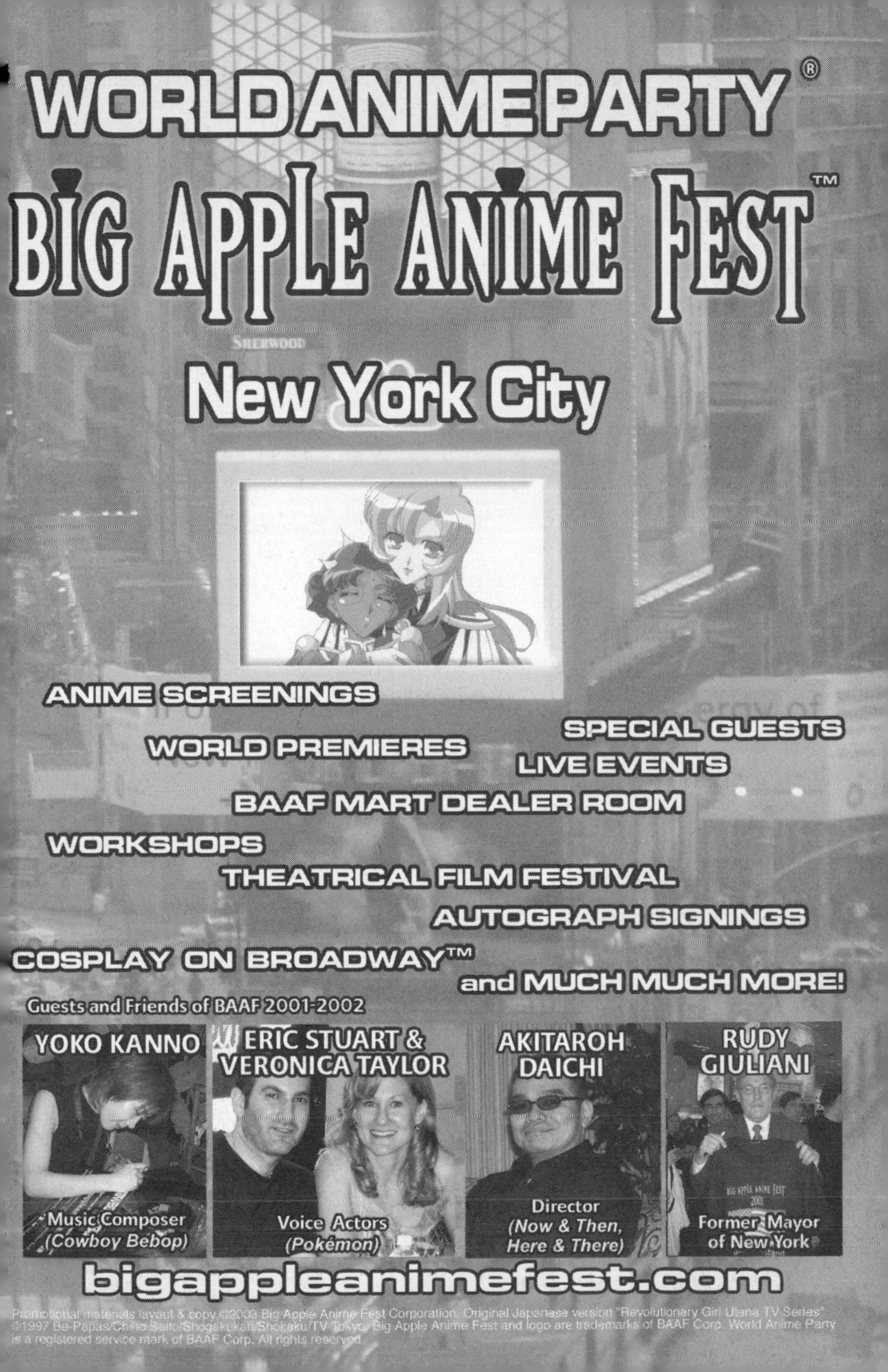

WORLD ANIME PARTY®
BIG APPLE ANIME FEST™
New York City
ANIME SCREENINGS
SPECIAL GUESTS
WORLD PREMIERES
LIVE EVENTS
BAAF MART DEALER ROOM
WORKSHOPS
THEATRICAL FILM FESTIVAL
AUTOGRAPH SIGNINGS
COSPLAY ON BROADWAY™
and MUCH MUCH MORE!
Guests and Friends of BAAF 2001-2002
YOKO KANNO
Music Composer
(Cowboy Bebop)
ERIC STUART & VERONICA TAYLOR
Voice Actors
(Pokémon)
AKITAROH DAICHI
Director
(Now & Then, Here & There)
RUDY GIULIANI
Former Mayor of New York
bigappleanimefest.com
Promotional materials layout & copy ©2003 Big Apple Anime Fest Corporation. Original Japanese version "Revolutionary Girl Utena TV Series" ©1997 Be-Papas/Chiho Saito/Shogakukan/Shokaku/TV Tokyo. Big Apple Anime Fest and logo are trademarks of BAAF Corp. World Anime Party is a registered service mark of BAAF Corp. All rights reserved.